The Age of Enlightenment

Volume 2

The Age of Enlightenment

Edited by Simon Eliot
and Beverley Stern

Volume 2

**Ward Lock Educational
in association with
The Open University Press**

ISBN 0 7062 3922 9

First published 1979
Reprinted 1981, 1983, 1984, 1989, 1990, 1991

Set in 10 on 11 point Garamond
Printed and bound in Hong Kong
for Ward Lock Educational
1 Christopher Road,
East Grinstead, Sussex, RH19 3BT
A Ling Kee Company

CONTENTS

Acknowledgments   vii

List of Plates   ix

Introduction   xi

Batty Langley   *The Builder's Treasury* (1740)   1

Laugier   *Essay on Architecture* (1753)   8

William Chambers   *On Civil Architecture* (1759, 1791)   24

James Stuart and
Nicholas Revett   *The Antiquities of Athens* (1762)   39

Le Blanc   *Letter to the Comte de Caylus* (1747)   42

Cochin   *A Petition . . . by a Society of Artists* (1754)   48

Cochin   *On the 'Greek Manner'* (c.1780–1790)   53

Blondel   *On Bad Taste in Interior Decoration* (1771)   55

La Font de Saint
Yenne   *Reflections on . . . the Present State of Painting in France* (1747)   57

William Hogarth   *The Analysis of Beauty* (1753)   64

William Hogarth   *The Anecdotes of William Hogarth* (1737, 1763)   77

Horace Walpole   *On Modern Gardening* (1771)   82

Joshua Reynolds   *The Fourteenth Discourse: On Gainsborough* (1788)   90

Diderot   *Salons of 1761, 1763, 1765, 1767, 1769, 1781*   103

D'Alembert   *A History of the Sciences* (1751)   126

Diderot   *Art* (1751)   144

Diderot   *The Stocking Machine* (1751)   155

Buffon   *How to Study Natural History* (1749)   160

Buffon   *History and Theory of the Earth* (1749)   191

Buffon   *An Examination of Some Other Theories of The Earth* (1749)   210

Buffon   *The Ass* (1753)   217

Buffon   *Of Animals Common to Both Continents* (1761)   227

D'Alembert   *On Men of Letters* (1753)   237

Samuel Johnson	*Letter to Lord Chesterfield* (1755)	240
Beaumarchais	*The Marriage of Figaro* (1784) *Opening Scene*	242
Beaumarchais	*The Marriage of Figaro* (1784) *Figaro's Soliloquy*	246
Kant	*Answer to the Question: What is 'Enlightening'?* (1784)	249
Index		256

ACKNOWLEDGMENTS

We would like to thank all those members of the Course Team who helped in the preparation and writing of the various introductions and notes, in particular: Stuart Brown, Colin Cunningham, Roger Day, Clive Emsley, Francis Frascina, David Goodman, Lorna Hardwick, Pat Howard, Rosalind Hursthouse, Arnold Kettle, Tony Lentin, Graham Martin, Gill Perry, Aaron Scharf, Gerald Steele and Belinda Thompson. We would also like to thank our secretaries, Ann Hulme and Wendy Macey, for their heroic efforts on what to them (and us) seemed a never-ending series of drafts and redrafts.

Most of all, we want to express and record our thanks to Nick Furbank, Course Team Chairman, for all his judicious guidance, advice and practical help, without which this book would have been much poorer and more incoherent.

Before the tempering experience of editorial work we had thought that such acknowledgements were merely formal academic gestures. We are now much wiser.

The Open University and the Publishers would like to thank the following for permission to reproduce copyright material. All possible care has been taken to trace ownership of the selections included and to make full acknowledgement for their use.

The Bobbs-Merrill Company Inc. for the extract from Jean Le Rond D'Alembert: Preliminary Discourse to the Encyclopedia of Diderot translated by Richard N. Schwab and 'Art' from *Encyclopedia: Selections* by Diderot, D'Alembert and A Society of Men of Letters, translated by Hoyt and Cassirer; Faber & Faber Ltd for extracts from *Early Neo-Classicism in France* by S. Eriksen edited and translated by Peter Thornton; David Higham Associates for extracts from *Philosophical Dictionary* translated by Theodore Besterman published by Penguin Books; Oxford University Press for extracts from *Diderot: Salons* edited by Jean Seznec and Jean Adhémar and for the extract from James Boswell's *The Life of Samuel Johnson*; Penguin Books Ltd for extracts from Beaumarchais: *The Barber of Seville* and *The Marriage of Figaro* translated by John Wood.

LIST OF PLATES

(Illustrations taken from books are not dated unless they have been reprinted from a second or later edition, in which case the original date of publication is given. The figures in brackets indicate each work's actual dimensions.)

Plate 1: Batty Langley, *Tuscan Book Case*, (23.3cm x 18.5cm), from *The City and Country Builder's and Workman's Treasury of Designs*, 1740.

Plate 2: Batty Langley, *Dorick Book Case*, (23.3cm x 18.5cm), *ibid.*, 1740.

Plate 3: Batty Langley, *Ionick Book Case*, (23.3cm x 18.5cm), *ibid.*, 1740.

Plate 4: Batty Langley, [*Chinese style*] *Book Case*, (23.3cm x 18.5cm), *ibid.*, 1740.

Plate 5: Batty Langley, [*Corinthian*] *Book Case*, (23.3cm x 18.5cm), *ibid.*, 1740.

Plate 6: William Chambers, *Primitive Buildings etc. c.*1759, (41.5cm x 29.5cm), from *A Treatise on the Decorative part of Civil Architecture*, ed. Gwilt, 1825.

Plate 7: William Chambers, *The Orders of the Antients, c.*1759, (29cm x 41cm), *ibid.*, 1825.

Plate 8: William Chambers, *The Roman or Composite Order, c.*1759, (40.5cm x 29cm), *ibid.*, 1825.

Plate 9: *Orfevre Grossier, Ouvrages* [*Rococo Work by Silver and Goldsmiths*], (32.0cm x 20.8cm), from *Encylopédie, Recueil de Planches*, Vol. VIII, 1771.

Plate 10: *Elévation du côté de la cheminée du Salon au premier étage des nouveaux appartements du Palais Royal* [*Design (1760) for one of the 'new' rooms in the Palais Royal*], (20.3cm x 33.5cm), from *Encyclopédie, Recueil de Planches*, Vol.I, 1762.

Plate 11: William Hogarth, *First Plate*, (36.2cm x 48.4cm), from *The Analysis of Beauty*, 1753.

Plate 12: William Hogarth, *Second Plate*, (36.7cm x 49cm), from *The Analysis of Beauty*, 1753.

Plate 13: Joshua Reynolds, *Mrs Siddons as the Tragic Muse, c.*1784, oil on canvas, (236cm x 146cm), Henry E. Huntington Library and Art Gallery, California.

Plate 14: Gabriel de Saint-Aubin, *Le Salon du Louvre en 1767, c.*1767, water-colour and gouache, (25cm x 48cm), collection particulière, Louvre, Paris.

Plate 15: Gabriel de Saint-Aubin, Two pages from the *Livret du Salon de 1761*, pen and ink, (9cm x 15.5cm), Print Room, Louvre, Paris.

Plate 16: Jean-Baptiste–Siméon Chardin, *Le Bénédicité*, *c*.1740–46, oil on canvas, (50cm x 66cm), The D. G. Van Beuningen Collection, Boymans – Van Beuningen Museum, Rotterdam.

Plate 17: Jean-Baptiste Greuze, *Le Paralytique* or *La piété filiale*, *c*.1762, oil on canvas, (91.4cm x 137.1cm), Hermitage Museum, Leningrad.

Plate 18: François Boucher, *Angélique et Médor*, 1763, oil on canvas, (oval 65cm x 55cm), Private collection, New York.

Plate 19: François Boucher, *Jupiter et Callisto*, 1763, oil on canvas, (oval 65cm x 55cm), Private collection, New York.

Plate 20: Claude-Joseph Vernet, *Le Matin*, *c*.1765, oil on canvas, (91.4cm x 152.3cm), Louvre, Paris.

Plate 21: Joseph-Marie Vien, *Saint Denis prêchant la foi en Gaule*, *c*.1767, oil on canvas, (647.5cm x 375.8cm), Church of Saint Roche, Paris.

Plate 22: François-Gabriel Doyen, *Le Miracle des Ardents*, *c*.1767, oil on canvas, (670.3cm x 365.6cm), Church of Saint Roche, Paris.

Plate 23: Jean-Baptiste Greuze, *Septime Sévère et Caracalla*, *c*.1769, oil on canvas, (124cm x 160cm), Louvre, Paris.

Plate 24: Jacques Louis David, *Bélisaire*, *c*.1781, oil on canvas, (288cm x 312cm), Museum, Lille.

Plate 25: *Travail du Bas au Metier* [*The Stocking Machine*], (32.7cm x 43.3cm), from *Encyclopédie, Recueil de Planches*, Vol .II, 1763.

Plate 26: *Le Âne* [*The Ass*], (19cm x 15cm), from *Histoire naturelle*, Vol. IV, 1753.

Plate 27: Le Squelette d'Âne [*Skeleton of the Ass*], (19cm x 15cm), from *Histoire naturelle*, Vol. IV, 1753.

LOCATION OF PLATES

Plates 1–5	*pages* 3–7
Plates 6–8	*pages* 25–7
Plates 9–24	*opposite page* 112
Plate 25	*pages* 158–9
Plates 26 and 27	*pages* 218–9

INTRODUCTION

One day in the late 1780s Goethe happened to be holding a prism and, remembering that Newton in his *Optics* had claimed that, by means of a prism, it was possible to divide light into individual colours, he turned the glass towards a whitewashed wall. Behold, there was no play of colours, the wall remained as white as before. In a flash, Goethe knew that Newton had been wrong, and for the next eighteen years he laboured, in his own *Theory of Colours*, to prove it. What he became eager to prove was that Newton had been wrong in the profoundest possible way, and a way which had infected the whole eighteenth century. For what had Newton been doing with his prism and his technique for resolving white light into the primary colours of the spectrum? He had been *torturing* that holy thing, 'Light', he had been, 'putting Nature on the rack'. The prism was the epitome of all that was wrong with Rationalism and so-called 'Enlightenment'; it was a way of dividing up, of separating and categorizing, of violating the living unity of Nature. Its chief instrument was mathematics, and this too was a dangerously overrated science, which made false abstractions from nature and which discovered nothing – merely elaborated a tautology. The need, he told himself, was to overthrow this whole evil fortress, this 'Bastille' of Newtonianism. Thus by a curious reversal the *ancien régime* and its enemy the Enlightenment' became, for Goethe, one and the same.

As for *true* 'Enlightenment' – ah, that was a different matter! Light – not the light passively received by the eye but light emitted by the eye – this was indeed godlike, for Goethe. 'Were there no sunshine in thine eye, how could it perceive the sun?' he wrote, quoting from the neo-Platonist Plotinus but with the authentic accent of the Romantic movement. 'Were God's own power not inherent in ourselves, how could Divinity enchant us?'

In this anecdote we perceive how fertile and perennial, but also how full of paradoxes, is that metaphor by which human thought and vision are considered in terms of 'light'. Goethe, brought up in the eighteenth-century 'Enlightenment', comes to reject it in the name of light.

'Enlightenment', in the eighteenth-century sense, is one of those useful but difficult terms, like 'romantic' or 'classical', which paradoxically are about as indefinable as they are indispensable. A good definition is that of Norman Hampson in *The Enlightenment* (Penguin Books, London 1968), who suggests that there is a cluster of characteristic attitudes which, when they occur in a high enough concentration, we call the Enlightenment. Among such attitudes would be: anticlericalism tending in certain cases to antireligion; a celebration of the pagan classical past as a healthy alternative to Christianity; a stress on the exercise of reason; a growing desire for the systematic, particularly scientific, investigation of nature, and a belief that this would reveal a set both of natural and moral laws; a deep mistrust of excess; and a delight in order brought about by a balance of competing forces. All these attitudes can be found in other countries and in other times, what makes them characteristic of the 'Enlightenment' is that they occurred with greater frequency and with a higher concentration in Europe in the eighteenth century than at any other time. This anthology represents an attempt to assemble a group of writers who display in various combinations, and to various degrees, these attitudes and others generally recognized as characteristically 'enlightened'. Rather than offering a precise definition of the Enlightenment we hope that this work will contribute some useful material to a continuing debate. In order to stir up that debate we have also occasionally included writers who exhibit strong anti-Enlightenment characteristics (such as Whitefield) or whose status as Enlightenment figures is questionable (such as Fielding, Johnson and Rousseau).

The Age of Enlightenment was produced to serve an Open University course, and its shape reflects the particular choices and exigencies of that course. Thus it includes an extract from Fielding, but none from Richardson, Sterne or Smollet for the simple reason that the English novel studied in the course is Fielding's *Tom Jones*. It also includes, and this is more contentious, very little Rousseau, because the course team decided, after some debate, not to designate any work by Rousseau as a central 'text' in the course.

Again, the anthology derives some of its characteristic shape from the inclusion of certain central 'texts' studied in the course, in particular the lengthy extracts from Gibbon, Hume, Buffon, and Adam Smith. The selection of shorter material is designed to put these key texts and others into an illuminating 'context'. In some ways then, *The Age of Enlightenment* attempts to combine the functions of a course reader and a conventional anthology.

We have shown, with a few exceptions, a distinct preference for longer rather than shorter extracts. Inevitably this has meant a smaller number of excerpts than is normal in an anthology of this size. We felt that quotation at length was the only way in which we could offer the student as genuine an experience of reading eighteenth-century texts as possible and, in doing so, do proper justice to the authors of those texts.

The material, as will be seen, has been arranged around certain broad themes. Within each group themes and questions are raised which are then reflected by certain other groups, so that the juxtaposition of two such groups is often illuminating in a variety of ways. We are not claiming that this is the only logical order in which such material could be organized, but we hope it is a stimulating one. We have avoided sectioning off each group with a separate title, for this would give the groups an independent dignity and status which would have been highly misleading. However, to emphasize the interrelationship of documents and writers, in the introduction to each piece we have included references to other pieces which raise similar issues or display similar or dramatically contrasting attitudes. In this way we hope to create a web of cross-references which might go a little way to representing the exciting, rich interchange of ideas which itself was a leading characteristic of the 'Enlightenment'.

The different groups of texts are linked by various means. Sometimes the connection is thematic, e.g. Gibbon followed by Architecture and Interior Design is justified by their common use of Roman civilization as a symbol of balance and order, civil or aesthetic. Sometimes, as in the period itself, texts are linked by the polymaths who wrote them. In Volume One the writer who acts as a link or 'hinge' is Voltaire, who participates in the Providence debate and opens the Politico-Constitutional one. In Volume Two it is Diderot, who rounds off 'Art History' and is involved in the *Encyclopédie* group.

The anthology opens with a group of excerpts (Voltaire, Johnson, Fielding) on the debate about the concept of 'classic' in literature. This juxtaposes English Augustan and French Neoclassical arguments and illustrates the power of this concept, and the problems of its definition, which run right through enlightenment thinking. The difference between English and French attitudes comes out clearly in regard to Shakespeare. Voltaire, brought up in the traditions of the age of Louis XIV, which assume that literature's task is to present a generalized and idealized version of human life, avoiding all reference to the particular and the 'low', is unable to see in Shakespeare's *Hamlet* much more than 'the production of a drunken savage'. Dr Johnson, on the other hand, though a champion of Augustan 'correctness', chooses to publish an edition of Shakespeare. The difference between Johnson and Voltaire comes to a focus especially in regard to 'Nature' (a key word for the eighteenth century in this, as in others of its many senses). Voltaire holds: 'It is not enough to say, as some of your [English] compatriots do, that it [*Hamlet*] is all pure Nature; our reply has to be that it is that very Nature that needs to be carefully veiled'. Johnson's adhesion to 'nature' is altogether more absolute, and it is on Shakespeare's 'adherence to general nature' that he rests the case for his greatness. In his attitude towards Pope's *Homer*, however, Johnson comes closer to Voltaire. Pope, he says, has added many graces and elegances to Homer not present in the original, but 'Elegance is surely to be desired, if it be not gained at the expense of dignity. A hero would wish to be loved as well as to be reverenced.' These are words that Voltaire, who contributed the article on 'Elegance' to the *Encyclopédie*, might well have used. To round up this topic, it is worth noticing in Fielding's Preface to *Joseph Andrews*, the puzzlement of an author, who has, or so he feels, created a new *genre* of writing – the novel – and does not know what to call it, so falls back uncomfortably on the traditional and 'classic' literary categories. He terms it 'a comic epic poem in prose', a term expressive of his problem or challenge in the writing of it, that is to say how to reconcile the 'classical' and elevated with the realistic and 'low'.

This 'classicism' group of extracts is followed by two clusters of texts centred on the contrasting topic of religion, namely, religion and the debate about Providence. The 'Religion' group (Toland, Butler, Whitefield, Hume) runs from the deistic rationalism of Toland to the enthusiasm of Whitefield. Hume's *Of Miracles* which, it might be argued, represents the culmination of reason applied to revelation, closes the religion section, and his *Of a Particular Providence* opens the Providence debate (Hume, Voltaire, Rousseau, Johnson). The debate about the intelligible world order in Providence is paralleled by the similar conviction in the Politico-Constitutional group (Voltaire, Montesquieu, Quesnai, Adam Smith) that there are natural, ordered, reasonable principles behind the apparently chaotic functioning of politics and economics. This group spans some forty years and provides an impression of contemporary debate on political, constitutional and economic matters. In both Voltaire's theoretical comparison between the governments of England and France, and Montesquieu's philosophical study of laws, will be found the admiration with which the philosophes regarded the British constitutional model. The extracts by the French physiocrat Quesnai and by Adam Smith illustrate two influential and systematic approaches to political economy. Classicism as a theme re-emerges in Gibbon's study of what, to the eighteenth century, would have been the greatest of all politico-constitutional systems, the Roman Empire. Gibbon is also linked to the Politico-Constitutional group by the distinct influence Montesquieu's ideas had on his writings.

The classical world as an ordered system and a reservoir of powerful imagery is a theme which is echoed in the Architecture section (Langley, Laugier, Chambers, Stuart and Revett) and re-echoed in the ideas of the French Neoclassical theorists (Le Blanc, Cochin, Blondel). La Font de Saint Yenne's study of painting as interior decor links us into the painting and landscape gardening group (Hogarth, Walpole, Reynolds, Diderot) where the attempt to define stable, classical rules is constantly disturbed by the pressures of actual practice. Diderot, in his role as an enlightenment polymath, provides us with the 'hinge' on which the anthology pivots from Art History to the *Encyclopédie* /Science section which follows it (D'Alembert, Diderot, Buffon). The same desire to discover, through systematic investigation, a coherent world order can be found in the *Encyclopédistes* and Buffon as was displayed by Quesnai, Montesquieu and Adam Smith. D'Alembert's piece on *Men of Letters* brings us round almost full circle back to a literary issue, but this time it is an issue deeply embedded in a wider social question, the problem of patronage and the need for intellectual independence (D'Alembert, Johnson, Beaumarchais). Kant's attempt to answer the question *What is Enlightening?* seems an appropriately provocative end to an anthology one of whose main aims is to fuel the debate on that very question.

Our policy on translation has been to reprint whenever possible the English version published closest to the date of publication of the original, in an attempt to retain as far as possible the 'flavour' of the period. The chief exceptions to this are the twentieth-century American translation of D'Alembert's *Preliminary Discourse* to the *Encyclopédie* and the specially commissioned translation of Diderot's

Salons.

Our desire to preserve the 'flavour' of the period has led us, wherever possible, to retain the author's original spelling and punctuation, even though this inevitably meant that there would be occasional inconsistencies between texts, and sometimes even within a single text. Most eighteenth-century writers were less particular about such things than we are today.

Our policy on editorial notes, like most editorial policies, has of necessity been flexible. For texts not readily accessible in good modern editions we have provided as full a set of notes as possible. For those texts (such as Gibbon) where reliable editions are available the notes are much less copious. The author's original footnotes are printed at the foot of each page and and are indicated in the text by an italic superior number. Editorial notes are printed at the end of each excerpt and are denoted in the text by the use of an upright superior number. There is a certain amount of duplication in the editorial notes, particularly in the case of short ones where it was as simple to repeat the information as to refer the reader to another note. In the case of longer notes the reader is referred to their first full appearance. This flexible policy has been extended to the author's footnotes. In the case of such writers as Hume, Montesquieu and Buffon we have reproduced a selection of the most relevant of the original footnotes. In the case of Gibbon, where the footnotes are such an integral part of the 'performance', we have reprinted them all. As befits a book based almost exclusively on contemporary material the bibliographic source information is as comprehensive as possible. Full details of the first edition are given and, if we are not reprinting from that, then details of the edition from which our text is taken are also included. The date following the title of each piece normally refers to the year of first publication. In cases where publication was delayed then the date of writing (if known) or of first public performance (in the case of Beaumarchais) is used instead.

BATTY LANGLEY

The Builder's Treasury (1740)

From Batty Langley, *The City and Country Builder's, and Workman's Treasury of Designs: or the Art of Drawing and Working the Ornamental Parts of Architecture*, Printed for J. Ilive, London, 1740.

Batty Langley (1696–1751) is best known as the author of some twenty or so books designed to enable the average builder to keep abreast of current fashions. He began practice as a landscape gardener, worked as both architect and surveyor and manufactured architectural ornaments in his own brand of artificial stone. Though he did not do well as an architect the many illustrations in his series of books afforded him considerable success as the provider of patterns which were copied in houses of all grades up and down the country. His recipes were founded on the simplest principle of the five Classical Orders (he also 'invented' Gothic Orders) and their ornamental parts could be transferred to any building or article of furniture. However, the principles of proportion that underlie his designs make his series of bookcases, doors and fireplaces remarkably agreeable. The method was capable of virtually endless adaptation and the curved top of the bookcase in Plate 4 fits with the 'Chinese' taste that developed in the 1740s. (For another example of 'Chinese' taste see Walpole, p. 88 note 28). Although the plates come from the first edition, the following introduction is reprinted from the third edition (1745).

The great Pleasure that Builders and Workmen of all Kinds have of late Years taken in the Study of Architecture; and the great Advantages that have accrued to those, for whom they have been employed; by having their Works executed in a much neater and more magnificent Manner than was ever done in this Kingdom before; has been the real Motive that induced me, to the compiling of this Work, for their further Improvement.

Besides, as the Study of Architecture is really delightful in all its Process; its Practice is evidently of the greatest Importance to Artificers in general; and its Rules so easy, as to be acquired at leisure Times, when the Business of Days is over, by Way of Diversion: 'Tis a Matter of very great Surprize to me; how any Person dare presume to discourage others from the Study thereof, and thereby render them very often less serviceable to the Public than so many Brutes.

But to prevent this Infection from diffusing its poisonous Effluvia's any further; and in Consideration that amongst all Sorts of People, there are some, in whom Nature has implanted that noble Faculty of the Soul, called REASON, *whereby we judge of Things*: I have therefore, at a very great Expense, compiled this Work for the common Good of all *Men of Reason*, whose Businesses require the Knowledge of this Art, and who desire to become Proficients therein.

The first Work to be done in order thereto, is perfectly to understand the Five Orders of Columns, which here I have placed precedent to the Designs for that Purpose; and which I peremptorily admonish, be well understood, before any Proceeding be made to attempt the Art of Designing.

The Five Orders of Columns have their Members so easily adjusted, that the Reader, after having once read their Explanations, need never read them a second Time. Nor will their general Proportions escape his Memory, after having practised them about half a Dozen Times[. . .]

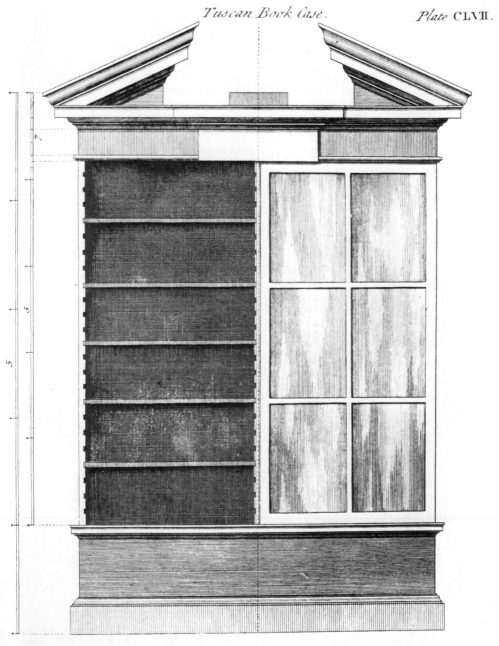

Batty Langley Invent 1739.   Tho: Langley Sculp.

Plate 1   Batty Langley   Tuscan Book Case

Dorick Book Case.   Plate CLIX.

8 Diameters

Batty Langley Invent 1739.   T. Langley Sculp.

Plate 2   Batty Langley   Dorick Book Case

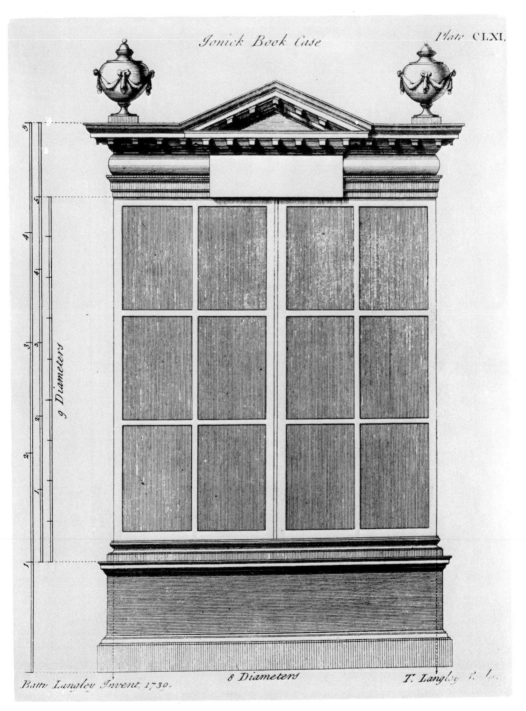

9 Diameters

Batty Langley Invent. 1730.

8 Diameters

T. Langley

Plate 3   Batty Langley   Ionick Book Case

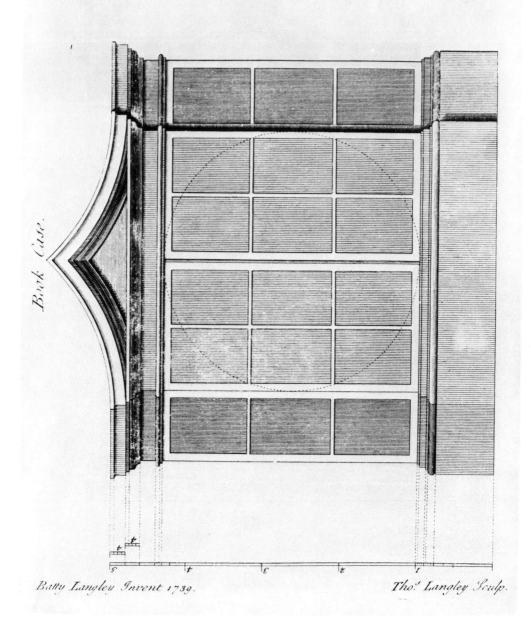

Plate CLXIII.

Book Case.

Batty Langley Invent 1739.

Tho.ˢ Langley Sculp.

Plate 4   Batty Langley   [Chinese style] Book Case

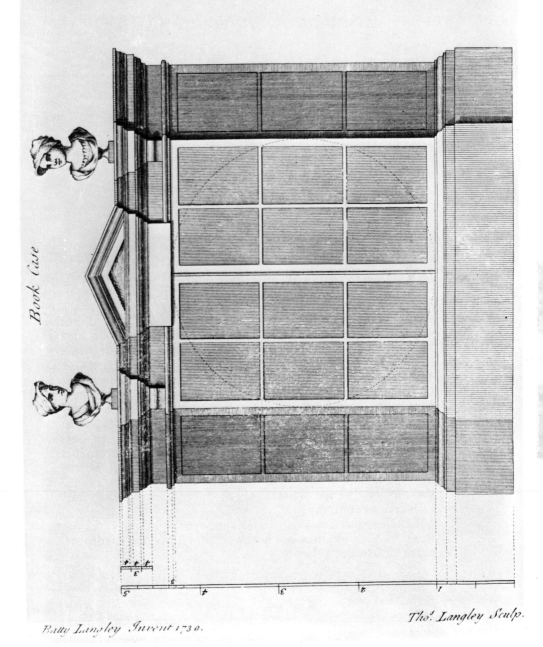

Plate CLXIV.

Book Case

Batty Langley Invent 1730.

Tho.ᵗ Langley Sculp.

Plate 5   Batty Langley   [Corinthian] Book Case

LAUGIER

Essay on Architecture (1753)

From Marc-Antoine Laugier, *Essai sur L'Architecture*, Chez Duchesne, Paris, 1753. Second edition: Nouvelle Edition, Chez Duchesne, Paris, 1755.
Reprinted from first translation: Printed for T. Osborne and Shipton in Gray's Inn, London, 1755.

M. A. Laugier (1713–69) published his *Essay on Architecture* in 1753 to expound the rationalist view of classical architecture. He was a Jesuit priest and a perceptive critic of architecture. His book is the only theoretical treatise to attempt to categorize architecture along the lines followed by the 'encyclopédistes'. The book lays down the rules for good design and, after tracing the supposed origins of building from a suitably Arcadian source, sets out to provide detailed instructions for the proportion and disposition of the parts of a building. There are sections on the layout of streets and gardens and a detailed chapter on how to build churches. Laugier's technique of returning to a mythical state of early simplicity in order to explain the origin of architecture, is curiously reminiscent of Rousseau's use of the mythical 'natural state' of man to explain later social and political developments as he saw them. Laugier's admiration for the artistic achievements of Louis XIV both links him to Voltaire (Vol. 1, p. 7), Le Blanc (p. 45) and La Font (p. 59) and illustrates the dangers of assuming that all 'enlightened' writers held the seventeenth century and all its works in contempt.

Laugier's book was enormously influential, in particular in the work of Soufflot, whose church of St. Geneviève incorporates much of Laugier's theory.

PREFACE

We have various treatises of Architecture, which explain with sufficient exactness the measures and proportions which enter into the detail of the different orders, and which furnish models for all kind of buildings. We have not as yet any work, which establishes in a solid manner the principles of it, which manifests the true spirit of it, or which proposes rules proper to direct the talent and to fix the taste. It appears to me that in those arts that are not purely mechanical, it is not sufficient to know how to work only, we ought to learn how to think upon them. An artist ought to give a reason for everything he does. For this end he has occasion for fixt principles to determine his judgement and justify his choice so that he may tell if a thing be good or bad, not purely by instinct, but by reasoning, and as a man instructed in the fine paths of beauty.

Observations have been carried to a great extent in all the liberal arts: abundance of people of talents have applied themselves to make us sensible of the delicacies of them. They have wrote very learnedly of poetry, painting and music. The mysteries of these ingenious arts have been so nicely examined, that there remains very few discoveries to be made in them. There are such judicious criticisms and reflected precepts of them, that determine their real beauties. Imagination has put them on the way, and served as reins to restrain them in their proper limits. The just rate is fixed upon the merit of their sallies and the disorders of their wandrings. If we want good poets, good painters or good musicians, it could not be for want of theory, it would be the defect of their talents.

Architecture alone has hitherto been abandoned to the caprice of Architects, which have given us precepts of it without discernment. They have determined its rules at hazard upon the bare inspection of ancient buildings. They have copied their defects with the same scruples as their beauties, wanting principles to distinguish their difference, they have imposed on themselves the obligation of confounding them – vile imitators, all that has been declared legitimate: limiting all their inquiries by consulting the fact, they have wrongfully concluded the right, and their lessons have only been a fountain of errors.

Vitruvius[1] has only learnt us what was practised in his time; and although sane lights escape from him, that shews a genius capable of penetrating into the true secrets of his art, he does not confine himself to the tearing of the veil that covers them, and avoiding always the abyss's of theory; he leads us through the roads of practice, which frequently makes us wander from the end. All the moderns except Mr. Cordemoy,[2] only comment upon Vitruvius, and follow him in all his wandrings with confidence.

I say Mr. de Cordemoy excepted: this author more profound than the greatest part of others, hath discovered the truth, which was hid to them. His treatise of Architecture is extremely short, but he has comprehended therein excellent principles and views extremely reflected. He was capable in unravelling a little more, to have drawn from thence consequences which would have spread a light upon the obscurities of his art, and banished the shameful uncertainty which renders the rules thereof arbitrary.

It is then to be wished that some great architect may undertake to protect Architecture from the caprice of opinions, in discovering to us the fixt and determined laws thereof. Every art, all sciences have a determined object. To arrive at this object, all the paths cannot be equally good, there is but one that leads directly to the end, and it is that road only that we ought to be acquainted with. In all things there is but one manner of doing well. What then is this art? but that established manner upon evident principles, and applied to the object by invariable principles.

In expectation that some one much more able then myself, may undertake to clear up this chaos of the rules of Architecture, that none of them may remain hereafter, but for which a solid reason may be given. I am endeavouring to produce an inconsiderable ray of light for that end. In considering with attention our great and fine edifices, my soul hath experienced various impressions. Sometimes the charm was so strong that it produced in me a pleasure mixed with transport and enthusiasm: at other times without being so lively drawn away, I found myself employed in an agreeable manner; it was indeed a less pleasure, but nevertheless a true pleasure. Often I remained altogether insensible; often also I was surfeited, shocked, and mutinied. I reflected a long time upon all these different effects. I repeated my observations until I was assured that the same objects always made the same impressions upon me. I have consulted the taste of others, and putting them to the same proof, I found in them all my sensibilities more or less lively, according as their souls had received from nature a less or greater degree of heat. From thence I concluded first that there were in Architecture essential beauties independent of the habitude of the senses, or of the agreement of them. Secondly, that the composition of a piece of Architecture was as all the operations of the mind, susceptible of coldness or vivacity, of exactness and disorder. Thirdly, that there should be for this art as for all others a talent which is not acquired, a measure of genius that is given by nature, and that this talent, this genius, ought nevertheless to be subjected and confined by laws.

In meditating always more upon the various impressions that the different compositions of Architecture made upon me, I was desirous of searching into the cause of their effect. I have called upon self for an account of my own sentiments. I was willing to know why such a thing ravished me, another only pleased me; this was without agreements; that were to me insupportable. This inquiry at first presented to me nothing but darkness and uncertainties. I was not discouraged, I have fathomed the abyss, until I believed I had discovered the bottom. I have not ceased to interrogate my soul until it had rendered me a satisfactory answer.[3] All at once it has given to my eyes a great light. I have beheld distinct objects, where before I could not see anything but mists and clouds: I have seized these objects with ardour, and in making use of their light I have discovered by little and little my doubts to disappear, my difficulties to vanish, and I am at last able to demonstrate to myself, by principles and consequences, the necessity of all the effects; the causes of which I was ignorant. Such is the road I have followed to satisfy myself. It has also appeared to me that it would not be un-useful to impart the success of my endeavours to the public. Although I should only engage my reader to examine if I have not contradicted myself, to criticise with severity my decisions, even to try them to penetrate further into the same abyss, Architecture would thereby be infinitely benefited. I can say with truth, that my principal aim is to put the public, and especially artists in a way to doubt, to conjecture, and to content themselves with difficulty: too happy if I can lead them to make inquiries that might discover my defects, correct my inaccuracies, and to excel my own reasonings.

This is only an Essay, wherein I do but properly hint the things, and pave the way, leaving to others the care of giving to my principles all their extent and all their application; with an intelligence and sagacity which I should not be capable of. I shall say enough herein to furnish architects with fixt rules for working and with infallible means of perfection. I have endeavoured to render myself as intelligible as possible. I have not been able to avoid very often terms of art; they are well enough known. At least their explanation may be found in dictionaries which gives the true sense of them. As my principal design is to form the taste of architects, I avoid all the details found elsewhere, and I find it unnecessary to load this little work with figures which might trouble and distaste the reader.

INTRODUCTION

Architecture of all the useful arts is that which requires the most distinguished talents, as well as the most extensive knowledge. Perhaps as much genius, spirit and taste is required therein as for the forming a Painter or a Poet of the first rank. It is a great mistake to think that mechanism only is required; that all is confined to laying foundations, and building walls, all according to rules; the practice of which supposes eyes accustomed to judge of a line, and hands to manage the travel.

When we speak of the art of building, of the confused heaps of troublesome rubbish, of heaps of shapeless materials, dangerous scaffolds, a frightful game of machines, a multitude of ragged labourers; this is all that presents itself to the imagination of the vulgar, it is the rind, the least agreeable of any art, the ingenious mysteries of which are understood by few, and excite the admiration of all who discern them. Therein are discovered inventions, the boldness of which intimates an extensive and most fruitful genius. Proportions, the use of which declares a severe and systematic precision. Ornaments, the elegance of which discloses a most excellent and delicate thought. Whoever is capable of discerning such a variety of beauties, far from confounding architecture with the lesser arts, will be tempted to place it in the rank of the most profound sciences.

11

The sight of an edifice, built with all the perfection of art, creates a pleasure and enchantment, which becomes irresistible. This view raises in the soul noble and most affecting ideas. We experience therein that sweet emotion, and that agreeable transport that such works excite, which bear the impression of true superiority of genius. A fine building speaks most eloquently for its architect. Mons. Perrault[4] in his writings only appears a knowing man; the colonade of the Louvre determines him the great one.

Architecture owes all that is perfect in it to the Greeks, a free nation, to which it was reserved not to be ignorant of any thing in the arts and sciences. The Romans, worthy of admiring, and capable of copying the most excellent models that the Greeks helped them to, were desirous there to join their own, and did no less then show the whole universe, that when perfection is arrived at, there only remains to imitate or decay.

The barbarity of succeeding ages having buried the liberal arts under the ruins of that empire, which alone retained its taste and principles, created a new system of Architecture, wherein unskilful proportions, ornaments ridiculously connected and heaped together, presented stones as paper work, unformed, ridiculous, and superfluous. This modern architecture hath been but too long the delight of all Europe. Most of our great churches are unfortunately destined to preserve the traces of it to the remotest posterity. To say the truth, with numberless blemishes, this architecture hath had some beauties, and altho' there governs in its most magnificent productions a heavy and gross spirit of invention, we may yet admire the bold traces, the delicacy of the chisel, the majestic and disengaged air that one beholds in certain pieces, which through all their ways have something forlorn and inimitable.[5] But at length more happy genius's discovered from the ancient monuments proofs of the universal wandrings, and also resources to return from them; made to taste the wonders that had in vain been exposed to every eye for so many ages. They meditated on the reports of them, they imitated their skill, and by the force of inquiry, examination, and trial, they again revived the study of good rules, and re-established Architecture in all its rights. They abandoned the ridiculous geugaws of the Goths and Arabians, and substituted in their room manly and elegant appearances of the Doric, Ionic and Corinthian. The French slow of invention, but quick to improve happy imaginations, envied Italy the glory of reviving the magnificent creations of Greece. Every place is full now of monuments that attest the ardour, that established the success of our fathers emulation. We have had our Bramanti, our Michael Angelos, our Vigniolis.[6] The past age, an age where in regard to talents, nature amongst us, hath displayed, and perchance exhausted, all its fruitfulness. The past age has produced in feats of Architecture performers worthy of the best times. But at the moment that we arrive at perfection, as if barbarity had not lost all its rights with us, we are fallen again into the base and defective: every thing seems to threaten at last an entire downfall.

This danger that approaches every day nearer, which may yet be prevented, engages me to propose herein modestly my reflections upon an art for which I have always had the greatest love. In the design I propose, I am not moved by the passion of censure; a passion I detest; nor by the desire of telling new things, a desire I think at least frivolous. Full of esteem for our artists, many of whom are of known abilities: I confine myself to communicate to them my ideas and my doubts, of which I desire them to make a serious examination. If I bring to mind real abuses, as certain usages universally received amongst them, I do not pretend that they should refer themselves to my opinion only, which I submit frankly to their critical judgment. I only request, they will divest themselves of certain prejudices too common, and always hurtful to the progress of the arts.

Don't let them say that not being of their profession I cannot speak of it with sufficient knowledge: it is assuredly the most vain of difficulties. We daily judge of tragedies without having ever made verses. The knowledge of rules is not prohibited to any body, altho' the execution is given but to some.[7] Let them not oppose me with respectable authorities, without being infallible. It would undo all only to judge of what ought to be by what is. The greatest have sometimes erred. It is not therefore a sure means of avoiding error to take always their example for a rule. Don't let them interrupt me by pretended impossibilities: idleness finds many of them, when reason sees none. I am persuaded that those of our architects that have a true zeal for the perfection of their art, will accept of my good-will. They will find, perchance in this writing, reflections that had escaped them. If they make a solid judgement of them they will not disdain to make use of them: this is all I ask of them.

(Such attitudes as regret that an unknown hand carried the torch of truth in the still unfathomed mysteries; rejection of enlightenment through aversion to its source; blind contempt of a zealous amateur seeking to point out the routes leading to the goal of those now straying from it; passionate denial of the success his efforts may have through fear of more attentive critics, more severe judges from now on; such attitudes are only for those Artists bereft of talent and feeling.)[8]

CHAPTER I.

General principles of Architecture.

It is with Architecture as with all other arts; its principles are founded upon simple nature, and in the proceedings of this are clearly shown the rules of that. Let us consider man in his first origin without any other help, without other guide, than the natural instinct of his wants. He wants an abiding place. Near to a gentle stream he perceives a green turf, the growing verdure of which pleases his eye, its tender down invites him, he approaches, and softly extended upon this enameled carpet, he thinks of nothing but to enjoy in peace the gifts of nature: nothing he wants, he desires nothing; but presently the Sun's heat which scorches him, obliges him to seek a shade. He perceives a neighbouring wood, which offers to him the coolness of its shades: he runs to hide himself in its thickets and behold him there content. In the mean time a thousand vapours raised by chance meet one another, and gather themselves together; thick clouds obscure the air, a frightful rain throws itself down as a torrent upon this delicious forest. The man badly covered by the shade of these leaves, knows not how to defend himself from this invading moisture that penetrates on every part. A cave presents itself to his view, he slides into it, and finding himself dry applauds his discovery. But new defects make him dislike his abode, he sees himself in darkness, he breathes an unhealthful air; he goes out of it resolved to supply by his industry the inattentions and neglects of nature. The man is willing to make himself an abode which covers but not buries him. Some branches broken down in the forest are the proper materials for his design. He chooses four of the strongest, which he raises perpendicularly and which he disposes into a square. Above he puts four others across, and upon these he raises some that incline from both sides. This kind of roof is covered with leaves put together, so that neither the sun nor the rain can penetrate therein; and now the man is lodged. Indeed cold and heat will make him sensible of their inconveniences in his house, open on every part; but then he will fill up between the space of the pillars, and will then find himself secure. Such is the step of simple nature: It is to the imitation of her proceedings, to which art owes its birth. The little rustic cabin that I have just described, is the model upon which all the magnificences of architecture have been imagined, it is in coming near in the execution of the simplicity of this first model, that we avoid all essential defects, that we lay hold on true perfection. Pieces of wood raised perpendicularly give us the idea of columns. The horizontal pieces that are laid upon them, afford us the idea of entablatures. In fine the inclining pieces which form the roof give us the Idea of the pediment. See then what all the masters of art have confessed: But then we ought here to be very much on our guard. Never principle was more fruitful in consequences. It is easy from hence to distinguish the part that enters essentially into the composition of an order of architecture, from those which are introduced only by necessity, or which have not been added thereto but by caprice. It is in the essential parts that all the beauties consist; in the part, added thereto by caprice, consist all the defects: this requires explaining. I am endeavouring to throw all the light upon it possible.

Do not let us lose sight of our little rustic cabin. I can see nothing therein, but columns, a [ceiling] or entablature; a pointed roof whose two extremities each of them forms what we call a pediment. As yet there is no arch, still less of an arcade, no pedestal, no attique, no door, even nor window. I conclude then with saying, in all the order of architecture, there is only the column, the entablature, and the pediment that can essentially enter into this composition. If each of these three parts are found placed in the situation and with the form which is necessary for it, there will be nothing to add; for the work is perfectly done. There is remaining with us in France a very fine monument of the ancients, it is what they call at Nismes[9] the square house, connoisseurs or not connoisseurs, everybody admires this beautiful building: What is the reason? because all therein is agreeable to the true principles of architecture. A long square, wherein thirty columns support an entablature, and a roof terminated at the two extremities by a pediment, this is all it contained; this collection hath such a simplicity and grandeur that strikes every eye.

(The Author of the *Examen*[10] does not approve of my establishing a relationship between the essential parts of our buildings and those of the rustic hut. He should have set out the laws which make this relationship null and void. For if it is based on solid grounds as I have alleged and as all Masters of Art have hinted, there are no possible grounds to attack the rules which I establish in the following articles. They are all necessary consequences of this simple principle. If anyone wants to refute my arguments, it all comes to this: show that the principle is false or that the conclusion is badly drawn. As long as neither of these two weapons is used against me, all attacks are in vain. All declamations, all abuse even will be made to no purpose. The discerning Reader will always come back to the question: Is the principle false? Is the deduction wrong? The only reason that objections are made to the relationship established between our buildings and the rustic hut, is that distance must be permitted us from this rough and shapeless construction. In truth we have come far from it, through the universal taste for decoration we have substituted for the carelessness of crude construction; but the essential remains. There is the rough sketch nature gives us; art must only use its resources to embellish, pare down or polish the work, without altering its basic design.[. . .])

ARTICLE I.

The Column.

1st, A Column ought to be exactly perpendicular; because being designed to support all the weight, it is the perfect line that gives it its strength. 2dly, The column ought to be detached, to express more naturally its origin and design. 3rdly, The column should be round, as nature forms nothing square. 4thly, The column should have its diminution from the bottom to the top, as imitating nature, which gives this sort of diminution to all plants. 5thly, A column should bear immediately upon the pavement, as the pillars of the rustic cabin bear immediately upon the ground. All these rules are found justified in our model. We should therefore look on every thing as defective, which deviates from thence without a real necessity.

1st Defect is when instead of detaching the columns, they hold them engaged in the wall. Most certainly the column loses infinitely of its grace, if the least obstacle takes from it, or takes from its circumference, we would live in covered places and not in open halls: Then there is a necessity to fill up the spaces between the columns, and by consequence the columns are engaged. In this case this engagement of the column would not be looked upon as a defect, it will be a licence authorised by necessity: But it is always to be remembered, that every licence declares an imperfection; that we must use them discreetly, and in an impossibility only of doing better. When we are obliged to engage the columns, we should engage them as little as possible, a fourth part at most and still less, so that even in their use they may always retain something of that air of freedom and disengagement, which gives them so much grace. We should always avoid the shameful necessity of using engaged columns. The best way would be to reserve columns for porticos, where they may be perfectly disengaged, and always to suppress them, wherein we are constrained by necessity to fix them against a wall: In short whenever we are subjected to this convenience, which prevents disengaging the column, to let it be entirely seen. Can we believe that the portal of St. Gervais[11] would not be more perfect, if the columns of the Doric order were detached as those are of the superior orders? Was there any thing impossible in it? It is having very little human respect, to dare to censure a work, that the public has always been accustomed to look upon as a masterpiece without a fault. In exposing the imperfections of this edifice, I acquire the right of not sparing any other, without wounding the fondness of every one that it may affect. You will see then I shall speak without reserve. After what I have been saying one will not be so surprised, that connoisseurs set so little a value upon the portal of the Jesuits church in St. Antony's Street.[12] Without reckoning the other faults, which are there to be found in great numbers, the three orders of columns engaged make a most disagreeable effect. It is not there, as Mr Cordemoy has ingenuously confessed, that an architecture in basso relievo wherein the clearest sight will not please its self. I have often groaned at the madness of some architects for the attached columns, but I should never have thought that it could enter into the mind of man to engage columns one in another; there is not a more monstrous and insupportable defect. Novices themselves in the art do agree in this; nevertheless this fault is found repeated upon all the fronts of the inward court of the Louvre. So gross a blunder in so great a work may be placed in the rank of the humiliations of the human mind.

2nd Defect. This is in the place of round pillars to employ square pilasters. Pilasters[13] are but a bad representation of columns. Their angles declare the narrowness of the art, and deviate sensibly from the simplicity of nature. There is in them lively and incommodious stops that obstruct the view. Their surfaces without the roundings give a flat air to the whole order. They are not susceptible of that diminution that makes one of the greatest harmonies of the column. Wherever they are

16

made use of the columns would be used with as much advantage. We ought then to look upon them as a low innovation, which not being founded in nature in any manner could not be adapted but by ignorance, and is not yet allowed of but by custom. The taste of pilasters has prevailed every where: alas! where are they not found? Nevertheless to get rid of this taste, one need only reflect upon the grand effect, that the columns always produce, an effect, which is entirely destroyed by pilasters. Change the joint columns of the portico of the Louvre, and you will rob it of all its beauty. Compare the two sides of this magnificent portico with the pavilions in the front that terminates it, what a difference is there! there is not a valet or any servant who does not enquire why the pavilions were not finished as the rest of the work. This regret is inspired by the taste of what is truly beautiful, a natural taste of all the world. It is the same order of architecture which governs upon all the fronts: but the portico exposes columns, the pavilions present pilasters: This variety alone suffices to trouble all the pleasure, that a more uniform collection would have occasioned. In entering into the spaces of the chapel of Versailles, every one is struck with the beauty of the columns, with the smartness of the intercolumnation; but as soon as one arrives at the spring of the round point, there is no body who may not see with chagrin that fine train of columns interrupted by a slovenly pilaster. We must therefore conclude that the use of pilasters is one of the greatest abuses that has been introduced into architecture; and as one abuse never comes alone, they have given us folded pilasters in the angles, pilasters arched in the circular plans, hidden pilasters confounding one in the other. The pilaster is a trifle that they put to all sort of uses. They marry it with the column, and it seems as if placed there as an inseparable companion: was there ever a more ridiculous allotment? Of what use is this pilaster engaged behind a detached column? Indeed I know nothing of it, and I defy them to give one reason for it. Is there any sense in uniting two things so incompatible? The column has its diminution, the pilaster cannot have any; from whence it happens that this will appear either too straight at bottom, or too large at top. Is there any space to fill up? It is filled up with a pilaster. Is there any defect to hide, any place to enrich? There is a half or a quarter of a pilaster cut. The ancients were not more scrupulous than the moderns upon this article. They even have sometimes shown less delicacy than these: for they have made porticos alternatively mixed with columns and pilasters. In a word the pilaster is a thing I cannot bear with. This aversion was born with me: The more I have studied architecture, the more I have found in it true principles wherewith to justify in myself this aversion. They make use of pilasters; shall one say to avoid the expence of columns? I answer if we are governed only by the consideration of expense, there remains the part only of suppressing every order of architecture. One may without this help form buildings which shall have beauty. But if we would make use of the great orders of architecture, I shall never pardon the retrenching the column, which is their most essential part.

17

3rd Defect. This is instead of the ordinary diminution of the columns to give them a swelling about the third of the height of their shank.[14] I do not believe nature ever produced any thing to justify this swelling. Let us do justice to our artists. It is a long time since that the fluted pillars have been practised, there are none to be found in our latest works. The rustic columns[15] are no less vicious than the fluted. Philibert of Ormus,[16] who was a great admirer, of them and who has filled the palace of the Tuilleries with them, had not so pure a taste that his authority ought to establish their admittance. This great man deserved distinguished praises. Architecture will always reckon him amongst the number of the most excellent masters. It is to him we owe the revival of this fine art amongst us, but his works still taste of the depravity of former ages. The rustic columns are but a capricious imagination. It is not an entire column that one sees; they are different cut pieces of columns, heaped one upon another in an unequal model, the effect of which has something pitiful and extremely harsh. The fine palace of Luxemburg[17] is not indifferently disfigured by these rustic columns. The twisted columns are still worse. He that invented them had undoubtedly ability, for these required a great deal to execute them well; but if he had had taste and judgment, most certain he would not have taken so much pains to execute so ridiculous an imagination. The twisted columns are in truth in architecture, what in human bodies is called a leg broken in wrestling, but the singularity of it has at first given pleasure to some who were enemies to the natural taste. They have thought the work fine, because it was difficult. Others still of a lower taste have given us pieces of columns straight, upon which they have miserably enchased the two thirds of a column twisted. Others in short ensnared by the same taste, but overcome by the difficulty of the execution, have been desirous to satisfy themselves in twisting the channelling of an upright column. These extravagancies have above all been effected in repairs of altars. I admire the canopies of St. Peter's at Rome, of the Val de Grace and the invalids,[18] but I shall never forgive the great men that have given the design of them, for having made use of the twisted columns. Do not let us run into the counterfeit brillant; it only proves the want of genius; let us confine ourselves to the simple and natural, it is the only path of beauty.

4th Defect. This is in the room[19] of making the columns rest immediately upon the pavement, to hoist them upon pedestals. The columns being, if I may say so, the legs of the edifice, it is absurd to give them other legs. The pedestals of which I speak have been invented through want. When they have had columns that were too short, they have taken the method of mounting them on scaffolds to supply their want of elevation. The same inconvenience has made them have recourse to double pedestals, when one only was not sufficient. Nothing can give to architecture a more heavy and ridiculous air than these enormous and angular masseys, that they make use of as a surbase[20] to the column. The portico of the palace of Soubise[21] is intolerable, because of the frightful pedestals: and if the columns touched the bottom, it would be a charming work. The columns may bear upon a continued massy wall, that is to say upon the foot of a pedestal without a base, without cornish,[22] and of a middle height; and this always when we build a portico whose interior pavement is higher than the pavement of the place that the portico surrounds. Far from blaming this practice, I am persuaded that it will have great success. The columns may also sometimes bear each of them upon a little separate base, when the spaces between the columns are filled up by a supported ballustrade, as the space of the chapel of Versailles, and in the portico of the Louvre. This second manner is less perfect: it would even be deficient, if it was not excused through the necessity of placing a supported ballustrade to a portico which is found raised to the first story. But when upon a level they place pedestals under the columns, it is a fault nothing can excuse. The altars of our churches offer most of them this ridiculous spectacle. They would have columns there; it would have cost too much to have them of a model great enough, to make them bear immediately upon the pavement, from thence arose the necessity of pedestals. At the principal altar of the Jesuits church in St. Antony's-street, one sees for that reason columns raised upon two pedestals, one upon the other. I shall not recite, but this time, this monstrous performance. All that one can say for it, is that of all the gross faults made in architecture there has not been one therein that has been forgot. In a word pedestals are only good to support a statue, and it is an essential want of taste to appoint them for any other use. Let what will be said, that pedestals have been admitted in all times, that Vitruvius and all his commentators have assigned to every order his own: That in the finest pieces of ancient edifices are found some of them; I have my principle, from which I will never depart. Every invention which is against nature, or for which one cannot give a solid reason, had she the greatest approvers, is a bad invention, and we must proscribe it.

CHAPTER II.

The different orders of Architecture.

The number of the orders of Architecture is not absolutely fixed. The Greeks have no more of them than three. The Romans have reckoned even to five of them, and the French are willing to add thereto a sixth. As this is an affair of taste and genius, it naturally appears fit to leave to artists an entire liberty in this respect. We are not in a worse condition than the Greeks and Romans: since the first have invented three orders of Architecture, and that the second have pretended to add thereto two others of their kind; why should it not then be permitted for us to pave a new way according to their example? It is certain we have a right thereto, and provided that we use it with as much success as the Greeks, we shall deserve to partake in this point of their true glory. The fact is that till the present time all our efforts have not made any real invention. Perchance we shall one day see some happy genius take a flight, and lead us by unknown ways to the discovery of a beauty that has escaped the ancients. We will hope all from the bounties of nature, which very likely has not yet distributed all her gifts. In taking things in their actual position, it seems to me that we have properly but three orders of Architecture, the Doric, Ionic and Corinthian. They are the only ones wherein one can observe invention and particular character, whilst the Tuscan and Composite have nothing but borrowed, and do not differ from the forgoing ones but in a very accidental manner. The Tuscan is only a gross Doric, and the Composite an agreeable mixture of the Ionic and Corinthian. It is then true, that architecture has only midling obligations to the Romans, and that it owes all that is precious and solid to the Greeks alone. I will not speak here of the Gothic and Arabic or Moorish orders which have governed a long time, they have nothing remarkable; the one, but its excessive heaviness, the other, but its excessive lightness. There is in both so little invention, of taste and exactness, that one only looks upon them as the subsisting proofs of the barbarity that has filled up the space of time for ten ages. From the revival of the fine arts our Architects have had the noble ambition to immortalize the french name by some new invention in Architecture. Philibert of Orme is he who has made the greatest effort, to penetrate beyond the limits wherein til his time we were constantly confined. He was desirous of giving us a new order, but though he was otherwise a very able man and perchance more able than any one of those that have followed him, he has shewn in the execution of his project a great barrenness of genius. All is reduced to a new composite ill enough understood; for it is generally neglected. It has been long since remarked, that invention is not our talent. We value ourselves more for perfecting the inventions of others, and to improve upon them. However it be, three orders only are our real riches. The Doric is the first and the heaviest: Designed for those works that require great solidity. The proportions thereof are regulated after such a manner as to give it the greatest strength possible, without banishing delicacy. The Corinthian is the last and the lightest: Designed for works that require more elegancy; they have so regulated the proportions of it, to give it the greatest delicacy possible, without excluding strength. The Ionic is between both. It has neither all the solidity of the Doric, nor all the elegancy of the Corinthian. It partakes of each. These three orders so understood seem to fill all the extent of the art, in supplying all our wants and all our tastes. The Doric and Corinthian are two extremes beyond which one cannot go without meeting on one side the massey, on the other the weak. Between these two extremes the Ionic gives us a just and happy medium. See then all the gradation from the solid to the delicate ingeniously filled up. It will then be extremely difficult to add any thing to so happy an invention.

ARTICLE VI

The manner of enriching the various orders of Architecture

An order of Architecture may be enriched three ways: either by the richness of the materials, or the richness of the workmanship, or by both together. By the richness of the materials, when we use therein marble, brass or gold. By the richness of the labour when we ornament the members with carving. By them both together; when marble, brass or gold have been joined to what is most excellent in sculpture. It is very rare that we can use marble, brass and gold. The expense thereof is too considerable. It is not in a great degree but in princes houses, and in our churches, that one can have such materials to work upon. Whatever they are there are many things to be observed in the method of using them. The various colours of marble require a particular attention to make a sortment of them agreeable to a good taste. We must not be led away by the price that the novelty only has given to certain marbles, nor believe that the work will be exactly fine, because it will have marble, either than comes a great away or that the quarry is exhausted. The granite and porphyric are in the case, and they are not for that reason the most agreeable colour. The eye does not know whether it be scarce or the only one, and this then is a perfection, which is not to be regarded, but it's known very well if a colour is fine, and herein it is necessary to satisfy the sight. Upon this principle we should place in the rank of the most beautiful marble such whose colours are very lively, the veins of which are well shown, well shaded, or thrown into a certain disorder and with a humorous sharpness. To make the sortments as we ought of marble, see here the rules which we ought to follow as near as possible.

First, we should reserve the white marble without veins for such places wherein there is to be sculpture. The veins of the marble always spoil what the chisel has touched; they confound the windings,[23] and produce inequalities of light very disadvantageous to the neatness of the work.

Secondly, we must use white veined marble for all the bottom[24] work, and reserve the marble that is variously coloured for the columns, the frizes and all panels of incrustation.

Thirdly, it is necessary that the colours of the marble agree as much as possible with the character of the subject. It would be equally absurd to employ green marble, red, yellow, or any other shining colours in a mausolaeum, and to be lavish of black marble in the ornaments of an altar.

Fourthly, we must avoid those sorts of marble that are too cutting,[25] and get more those of one and the same colour. The too great abounding of brown colours render the work sad, and diminishes the light. The soft colours, if they are too governing,[26] render the work cold and insipid. It is then essential to mix one with the other, and to make one of value by the other. There is still herein a harmony which we ought to study the agreements of.

The decorations of marble always want to be relieved by that of gilding. Brass gilt is what agrees the best, but the expence of it is very great. Through economy we often make use of wood or lead gilt. Wood takes the gilding very well, but the moisture of the marble makes it perish. Lead is not subject to this inconvenience, but it never takes the gilding well. We must never be lavish in gilding. It is sufficient that there be enough to enliven the sadness of the marble too strong in colour.

The second manner of enriching Architecture is to carve the members of it. I have already said to avoid confusion one should never carve the whole, and the best would be to carve alternately. There remains for me to observe various particularities concerning carved work, and which decides the success of it. The contours thereof ought to be well terminated,[27] and very plain. If they are well terminated, the work will be properly done; if they are very natural, it will be done with much grace. The design of it must be natural. Our architects have for some time given in to a capricious humour that has had the vogue.[28] All the contours of their ornaments were capriciously disfigured. This singularity has not been wanting to succeed immediately in a nation as inconstant, and as light as our own. If it had reigned a long time, we were about to comfort ourselves upon the foolish inventions of the vandals. Happy it is we are returned from it, and this dangerous epidemicy is upon its conclusion. In pieces of sculpture we should avoid the round swelling, because the thickness of its massys is always a heavy air to Architecture: we should always keep to the bas relief. The sculptures of the chapel of Versailles may serve as a model. Every thing there is plainly designed, properly terminated, and of a middle relief, and from thence it comes that the eye is extremely satisfied therewith.

I have nothing to say upon the third manner of enriching an order of Architecture. The rules I have given upon the two preceding, ought to reunite in this.

Notes

1   Marcus Vitruvius Pollio, an architect and military engineer in Rome under Augustus (27 B.C.–A.D.14), wrote the treatise *On Architecture* which became the basis for Palladio's and later classical architects' theories.

2   Jean Louis de Cordemoy, L'Abbé de Cordemoy, was an early neoclassical theorist, strongly influenced by Perrault, who wrote *Nouveau traité de toute l'architecture* (1706). In this he argued that architectural forms should be simple, clear, and never used merely for decoration. He strongly favoured Greek as opposed to Roman architecture, a view clearly shared by Laugier.

3   This technique of self-enquiry is reminiscent of the philosophical approach used by René Descartes (1596–1650).See p. 141, note 15.

4   Claude Perrault (1613–88), doctor and amateur architect, built the east front of the Louvre in 1677. He also published an edition of Vitruvius in 1673.

5   Here Laugier is more generous to gothic architecture than most of his neoclassical contemporaries would have been. The sense of loss (occasioned by the fall of the Roman Empire) that pervades this paragraph should be compared with that of Gibbon.

6   See Chambers, p. 37 note 8.

7   Compare this claim of the layman's right to criticize with a similar argument put

forward by La Font de Saint Yenne (p. 58).

8   Paragraphs in round brackets come from the second edition (1755) and are newly translated by Rosemary Smith.

9   The Maison Carrée at Nîmes (16 B.C.); a temple built in the Corinthian Order during the Augustan Period.

10   *Examen d'un essai sur l'architecture*, Paris, 1753.

11   Parisian Church whose facade (built in 1616, probably by Salomon de Brosse (1571–1626)) displayed all three superimposed orders.

12   Probably the Church of St. Paul and St. Louis in Paris which was based on Vignola's Jesuit Church in Rome, the Gesù, begun in 1568.

13   A pilaster is a rectangular column projecting only slightly from a wall.

14   Laugier is referring here to a misuse of entasis. Entasis was a very slight convex curve used in columns to correct the optical illusion of concavity created by perfectly straight columns. Misuse, as far as Laugier was concerned, occurred when this entasis was exaggerated or when Palladio's formula (of letting the column rise vertically for the first third of its length and then tapering it) was misapplied.

15   A column whose shaft is interrupted by square blocks.

16   Philibert Delorme (1510–70), French Renaissance architect and engineer. He wrote the influential *Le Premier tôme de l'Architecture de Philibert de l'Orme* (1567).

17   Château de Luxembourg built 1615–24 by Salomon de Brosse.

18   Val de Grâce: Paris church built and decorated 1645–63 (architects: Mansart (1598–1666) and, later, Lemercier (*c.* 1580–1654)). Les Invalides: this refers to the second chapel on the site built in the baroque style between 1679 and 1691 by J. H. Mansart (1646–1708).

19   i.e. instead of.

20   i.e. an extra base.

21   The Hôtel de Soubise, rebuilt by Germain Boffrand (1667–1754) between 1735 and 1739 in the Rococo style.

22   i.e. cornice.

23   i.e. the outline.

24   i.e. the background.

25   i.e. glaring or clashing.

26   i.e. dominating.

27   i.e. defined.

28   The style which Laugier found so offensive is generally called Rococo. It was particularly popular in France and Germany but it never fully established itself in England.

WILLIAM CHAMBERS

On Civil Architecture (1759, 1791)

From William Chambers, *A Treatise on Civil Architecture*, Printed by J. Haberkorn, London, 1759. Reprinted from edition edited by Joseph Gwilt, Priestly and Weale Ltd, London, 1825.

Sir William Chambers (1723–96), the son of a Scottish merchant, began his architectural training at the École des Arts in Paris (run by J. F. Blondel, see p. 55) in 1749. He travelled in Italy and had earlier been to India and Canton with the East India Company. He was appointed architectural tutor to the young George III and as a result became the most influential establishment architect (though less prolific than Robert Adam) from the late 1760s on. His *Treatise on Civil Architecture* rapidly became the standard textbook in English superseding the many pattern books and more superficial practical–theoretical works. Chambers had little time for the Gothic taste and disliked what he called the 'Attic deformity' of Greek architecture. His own style was a comfortable blend of French neoclassicism with the established English Palladianism. His book, like Laugier's Essay (see p. 8), provides a theoretical justification for classical architecture but is a great deal more specific in its instructions for the use of classical motifs, and he differed from Laugier in being far readier to abandon principles in the face of constructional or decorative necessity or convenience.

Although *Civil Architecture* was originally published in 1759 much of what follows was first included by Chambers in the third 'considerably augmented' edition of 1791. He also took the opportunity the third edition afforded him of changing the title from *Treatise on Civil Architecture* to *A Treatise on the Decorative part of Civil Architecture*. Interestingly enough the 1759 edition prints a list of subscribers, among whom can be found J.-F. Blondel, Gainsborough and Joshua Reynolds.

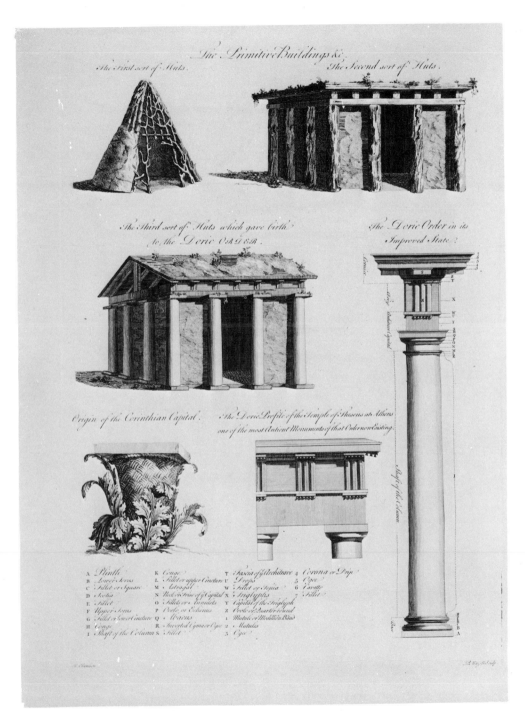

The Primitive Buildings &c.

The First sort of Huts.

The Second sort of Huts.

The Third sort of Huts which gave birth to the Doric Order.

The Doric Order in its Improved State.

Origin of the Corinthian Capital.

The Doric Profile of the Temple of Theseus at Athens one of the most Antient Monuments of that Order now Existing.

A	Plinth	K	Conge	T	Fascia of the Architrave	4	Corona or Drip
B	Lower Torus	L	Fillet or upper Cincture	V	Drops	5	Ogee
C	Fillet or Square	M	Astragal	W	Fillet or Tenia	6	Cavetto
D	Scotia	N	Plackor Frise of Capital	X	Triglyphs	7	Fillet
E	Fillet	O	Fillets or Annulets	Y	Capital of the Triglyph		
F	Upper Torus	P	Ovolo or Echinus	Z	Ovolo & Quarter round		
G	Fillet or lower Cincture	Q	Abacus	1	Mutule or Medillion Band		
H	Conge	R	Inverted Cymaor Ogee	2	Mutules		
I	Shaft of the Column	S	Fillet	3	Ogee		

Plate 6   William Chambers   Primitive Buildings etc.

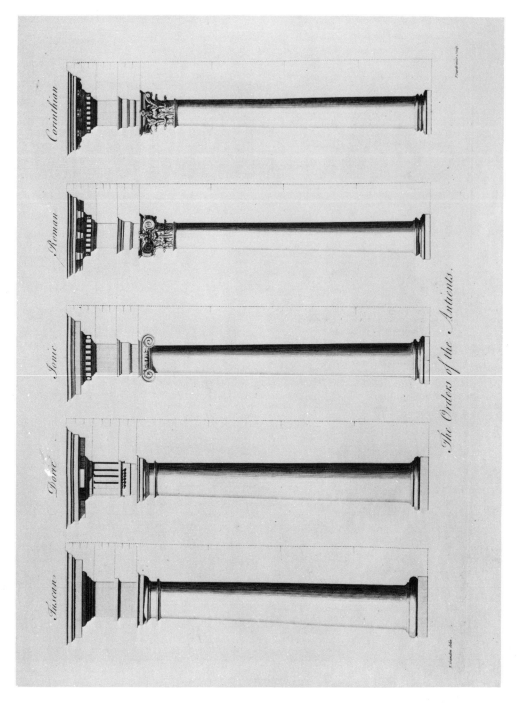

Plate 7   William Chambers   The Orders of the Antients

THE ROMAN OR COMPOSITE ORDER.

Plan of the Capital.

Soffit of the Corona.

Angular View of the Capital.

Composite Base.

Plate 8   William Chambers   The Roman or Composite Order

INTRODUCTION

Civil Architecture[1] is that branch of the builder's art, which has for its objects all structures, either sacred or prophane, calculated to supply the wants and comforts; or to promote, extend, and diversify, the pleasures of life: either contrived to facilitate the business; give lustre to the duties; or display the state and distinctions of society. Its purpose is to erect edifices, in which strength and duration, shall unite with beauty, convenience, and salubrity; to ascertain their value; and to build them with every attention to safety, ease, and economy.

Many, and singularly opposite, must be the qualities and attainments of him, who aspires to excel, in an art so variously directed. "Architecture," says father Laugier,[2] "is of all useful arts, that which requires the most distinguished talents; there is perhaps as much genius, good sense, and taste requisite, to constitute a great architect; as to form a painter or poet of the first class. It would be a strange error to suppose it merely mechanical; and confined to digging foundations, or building walls, by rules of which the practice, supposes nothing more than eyes accustomed to judge of a perpendicular, and hands expert in the management of a trowel. In contemplating the builder's art, all indeed that strikes a vulgar imagination, are, confused mounds of incommodious ruins; formless heaps of collected materials; dangerous scaffolding; a frightful clatter of hammers, tools, and working machinery; an army of slovenly bespattered labourers and workmen: but these are only as it were, the rough bark of an art, the ingenious mysteries of which, though only discoverable to few observers, excite the admiration of all who comprehend them. They perceive inventions of which the boldness, implies a genius, at once fertile and comprehensive; proportions of which the justness, announces a severe and systematic precision; ornaments of which the excellence, discovers exquisite and delicate feelings: and whoever is qualified to taste so many real beauties, will, I am certain, far from attempting to confound architecture with the inferior arts, be strongly inclined to rank it amongst those that are most exalted."

Vitruvius[3] requires that the architect should have both ingenuity and application, observing, that wit without labour, or labour without wit, never arrived at perfection. "He should," says he, "be a writer and draughtsman, understand geometry, optics, and arithmetic; be a good historian and philosopher, well skilled in music, and not ignorant in either physic, law, or astrology. The same author farther requires that he should be possessed of a great and enterprizing mind; be equitable, trusty, and totally free from avarice; without which, it would be impossible to discharge the duties of his station with due propriety: ever disinterested, he should be less solicitous of acquiring riches, than honour, and fame, by his profession."[...]

In fact, the business of an architect requires him rather to be a learned judge, than a skilful operator; and when he knows how to direct, and instruct others, with precision; to examine, judge, and value, their performances with masterly accuracy; he may truly be said to have acquired all that most men can acquire; there are but few instances of such prodigies as Michael Angelo Buonaroti,[4] who was at once the first architect, painter, geometrician, anatomist and sculptor, of his time. [. . .]

Some part of all this knowledge, though it might have been necessary to an artist of the Augustan age, is not absolutely so now; some part of it too, seems rather ostentatiously introduced; more to enumerate the learned writer's own qualifications than such as were indispensably necessary, to every man of his profession: the remaining part shall be mentioned in its place; while I venture to give an opinion, concerning the requisite qualifications of an architect: differing in some particulars, from those above given; but more adapted, I flatter myself, to the wants, customs, and modes of life of our contemporaries, as well as to the duties and avocations of a modern architect.

Architecture being an active as well as speculative art, in which exertions of the body, the organs of sense, and of utterance, are equally necessary with efforts of the mind; it naturally follows, that such as intend to make it their profession, should enter the lists with a good stock of health, vigor and agility; they should neither be lame nor unwieldy; neither awkward, slow, nor helpless; neither purblind nor deaf; nor have any thing ridiculous about them, either natural or acquired. Their understanding should be sound; the sight and apprehension quick; the reasoning facilities clear, and unwarped by prejudices; the temper enterprising, steady, resolute, and though benevolent, rather spirited than passive, meek, or effeminate.

The necessity of these qualities, in one destined to direct and manage great works, to govern and control numerous bands of clerks, inspectors, artists, artificers, workmen, and labourers, must be sufficiently obvious. And as at the present time, few engage in any profession, till qualified for the world by a proper school education at least; it must be supposed, that to a competent proficiency in the learned languages, the student adds a thorough knowledge of his own; so as to speak and write it correctly at least, if not elegantly; that he is a good penman; versed in accounts; a ready practitioner in arithmetic; and has received and profited by such other instructions, as tend to fix the moral character; to inculcate integrity; to polish the minds, and improve the manners of youth. [. . .]

To these qualifications, mental and corporeal, must be united genius, or a strong inclination and bias of mind towards the pursuit in question; without which little success can be expected. This quality, whether it be the gift of God, or a fortuitous propensity; whether innate or acquired, has not unaptly been compared to those instincts implanted by nature in different animals; by which, they are enabled to comprehend, and to perform certain things with much ease, while others, not having the same natural disposition, neither comprehend, nor can perform them; thus the man of genius, or he whose mind is peculiarly adapted to the contemplation of his subject, comprehends with ease, distinguishes with perspicuity, treasures up with nice selection, whatever is ingenious, extraordinary, useful, or elegant; his imagination ever active in a favorite pursuit, will abound in ideas, combinations, and improvements, equally new, striking, and agreeable; while he who mistakes his way, and applies to studies for which nature, or early impressions, have not prepared him, labours sluggishly, without relish, as without effect; like Sisyphus, ever toiling up a hill, the summit of which he is never to reach.

As many sorts of knowledge, very opposite in their natures, come under the architect's consideration, his genius must be of a complex sort, endowed with the vivacity and powers of imagination, requisite to produce sublime or extraordinary compositions; and at the same time, with the industry, patience, and penetration, necessary to investigate mathematical truths, discuss difficult, sometimes irksome subjects, and enter into details of various sorts, often as tiresome, as they are necessary; a genius equally capable of expanding to the noblest and most elevated conceptions or of shrinking to the level of the meanest and minutest enquiries; as Doctor Johnson expresses it, a mind, that at once comprehends the vast, and attends to the minute.

But though genius be the basis of excellence, it can alone, produce but little; the richest soil when neglected, affords no other crop than weeds; and from the happiest disposition without culture, without knowledge of rules to guide, or judgment to restrain, little more can be expected than capricious conceits, or luxuriant extravagancies.

Of mathematical knowledge, geometry, trigonometry, and conic sections should be understood, as teaching the construction, properties, contents, and divisions of the forms used in building. Likewise mechanics and hydraulics, which treat of the formation, and ascertain the effects of all kinds of machinery, simple or complex, used in building; likewise of the raising, conveyance, and application of water, as well for the common uses of life, as to produce many extraordinary effects, very ornamental in gardening, and efficacious in manufactures.

These sciences furthermore treat of the gravitation of bodies, and in what manner, and by what laws, they move and act upon each other, under different circumstances; with many other particulars of frequent and material use in an art, where vast weights are to be moved, and in which structures, of whatever form, must be calculated to carry great and indeterminate burthens, to stand the shock of heavy laden carriages, and to resist the utmost fury of the elements.

By optics, particularly that part which is called perspective, the artist is enabled to judge with precision, of the effects of his compositions when carried into execution, and also to represent them more pleasingly in design, as well for his own satisfaction, as to give his employers a more perfect idea of his intentions than could be collected from geometrical drawings. And an acquaintance with the other branches will be useful on many occasions, in the distribution of light, to produce particular striking effects, and in the disposal of mirrors, to create deceptions, multiply objects, and raise ideas of far greater than the real magnitude or extent of that which is exhibited to view.

As to a painter, or sculptor, so to an architect, a thorough mastery in design is indispensably necessary; it is the *sine quâ non*, and the *mai a bastanza* of Carlo Maratta,[5] is fully as applicable in one art as in the others; for if the architect's mind be not copiously stored with correct ideas of forms, and habituated by long practice to vary and combine them as the fancy operates: or if his hand has not the power of representing with precision and force, what the imagination suggests, his compositions will ever be feeble, formal, and ungraceful, and he will stand unqualified to discharge the principal part of his duty, which is, to invent and dispose all that enters into his design, and to guide the painter, sculptor, and every other artist or artificer, by advice and precise directions, as far at least, as relates to the outline and effect of their performances, that all may be the effort of one mind, master of its object, and all the parts be calculated to produce a general uniformly supported whole; which never can be the case where artists and artificers are left to themselves, as each, naturally enough, considers the perfection of his own part, sometimes without comprehending, and always without attention to, the whole composition. Even Bernini,[6] though an able architect, could seldom refrain from sacrificing architecture to the graces of sculpture and painting, the ill consequences of which, are sufficiently conspicuous in several of his works, but particularly in his piazza of St. Peter's, where the statues placed upon the colonnades, instead of standing upright as they should do, in all such situations, are so whimsically contorted, that at a little distance they seem to be performing a dance, and very considerably injure the effect of that magnificent approach to the first building in the Christian world.

To the knowledge, practice, and facility of hand just mentioned, composers in architecture must unite a perfect acquaintance with all kinds of proportions, having relation either to the grandeur, beauty, strength, or convenience of structures, their variations as occasions require, and the different effects which situation, distance, light, or other circumstances have upon them; which is a science of very considerable difficulty, and only to be attained by much experience and close observation.

He furthermore must be well versed in the customs, ceremonies, and modes of life of all degrees of men his cotemporaries, their occupations and amusements, the number and employments of their domestics, equipages and appurtenances, in what manner the business allotted to each is performed, and what is requisite or proper to facilitate the service, with many other particulars which, though seemingly trifling, must not be unknown to him who is to provide for the wants, and gratify the expectations of all.

Neither must he be ignorant of ancient history, fable and mythology, nor of antiquities, as far as relates to the structures, sculpture, ornaments, and utensils of the Egyptians, Greeks, Romans, and

Etrurians;[7] as the established style of decoration collects its forms, combinations, symbols, and allusions, from these abundant sources, which time, and the concurring approbation of many ages, have rendered venerable.

The painter's canvas, and the sculptor's block, are their ultimate objects; but the architect's attention must at once be directed to the grandeur or beauty, strength, duration, fit contrivance, and economical execution of his compositions; qualities that ever clash, and which it often is exceedingly difficult to reconcile. His different plans, elevations, and sections, must all be considered at the same time, and like the parts of a piece of music, be contrived to harmonize and set each other off to most advantage.

To the excellence of the designer's art, must yet be added, the humbler, though not less useful skill, of the mechanic and accountant; for however able the draughtsman, he should not deem himself an architect, nor venture upon practising in that capacity, till master of the executive parts of this profession.

These imply an acquaintance with all the known approved methods of building every kind of structure, securely, and for duration. How difficulties arising from situation, nature of soils, or other adventitious circumstances, are to be surmounted; and precisely what precautions the occasion may require, in order to avoid superfluous expence, by avoiding to employ superfluous remedies.

They farther imply a power of conducting large works, with order and economy; of measuring correctly according to established usages, of regulating the accounts with accuracy, of employing with discernment, directing and governing with skill and temper, many men of different professions, capacities and dispositions; all without violence or clamour, yet with full effect.

To mastery in these particulars must be added, proficiency in all the arts, liberal or mechanic, having relation to the building or adorning structures; a capacity of determining exactly, the goodness of the different materials used, with the degree of perfection and consequent value at all times, of every kind of work, from the stately splendid productions of the pencil and chissel, to the most trifling objects employed in a fabric: together with all the circumstances constituting their value; as upon these, its occasional fluctuation must depend.

Considerable as this detail may seem, it is yet insufficient. A builder, like a chemist, must analyze his substances; be so much master of the constituent parts of his composition, their necessary forms and dimensions, that, as those of the profession term it, he may be able to take the whole building to pieces, and estimate from his designs, the total amount of the structure, before a single stone is prepared.

To ignorance, or inattention in this particular, of which for serious reasons, no architect should ever be ignorant, or careless, must be ascribed the distressful, often the ruinous, uncertainty of common estimates; for some, who condescend to estimate their own productions, know perhaps, but imperfectly, how their designs are to be carried into execution, and consequently omit in the valuation, much that must be done. And some, who being too great for such minute investigations, employ others to estimate, without describing thoroughly the manner in which they intend to proceed, leave them so much in the dark, that even if capable, they can do little more than guess at the value, and are seldom or ever right in their conjectures.

Others there are, who being either unqualified, or too idle to calculate themselves, and perhaps too parsimonious to employ any other person, for it is a work of time, and considerable expense, value by the square; an operation, both easy and expeditious, but of all, the most fallacious, excepting in common buildings, of similar forms and dimensions, built and finished in the same manner; where, the amount of what has been done, may be a guide to value by. But in extraordinary works, these rapid estimators never hit the mark, and are generally so far wide of it, as to draw shame and reproaches on themselves; regret, difficulties, sometimes ruin, both on the employer and the tradesmen employed.

As one, in whose honour and judgment the employer confides, and to whom the employed look up for protection and justice; as mediator and judge between them, on subjects generally important: the architect's skill, vigilance, and activity, should equal the consequence of his station, and studious to sustain his character, attentive to justify the confidence reposed in him, he must neither inadvertently, nor otherwise, bring on unexpected ruinous expenses; neither countenance, nor suffer, imposition on the one hand; oppressive parsimony, or ill directed liberality, on the other.

Ornamental gardening, which in Italy, France, and other countries of the European continent, constitutes a part of the architect's profession; is here in other hands: and, with a few exceptions, in very improper ones. Should that pleasing art be ever practised by men, who have made composition in general, a study; who by having seen much, have stored the fancy with copious imagery; and by proficiency in the arts of design, formed a correct and elegant taste; we might expect to find much more variety and far higher perfection in works of that sort, than can now be expected, or is yet to be boasted of.

It seems almost superfluous to observe, that an architect cannot aspire to superiority in his profession, without having travelled; for it must be obvious, that an art founded upon reasoning and much observation, is not to be learnt without it; books cannot avail; descriptions, even drawings or prints, are but weak substitutes of realities: and an artist who constantly inhabits the same place, converses with the same people, and has the same objects always obtruding on his view, must necessarily have very confined notions, few ideas, and many prejudices. Travelling rouses the imagination; the sight of great, new, or uncommon objects, elevates the mind to sublime conception; enriches the fancy with numerous ideas; sets the reasoning faculties in motion: he who has beheld with attentive consideration, the venerable remains of ancient magnificence; or studiously examined the splendor of modern times, in the productions of the sublime Buonarroti, Bramante, Vignola, Palladio, Raffaello, Polidoro, Peruzzi, Sansovino, Sanmicheli, Ammanati, Bernini, Pietro da Cortona,[8] and many other original masters; whose works are the ornament and pride of the European continent; must have acquired notions, far more extensive, and superior to him, whose information has been gleaned from the copiers, or feeble imitators, of these great men, and their stupendous works: he must be in composition more animated, varied, and luxuriant; in design, more learned, correct, and graceful: ever governed by a taste formed at the fountain's head, upon the purest models; and impressed with the effect of those great objects, which some time or other in life, have been the admiration of most who either claim distinction, or aspire to elegance; he must always labour with greater certainty of success.

Thus habituated to consider with the rigour of critical accuracy, we learn to see objects in their true light; without attention, either to casual approbation or dislike: to distinguish truth through the veil of obscurity, and detect pretence however speciously sustained. Travelling to an artist, is, as the university to a man of letters, the last stage of a regular education; which opens the mind to a more liberal and extensive train of thinking, diffuses an air of importance over the whole man, and stamps value upon his opinions: it affords him opportunities of forming connections with the great, the learned, or the rich; and the friendships he makes while abroad, are frequently the first causes of his reputation, and success at home.

OF THE ORDERS OF ARCHITECTURE IN GENERAL

The orders of Architecture, as has been observed, are the basis upon which the whole decorative part of the art is chiefly built, and towards which the attention of the artist must ever be directed, even where no orders are introduced. In them, originate most of the forms used in decoration; they regulate most of the proportions; and to their combination multiplied, varied, and arranged in a thousand different ways, architecture is indebted, for its most splendid productions.

These orders, are different modes of building, said, originally to have been imitated from the primitive huts; being composed of such parts as were essential in their construction, and afterwards also in the temples of antiquity; which, though at first simple and rude, were in the course of time, and by the ingenuity of succeeding architects, wrought up and improved, to such a pitch of perfection, that they were by way of excellence distinguished by the name of orders.

Of these there are five: three said to be of Grecian origin, are called Grecian orders; being distinguished by the names of Doric, Ionic, and Corinthian: they exhibit three distinct characters of composition; supposed to have been suggested, by the diversity of character in the human frame. The remaining two being of Italian origin, are called

Latin orders; they are distinguished by the names of Tuscan and Roman, and were probably invented with a view of extending the characteristic bounds, on one side, still farther towards strength and simplicity; as on the other, towards elegance and profusion of enrichments.

The ingenuity of man has, hitherto, not been able to produce a sixth order, though large premiums have been offered, and numerous attempts been made, by men of first rate talents, to accomplish it. Such is the fettered human imagination, such the scanty store of its ideas, that Doric, Ionic, and Corinthian, have ever floated uppermost; and all that has ever been produced, amounts to nothing more, than different arrangements and combinations of their parts, with some trifling deviations, scarcely deserving notice; the whole generally tending more to diminish, than to increase the beauty of the ancient orders.

The substitution of cocks, owls, or lions' heads, &c. for roses; of trophies, cornucopias, lilies, sphinxes, or even men, women, and children, for volutes; the introduction of feathers, lyres, flower de luces,[9] or coronets, for leaves; are more alterations, than improvements; and the suspension of festoons of flowers, or collars of knighthood, over the other enrichments of a capital, like lace on embroidery: rather tends to complicate and confuse the form, than to augment its grace, or contribute to its excellence.

The suppression of parts of the ancient orders, with a view to produce novelty, has of late years, been practised among us, with full as little success. And though it is not wished to restrain sallies of imagination, nor to discourage genius from attempting to invent; yet it is apprehended, that attempts to alter the primary forms invented by the ancients, and established by the concurring approbation of many ages, must ever be attended with dangerous consequences, must always be difficult, and seldom, if ever, successful. It is like coining words, which, whatever may be their value, are at first but ill received, and must have the sanction of time, to secure them a current reception.

An order is composed of two principal members, the column and the entablature, each of which is divided into three principal parts. Those of the column are the base, the shaft, and the capital; those of the entablature are the architrave, the frize, and the cornice. All these are again subdivided into many smaller parts, the disposition, number, forms, and dimensions of which, characterize each order, and express the degree of strength or delicacy, richness or simplicity, peculiar to it.

In the opinion of Scamozzi,[10] columns should not be less than seven of their diameters in height, nor more than ten; the former being, according to him, a good proportion in the Tuscan, and the latter in the Corinthian order. The practice of the ancients in their best works being conformable to this precept, I have, as authorized by the doctrine of Vitruvius, made the Tuscan column seven diameters in height, and the Doric eight, the Ionic nine, as Palladio and Vignola have done, and the Corinthian and Composite ten; which last measure is a mean between the proportions observed in the Pantheon,[11] and at the three columns in the Campo Vaccino,[12] both which are esteemed most excellent models of the Corinthian order.

The height of the entablature, in all the orders, I have made one quarter of the height of the column, which was the common practice of the ancients, who, in all sorts of entablatures, seldom exceeded, or fell much short of, that measure.

Nevertheless Palladio, Scamozzi, Alberti, Barbaro, Cataneo, Delorme,[13] and others of the modern architects, have made their entablatures much lower in the Ionic, Composite, and Corinthian orders, than in the Tuscan or Doric. This, on some occasions, may not only be excusable, but highly proper; particularly where the inter-columniations are wide, as in a second or third order, in private houses, or inside decorations, where lightness should be preferred to dignity, and where expense, with every impediment to the conveniency of the fabric, are carefully to be avoided; but to set entirely aside a proportion which seems to have had the general approbation of the ancient artists, is surely presuming too far.[. . .]

Columns, in imitation of trees from which they drew their origin, are tapered in their shafts. In the antiques, the diminution is variously performed; sometimes beginning from the foot of the shaft, at others from one quarter, or one third of its height, the lower part being left perfectly cylindrical. The former of these methods was most in use amongst the ancients, and being the most natural, seems to claim the preference, though the latter has been almost universally practised by modern artists, from a supposition, perhaps, of its being more graceful, as it is more marked and strikingly perceptible. [. . .]

OF ORNAMENTS

[. . .] Variety in ornaments, must not be carried to an excess. In architecture they are only accessories, and therefore they should not be too striking, nor capable of long detaining the attention from the main object. Those of the mouldings in particular, should be simple, uniform, and never composed of more than two different represen-tations upon each moulding: which ought to be cut equally deep, be formed of the same number of parts, all nearly of the same dimensions; in order to produce one even uninterrupted hue throughout; that so the eye may not be more strongly attracted, by any particular part, than by the whole composition.

When mouldings of the same form and size, are employed in one profile, they should be enriched with the same kind of ornaments; by which means, the figure of the profile will be better apprehended, and the artist will avoid the imputation of a puerile minuteness, neither much to his own credit, nor of any advantage to his works.[. . .]

OF PILASTERS

[. . .] Pilasters differ from columns in their plan only, which is square, as that of the column is round. Their bases, capitals, and entablatures have the same parts, with all the same heights and projections as those of columns, and they are distinguished in the same manner, by the names of Tuscan, Doric, Ionic, Composite, and Corinthian.

Of the two, the column is, doubtless, most perfect. Nevertheless, there are occasions in which pilasters may be employed with great propriety; and some, where they are, on various accounts, even preferable to columns.

I am not ignorant that several authors are of a different opinion: a certain French Jesuit[14] in particular, who some thirty years ago, first published an essay on architecture, which from its plausibility, force, and elegance of diction, went through several editions, and operated very powerfully on the superficial part of European connoisseurs. He inveighs vehemently against pilasters, as against almost every other architectonic form but such as were imitated by the first builders in stone, from the primitive wooden huts; as if, in the whole catalogue of arts, architecture should be the only one confined to its pristine simplicity, and secluded from any deviation or improvement whatever.[. . .]

Concerning the reverend father's inborn aversion, much need not be said, and several others of his objections, as they consist more of words than meaning, seem not to require any refutation. [. . .]

Notes

1   'Civil' as opposed to Naval or Military Architecture.
2   Abbé Laugier author of the *Essay on Architecture*.
3   Marcus Vitruvius Pollio, an architect and military engineer in Rome under Augustus (27 B.C.–A.D. 14) wrote the treatise *On Architecture* which became the basis for Palladio's and later classical architects' theories.
4   Michelangelo (1475–1564), one of the most famous artists of the Renaissance. He was also in charge of the fortification of Florence and built a large part of St. Peter's in Rome.
5   *sine qua non*: 'The essential quality' (literally 'without which not'); *mai a bastanza*: 'the feature you can't get enough of'. Maratta (1625–1713), a painter of the late baroque, rejected its more dramatic elements and worked in a neoclassical style that appealed immensely to the eighteenth century.
6   Gian Lorenzo Bernini (1598–1680), baroque architect and sculptor, designed the great square and colonnade in front of St. Peter's Rome.
7   The eighteenth century did not distinguish native Etruscan work from Greek or Greek influenced work found in Italy. The latter is now generally termed Apulian. Etrurian could refer to all three though Apulian vases were what principally interested collectors. The confusion was enshrined in Wedgwood's choice of the name Etruria (1766) for the new works at Stoke-on-Trent in which he was making 'antique' vases.
8   A selection of architects, not all well known. Michelangelo Buonarotti (1475–1564), Bramante (1444–1514), Vignola (1507–73), Palladio (1508–80), Raphael (1483–1520), probably Polidoro da Caravaggio (c. 1495–1543), Peruzzi (1481–1536), Sansovino (1486–1570), Sanmichele (c.1484–1559), Ammanati (1511–92), Bernini (1598–1680), Pietro da Cortona (1596–1669).
9   Fleurs de lys.
10   Vincenzo Scamozzi (1552–1616) the most important of Palladio's immediate followers.

11   The Pantheon in Rome built A.D. 126.
12   The Roman Forum was called the 'Field of Cows' because it was used for pasture throughout the Renaissance.
13   Alberti (1407–72) wrote *Ten Books on Architecture* (published 1452–85) the first Renaissance treatise on building. Barbaro published a commentary on Vitruvius (1556). Cataneo – lesser known late Renaissance architect. P. Delorme (*c*.1510–70), French architect influential through his publications. (See Laugier p. 23, note 16.)
14   Abbé Laugier, see p. 22, note 2.

JAMES STUART
and NICHOLAS REVETT

The Antiquities of Athens (1762)

From James Stuart and Nicholas Revett, *The Antiquities of Athens*, Printed by John Haberkorn, London, 1762. Vol. I.

James 'Athenian' Stuart (1713–88) and Nicholas Revett (1720–1804) were among several Europeans to visit Greece in the mid-eighteenth century. They spent four years from 1751 in Greece, Stuart (who was both architect and painter – he succeeded Hogarth as Serjeant Painter at the Office of Works in 1764) making topographical drawings and Revett measured drawings of the buildings. The results of their work were published by the Society of Dilettanti in a lavish book illustrating the 'different Greek modes of decorating buildings' in 1762 (further volumes followed in 1789, 1795 and 1816). Stuart, who was clearly a bad businessman but a convivial fellow (unlike Robert Adam) quite failed to capitalize on his book and its effect on architecture was minimal. However, it was immediately appreciated as a major work of scholarship making clear the true nature of the Greek orders and their usage as opposed to their Roman copies. This stress on the importance of the Greek contribution to the classical orders can also be found in Cordemoy (see p. 22, note 2) and M. A. Laugier (p. 12).

PREFACE

The ruined Edifices of Rome have for many years engaged the attention of those who apply themselves to the study of Architecture; and have generally been considered, as Models and Standard of regular and ornamental Building. Many representations of them drawn and engraved by skilful Artists have been published, by which means the Study of the Art has been everywhere greatly facilitated, and the general practice of it improved and promoted. Insomuch that what is now esteemed the most elegant manner of decorating Buildings, was originally formed, and has been since established on Examples, which the Antiquities of Rome have furnished.

But although the World is enriched with Collections of this sort already published, we thought it would be a Work not unacceptable to the lovers of Architecture, if we added to those Collections, some Examples drawn from the Antiquities of Greece; and we were confirmed in our opinion by this consideration principally, that as Greece was the great Mistress of the Arts, and Rome, in this respect, no more than her disciple, it may be presumed, all the most admired Buildings which adorned that imperial City, were but imitations of Grecian originals.

Hence it seemed probable that if accurate Representations of these Originals were published, the World would be enabled to form, not only more extensive, but juster Ideas than have hitherto been obtained, concerning Architecture, and the state in which it existed during the best ages of antiquity. It even seemed that a performance of this kind might contribute to the improvement of the Art itself, which at present appeared to be founded on too partial and too scanty a system of ancient Examples.

For during those Ages of violence and barbarism, which began with the declension and continued long after the destruction of the Roman Empire, the beautiful Edifices which had been erected in Italy with such great labour and expence, were neglected or destroyed; so that, to use a very common expression, it may truly be said, that Architecture lay for Ages buried in its own ruins; and although from these Ruins, it has Phenix-like received a second birth, we may nevertheless conclude, that many of the beauties and elegancies which enhanced its ancient Splendor, are still wanting, and that it has not yet by any means recovered all its former Perfection.

This Conclusion becomes sufficiently obvious, when we consider that the great Artists, by whose industry this noble Art has been revived, were obliged to shape its present Form, after those Ideas only, which the casual remains of Italy suggested to them; and these Remains are so far from furnishing all the materials necessary for a complete Restoration of Architecture in all its parts, that the best collections of them, those published by Palladio and Desgodetz,[1] cannot be said to afford a sufficient variety of Examples for restoring even the three Orders of Columns; for they are deficient in what relates to the Doric and Ionic, the two most ancient of these orders.

If from what has been said it should appear, that Architecture is reduced and restrained within narrower limits than could be wished, for want of a greater number of ancient Examples than have hitherto been published; it must then be granted, that every such example of beautiful Form or Proportion, wherever it may be found, is a valuable addition to the former Stock; and does, when published, become a material acquisition to the Art.

But of all the Countries, which were embellished by the Ancients with magnificent Buildings, Greece appears principally to merit our Attention; since, if we believe the Ancients themselves, the most beautiful Orders and Dispositions of Columns were invented in that Country, and the most celebrated Works of Architecture were created there [. . .]

They [the arts of the Greeks] were indeed at length assiduously cherished and cultivated at Rome. That City being now Mistress of the World and possessed of unbounded Wealth and Power, became ambitious also of the utmost embellishments which these Arts could bestow. They could not, however, though assisted by Roman Munificence, reascend to that height of Perfection, which they had attained in Greece during the happy period we have already mentioned. And it is peculiarly remarkable, that when the Roman Authors themselves, celebrate any exquisite production of the Art; it is the work of Phidias, Praxiteles, Myron, Lysippis, Zeuxis, Appelles,[2] or in brief of some Artist, who adorned that happy Period; and not of those who had worked at Rome, or had lived nearer to their own times than the Age of Alexander.

It seemed therefore evident that Greece is the Place where the most beautiful Edifices were erected, and where the purest and most elegant Examples of ancient Architecture are to be discovered.

But whether or no, it be allowed, that these Edifices deserved all the encomiums which have been bestowed on them; it will certainly be a study of some delight and curiosity, to observe wherein the Grecian and Roman style of Building differ; for differ they certainly do; and to decide, by a judicious examination, which is the best.

Notes

1   Andrea Palladio (1508–80) Italian architect and theorist. Wrote the highly influential *Quattro libri dell'architettura* (1570) and gave his name to the Palladian movement. Antoine Desgodetz, or Desgodets (1653–1728), architectural theorist and professor at the Académie. He was strongly influenced by J. L. de Cordemoy (see p. 22, note 2). He wrote *Les Édifices antiques de Rome* (1682), *Traité des Ordres d'architecture* (1711) and the posthumously published *Les lois des batîments* (1748). The RIBA Library has a copy of *Les Édifices* annotated in his own hand by James Stuart.

2   Phidias: Greek sculptor (*c*.490–*c*.417 B.C.)
     Praxiteles: Greek sculptor (*fl.c*. 364 B.C.)
     Myron: Greek sculptor (*c*.480–?B.C.)
     Lysippis: Greek sculptor (Fourth century B.C.)
     Zeuxis: Greek painter (*fl.* 424–380 B.C.)
     Appelles: Greek painter (Fourth century B.C.)

LE BLANC

Letter to the Comte de Caylus[1] *(1747)*

From Jean-Bernard le Blanc, *Lettres de Monsieur l'Abbé Le Blanc concernant le gouvernement, la politique et les moeurs des Anglois et des Francois,* Paris, 1747. Reprinted from the first translation: London and Dublin, 1747.

Jean-Bernard Le Blanc (1706–81), known as l'Abbé Le Blanc, was a poet, art critic and man of letters. He was educated at the Jesuit Collège des Godrans in Dijon, where he was a fellow pupil of Buffon. In 1728 he moved to Paris and soon made friends in literary circles, including Mme Geoffrin. He spent some time from 1737 to 1738 in England. Like Voltaire (see Vol. 1, p. 122) Le Blanc produced a series of letters, one of which we reproduce below, comparing the English and French nations. Like both Voltaire and Laugier, Le Blanc clearly admires the France of Louis XIV, despite its 'unenlightened' state. In his 1747 review of the Salon, Le Blanc upheld the right of the man of letters to pass judgment on works of art, an idea put forward by La Font de Saint-Yenne in 1746 (See La Font extract p. 58). A similar assertion of the rights of the non-specialist, along with an appeal to Nature as a source of aesthetic principles, can be found in Laugier (p. 8). Le Blanc's dislike of 'Gothick barbarity' was shared by Gibbon and to a lesser extent by Laugier.

His strongly anti-Rococo views brought him to Mme de Pompadour's attention. In 1749 he was appointed Historiographer of the King's Buildings shortly before his educational visit to Italy. The other members of the party were Soufflot and C. N. Cochin (see p. 48). Le Blanc's enthusiasm for the neoclassical style was an undoubted influence on the young Marigny. (See p. 54, note 1.)

You are acquainted with the *Vitruvius Britannicus;*[2] and as you are not only a master of the rules of all the arts, but have that exquisite taste, which is much superior to the rules themselves, because it is the hidden principle of them; don't you think the author of that work has had all the remarkable buildings in England, designed and engraved on purpose to shew us, that architecture is a science, which is not yet naturalised here? It is one of those that depend on taste, and therefore may be still a long time foreign in this island. It is not that architecture is void of known principles and certain rules, some of them, founded on nature; as this, for example; *That the strongest ought to support the weakest*; and others successively established and unanimously agreed to, as the result of the experience of our predecessors: but the most difficult and most extensive part of it, that of decoration, and the ornaments it is capable of receiving, taste alone must give; and taste gives nothing in this country.

Architecture is one of those things, which most particularly indicate the magnificence of a nation; and from magnificence, we easily conclude grandeur. Though we would only judge of the Romans, by the ruins which are left us of their stately amphitheatres, would they not nevertheless be the object of our admiration? All that history relates of the Aegyptians, makes less impression on us, than those vast pyramids, which have subsisted in their country for so many ages. What an idea, will the front of the Louvre[3] leave to posterity, of the power of that monarch who erected it, and of the degree of perfection, to which the arts were carried, in his reign!

Italy is the country of Europe that has produced the most master-pieces of modern architecture. The English have yet only the merit of having copied some of them. The architect, who built their famous church of St. Paul, at London, has only reduced the plan of St. Peter's at Rome, to two thirds of it's size; the proportions excepted, which he has very ill observed: and a man, who understands but little of architecture, may easily perceive that throughout the whole, wherever he deviates from his model, he has committed the greatest errors.

The greatest part of the country houses, for there are few in London, that deserve to be spoke of, are also in the Italian taste; but it has not been always justly applied. One of the first things an architect should consider, is the climate where he builds; what is proper for a country as hot, and where the air is as clear as that of Naples; is improper in a much colder climate, and where the sky is not so serene. The Italians in their houses, ought to screen themselves from the excessive heat, the English, who do not see the sun so often as they would, ought to admit it, as much as possible. A pleasure-house for a vigna[4] in Rome, is not a model for a country house, in the neighbourhood of London.

Those Englishmen who want to pass for men of taste have to do many things against the grain; they are forced in every thing to constrain their own taste and affect a foreign one. They pay very dear, say they, to hear musick that displeases them; their tables are covered with meats to which they cannot accustom their palates; they wear cloaths that are troublesome to them, and live in houses where they are not at their ease. This is not the only country where we find men who are the dupes of this sort of madness, who sacrifice their ease to the fashions of a real pleasure to what is only the shadow of it. How must this folly make true philosophers laugh!

The celebrated INIGO JONES, has adorned London with some edifices of taste, and amongst the rest, with the magnificent Banqueting-house at Whitehall, one of the finest pieces of architecture in Europe. On the oher hand my lord BURLINGTON[5] who has joined example to precept, by the fine house which he has built for himself in London, and some things which he has published concerning architecture; has endeavoured to give his countrymen a taste for it. But these models have not made the English architects more expert; for whenever they attempt to do any thing more than barely to copy, they erect nothing but heavy masses of stone, like that of Blenheim-Palace,[6] the plan and front of which you will find in the *Vitruvius Britannicus*.

The English also, in the ornaments of their buildings, very often affect a taste that is perfectly childish. They have built for the queen in Richmond-park, a small structure to place her country library in; which they call Merlin's-cave. 'Tis only an octogon pavilion, with a Gothick arched roof; and has nothing in it answerable to the idea that its name gives us of it. You find no other curiosity there, except that sorcerer and some other figures in wax as large as life. So far from finding any thing in this building that savours of enchantment and the magician's power, it is impossible to conceive of anything of a worse taste.

The English are not always happy in their inventions; they are unacquainted with the exactness of proportions, and elegancy of forms in every thing: and therefore succeed no better in the taste of their furniture than in that of the ornaments of their houses. We regard the Italians as our masters in the architecture and external ornaments of large buildings; but the French seem to understand the distribution and internal proportions, the best of any nation in Europe; and the bad taste of the English particularly shews itself in these.

However, the love of truth does not permit me to flatter my countrymen in their faults. I shall be bold enough to own and condemn the pernicious effects of our natural levity. We now a-days in every thing that depends upon design, as well as in the productions of the understanding, begin to deviate from that noble simplicity which the great masters of antiquity followed in all things; and ours have endeavoured to imitate. It was not for want of invention, that both the one and the others adopted this; and those who affect to deviate from it, prove their bad taste much more than the fruitfulness of theirs. Whatever they say, to hide their ignorance or want of capacity, it is much easier to follow our own humour, and tack scraps of verses together, than to contrive a fine scene, and represent nature truly in it. This seeming abundance is a real sterility. He that has both a fruitful genius and fine taste, thinks he ought to reject all superfluous beauty. But in this sort of riches as well as others, a man must be rich indeed, not to regret the loss of those, he has ill employed. A bungling designer invents ornaments of all forms, and crowds them on one another; a man of BOUCHARDON's[7] genius, invents only noble ones, and distributes them with judgment. The Goths were as prodigal of them, as the Greeks avaricious; but the example of the last shews us, that the force of genius, and perfection of art, are to arrive at this happy simplicity.

I am certain, sir, you see with regret, that we already affect in several instances to deviate from the taste of Louis XIV's time; the golden age for letters and fine arts in France. Nothing is more monstrous, as HORACE observes, than to couple together being of different natures; and yet it is what many of our artists at this time glory in doing. A cupid is the contrast of a dragon; and a shell, of a bat's wing; they no longer observe any order, any probability, in their productions. They heap cornices, bases, columns, cascades, rushes and rocks, in a confused manner, one upon another; and in some corner of this chaos, they will place a cupid in a great fright, and have a festoon of flowers above the whole. And this is what they call designs of a new taste. Thus by going beyond the due limits, we are returned to the Gothick barbarity. Perhaps there are things, where too much symmetry is a fault, but it is commonly a greater, to observe none; there should always be a symmetry in the whole mass, though not in all its parts. It is indispensably necessary in architecture. A building, of whatsoever sort, is a whole composed of parts, that ought to correspond with each other; and it is in the ornaments we should use variety. Statues placed facing each other in a niche, have a bad effect, if they do not appear very nearly of the same size; but they offend the eye as much if their attitudes are exactly the same. Thus in a flower-garden; the beds, both in their middles, and at their ends, should have the same proportions and points which answer to each other but to observe exactly the same regularity, in the disposition of every one of the flowers, which are planted there to vary the prospect, would be to affect a symmetry equally childish and insipid. But how far are we at present, with regard to ornaments, from this defect! We will have nothing that looks like symmetry. If they adorn the frontispiece of a house, with the arms of the person who built it; they place the escutcheon in a diagonal line, with the coronet on one side of it, so that it looks if it were going to fall down. They forsake the perpendicular and horizontal lines as much as possible; and place nothing now, either upright or level.

Our architects in time past were too wise to take those liberties, which the moderns think so ingenious. In this more adventurous age, they would have every thing make a shew, and turn things topsy-turvy in such a manner, that I am afraid this ill taste may prove their heads are topsy-turvy likewise. Our sensible artists, often blush at things they are obliged to do; but the torrent bears them down, and they are forced to do like the rest, to get employment. They ask them for things of the new fashion; of those shapes, which bear no resemblance to any thing; and they let them have them.

This fashion is most visible in that part of our furniture, which is designed chiefly for ornaments; and indeed taste which admits of every thing at this time, runs perhaps more ridiculous lengths than ever it did. What do those pendulum-clocks, so much in fashion, resemble; which

45

have neither basis nor console,[8] but seem to spring out of the wainscot, to which they are fastened? Those stags, dogs, huntsmen, or Chinese figures, which they dispose in so odd a manner about the dial-plate; are they its natural ornaments? Those cartouches[9] whether at the top, the bottom, or on the sides, which have nothing to answer them; are they really of a good taste? A shape that is, as we may say, undetermined, and unlike all known shapes, is so far from being pleasing; that we can't conceive any thing elegant, which is not terminated, and does not resemble something. There is in all sorts of things, a *Right*, without which there can be no beauty; and it is the sense of this *Right*, that constitutes taste.

What is there more ridiculous, than varnishing the brasses which are placed for ornament in a chimney? What more absurd, than fastening pagods of China-ware to them? Thus by varying shapes too much, we run into extravagance; and by crowding too much riches into ornaments, fall into foppery. We hardly avoid one excess before we are guilty of a greater. Nothing is so difficult as to eradicate bad taste: it is a hydra with many heads, one of which you have no sooner cut off, but another springs up. There are some happy mortals, who by superior strength compass the destruction of it. Thus MOLIERE, in his time, by the beauty of his plays, forced the people to abandon the silly jests, playing with words and double-meanings to which they were accustomed. Thus the *Puget*[10] of our time, may, by the productions of an invention as wise as fruitful, and an exquisite judgment, restore the true taste to design, by recalling us to beautiful nature; and make every thing, that ignorance and bad taste has lately produced, fall into contempt. That of this time, sir, is so depraved, that I do not think it can continue much longer; and the attention and encouragement which you give to the arts, must necessarily hasten its fall.

> I have the honour to be,
> Sir, your most humble, &c.

Notes

1   Comte de Caylus (1692–1765). Antiquarian and collector, engraver and writer on art. The Comte de Caylus is acknowledged as one of the founders of archaeology as a scientific discipline. He travelled widely in Italy and the Near East, collecting antique remains, which he later published in seven volumes as *Recueil d'Antiquités Egyptiennes, Etrusques, Grècques, Romaines et Gauloises*, 1752–67. A strong supporter of Classicism in art and a generous patron of certain academic painters, he was a life-long enemy of Diderot.

2   *Vitruvius Britannicus*. Colen Campbell's architectural treatise, published 1715–25, was the central text for Palladian architects.

3   Le Blanc is referring to the great colonnaded east front of the Louvre, completed to designs by Claude Perrault, Le Brun and Le Vau in c 1677, during the reign of Louis XIV.

4   Vigna: a vineyard or garden.

5   Richard Boyle, Lord Burlington, 3rd Earl (1694–1753). Architect and patron of the arts. He designed his own villa at Chiswick on a Palladian model. He financed the publication of Kent's *Designs of Inigo Jones*, 1727, and published Palladio's

drawings of Roman baths: *Fabbriche Antiche*, 1730.

6   Blenheim Palace was built between 1705–20 by Vanbrugh and Hawksmoor for the Duke of Marlborough.

7   Edmé Bouchardon (1698–1762). Sculptor, medallist and draughtsman. His work marks the beginning of the Classical reaction against the Rococo. He designed the equestrian statue of Louis XV to stand in Place Louis XV, now Place de la Concorde. It was destroyed during the Revolution.

8   A console is an ornamental bracket with a curved outline. Le Blanc is referring to the typical Rococo wall clock of asymmetrical design, decorated with elaborate gilt bronze mounts.

9   A cartouche is an ornamental scroll, usually bearing an inscription.

10   Pierre Puget (1620–94) sculptor. Puget was largely responsible for introducing the full-blown Baroque style to French sculpture. His work did not meet with official approval and much of it was done outside Paris.

COCHIN

A Petition... by a Society of Artists (1754)

From Charles-Nicolas Cochin, 'Supplication aux Orfèvres, Ciseleurs, Sculpteurs en bois pour les appartements et autres, par une société d'Artistes', *Mercure de France*, December, 1754. Reprinted from Svend Eriksen, *Early Neo-Classicism in France*, ed. P. Thornton, Faber, London, 1974.

Charles-Nicolas Cochin (1715–90) was an engraver and designer. He was born into a family of artists, and was taught engraving by his father and by Le Bas. Among his designs and illustrations were many for the royal *fêtes*, and a series of portrait medallions of prominent figures of his time, including the Englishmen Horace Walpole and David Garrick. He too was chosen by Mme de Pompadour to accompany her brother on his study tour of Italy, 1749–51 (see Le Blanc p. 42). In 1752 he was appointed Keeper of the King's Drawings and in 1755, Secretary to the Academy of Painting and Sculpture. In this role he was able to exercise considerable influence on art. He was closely associated with Diderot and Chardin and left one of the fullest accounts of Chardin's life, written in 1780 (a year after the artist's death).

His publications included *Observations sur les antiquités de la ville d'Herculaneum*, 1754, and *Voyage d'Italie*, 1758. In 1754–55 he published two articles in the *Mercure de France* attacking the Rococo, the first of which is below. The second, dated February 1755, purported to be an indignant reply on behalf of the Rococo architects. In fact, Cochin simply used it to make out a still stronger case for a return to the Antique principles of decoration.

Be it most humbly represented to these gentlemen that however great the efforts made by the French nation for several years past to accustom its reason to bend to the waywardness of their fancy, it has not been entirely able to succeed. Wherefore these gentlemen are petitioned to be so obliging as to observe henceforward certain simple rules dictated by good sense, from which we cannot tear the principles of our understanding. It would be a very meritorious act on the part of these gentlemen if they would condescend to our weakness and pardon us the real impossibility in which we find ourselves of extinguishing all the lights of our reason out of complaisance towards them.

Example. Goldsmiths are prayed that whenever they execute a life-size artichoke or celery stalk on the lid of a *pot à oille*[1] or on some other piece of plate, to be good enough not to set beside it a hare as big as a finger, a lark as large as life and a pheasant about a quarter or a fifth of its real size; children of the same size as a vine leaf, or figures supposed to be life-sized which are borne up by an ornamental leaf that could hardly support a little bird without bending; trees whose trunks are not as big as a single one of their leaves, and a quantity of other things of an equal force of reasoning.

We should also be infinitely obliged to them if they would be good enough not to alter the intention of things and to remember, for instance, that a candlestick ought to be straight and perpendicular in order to support its light, not twisted as if someone had forced it out of shape; that its pan ought to be concave so as to hold the wax that runs down and not convex so as to let it drop in a sheet on the candlestick, besides a quantity of other charming devices no less unreasonable which it would take too long to mention.

Similarly Messrs the carvers of panelling in the trophies[2] that they carve are prayed to be pleased not to make a scythe smaller than an hour-glass, a hat or a tambourine larger than a bass viol, a man's head smaller than a rose, a bill-hook as large as a rake, &c. It is with much regret that we find ourselves obliged to beg them to confine their genius within these laws of proportion, however simple they may be. We are but too conscious that in subjecting themselves to good sense quite a number of personages who now pass for great geniuses will find themselves without any genius at all, but it is now no longer possible for us to lend them our countenance. Before uttering loud protests we have endured with all possible patience and made unbelievable efforts to admire these inventions which are so marvellous that they are beyond the province of reason, yet our coarse commonsense invariably excites us to find them ridiculous. But we shall restrain ourselves from raising objections to the taste that reigns in the interior decoration of our buildings. We are far too good citizens to desire to reduce to sudden beggary so many honest folk who know nothing else. We do not even wish to ask them for a little restraint in the use of those palm trees[3] which they cause to grow so abundantly in our apartments, on chimney-pieces, round mirrors, against walls, in fact everywhere; this would be to deprive them of their last resource. But perhaps we may at least hope to obtain from them that when things can be made right-angled they will be kind enough not to twist them, that when arches can be semi-circular they will be kind enough not to vitiate their outlines by those serpentine contours which they seem to have learnt from the writing masters and which are so fashionable that they are used even in making plans of buildings.[4] They are called 'forms' by those who use them, but they forget to add the epithet 'bad' which is inseparable from them. We give our consent nevertheless to their serving up this twisted merchandise to all provincials and foreigners who shall be poor enough connoisseurs to prefer our modern taste to that of the last century. The more these inventions are scattered among foreigners the more we may hope to maintain the superiority of France.[5] We beg them to consider that we furnish them with fine straight wood and that they ruin us with expense by working it into all these sinuous forms, that in bending our doors in order to subject them to the circularities which it pleases the good taste of our modern architects to give to all our rooms, they make us expend much more than if they were to make them straight, and that we find no advantage in them since we pass just as well through a straight door as through a rounded door. As for the curves of the walls of our apartments we find no other convenience in them save that we no longer know where to place or how to arrange our chairs or other furniture against them. The carvers are begged to be kind enough to put faith in the assurances we give them, we who have no interest in deceiving them, that regular straight, right-angled, round and oval forms are as rich a decoration as all their inventions and that since to execute them precisely is more difficult than to execute all those grasses, bats-wings and other paltry ornaments which are in current use, they will do more honour to their talents. And that finally the eyes of a great many honest folk, of whom we are one, will be under an inexpressible obligation to them if they are no longer annoyed by irrational disproportion and by so great an abundance of twisted and extravagant ornaments.

And if we ask too many things at once, let them at least grant us this one grace, that from henceforth the principal moulding[6] which now ordinarily they torment, shall become and shall remain straight in conformity with the principles of good architecture. We shall then consent to their making their ornaments twist about and above it as much as meets their good pleasure, and we shall consider ourselves the less unfortunate because a man of good taste, should such an apartment fall to his lot, will be able to knock away all such stuff with a chisel, and rediscover the plain moulding, which will provide him with a sensible decoration that will cause his reason no suffering.

Our readers will readily perceive that a fair number of the complaints we have addressed to the carvers might with good reason also be addressed to the architects, but the truth is that we do not dare do it. These gentlemen are not so easily ruled; there is hardly one of them who entertains any doubt of his talents and does not boast of them with entire confidence. We do not presume sufficiently on our credit amongst them to flatter ourselves that even with the best reasons in the world we might work their conversion. Had we felt boldness enough we should respectfully have invited them to be kind enough to examine from time to time the old Louvre, the Tuileries and several other royal buildings of the last century which are universally recognised as fine things, and not to give us occasion so frequently for thinking that they have never seen these buildings, which yet are so near them. We should have begged them to spare us those wretched angled forms upon which it seems they are agreed for the salient part of all façades and we should have assured them in the sincerity of our conscience that all obtuse and acute angles (unless introduced from necessity, as in fortifications) are disagreeable in architecture, and that only the right angle produces a good effect. They would lose thereby their octagonal saloons, but why should a right-angled saloon not be as beautiful? It would no longer be necessary to suppress cornices in interiors so as to evade the difficulty of distributing the ornaments proper to them successfully. They would not have been reduced to substituting grasses or similar miserable fancies for the modillions, denticules,[7] and other ornaments invented by persons who were more learned than they and since received of all nations after mature examination. We should have begged them to respect the natural beauty of the stones that they draw from the quarry straight and with right angles, and to be kind enough not to spoil them in order to make them assume forms which cause us the loss of half of them and give public proofs of the derangement of our brains. We should have begged them to deliver us from the tediousness of seeing arched windows on every house from the ground floor to the garrets, in such fashion that it seems as if a pact had been sworn to make no others. Even the window-frames desire to join in the parade and twist themselves about in the prettiest manner in the world with no other advantage save that of giving a great deal of trouble to the carpenter and difficulty to the glazier when he has to cut panes into these Baroque forms.

We should also have had some small representations to make to them on the subject of that general mould into which it seems they cast all carriage-gates by making the moulding of the cornice always turn up into an arched form without being followed by those of the architrave,[8] so that the cornice tells falsely and if they add their cherished console,[9] useless though it be, they do not know where to place it. Beyond the middle of the pilaster it is ridiculous, in the middle it does not receive the fall of the arch. Even while granting them that the mansard roof[10] is a marvellous and wonderful invention, worthy of being transmitted to our remotest posterity could it but be constructed of marble, we should none the less have been able to beg them to be kind enough to be a little more sparing of it, and in its place to offer sometimes an attic storey,[11] which being perpendicular and of stone would appear more regular and more in keeping with the rest of the building. For at last one becomes tired of always seeing a blue house on top of a white.

How many favours should we not have had to ask from them, but in vain should we hope they might be willing to grant us even one. So far as they are concerned all we can do is to sigh in secret and wait until such time as their invention is exhausted and they themselves become tired

51

of it. It seems that this time is approaching, for they do nothing but repeat themselves and there is room for us to hope that the desire to do something novel will bring back the old style of architecture.

Notes

1   Pot à oille: entrée dish.

2   Trophies are sculpted or carved groups of arms or armour commemorating victories. Often interspersed with floral motifs to form a festoon, they are usually found above a door or mirror.

3   Palm trees. The palm leaf was a popular decorative motif in the eighteenth century.

4   Plans of buildings. Rounded contours were finding their way into the ground-plans of buildings. Round and oval rooms were popular, and they often caused curving projections on the facade.

5   In the eighteenth century, France held the unrivalled position of cultural centre of Europe. The originally French Rococo style spread quickly to Russia, Austria, Spain, N. Italy and above all to Germany. Frederick the Great, like the other European rulers, enticed a number of French artists and craftsmen to work for him and modelled his palaces on those of the French monarchy.

6   The moulding is the continuous curved surface, often carved with a repeating pattern, that links two architectural surfaces, e.g. the cornice and the architrave.

7   Modillions, denticules. Both are characteristic motifs of classsical architecture and are used in series to support the upper part of a cornice. The modillion is a small bracket or console, and the denticule, a small square block.

8   The architrave is the lowest of the three main divisions of the entablature, i.e. cornice, frieze and architrave. The word is also used to describe any moulding surrounding a window or, as in this case, a doorway.

9   A console is an ornamental bracket, often placed centrally above a doorway or window.

10   A mansard roof is one that has a double slope, the lower part more steeply pitched than the upper. Named after the French architect François Mansart (1598–1666), it had in fact been used at the Louvre before his day.

11   The attic storey, in Classical architecture, is the storey above the main entablature, in strictly architectural relation to it.

COCHIN

On the 'Greek Manner' (*c.* 1780–1790)

From Charles-Nicolas Cochin, *Mémoires inédits*, ed. Charles Henry, Paris, 1880. Reprinted from Svend Eriksen, *Early Neo-Classicism in France*, ed. P. Thornton, Faber, London, 1974.

In his *Memoirs*, unpublished during his lifetime, Cochin gave the following account of the changes in taste in the second half of the eighteenth century. He described some of the abuses that resulted from the first rejection of the Rococo in favour of the 'Greek taste'.

[. . .] Later the truly decisive epoch was the return of M. de Marigny[1] and his company from Italy. We had seen and reflected on what we had seen. The absurdity appeared perfectly evident to us all and we were not silent. Our protests won so far in the sequel that Soufflot preached by his example. He was followed by Potain and several other good architects who returned from being pupils in Rome. I helped too – like the fly that stung the coach horse. I wrote in the *Mercure* against the late extravagances and covered them with a quite sufficient share of ridicule.

At last everybody turned or attempted to turn back to the path of the good taste of the previous century, and since everything has to be twisted into a nickname in Paris it was called architecture in the Greek manner. Soon even braids and ribbons were made in the Greek manner: it remained as good taste only in the hands of a small number of people and became extravagance in the hands of all the rest.

Our old architects who had never been out of Paris also wanted to show that they could work well in the Greek taste, and it was the same with beginners and even with master-masons. All these worthy people misplaced the ornaments of antiquity, distorted them, decorated window-sills with extremely heavy guilloche[2] work and committed a thousand other blunders. The painter Le Lorrain[3] made extremely heavy designs for all the ornaments in the suite of M. de la Live, a rich amateur who dabbled in drawing. They caused an even greater stir because M. de Caylus[4] praised them so enthusiastically: it was from this source that there came to us garlands like well-ropes, and clocks with rotating bands instead of dials and shaped like vessels that the Ancients had made to hold cordials; all very pleasing inventions in themselves but, now that they are imitated by all kinds of ignorant persons, we find Paris flooded with all sorts of stuff in the Greek manner. There ensued what will always happen, which is that the number of good things in whatever taste may prevail will always be very small and that ignorance will always find means to lord it in architecture. Yet although very bad things are still executed at least they are closer to what is good than the bad taste which preceded them, and whoever has some natural taste will be less far from the path which leads to what is good than men were before, always provided that this taste does not become (by the fault of those who travesty it) so cried down that it can no longer be tolerated.

Notes

1   M. de Marigny (1727–81) was the brother of Mme de Pompadour. Thanks to her influence, he was appointed to the all-powerful position of Surintendant des Batiments in 1751. Consequently, at the age of 24, he was in charge of all the arts, the Academies, the royal manufacturers, all public buildings and gardens. His tour of Italy in 1749–51 with Le Blanc, Cochin and Soufflot was a formative influence on his taste and he consistently favoured the revival of Classical forms in architecture.

2   Guilloche work is a pattern of interlacing bands forming a plait, used as an enrichment on a moulding.

3   L-J. Le Lorrain (*c.* 1714–59). Painter and furniture designer. After studying in Rome for eight years, where he copied the paintings in the Vatican and designed architectural settings for a number of festivals, Le Lorrain returned to Paris and was patronized by the Comte de Caylus. In 1754 he designed some Classical wall decorations for Count Tessin of Sweden and, in 1756, the Greek style furniture for La Live de Jully. In 1758 he went to Russia to work at the newly-founded St. Petersburg Academy of Fine Arts, but died shortly after his arrival.

4   For note on M. de Caylus, see p. 46, note 1.

BLONDEL

On Bad Taste in Interior Decoration (1771)

From Jean-Francois Blondel, *Cours d'Architecture*, Volume I, Paris, 1771. Reprinted from Svend Eriksen, *Early Neo-Classicism in France*, ed. P. L. Thornton, Faber, London, 1974.

Jean-Francois Blondel (1705–74) was an architect and an architectural theorist who opposed the Rococo style and upheld the classical principles of French seventeenth century architecture. His influence as a teacher and writer on architecture was crucial. In 1743 he started his own school of architecture (at which William Chambers studied, see p.24) and from 1762 onwards he lectured as professor at the Academy of Architecture in the Louvre. The following extract is from the *Cours d'Architecture* which were published in six volumes from 1771 to 1777. After Blondel's death, the publication was completed by Pierre Patte. Incidentally, Blondel was the author of the article on Architecture in the *Encyclopédie*.

[. . . .] Have we not seen the frivolous ornaments of interiors pass from thence to exteriors, an abuse which long subsisted? Today, with an illogicality equally to be condemned, the grave style of exteriors is applied to interiors. Our furniture is given what experience has taught us to avoid, I mean those right-angled forms whose corners hurt the eye and impede the movement of persons who are assembled in our dwellings. Often men adduce the pretext that these forms are imitated from the Greeks, without considering that those peoples only employed them in their temples or in the exterior decoration of their public buildings and that they are never, or only very rarely suitable for works of decorative art or objects of daily use. What can be more absurd for instance than to load the panelling of a boudoir with the same festoons of oak and laurel leaves with which triumphal arches, intended to transmit to posterity the victories of a hero, were adorned in Rome. This is an inattention which is perhaps even more disgusting than the rocailles[1] and Chinese ornaments[2] which for twenty years have been lavishly employed in all our buildings and even within the interiors of our temples.

Notes

1   Rocailles were shell-like, curvilinear and often asymmetrical decorative forms.
2   The use of Chinese ornaments – Chinoiserie – was very popular in eighteenth-century Rococo decoration in France.

LA FONT DE SAINT YENNE

Reflections on . . . the Present State of Painting in France (1747)

From La Font de Saint Yenne, *Réfléxions sur quelques causes de L'état présent de la peinture en France*. A La Haye chez Jean Neaulme, 1747. Translation by Belinda Thomson.

Little biographical information is available about La Font de Saint Yenne, art critic and connoisseur. His early career was spent in Lyon where he was a member of the Academy and made designs for the tapestry manufacture; later he settled in Paris. He also travelled to Flanders and Holland and was familiar with art collections there. He is remembered today as one of the founders of art criticism as a respectable intellectual pursuit. He stood out against current artistic opinion and maintained, in his 1746 Salon review, that a man of letters, or indeed any enlightened member of the Salon-going public, had a right to express his own subjective impressions, even though he had no technical knowledge of painting. His controversial review, the first of its kind, from which the following extract was taken, was coupled with a more general appraisal of the state of the arts in France. La Font was deeply concerned with the status and quality of French art. He deplored the current taste for Flemish painting, with its low-life subjects, because it had almost ousted the more serious art of the Italian school from contemporary collections. Anxious that young artists and the public should have the very best examples of art to study, he suggested that the Louvre be opened as a public gallery, displaying the unrivalled royal picture collection which was at that time stored in a number of locations and not open to view. His idea was in fact taken up by the Marquis de Marigny (see p. 54, note 1), but not eventually realized until after the Revolution.

La Font de Saint Yenne's stress on the importance of 'history' painting should be compared with Sir Joshua Reynold's similar view on the subject (see p. 90).

An exhibited picture is the same as a book on the day of publication, and as a play performed in the theatre: everyone has the right to make his own judgement. We have gathered together the judgements of the public which showed the greatest amount of agreement and fairness, and we now present *them*, and not at all our own judgement, to the artists, in the belief that this same public whose judgements are so often bizarre and unjustly damning or hasty rarely errs when all its voices unite on the merit or weakness of any particular work.

It is by taking scrupulous pains and with the genuine intention of offending no-one that we present the judgements of discerning connoisseurs, men enlightened by principles and still more by that natural light that we call feeling, because it makes one feel from the first glance the dissonance or the harmony of a work; indeed it is this feeling which is the basis of taste, I mean of that steady and unalterable taste for true beauty which can almost never be acquired where it is not the endowment of a fortunate birth.

Few artists will attain a reputation of the first order without the help of advice and criticism, not only from their colleagues most of whom only judge the beauties and faults of their art in relation to a cold, dry set of rules or by a routine of comparison with their own often dull and repetitive style, but also from a disinterested and enlightened spectator who, although not a practising painter himself, judges with natural taste and without a servile adherence to the rules. These are the people one cannot consult too frequently about the suitability of the tones, the choice of the details and their particular and general effects and about the harmony of that beautiful whole which charms the eye.

Of all the genres of painting, history is without question the most important. The history painter alone is the painter of the soul, the others only paint for the eye. He alone can bring into play that enthusiasm, that divine spark which makes him conceive his subjects in a powerful, sublime manner; he alone can create heroes for posterity, through the great actions and the virtues of the famous men he presents; so the public does not coldly read about but actually sees the performers and their deeds. Who does not know the advantage the faculty of sight has over all the others, and the power it has over our soul to bring about the deepest, most sudden impression?

But where shall our young pupils find the heat and fire of those eloquent expressions, the source of those great ideas, of those striking or interesting features that characterize true history painting? Why, in the same sources that have always been drawn upon by our greatest poets. In the great writers of Antiquity: in the *Iliad* and *Odyssey* of Homer, so rich in sublime images; in the *Aeneid*, so rich in heroic actions, pathetic narratives and grand sentiments; in Horace's *Ars Poetica*, an inexhaustible treasure of good sense for arranging the composition of an epic or tragic painting, and in Despréaux[1] his imitator; in Tasso,[2] in Milton. These are the men who have unlocked the human heart and known how to read it, to render its troubles, its rages, its torments for us with an eloquence and truth which both teach us and fill us with pleasure.

What if the history painter is religious and wishes to devote his brush to subjects of piety? What an abundant source of great events, supernatural and yet true and respectable, of majestic pathos is to be found in our sacred books, and above all in the five great prophets, Isaiah, Ezekial, Jeremiah, Daniel, and the Prophet King.

Was it not the latter who inspired the famous Rousseau,[3] that sublime and exact poet, whose genius, by its strength and beauty, has brought so much honour to his century and to French poetry! Does he not owe the entrancing beauties of his sacred Odes to David?

Everyone knows the perfect relationship the painter has with the poet. He will lack passion and life, and his inspiration will quickly cool unless he fires it by repeated intercourse with those great men I have just spoken of. When I advise such study for our history painters, I presume it to have been preceded and backed up by the study of our most famous painters in this genre, both past and present. Raphael, Domenichino, the Carracci, Giulio Romano, Pietro da Cortona, etc., and closer to home, Rubens, Poussin, Le Sueur, Le Brun, Coypel,[4] Le Moine[5] in his ceiling at Versailles, which is a master-piece of art and comparable to the most beautiful of its kind, both in France and in Italy: in short all the excellent works whose economy, arrangement, effects produced by skilled composition he will have had to consider deeply, and to copy the pieces most admired for their drawing or colour. Without a plentiful collection of this excellent material, he will never manage to construct the solid and durable edifice of a great reputation.

After having given history painters the standing and praise they deserve, would that I could lavish praise on those of today, and raise them, or at least compare them to those of the last century! O blessed century, when the progress and perfection in all the Arts made France a rival to Italy! I am, however, far from thinking that France's genius has been extinguished or her vigour lost. The celebrated painters of our school I have just mentioned, who raised the century of Louis XIV to the level of Leo X[6] in the Fine Arts, and surpassed it even by the great number, would still find admirers today, were it not that the taste of the nation has greatly changed, and had there not been, to accompany the upheavals that passing years and the sway of novelty necessarily bring to States and minds, an excessive taste for ornamentation, the success of which has been extremely harmful to painting.

An account of the effects of mirrors, which form pictures in which the imitation is so perfect, that our eyes have an illusion equal to nature, would sound like a fairy-tale and a figment of the imagination, if the reality was not already too well-known to us; these mirrors which were comparatively rare in the last century and are extremely abundant in this have dealt a fatal blow to art, and have been one of the principle causes of its decline in France, banishing the great history subjects which were its triumph from their former positions and monopolizing the decoration of salons and galleries. I admit that the miraculous-sounding advantages of these mirrors deserved the fashionable success they have had, in many respects. Breaking through walls to enlarge apartments and adjoin others to them; reflecting the rays of light from the sun or from candles with increased brilliance; how could man, the born enemy of darkness and everything suggesting its horror, prevent himself loving a form of embellishment which brightens as well as lightens his room and which, while deceiving his eyes, does not deceive him as to the genuine pleasure he receives? How could he prefer to it the ideal beauties of painting which is often dark, where the enjoyment depends solely upon the illusion to which one must submit, and which often has not affect on the vulgar or ignorant man?

We should not then be surprised by the rapid success of a discovery so favourable to the general pleasure and to the particular taste of a nation greedy for all that is sparkling and new, although its charms are strictly material and entirely limited to the delight of the eye.

Everything possible has been done to perfect its manufacture and to increase their number ad infinitum.[7] But since it was impossible to entirely line the walls of large apartments with mirrors, either because of the considerable cost involved or lest such uniformity should have led to surfeit, the idea came about of filling the intervals with panels, sometimes enriched with gilding and coated with colour varnishes; the brilliance and polish of these attractive varnishes being, the next best means, after mirrors, of reflecting light.

And so the science of the brush has been forced to yield to the brilliance of glass; its abundance and the mechanical facility of its perfection have banished the finest of the arts from our apartments; the only refuge left to it being to fill in a few miserable gaps, overdoors, overmantels and the tops of a few pier-glasses reduced in height for the sake of economy.[8] In this way, restricted by lack of space to paltry little subjects which are in any case far above eye level, painting, is reduced in these large rooms, to cold, insipid, totally uninteresting represent-ations: the four Elements, the Seasons, the Senses, the Arts, the Muses and other commonplaces which are the triumph of the plagiarist journeyman painter, requiring neither genius nor imagination, pitifully worked and reworked for more than twenty years in a hundred thousand ways.

I ought to pass over in silence, for the honour of this fine art, the unworthy places in which painting has taken refuge since its expulsion from our apartments. Could our fathers have foreseen that one day art lovers would come to admire the beauties of a skilful brush in such vile hovels, in dusty sheds and filthy coach-houses? Nothing is more true, nevertheless, than that up until the time when camaieux[9] became the most popular form of carriage decoration, for several years one saw in their place paintings, of a price and quality superior to, or at least equal to those decorating the apartments of the masters' of those houses. These paintings were only brought out of their shameful stores to be dragged through the streets, to suffer the ravages of the mud, to be defenselessly exposed every day to the danger of being knocked to pieces by the dirtiest rubbish-wagons, by carts, or by the innumerable hazards of the public highway, unavoidable in such a large city. What must foreigners find the most incomprehensible... our shameful disregard and ridiculous abuse of this fine art, or the excess and eccentricity of our ornament, carried to such a high degree of extravagance?

For mythological and historical subjects, there did·remain one fruitful area, favourable to the painter whose great talent lay in illusionism and foreshortening, which gave full scope to the magical art of perspective – and that was the ceiling. But, accustomed to the brilliance of mirrors – which unfortunately have so far been impossible to install in new ceilings, where, I am quite convinced, I shall one day see them admired, the public rejected embellishments of an intellectual character, requiring some consideration and knowledge, in favour of the material whiteness of plaster carved into filigree work at the base of the coving[10] and in the corners and at the central point carved into ornaments of the same substance, ofted gilded, sometimes painted, imperceptible grotesques[11] for the most part, that Voltaire so aptly criticised in his *Temple du Goût*:[12]

> 'I will cover ceilings, canopies, covings with a hundred singeries[13] carefully worked,
> An inch or two large so they can be seen from afar.'

And elsewhere:

> 'The whole thing glazed, varnished, whitewashed, gilded;
> And admired, for sure, by idle gazers.'

These, then, are the main causes of the present decline in painting, I am in no doubt that they have forced several pupils, into whose hands the gods had placed paintbrushes, to abjure their talent and abandon themselves, like our writers have done to works of wit, to the futile subjects of fashion and of the day; or else to the most lucrative genre of this art, which is, and has been for several years, the portrait.

A painter today, obstinately attached to history painting through the elevation of his thoughts and the nobility of his expressions, will see himself reduced to a few works for churches, for the Gobelins,[14] or to a very small number of easel paintings which have been almost entirely banished from decorative schemes because, it is said, they spoil the silk tapestries whose lustre and uniformity is at present preferred to the skilful variations of the brush and to all the products of the imagination. What resource will be left to the history painter if he is not in a position to feed his family on more solid fare than glory? He will sacrifice his personal tastes and natural talents to his needs, in order not to see his fortunes waning, despite his skill and efforts, in contrast to the rapid financial gains made by his colleagues the portrait painters, especially those working in pastel. He will suppress his inner callings and divert his brush from the path to glory to follow that of material well-being. He will, in all honesty, suffer for a time to see himself forced to flatter a simpering, often misshapen or aged face, which almost always lacks physiognomy; reproducing obscure, characterless people, without name, without position, without merit; people who are often despised, sometimes even hateful, or at the very least indifferent to the public, to their posterity, even to their heirs who will abandon their features to the dust of the attic and the teeth of mice; or who will coldly watch them pass from an auction sale to hang in furnished rooms and render the householder more illustrious. We should not then be surprised that today the portrait is the genre of painting in readiest supply, the most cultivated and the most advantageous to even the most mediocre talent. Its credit is of long-standing, and based on several good reasons.

Although the present widespread taste for the beauties of a damask tapestry,[15] picked up by richly gilded and attractively sculpted frames has banished history paintings from apartments, as if they were boring and superfluous ornaments, portraits have managed to replace them and secure from the caprices of fashion an exception in their favour.

Self-love, whose rule is even more imperious than that of fashion, has had the art of presenting to the eyes, of ladies especially, mirrors of themselves that are all the more beguiling for being false and which, for that reason, are preferred by most people to real mirrors which are too truthful. In effect, what sight can be compared, either for a real or for an imaginary beauty, to that of eternally seeing herself endowed with the grace and the cup of Hebe, the goddess of youth? Or to that of displaying every day, beneath the apparel of Flora, the budding charms of spring of which she is the image? Then again, seeing herself decked out with the attributes of the goddess of the forests, a quiver on her back, her hair attractively dishevelled, an arrow in her hand, how could she not believe herself to be the rival of that charming god who wounds all hearts?[16] The example of the really beautiful woman for whom the striking poses of these metamorphoses added yet a new beauty, beguiled the less attractive woman. She imagined she would have the same graces as soon as she was in the same costume. She never doubted that the youth of Hebe would avenge her for the insults of Time, the least gallant, most impolite of all the gods. She easily persuaded herself that our sex, always seeking to please, when forced to see two physiognomies at her home, would prefer that of the youthful goddess to that of the dowager divinity, or at least that he would take into consideration her efforts, and the time she was spending each day in trying to resemble her earlier self. After all, what more pardonable an error could the fair sex make? If old age is indeed Hell for pretty women, as one of the greatest wits of Louis XIV's court maintained,[17] why don't the arts, especially painting, make every endeavour to hide from them the passing of a state which provided all their happiness, and to distance them from, even rid them altogether, if it be possible, of the sight of their chief torment?

Notes

1   Despréaux: Nicolas Boileau-Despréaux (1636–1711). Playwright, poet and theorist. Boileau's *Art poétique* (1674) was based on Horace's *Ars Poetica* and laid down many of the principles on which French literary classicism was based.

2   Torquato Tasso (1544–95). Italian poet. Patronized for a time by the d'Este court and subsequently imprisoned for seven years, his best known works are the narrative poem *Rinaldo* (1562) and the epic poem *Gerusalemme Liberata* (1574).

3   J-B. Rousseau (1671–1741). French lyric poet and dramatist. His most famous work was probably his *Ode à la Fortune* but his epigrams were also successful.

4   Coypel. The family numbered several artists, but La Font is almost certainly referring to Antoine Coypel (1661–1722). Trained in the Baroque tradition, he was responsible for introducing a more colouristic, light-hearted style to French decorative painting. He painted the ceiling of the Versailles chapel, and several decorations for the Duc d'Orléans at the Palais Royal. The latter appointed him Premier Peintre in 1716.

5   *F. Le Moine* (1688–1737). French painter. On a visit to Italy in 1723, Le Moine was enormously impressed by the decorative schemes of the Baroque masters Lanfranco and Pietro da Cortona. On returning to France he was commissioned to paint the vast ceiling of the Salon d'Hercule at Versailles.

6   Leo X's papacy, 1513–21, coincided with high points in the careers of Raphael and Michelangelo.

7   Whereas at Versailles' Galerie de Glaces several sheets of mirror had been needed to fill the enormous frames, by the mid-eighteenth century the technique of making large mirrors had been mastered. Despite La Font's warnings, 'mirror rooms' became fashionable for a time. Marie-Antoinette, for instance, had a bathroom entirely lined with mirrors.

8   Panelling and mirrors tended to form the main part of eighteenth-century wall decoration, but an architect would leave a number of clearly defined spaces, above doorways, mirrors and mantel-pieces to be filled with suitable paintings.

9   Camaieux: a type of painting used particularly in interior decoration made up of different tones of the same colour.

10 Coving: the concave moulding produced by the sloped or arched junction of wall and ceiling.

11 Grotesques: fanciful ornamental motifs, in paint or stucco, consisting of arabesques, medallions, sphinxes, foliage, etc.

12 Voltaire's *Temple du Goût*, c. 1732, was an essay in criticism composed in verse and prose which attacked all that was false or feeble in the arts – in particular, the Rococo.

13 Singeries: a form of grotesque ornamentation incorporating monkeys, often in human guise, into the design.

14 Gobelins: the royal Gobelins tapestry factory was set up by Colbert in 1667, during the reign of Louis XIV. It depended upon painters for its designs. Technical advances made in the eighteenth century enabled weavers to make tapestries resemble paintings more and more closely.

15 Silk tapestries – damasks – imported from the Orient, were becoming a fashionable form of wall covering.

16 '. . . all hearts'. Flattering portraits of aristocratic ladies dressed up to look like goddesses, were popularized by such painters as J-M. Nattier (1685–1766) and L-M. Van Loo (1707–71). They inherited the genre from N. Largillière (1656–1746).

17 The Duc de la Rochefoucault (1613–80). Famous for his *Maximes* (1665) which were originally written to amuse fashionable salon society. They reflect his deeply pessimistic attitudes to human behaviour.

WILLIAM HOGARTH

The Analysis of Beauty (1753)

From William Hogarth, *The Analysis of Beauty, written with a view of fixing the fluctuating IDEAS of TASTE*, Printed by.J. Reeves, for the author, and sold by him at his House in Leicester-fields, London, 1753.

Hogarth's theoretical convictions and their practical application were set down by the artist in literary form in the *Analysis*. Two plates, illustrated here (Plates 11 and 12) were meant as graphic demonstrations to illustrate his idea of beauty, though it must be admitted that clarity in their organization is rather lacking. While the book gained for Hogarth a number of supporters, in Germany and France as well as at home, his detractors were many; they were voluble and exceedingly hostile. 'Written [as the title page asserts] with a view of fixing the fluctuating IDEAS of TASTE' it struck others as a presumptuous undertaking by a novice in an intellectual minefield. (A similar desire to establish unquestionable rules in taste can be found in Laugier, see p. 9.) It was not only Hogarth's theories which were lampooned; the eccentricities of his verbal style were abused as well.

The pugnacious and satirical tone which permeates the *Analysis* was in itself an affront to those who fancied themselves as the sole arbiters of good taste. Hogarth paid dearly for his impudence in attempting to undermine deeply-entrenched aesthetic theories, the foundations of which lay in the Italian Renaissance. Those theories were sustained and embellished by contemporaries such as Richardson and Shaftesbury.[1] Hogarth's antipathy for 'High' art sprang essentially from his dislike of vanity. For he, like Fielding, repudiated the connoisseurs of art, their derivative styles and synthetic structures which dominated the art and literature of the period. Hogarth's dedication was not to rules and the perpetuation of order and harmony in art, but to naturalness and the limitless variety to be found in life itself. Look hard at nature, he says, not pictures: 'Shakespear, who had the deepest penetration into nature, has summed up all the charms of beauty in two words, INFINITE VARIETY ... ' Hogarth's empirical methods give evidence, in this volume, of a rare acuity of vision. In this, he anticipates some of the observations made in our own time by psychologists concerned with visual perception.

PREFACE

If a preface was ever necessary, it may very likely be thought so to the following work; the title of which (in the proposals published some time since) hath much amused, and raised the expectation of the curious, though not without a mixture of doubt, that its purport could ever be satisfactorily answered. For though beauty is seen and confessed by all, yet, from the many fruitless attempts to account for the cause of its being so, enquiries on this head have almost been given up; and the subject generally thought to be a matter of too high and too delicate a nature to admit of any true or intelligible discussion. Something therefore introductory ought to be said at the presenting a work with a face so entirely new; especially as it will naturally encounter with, and perhaps may overthrow, several long received and thorough established opinions: and since controversies may arise how far, and after what manner this subject hath hitherto been considered and treated, it will also be proper to lay before the reader, what may be gathered concerning it, from the works of the ancient and modern writers and painters.

It is no wonder this subject should have so long been thought inexplicable, since the nature of many parts of it cannot possibly come within the reach of mere men of letters; otherwise those ingenious gentlemen who have lately published treatises upon it (and who have written much more learnedly than can be expected from one who never took up the pen before) would not so soon have been bewildered in their accounts of it, and obliged so suddenly to turn into the broad, and more beaten path of moral beauty; in order to extricate themselves out of the difficulties they seem to have met with in this: and withal forced for the same reasons to amuse their readers with amazing (but often misapplied) encomiums on deceased painters and their performances; wherein they are continually discoursing of effects instead of developing causes; and after many prettinesses, in very pleasing language, do fairly set you down just where they first took you up; honestly confessing that as to GRACE, the main point in question, they do not even pretend to know any thing of the matter. And indeed how should they? when it actually requires a practical knowledge of the whole art of painting (sculpture alone not being sufficient) and that too to some degree of eminence, in order to enable any one to pursue the chain of this enquiry through all its parts: which I hope will be made to appear in the following work. [...]

INTRODUCION

I now offer to the public a short essay, accompanied with two explanatory prints, in which I shall endeavour to shew what the principles are in nature, by which we are directed to call the forms of some bodies beautiful, others ugly; some graceful, and others the reverse; by considering more minutely than has hitherto been done, the nature of those lines, and their different combinations, which serve to raise in the mind the ideas of all the variety of forms imaginable. At first, perhaps, the whole design, as well as the prints, may seem rather intended to trifle and confound, than to entertain and inform: but I am persuaded that when the examples in nature, referred to in this essay, are duly considered and examined upon the principles laid down in it, it will be thought worthy of a careful and attentive perusal: and the prints themselves too will, I make no doubt, be examined as attentively, when it is found, that almost every figure in them (how odly soever they may seem to be grouped together) is referred to singly in the essay, in order to assist the reader's imagination, when the original examples in art, or nature, are not themselves before him.

And in this light I hope my prints will be considered, and that the figures referred to in them will never be imagined to be placed there by me as examples themselves, of beauty or grace, but only to point out to the reader what sorts of objects he is to look for and examine in nature, or in the works of the greatest masters. My figures, therefore, are to be considered in the same light, with those a mathematician makes with his pen, which may convey the idea of his demonstration, though not a line in them is either perfectly straight, or of that peculiar curvature he is treating of. Nay, so far was I from aiming at grace, that I purposely chose to be least accurate, where most beauty might be expected, that no stress might be laid on the figures to the prejudice of the work itself. For I must confess, I have but little hope of having a favourable attention given to my design in general, by those who have already had a more fashionable introduction into the mysteries of the arts of painting, and sculpture. Much less do I expect, or in truth desire, the countenance of that set of people, who have an interest in exploding any kind of doctrine, that may teach us to *see with our own eyes.*

It may be needless to observe, that some of the last-mentioned, are not only the dependents on, but often the only instructors and leaders of the former; but in what light they are so considered abroad, may be (1)Fig.1.T.p.1[2] partly seen by (1) a burlesque representation of them, taken from a print published by Mr. Pond,[3] designed by Cavr. Ghezzi at Rome.

To those, then, whose judgments are unprejudiced, this little work is submitted with most pleasure; because it is from such that I have hitherto received the most obligations, and now have reason to expect most candour.

Therefore I would fain have such of my readers be assured, that however they may have been awed, and over-born by pompous terms of art, hard names, and the parade of seemingly magnificent collections of pictures and statues; they are in a much fairer way, ladies, as well as gentlemen, of gaining a perfect knowledge of the elegant and beautiful in artificial, as well as natural forms, by considering them in a systematical, but at the same time familiar way, than those who have been prepossessed by dogmatic rules, taken from the performances of art only: nay, I will venture to say, sooner, and more rationally, than even a tolerable painter, who has imbibed the same prejudices.

The more prevailing the notion may be, that painters and connoisseurs are the only competent judges of things of this sort; the more it becomes necessary to clear up and confirm, as much as possible, what has only been asserted in the foregoing paragraph: that no one may be deterred, by the want of such previous knowledge, from entring into this enquiry. [. . .]

CHAPTER I.

Of Fitness

Fitness of the parts to the design for which every individual thing is formed, either by art or nature, is first to be considered, as it is of the greatest consequence to the beauty of the whole. This is so evident, that even the sense of seeing, the great inlet of beauty, is itself so strongly biased by it, that if the mind, on account of this kind of value in a form, esteem it beautiful, tho' on all other considerations it be not so; the eye grows insensible of its want of beauty, and even begins to be pleased, especially after it has been a considerable time acquainted with it.

It is well known on the other hand, that forms of great elegance often disgust the eye by being improperly applied. Thus twisted columns are undoubtedly ornamental; but as they convey an idea of weakness, they always displease, when they are improperly made use of as supports to any thing that is bulky, or appears heavy.

The bulks and proportions of objects are governed by fitness and propriety. It is this that has established the size and proportion of chairs, tables, and all sorts of utensils and furniture. It is this that has fixed the dimensions of pillars, arches, &c. for the support of great weight, and so regulated all the orders in architecture, as well as the sizes of windows and doors, &c. Thus though a building were ever so large, the steps of the stairs, the seats in the windows must be continued of their usual heights, or they would lose their beauty with their fitness: and in ship-building the dimensions of every part are confined and regulated by fitness for sailing. When a vessel sails well, the sailors always call her a beauty; the two ideas have such a connexion!

The general dimensions of the parts of the human body are adapted thus to the uses they are designed for. The trunk is the most capacious on account of the quantity of its contents, and the thigh is larger than the leg, because it has both the leg and foot to move, the leg only the foot, &c.

Fitness of parts also constitutes and distinguishes in a great measure the characteristics of objects; as for example, the race-horse differs as much in quality, or character, from the war-horse, as to its figure, as the Hercules from the Mercury.

The race-horse, having all its parts of such dimensions as best fit the purposes of speed, acquires on that account a consistent character of one sort of beauty. To illustrate this, suppose the beautiful head and gracefully-turned neck of the war-horse were placed on the shoulders of the race-horse, instead of his own aukward straight one: it would disgust, and deform, instead of adding beauty; because the judgment would condemn it as unfit.

(1)Fig.3.p.1.   The Hercules, by Glicon (1), hath all its parts finely fitted for the purposes of the utmost strength, the texture of the human form will bear. The back, breast and shoulders have huge bones, and muscles adequate to the supposed active strength of its upper parts; but as less strength was required for the lower parts, the judicious sculptor, contrary to all modern rule of enlarging every part in proportion, lessened the size of the muscles gradually down towards the feet; and for the same reason made the neck larger in circumference than any part of the head; otherwise the figure would have been burdened with an unnecessary weight, which would have been a draw-back from his strength, and in consequence of that, from its characteristic beauty.

These seeming faults, which shew the superior anatomical knowledge as well as judgment of the ancients, are not to be found in the leaden imitations of it near Hyde-park.[4] These saturnine geniuses imagined they knew how to correct such apparent *disproportions*.

These few examples may be sufficient to give an idea of what I mean, (and would have understood) by the beauty of fitness, or propriety.

CHAPTER V.

Of Intricacy

The active mind is ever bent to be employed. Pursuing is the business of our lives; and even abstracted from any other view, gives pleasure. Every arising difficulty, that for a while attends and interrupts the pursuit, gives a sort of spring to the mind, enhances the pleasure, and makes what would else be toil and labour, become sport and recreation.

Wherein would consist the joys of hunting, shooting, fishing, and many other favourite diversions, without the frequent turns and difficulties, and disappointments, that are daily met with in the pursuit? – how joyless does the sportsman return when the hare has not had fair play? how lively, and in spirits, even when an old cunning one has baffled, and out-run the dogs!

This love of pursuit, merely as pursuit, is implanted in our natures, and designed, no doubt, for necessary, and useful purposes. Animals have it evidently by instinct. The hound dislikes the game he so eagerly pursues; and even cats will risk the losing of their prey to chase it over again. It is a pleasing labour of the mind to solve the most difficult problems; allegories and riddles, trifling as they are, afford the mind amusement: and with what delight does it follow the well-connected thread of a play, or novel, which ever increases as the plot thickens, and ends most pleased, when that is most distinctly unravelled?

The eye hath this sort of enjoyment in winding walks, and serpentine rivers, and all sorts of objects, whose forms, as we shall see hereafter, are composed principally of what, I call, the *waving* and *serpentine* lines.

Intricacy in form, therefore, I shall define to be that peculiarity in the lines, which compose it, that *leads the eye a wanton kind of chace*, and from the pleasure that gives the mind, intitles it to the name of beautiful: and it may be justly said, that the cause of the idea of grace more immediately resides in this principle, than in the other five,[5] except variety; which indeed includes this, and all the others.

That this observation may appear to have a real foundation in nature, every help will be required, which the reader himself can call to his assistance, as well as what will here be suggested to him.

To set this matter in somewhat a clearer light, the familiar instance of a common jack, with a circular fly, may serve our purpose better than a more elegant form: preparatory to which, let the (1) figure be (1)Fig.14.T.p.1. considered, which represents the eye, at a common reading distance viewing a row of letters, but fixed with most attention to the middle letter A.

Now as we read, a ray may be supposed to be drawn from the center of the eye to that letter it looks at first, and to move successively with it from letter to letter, the whole length of the line: but if the eye stops at any particular letter, A, to observe it more than the rest, these other letters will grow more and more imperfect to the sight, the farther they are situated on either side of A, as is expressed in the figure: and when we endeavour to see all the letters in a line equally perfect at one view, as it were, this imaginary ray must course it to and fro with great celerity. Thus though the eye, strictly speaking, can only pay due attention to these letters in succession, yet the amazing ease and swiftness, with which it performs this task, enables us to see considerable spaces with sufficient satisfaction at one sudden view.

Hence, we shall always suppose some such principal ray moving along with the eye, and tracing out the parts of every form, we mean to examine in the most perfect manner: and when we would follow with exactness the course any body takes, that is in motion, this ray is always to be supposed to move with the body.

In this manner of attending to forms, they will be found whether *at rest*, or *in motion*, to give *movement* to this imaginary ray; or, more properly speaking, to the eye itself, affecting it *thereby* more or less *pleasingly*, according to their different *shapes* and *motions*. Thus, for example, in the instance of the jack, whether the eye (with this imaginary ray) moves slowly down the line, to which the weight is fixed, or attends to the slow motion of the weight itself, the mind is equally fatigued: and whether it swiftly courses round the circular rim of the flyer, when the jack stands; or nimbly follows one point in its circumference whilst it is whirling about, we are almost equally made giddy by it. But our sensation differs much from either of these unpleasant ones, when we observe the curling worm, into which the worm-wheel is fixt (2): for this is always pleasing, either at rest or in motion, and whether that motion is slow or quick.

2)Fig.15.T.p.1.

That it is accounted so, when it is *at rest*, appears by the ribbon, twisted round a stick (represented on one side of this figure) which has been a long-established ornament in the carvings of frames, chimney-pieces, and door-cases; and called by the carvers, *the stick and ribbon ornament:* and when the stick, through the middle is omitted, it is called the *ribbon edge*; both to be seen in almost every house of fashion.

But the pleasure it gives the eye is still more lively when *in motion*. I never can forget my frequent strong attention to it, when I was very young, and that its beguiling movement gave me the same kind of sensation then, which I since have felt at seeing a country-dance; tho' perhaps the latter might be somewhat more engaging; particularly when my eye eagerly pursued a favourite dancer, through all the windings of the figure, who then was bewitching to the sight, as the imaginary ray, we were speaking of, was dancing with her all the time.

This single example might be sufficient to explain what I mean by *the beauty of a composed intricacy of form*; and how it may be said, with propriety, to *lead* the eye a *kind of chace*.

But the hair of the head is another very obvious instance, which, being designed chiefly as an ornament, proves more or less so, according to the form it naturally takes, or is put into by art. The most amiable in itself is the flowing curl; and the many waving and contrasted turns of naturally intermingling locks ravish the eye with the pleasure of the pursuit, especially when they are put in motion by a gentle breeze. The poet knows it, as well as the painter, and has described the wanton ringlets waving in the wind.

And yet to shew how excess ought to be avoided in intricacy, as well as in every other principle, the very same head of hair, wisped, and matted together, would make the most disagreeable figure; because the eye would be perplexed, and at a fault, and unable to trace such a confused number of uncomposed and entangled lines; and yet notwithstanding this, the present fashion the ladies have gone into, of wearing a part of the hair of their heads braided together from behind, like intertwisted serpents, arising thickest from the bottom, lessening as it is brought forward, and naturally conforming to the shape of the rest of the hair it is pinned over, is extremely picturesque. Their thus interlacing the hair in distinct varied quantities is an artful way of preserving as much of intricacy, as is beautiful.

CHAPTER IX.

Of Composition with the Waving-Line

There is scarce a room in any house whatever, where one does not see the waving-line employed in some way or other. How inelegant would the shapes of all our moveables be without it? how very plain and unornamental the mouldings of cornices, and chimney-pieces, without the variety introduced by the *ogee*[6] member, which is entirely composed of waving-lines.

Though all sorts of waving-lines are ornamental, when properly applied; yet, strictly speaking, there is but one precise line, properly to be called the line of *beauty*, which in the scale of them (1) is number 4: (1)Fig.49.T.p.1. the lines 5, 6, 7, by their bulging too much in their curvature becoming gross and clumsy; and, on the contrary, 3, 2, 1, as they straighten, becoming mean and poor; as will appear in the next figure (2) where (2)Fig.50.T.p.1. they are applied to the legs of chairs.

A still more perfect idea of the effects of the precise waving-line, and of those lines that deviate from it, may be conceived by the row of stays, figure (3), where number 4 is composed of precise waving-lines, and is (3)Fig.53.B.p.1. therefore the best shaped stay. Every whale-bone of a good stay must be made to bend in this manner: for the whole stay, when put close together behind, is truly a shell of well-varied contents, and its surface of course a fine form; so that if a line, or the lace were to be drawn, or brought from the top of the lacing of the stay behind, round the body, and down to the bottom peak of the stomacher; it would form such a perfect, precise, serpentine-line, as has been shewn, round the cone, figure 26 in plate I. – For this reason all ornaments obliquely contrasting the body in this manner, as the ribbons worn by the knights of the garter, are both genteel and graceful. The numbers 5, 6, 7, and 3, 2, 1, are deviations into stiffness and meanness on one hand, and clumsiness and deformity on the other. The reasons for which disagreeable effects, after what has been already said, will be evident to the meanest capacity.

It may be worth our notice however, that the stay, number 2, would better fit a well-shaped man than number 4; and that number 4, would better fit a well-formed woman, than number 2; and when on considering them, merely as to their forms, and comparing them together as you would do two vases, it has been shewn by our principles, how much finer and more beautiful number 4 is, than number 2: does not this our determination enhance the merit of these principles, as it proves at the same time how much the form of a woman's body surpasses in beauty that of a man?

From the examples that have been given, enough may be gathered to carry on our observations from them to any other objects that may chance to come in our way, either animate or inanimate; so that we may not only *lineally* account for the ugliness of the toad, the hog, the bear and the spider, which are totally void of this waving-line, but also for the

71

different degrees of beauty belonging to those objects that possess it.

CHAPTER X.

Of Compositions with the Serpentine-Line

The very great difficulty there is in describing this line, either in words, or by the pencil (as was hinted before, when I first mentioned it) will make it necessary for me to proceed very slowly in what I have to say in this chapter, and to beg the reader's patience whilst I lead him step by step into the knowledge of what I think the sublime in form, so remarkably displayed in the human body; in which, I believe, when he is once acquainted with the idea of them, he will find this species of lines to be principally concerned.

(1)Fig.56.B.p.2.   First, then, let him consider fig. (1), which represents a straight horn, with its contents, and he will find, as it varies like the cone, it is a form of some beauty, merely on that account.

Next let him observe in what manner, and in what degree the beauty (2)Fig.57.B.p.2.   of this horn is increased, in fig. (2). where it is supposed to be bent two different ways.

And lastly, let him attend to the vast increase of beauty, even to grace (3)Fig.58.B.p.2.   and elegance, in the same horn, fig. (3), where it is supposed to have been twisted round, at the same time, that it was bent two different ways, (as in the last figure.)

In the first of these figures, the dotted line down the middle expresses the straight lines of which it is composed; which, without the assistance of curve lines, or light and shade, would hardly shew it to have contents.

The same is true of the second, tho' by the bending of the horn, the straight dotted line is changed into the beautiful waving-line.

But in the last, this dotted line, by the twisting as well as the bending of the horn, is changed from the waving into the serpentine-line; which, as it dips out of sight behind the horn in the middle, and returns again at the smaller end, not only gives play to the imagination, and delights the eye, on that account; but informs it likewise of the quantity and variety of the contents.

I have chosen this simple example, as the easiest way of giving a plain and general idea of the peculiar qualities of these serpentine-lines, and the advantages of bringing them into compositions, where the contents you are to express, admit of grace and elegance.

And I beg the same things may be understood of these serpentine-lines, that I have said before of the waving-lines. For as among the vast variety of waving-lines that may be conceived, there is but one that truly deserves the name of *the line of beauty*, so there is only one precise serpentine-line that I call *the line of grace*. Yet, even when they are made too bulging, or too tapering, though they certainly lose of their beauty and grace, they do not become so wholly void of it, as not to be of excellent service in compositions, where beauty and grace are not particularly designed to be expressed in their greatest perfection.

Though I have distinguished these lines so particularly as to give them the titles of *the lines of beauty and grace*, I mean that the use and application of them should still be confined by the principles I have laid down for composition in general; and that they should be judiciously mixt and combined with one another, and even with those I may term *plain* lines, (in opposition to these) as the subject in hand requires. Thus the cornu-copia, fig. (4), is twisted and bent after the same manner, as (4)Fig.59.B.p.2. the last figure of the horn; but more ornamented, and with a greater number of other lines of the same twisted kind, winding round it with as quick returns as those of a screw.

This sort of form may be seen with yet more variations, (and therefore more beautiful) in the goat's horn, from which, in all probability, the ancients originally took the extreme elegant forms they have given their cornu-copias.

There is another way of considering this last figure of the horn I would recommend to my reader, in order to give him a clearer idea of the use both of the waving and serpentine-lines in composition.

This is to imagine the horn, thus bent and twisted, to be cut length-ways by a very fine saw into two equal parts; and to observe one of these in the same position the whole horn is represented in; and these two observations will naturally occur to him. First, that the edge of the saw must run from one end to the other of the horn in the line of beauty; so that the edges of this half of the horn will have a beautiful shape: and, secondly, that wherever the dotted serpentine-line on the surface of the whole horn dips behind, and is lost to the eye, it immediately comes into sight on the hollow surface of the divided horn.

The use I shall make of these observations will appear very consider-able in the application of them to the human form, which we are next to attempt.

It will be sufficient, therefore, at present only to observe, first, that the whole horn acquires a beauty by its being thus genteely bent two different ways; secondly, that whatever lines are drawn on its external surface become graceful, as they must all of them, from the twist that is given the horn, partake in some degree or other, of the shape of the serpentine-line: and, lastly, when the horn is split, and the inner, as well as the outward surface of its shell-like form is exposed, the eye is peculiarly entertained and relieved in the pursuit of these serpentine-lines, as in their twistings their concavities and convexities are alter-nately offered to its view. Hollow forms, therefore, composed of such lines are extremely beautiful and pleasing to the eye; in many cases more so, than those of solid bodies.

Almost all the muscles, and bones, of which the human form is composed, have more, or less of these kind of twists in them; and give in a less degree, the same kind of appearance to the parts which cover them, and are the immediate object of the eye: and for this reason it is that I have been so particular in describing these forms of the bent, and twisted, and ornamented horn.

There is scarce a straight bone in the whole body. Almost all of them are not only bent different ways, but have a kind of twist, which in some of them is very graceful; and the muscles annexed to them, tho' they are of various shapes, appropriated to their particular uses, generally have their component fibres running in these serpentine-lines, surrounding and conforming themselves to the varied shape of the bones they belong to: more especially in the limbs. Anatomists are so satisfied of this, that they take a pleasure in distinguishing their several beauties. I shall only instance in the thigh-bone, and those about the hips.

(5)Fig.62.R.p.2.   The thigh-bone fig. (5), has the waving and twisted turn of the horn,
(6)Fig.60.B.p.2.   58: but the beautiful bones adjoining, called the ossa innominata (6), have, with greater variety, the same turns and twists of that horn when it is cut; and its inner and outward surfaces are exposed to the eye.

How ornamental these bones appear, when the prejudice we conceive against them, as being part of a skeleton, is taken off, by adding a
(7)Fig.61.B.p.2.   little foliage to them, may be seen in fig.(7) – such shell-like winding forms, mixt with foliage, twisting about them, are made use of in all ornaments; a kind of composition calculated merely to please the eye. Divest these of their serpentine twinings and they immediately lose all grace, and return to the poor gothic taste they were in an hundred years
(8)Fig.63.B.p.2.   ago (8).[. . .]

CHAPTER XV.

Of the Face

[. . .] 2. With regard to character and expression; we have daily many instances which confirm the common received opinion, that the face is the index of the mind; and this maxim is so rooted in us, we can scarce help (if our attention is a little raised) forming some particular conception of the person's mind whose face we are observing, even before we receive information by any other means. How often is it said, on the slightest view, that such a one looks like a good-natured man, that he hath an honest open countenance, or looks like a cunning rogue; a man of sense, or a fool, &c. And how are our eyes riveted to the aspects of kings and heroes, murderers and saints; and as we contemplate their deeds, seldom fail making application to their looks. It is reasonable to believe that aspect to be a true and legible representation of the mind, which gives every one the same idea at first sight; and is afterwards confirmed in fact: for instance, all concur in the same opinion, at first sight, of a down-right idiot.

There is but little to be seen by childrens faces, more than that they are heavy or lively; and scarcely that unless they are in motion. Very handsom faces of almost any age, will hide a foolish or a wicked mind till they betray themselves by their actions or their words: yet the frequent aukward movements of the muscles of the fool's face, tho' ever so handsom, is apt in time to leave such traces up and down it, as will distinguish a defect of mind upon examination: but the bad man, if he be an hypocrite, may so manage his muscles, by teaching them to contradict his heart, that little of his mind can be gathered from his countenance, so that the character of an hypocrite is entirely out of the power of the pencil, without some adjoining circumstance to discover him, as smiling and stabing at the same time, or the like.

It is by the natural and unaffected movements of the muscles, caused by the passions of the mind, that every man's character would in some measure be written in his face, by that time he arrives at forty years of age, were it not for certain accidents which often, tho' not always prevent it. For the ill-natured man, by frequently frowning, and pouting out the muscles of his mouth, doth in time bring those parts to a constant state of the appearance of ill-nature, which might have been prevented by the constant affectation of a smile; and so of the other passions: tho' there are some that do not affect the muscles at all simply of themselves, as love and hope.

But least I should be thought to lay too great a stress on outward shew, like a physiognomist, take this with you, that it is acknowledged there are so many different causes which produce the same kind of movements and appearances of the features, and so many thwartings by accidental shapes in the make of faces, that the old adage, fronti nulla fides,[7] will ever stand its ground upon the whole; and for very wise reasons nature hath thought fit it should. But, on the other hand, as in many particular cases, we receive information from the expressions of the countenance, what follows is meant to give a lineal description of the language written therein.

It may not be amiss just to look over the passions of the mind, from tranquillity to extreme despair; as they are in order described in the common drawing-book, called, Le Brun's[8] passions of the mind; selected from that great master's works for the use of learners; where you may have a compendious view of all the common expressions at once. And altho' these are but imperfect copies, they will answer our purpose in this place better than any other thing I can refer you to; because the passions are there ranged in succession, and distinctly marked with lines only, the shadows being omitted.

Some features are formed so as to make this or that expression of a passion more or less legible; for example, the little narrow chinese eye suits a loving or laughing expression best, as a large full eye doth those of fierceness and astonishment; and round-rising muscles will appear with some degree of cheerfulness even in sorrow: the features thus suiting with the expressions that have been often repeated in the face, at length mark it with such lines as sufficiently distinguish the character of the mind. [. . .]

Notes
1   Richardson and Shaftesbury. Jonathan Richardson (1665–1745), painter and

writer on art. Anthony Ashley Cooper, 3rd Earl of Shaftesbury (1671–1713), writer on aesthetics, e.g. in *Characteristicks* (1711). Many other editions of Shaftesbury's theoretical treatises on art appeared through the century. Both men had a considerable influence on Lord Burlington, his followers (see note 4 here) and others among the nobility, in matters concerning beauty, morality and ideal form in the arts.

2   Hogarth's marginal figures refer to the location of his illustrations in the two prints which accompany the *Analysis of Beauty*; T=top; B=bottom, etc. The lack of sequence in numbering the sections of the prints is no doubt due to the priorities given to their overall design.

3   Arthur Pond (*c.* 1705–58) was one of the first English artists to attempt, in the early eighteenth century, to make caricature a popularly accepted form of art. But it wasn't until the early 1760s (about the time of Hogarth's death) that the technique began to catch on. Pier Leone Ghezzi (1674–1755) produced caricatures of contemporary Roman personalities which were well known in England at the time. Pond worked in the manner of Ghezzi, publishing his own caricature portraits from 1736, much to the disgust of Hogarth who impugned this new 'fashion' in art.

4   'leaden imitations . . . near Hyde-park'. A reference, probably, to the Italianate decorations at Burlington House in Piccadilly, and the part the architect, painter, and landscape gardener, William Kent (*the bête noire* of both Hogarth and Thornhill) played in them. Hogarth's print, *Masquerades and Operas* (1732/4), referred to at the time as 'The Bad Taste of the Town' was a satire aimed at aristocratic patrons of art and their preferences for the works and styles of foreign, rather than native, artists. Among other means in the print for ridiculing the connoisseurs of art, the gate at Burlington House features prominently, a statue of Kent surmounting it.

5   Hogarth's six principles of beauty were, to quote from the final paragraph of his introduction, '. . . Fitness, variety, uniformity, simplicity, Intricacy and Quantity; – all which co-operate in the production of beauty, mutually correcting and restraining each other occasionally.

6   '*ogee* member', i.e. having an S-shaped profile.
     Roughly, 'don't trust appearances'.

8   A reference to Charles Le Brun (1619–90), history painter and Minister of Art under Louis XIV of France. Le Brun's physiognomic prototypes for the expression of the emotions were illustrated in his *Method for drawing the Emotions* (1696 and translated into English in 1734).

WILLIAM HOGARTH

The Anecdotes of William Hogarth (1737, 1763)

From John Bowyer Nichols (ed.), *Anecdotes of William Hogarth*, J. B. Nichols and Son, London, 1833.

The *Anecdotes of William Hogarth* from which the following extracts were taken, was originally published in London in 1833, that is well after the death of the artist. A collection of essays and criticisms pertaining to Hogarth's work and character, it also contains autobiographical material 'originating'[1] in the writings of the artist himself.

The *Anecdotes* was compiled by John Bowyer Nichols (1779–1863). It was designed to combine and augment earlier editions of the *Biographical Anecdotes of William Hogarth* (1781, 1782 and 1785), the *Genuine Works of William Hogarth* (1817) and other works on the artist. The earlier *Anecdotes* was published by Nichols's father whose admiration for Hogarth he shared.

The *Anecdotes* also incorporates the first more or less complete catalogue of Hogarth's prints, drawings and paintings.[2] It retains its authority and usefulness to this day.

[. . .] The early part of my life had been employed in a business rather detrimental than advantageous to those branches of the art which I wished to pursue, and have since professed. I had learned, by practice, to copy with tolerable exactness in the usual way; but it occurred to me that there were many disadvantages attending this method of study, as having faulty originals, &c. and even when the pictures or prints to be imitated were by the best masters, it was little more than pouring water out of one vessel into another. Drawing in an academy, though it should be after the life, will not make the student an artist; for as the eye is often taken from the original, to draw a bit at a time, it is possible he may know no more of what he has been copying, when his work is finished, than he did before it was begun.

There may be, and I believe are, some who, like the engrossers of deeds, copy every line without remembering a word; and if the deed should be in law Latin, or old French, probably without understanding a word of their original. Happy is it for them; for to retain would be indeed dreadful.

A dull transcriber, who in copying Milton's "Paradise Lost" hath not omitted a line, has almost as much right to be compared to Milton, as an exact copier of a fine picture by Rubens hath to be compared to Rubens. In both cases the hand is employed about minute parts, but the mind scarcely ever embraces the whole. Besides this, there is an essential difference between the man who transcribes the deed, and he who copies the figure; for though what is written may be line for line the same with the original, it is not probable that this will often be the case with the copied figure; frequently far from it. Yet the performer will be much more likely to retain a recollection of his own imperfect work than of the original from which he took it.

More reasons, not necessary to enumerate, struck me as strong objections to this practice, and led me to wish that I could find the shorter path, – fix forms and characters in my mind, and, instead of *copying* the lines, try to read the language, and if possible find the grammar of the art, by bringing into one focus the various observations I had made, and then trying by my power on the canvas, how far my plan enabled me to combine and apply them to practice.

For this purpose, I considered what various ways, and to what different purposes, the memory might be applied; and fell upon one which I found most suitable to my situation and idle disposition.

Laying it down first as an axiom, that he who could by any means acquire and retain in his memory, perfect ideas of the subjects he meant to draw, would have as clear a knowledge of the figure, as a man who can write freely hath of the twenty-four letters of the alphabet, and their infinite combinations (each of these being composed of lines), and would consequently be an accurate designer.

This I thought my only chance for eminence, as I found that the beauty and delicacy of the stroke in engraving was not to be learnt without much practice, and demanded a larger portion of patience than I felt myself disposed to exercise. Added to this, I saw little probability of acquiring the full command of the graver, in a sufficient degree to distinguish myself in that walk; nor was I, at twenty years of age, much disposed to enter on so barren and unprofitable a study, as that of merely making fine lines. I thought it still more unlikely, that by pursuing the common method, and copying *old* drawings, I could ever attain the power of making *new* designs, which was my first and greatest ambition. I therefore endeavoured to habituate myself to the exercise of a sort of technical memory; and by repeating in my own mind, the parts of which objects were composed, I could by degrees combine and put them down with my pencil. Thus, with all the drawbacks which resulted from the circumstances I have mentioned, I had one material advantage over my competitors, *viz*. the early habit I thus acquired of retaining in my mind's eye, without coldly copying it on the spot, whatever I intended to imitate.[1] Sometimes, but too seldom, I took the life, for correcting the parts I had not perfectly enough remembered, and then I transferred them to my compositions.

My pleasures and my studies thus going hand in hand, the most striking objects that presented themselves, either comic or tragic, made the strongest impression on my mind; but had I not sedulously practised what I had thus acquired, I should very soon have lost the power of performing it.

Instead of burthening the memory with musty rules, or tiring the eyes with copying dry and damaged pictures, I have ever found studying from nature the shortest and safest way of attaining knowledge in my art. By adopting this method, I found a redundancy of matter continually occurring. A choice of composition was the next thing to be considered, and my constitutional idleness naturally led me to the use of such materials as I had previously collected; and to this I was further induced by thinking, that if properly combined, they might be made the most useful to society in painting, although similar subjects had often failed in writing and preaching. [. . .]

[The annexed letter Mr. John Ireland was informed was written by Hogarth; add to this authority, of which he had no doubt, it carries internal evidence of his mind. It is printed in the London Magazine for 1737, and thus prefaced:]

"The following piece, published in the St. James's Evening Post of June 7th, is by the first painter in England, – perhaps in the world in his way.

"Every good-natured man and well-wisher to the Arts in England, must feel a kind of resentment at a very indecent paragraph, in the Daily Post of Thursday last, relating to the death of M. de Morine, first painter to the French king; in which very unjust, as well as cruel reflections, are cast on the noblest performance (in its way) that England has to boast of; I mean the work of the late Sir James Thornhill[4] in Greenwich Hall. It has ever been the business of narrow, little geniuses, who by a tedious application to minute parts, have (as they fancy) attained to a great insight into the correct drawing of a figure, and have acquired just knowledge enough in the art to tell accurately when a toe is too short, or a finger too thick, to endeavour, by detracting from the merits of great men, to build themselves a kind of reputation. These peddling demi-critics, on the painful discovery of some little inaccuracy (which proceeds mostly from the freedom of the pencil), without any regard to the more noble parts of a performance (which they are totally ignorant of), with great satisfaction condemn the whole as a bad and incorrect piece.

1 Though averse, as he himself expresses it, to *coldly copying on the spot* any objects that struck him, it was usual with him when he saw a singular character, either in the street or elsewhere to pencil the leading features, and prominent markings upon his nail, and when he came home, to copy the sketch on paper, and afterwards introduce it in a print. Several of these sketches I have seen, and in them may be traced the first thought for many of the characters which he afterwards introduced in his works. J. IRELAND[3]

The meanest artist in the Emelian square,
Can imitate in brass the nails or hair;
Expert at trifles, and a cunning fool,
Able to express the parts, but not the whole.[5]

There is another set of gentry, more noxious to the art than these, and those are your picture jobbers from abroad, who are always ready to raise a great cry in the prints, whenever they think their craft is in danger; and indeed it is their interest to depreciate every English work as hurtful to their trade of continually importing ship-loads of dead Christs, Holy Families, Madonas, and other dismal dark subjects, neither entertaining nor ornamental, on which they scrawl the terrible cramp names of some Italian masters, and fix on us poor Englishmen the character of universal dupes. If a man, naturally a judge of painting, not bigotted to those empyrics, should cast his eye on one of their sham virtuoso pieces, he would be very apt to say, 'Mr. Bubbleman, that grand Venus, as you are pleased to call it, has not beauty enough for the character of an English cook-maid.' – Upon which the quack answers, with a confident air, 'Sir, I find that you are no connoisseur; the picture, I assure you, is in Alesso Baldminetto's[6] second and best manner, boldly painted, and truly sublime: the contour gracious; the air of the head in the high Greek taste; and a most divine idea it is.' – Then spitting in an obscure place, and rubbing it with a dirty handkerchief, takes a skip to the other end of the room, and screams out in raptures, – 'There's an amazing touch! A man should have this picture a twelvemonth in his collection before he can discover half its beauties!' The gentleman (though naturally a judge of what is beautiful, yet ashamed to be out of the fashion, by judging for himself) with this cant is struck dumb; gives a vast sum for the picture, very modestly confesses he is indeed quite ignorant of painting, and bestows a frame worth fifty pounds on a frightful thing, which, without the hard name, is not worth so many farthings. Such impudence as is now continually practised in the picture trade must meet with its proper treatment, would gentlemen but venture to see with their own eyes. Let but the comparison of pictures with nature be their only guide, and let them judge as freely of painting as they do of poetry, they would then take it for granted, that when a piece gives pleasure to none but these connoisseurs, or their adherents, if the purchase be a thousand pounds, 'tis nine hundred and ninety-nine too dear; and were all our grand collections stripped of such sort of trumpery, then, and not till then, it would be worth an Englishman's while to try the strength of his genius to supply their place; which now it were next to madness to attempt, since there is nothing that has not travelled a thousand miles, or has not been done a hundred years, but is looked upon as mean and ungenteel furniture. What Mr. Pope in his last work says of poems, may with much more propriety be applied to pictures:

'Authors, like coins, grow dear as they grow old;
It is the rust we value, not the gold'.[7]

Notes

1   Inverted commas are placed around 'originating' because Hogarth's fragmented notes were assembled and edited by John Ireland who acquired Hogarth's papers about thirty years after the artist's death.

2   The works are illustrated by 48 plates engraved after the originals.

3   John Ireland: see note 1.

4   Sir James Thornhill (1675/6–1734), Hogarth's father-in-law, was a highly esteemed and well-rewarded painter of the period. Following the Grand Baroque tradition, his most notable works include the Dome of St. Paul's and the Painted Hall and other rooms in Greenwich Hospital. His treatment of subjects from modern history in allegorical settings was of some influence on the young Hogarth. Hogarth's paintings at St. Bartholomew's Hospital (*The Pool of Bethesda* and *The Good Samaritan*, 1735–6) were in emulation of the grand manner of the recently deceased Thornhill.

5   Quintus Horatius Flaccus, or Horace, (65–8 B.C.), *Ars Poetica* (*The Art of Poetry*), lines 32–35. From an unidentified late seventeenth or early eighteenth century translation.

6   Alesso Baldminetto. Hogarth's parody of the name of an earlier Italian painter whose works in Hogarth's time were fashionable in England: Alesso Baldovinetti (1426–99).

7   Alexander Pope, from *The First Epistle of the Second Book of Horace Imitated* (1737), lines 35–36.

HORACE WALPOLE

On Modern Gardening (1771)

From Horace Walpole, *Anecdotes of Painting in England*, Vol. IV. Printed by Thomas Kirgate, Strawberry Hill, 1771.

Horace Walpole (1717–97) included the essay 'On Modern Gardening' at the end of Vol. IV of his *Anecdotes of Painting in England*. This was first printed in 1771 at the printing office in Strawberry Hill, Walpole's pseudo-Gothic villa in Twickenham. However, publication was delayed until 1780 out of consideration for the living artists (and relatives of deceased artists) whose works had been criticized in the *Anecdotes*. The essay was originally titled 'The History of the Taste in Modern Gardening' and was probably written between 1750–70 when Walpole was laying out the grounds of Strawberry Hill and was particularly interested in contemporary fashions in garden design.

In the following excerpt he supports the 'modern' style of gardening which, broadly speaking, follows irregular forms of nature as opposed to the formal geometrical designs favoured in the seventeenth century. A somewhat contrary view on symmetry in garden design can be found in Le Blanc (p. 45).

One of the first gardens planted in this simple though still formal style, was my father's at Houghton.[1] It was laid out by Mr. Eyre,[2] an imitator of Bridgman. It contains three-and-twenty acres, then reckoned a considerable portion.

I call a sunk fence[3] the leading step, for these reasons. No sooner was this simple enchantment made, than levelling, mowing and rolling, followed. The contiguous ground of the park without the sunk fence was to be harmonized with the lawn within; and the garden in its turn was to be set free from its prim regularity, that it might assort with the wilder country without. The sunk fence ascertained the specific garden, but that it might not draw too obvious a line of distinction between the neat and the rude, the contiguous out-lying parts came to be included in a kind of general design: and when nature was taken into the plan, under improvements, every step that was made, pointed out new beauties and inspired new ideas. At that moment appeared Kent,[4] painter enough to taste the charms of landscape, bold and opinionative enough to dare and to dictate, and born with a genius to strike out a great system from the twilight of imperfect essays. He leaped the fence, and saw that all nature was a garden. He felt the delicious contrast of hill and valley changing imperceptibly into each other, tasted the beauty of the gentle swell, or concave scoop, and remarked how loose groves crowned an easy eminence with happy ornament, and while they called in the distant view between their graceful stems, removed and extended the perspective by delusive comparison.

Thus the pencil of his imagination bestowed all the arts of landscape on the scenes he handled. The great principles on which he worked were perspective, and light and shade. Groupes of trees broke too uniform or too extensive a lawn; evergreens and woods were opposed to the glare of the champain,[5] and where the view was less fortunate, or so much exposed as to be beheld at once, he blotted out some parts by thick shades, to divide it into variety, or to make the richest scene more enchanting by reserving it to a farther advance of the spectator's step. Thus, selecting favourite objects, and veiling deformities by screens of plantation; sometimes allowing the rudest waste to add its soil to the richest theatre, he realized the compositions of the greatest masters in painting. Where objects were wanting to animate his horizon, his taste as an architect could bestow immediate termination. His buildings, his feats, his temples, were more the works of his pencil than of his compasses. We owe the restoration of Greece and the diffusion of architecture to his skill in landscape.

But of all the beauties he added to the face of this beautiful country, none surpassed his management of water. Adieu to canals, circular basons, and cascades tumbling down marble steps, that last absurd magnificence of Italian and French villas. The forced elevation of cataracts was no more. The gentle stream was taught to serpentize seemingly at its pleasure, and where discontinued by different levels, its course appeared to be concealed by thickets properly interspersed, and glittered again at a distance where it might be supposed naturally to arrive. Its borders were smoothed, but preserved their waving ir-regularity. A few trees scattered here and there on its edges sprinkled the tame bank that accompanied its meanders; and when it disappeared among the hills, shades descending from the heights leaned towards its progress, and framed the distant point of light under which it was lost, as it turned aside to either hand of the blue horizon.

Thus dealing in none but the colours of nature, and catching its most favourable features, men saw a new creation opening before their eyes. The living landscape was chastened or polished, not transformed. Freedom was given to the forms of trees; they extended their branches unrestricted, and where any eminent oak, or master beech had escaped maiming and survived the forest, bush and bramble was removed, and all its honours were restored to distinguish and shade the plain. Where the united plumage of an ancient wood extended wide its undulating canopy, and stood venerable in its darkness, Kent thinned the foremost ranks, and left but so many detached and scattered trees, as softened the approach of gloom and blended a chequered light with the thus lengthened shadows of the remaining columns.

Succeeding artists have added new master-strokes to these touches; perhaps improved or brought to perfection some that I have named. The introduction of foreign trees and plants, which we owe principally to Archibald duke of Argyle,[6] contributed essentially to the richness of colouring so peculiar to our modern landscape. The mixture of various greens, the contrast of forms between our forest-trees and the northern and West-Indian firs and pines, are improvements more recent than Kent, or but little known to him. The weeping-willow and every florid shrub, each tree of delicate or bold leaf, are new tints in the composition of our gardens. The last century was certainly acquainted with many of those rare plants we now admire. The Weymouth-pine[7] has long been naturalized here; the patriarch plant still exists at Longleat. The light and graceful acacia was known as early; witness those ancient stems in the court of Bedford-house[8] in Bloomsbury-square; and in the bishop of London's garden at Fulham are many exotics of very ancient date. I doubt therefore whether the difficulty of preserving them in a clime so foreign to their nature did not convince our ancestors of their inutility in general, unless the shapeliness of the lime and horse-chesnut which accorded so well with established regularity, and which thence and from their novelty grew in fashion, did not occasion the neglect of the more curious plants.

But just as the encomiums are that I have bestowed on Kent's discoveries, he was neither without assistance or faults. Mr. Pope undoubtedly contributed to form his taste. The design of the prince of Wales's garden at Carlton-house[9] was evidently borrowed from the poet's at Twickenham.[10] There was a little of affected modesty in the latter, when he said of all his works he was most proud of his garden. And yet it was a singular effort of art and taste to impress so much variety and scenery on a spot of five acres. The passing through the gloom from the grotto to the opening day, the retiring and again assembling shades, the dusky groves, the larger lawn, and the solemnity of the termination at the cypresses that lead up to his mother's tomb, are managed with exquisite judgment; and though lord Peterborough[11] assisted him

To form his quincunx[12] and to rank his vines,

those were not the most pleasing ingredients of his little perspective.

I do not know whether the disposition of the garden at Rousham, laid out for general Dormer,[13] and in my opinion the most engaging of all Kent's works, was not planned on the model of Mr. Pope's, at least in the opening and retiring shades of Venus's vale. The whole is as elegant and antique as if the emperor Julian had selected the most pleasing solitude about Daphne[14] to enjoy a philosophic retirement.

That Kent's ideas were but rarely great, was in some measure owing to the novelty of his art. It would have been difficult to have transported the style of gardening at once from a few acres to tumbling of forests: and though new fashions like new religions, (which are new fashions) often lead men to the most opposite excesses, it could not be the case in gardening, where the experiments would have been so expensive. Yet it is true too that the features in Kent's landscapes were seldom majestic. His clumps were puny, he aimed at immediate effect, and planted not for futurity. One sees no large woods sketched out by his direction. Nor are we yet entirely risen above a too great frequency of small clumps, especially in the elbows of serpentine rivers. How common to see three or four beeches, then as many larches, a third knot of cypresses, and a revolution of all three! Kent's last designs were in a higher style, as his ideas opened on success. The north terras at Claremont[15] was much superior to the rest of the garden.

A return of some particular thoughts was common to him with other painters, and made his *hand* known. A small lake edged by a winding bank with scattered trees that led to a seat at the head of the pond, was common to Claremont, Esher, and others of his designs. At Esher,

Where Kent and nature vied for Pelham's love,[16]

the prospects more than aided the painter's genius. – They marked out the points where his art was necessary or not; but thence left his judgment in possession of all its glory.

Having routed *professed* art, for the modern gardiner exerts his talents to conceal his art, Kent, like other reformers, knew not how to stop at the just limits. He had followed nature, and imitated her so happily, that he began to think all her works were equally proper for imitation. In Kensington-garden he planted dead trees, to give a greater air of truth to the scene – but he was soon laughed out of this excess. His ruling principle was, that *nature abhors a strait line*.[17] – His mimics, for every genius has his apes, seemed to think that she could love nothing but what was crooked. Yet so many men of taste of all ranks devoted themselves to the new improvements, that it is surprizing how much beauty has been struck out, with how few absurdities. Still in some lights the reformation seems to me to have been pushed too far. Though an avenue crossing a park or separating a lawn, and intercepting views from the seat to which it leads, are capital faults, yet a great avenue*¹* cut through woods, perhaps before entering a park, has a noble air, and

1 Of this kind one of the most noble is that of Stanstead,[19] the seat of the earl of Halifax, traversing an ancient wood for two miles and bounded by the sea. The very extensive lawns at that seat, richly enclosed by venerable beech woods, and chequered by single beeches of vast size, particularly when you stand in the portico of the temple and survey the landscape that wastes itself in rivers of broken sea, recall such exact pictures of Claud Lorrain, that it is difficult to conceive that he did not paint from this very spot.

> Like footmen running before coaches
> To tell the inn what lord approaches,[18]

announces the habitation of some man of distinction. In other places the total banishment of all particular neatness immediately about a house, which is frequently left gazing by itself in the middle of a park, is a defect. Sheltered and even close walks in so very uncertain a climate as ours, are comforts ill exchanged for the few picturesque days that we enjoy: and whenever a family can purloin a warm and even something of an old fashioned garden from the landscape designed for them by the undertaker in fashion, without interfering with the picture, they will find satisfactions on those days that do not invite strangers to come and see their improvements.

Fountains have with great reason been banished from gardens as unnatural; but it surprizes me that they have not been allotted to their proper positions, to cities, towns, and the courts of great houses, as proper accompaniments to architecture, and as works of grandeur in themselves. Their decorations admit the utmost invention, and when the waters are thrown up to different stages, and tumble over their border, nothing has a more imposing or a more refreshing sound. A palace demands its external graces and attributes, as much as a garden. Fountains and cypresses peculiarly become buildings, and no man can have been at Rome, and seen the vast basons of marble dashed with perpetual cascades in the area of St. Peter's, without retaining an idea of taste and splendor. Those in the piazza Navona are as useful as sublimely conceived.

Grottoes in this climate are recesses only to be looked at transiently. When they are regularly composed within of symmetry and architecture, as in Italy, they are only splendid improprieties. The most judiciously, indeed most fortunately placed grotto, is that at Stourhead, where the river bursts from the urn of its god, and passes on its course through the cave.

But it is not my business to lay down rules for gardens, but to give the history of them. A system of rules pushed to a great degree of refinement, and collected from the best examples and practice, has been lately given in a book intituled *Observations on modern Gardening*.[20] The work is very ingeniously and carefully executed, and in point of utility rather exceeds than omits any necessary directions. The author will excuse me if I think it a little excess, when he examines that rude and unappropriated scene of Matlocke-bath,[21] and criticizes nature for having bestowed on the rapid river Derwent too many cascades. How can this censure be brought home to gardening? The management of rocks in a province can fall to few directors of gardens; still in our distant provinces such a guide may be necessary.

The author divides his subject into gardens, parks, farms, and ridings. I do not mean to find fault with this division. Directions are requisite to each kind, and each has its department at many of the great scenes from whence he drew his observations. In the historic light, I distinguish them into the garden that connects itself with a park, into the ornamented farm, and into the forest or savage garden. Kent, as I have shown, invented or established the first sort. Mr. Philip Southcote founded the second or ferme ornée,[22] of which is a very just description in the author I have been quoting. The third I think he has not enough distinguished. I mean that kind of alpine scene, composed almost wholly of pines and firs, a few birch, and such trees as assimilate with a savage and mountainous country. Mr. Charles Hamilton, at Pain's-hill, in my opinion has given a perfect example of this mode in the utmost boundary of his garden. All is great and foreign and rude; the walks seem not designed, but cut through the wood of pines; and the style of the whole is so grand, and conducted with so serious an air of wild and uncultivated extent, that when you look down on this seeming forest, you are amazed to find it contain a very few acres. In general, except as a screen to conceal some deformity, or as a shelter in winter, I am not fond of total plantations of ever-greens. Firs in particular form a very ungraceful summit, all broken into angles.

Sir Henry Englefield[23] was one of the first improvers on the new style, and selected with singular taste that chief beauty of all gardens, prospect and fortunate points of view. We tire of all the painter's art when it wants these finishing touches. The fairest scenes, that depend on themselves alone, weary when often seen. The Doric portico, the Palladian bridge, the Gothic ruin, the Chinese pagoda, that surprize the stranger, soon lose their charms to their surfeited master. The lake that floats the valley is still more lifeless, and its lord seldom enjoys his expence but when he shows it to a visitor. But the ornament whose merit soonest fades, is the hermitage or scene adapted to contemplation. It is almost comic to set aside a quarter of one's garden to be melancholy in. Prospect, animated prospect, is the theatre that will always be the most frequented. Prospects formerly were sacrificed to convenience and warmth. Thus Burleigh[24] stands behind a hill, from the top of which it would command Stamford. Our ancestors who resided the greatest part of the year at their seats, as others did two years together or more, had an eye to comfort first, before expence. Their vast mansions received and harboured all the younger branches, the dowagers and ancient maiden aunts of the families, and other families visited them for a month together. The method of living is now totally changed, and yet the same superb palaces are still created, becoming a pompous solitude to the owner, and a transient entertainment to a few travellers.

If any incident abolishes or restrains the modern style of gardening, it will be this circumstance of solitariness. The greater the scene, the more distant it is probably from the capital; in the neighbourhood of which land is too dear to admit considerable extent of property. Men tire of expence that is obvious to few spectators. Still there is a more imminent danger that threatens the present, as it has ever done, all taste. I mean the pursuit of variety. A modern French writer has in a very affected phrase given a just account of this, I will call it, distemper.

He says, *l'ennui du beau amene le gout du singulier*.[25] The noble simplicity of the Augustan age was driven out by false taste. The gigantic, the puerile, the quaint, and at last the barbarous, and the monkish, had each their successive admirers. Music has been improved, till it is a science of tricks and slight of hand: the sober greatness of Titian is lost, and painting since Carlo Maratti,[26] has little more relief than Indian paper. Borromini[27] twisted and curled architecture, as if it was subject to the change of fashions like a head of hair. If we once lose sight of the propriety of landscape in our gardens, we shall wander into all the fantastic sharawadgis[28] of the Chinese. We have discovered the point of perfection. We have given the true model of gardening to the world; let other countries mimic or corrupt our taste; but let it reign here on its verdant throne, original by its elegant simplicity, and proud of no other art than that of softening nature's harshnesses and copying her graceful touch.

Notes

1   Houghton Hall, Norfolk was the home of Sir Robert Walpole, Horace Walpole's father.

2   P. E. Eyre was a landscape gardener who, as Walpole suggests, worked in a formal style derived from the geometrical designs of Charles Bridgeman.

3   Sunk fence, sometimes called a 'fosse' or 'Ha! Ha!', a ditch or trench used as a boundary.

4   William Kent (1684–1748) was a painter, architect and landscape gardener, seen by Walpole as 'the father of Modern Gardening'. (*Anecdotes of Painting*, sect. 4, Vol. IV.)

5   Flat level country or plain.

6   Archibald Campbell (1682–1761) was the third Duke of Argyll.

7   A white pine introduced into England at the beginning of the eighteenth century by Thomas Thynne, first Viscount Weymouth.

8   Residence of the fourth Duke of Bedford.

9   Prince George, son of George III, owned Carlton House in Pall Mall.

10   Alexander Pope's garden, near the River Thames, Twickenham. Pope began laying out these grounds in 1720.

11   Charles Mordaunt, the Earl of Peterborough.

12   A rectangular arrangement of five trees with one in each of the four corners and the fifth in the centre.

13   The twenty-five acre garden at Rousham was landscaped by William Kent for General Dormer of the Cotterell family.

14   A shrine on the River Orontes in Antioch, Syria, at the spot where Daphne (according to ancient mythology) turned into a tree when pursued by Apollo. The Emperor Julian is supposed to have made regular visits to the shrine.

15   The Surrey house of the architect Sir John Vanbrugh, expanded to form a villa for the Duke of Newcastle and destroyed later in the eighteenth century.

16   From Pope's *Epilogue to the Satires* Dialogue II, 11 66–7. Kent reconstructed the site at Esher Lodge for Henry Pelham during the 1730s.

17   Quoted from Frances Coventry, 'Strictures on the Absurd Novelties introduced into Gardening' in *The World*, April 12, 1753.

18   From Matthew Prior, *Alma: or Progress of the Mind*, 1715, Canto I, pp. 53–4.

19   Stanstead Park, Sussex.

20   Book by Thomas Whately, written in 1756 and published anonymously in 1770.

21   Matlock Bath in Derbyshire is situated on the River Derwent in a vale three miles long. Walpole records a visit to Matlock in September 1768 in his *Journal of Visits to Country Seats*.

22   Ferme ornée or ornamented farm. One of the earliest examples of this type of garden design can be found in Woburn Farm, established by Philip Southcote.

23   Father of better-known Sir Henry Charles Englefield, a specialist in literature and science.

24   Burleigh known as Theobalds, and the seat of Lord Burleigh, one of Walpole's ancestors.

25   'An excess of beauty leads the taste to novelty.'

26   An Italian painter and etcher (1625–1713) renowned for his many monumental altarpieces.

27   Francesco Borromini (1599–1667) was a famous Italian architect, noted for his many Baroque churches in Rome.

28   There was a great interest in the eighteenth century in the irregular and fantasy garden designs – the 'sharawadgis' – favoured by the Chinese. In 1782 Walpole added a note to an earlier part of this essay defending the English garden against French accusations that it was derived almost entirely from Chinese sources. Walpoie attacks the French notion of 'Le Gout Anglais–Chinois', claiming that Chinese designs are more remote from nature and asserting the originality of the English invention.

Joshua Reynolds

The Fourteenth Discourse: On Gainsborough (1788)

From Sir Joshua Reynolds, *A Discourse delivered to the students of the Royal Academy, on the Distribution of the Prizes, December 10 1788, by the President*, Printed by Thomas Cadell, London, 1789.

Sir Joshua Reynolds (1723–92) was elected first President of the Royal Academy in 1769, one year after its foundation. The Fourteenth Discourse was one of fifteen lectures which he delivered at the Academy's annual distribution of prizes between 1769–90. The institution included among its professors some of the most eminent painters in the country and offered students a rigorous training in the practice and principles of High Art. As formulated in Reynolds's discourses, these principles emphasized the superiority of history painting over other genres (such as portrait or landscape painting) and the value of an elevated or 'grand' style, evolved through careful study of works by Old Masters. These included classical Greek sculpture and paintings by the Renaissance artists Raphael and Michelangelo. A similar stress on the high value of history painting can be found in La Font de St. Yenne's *Réflexions* (see p. 58).

Reynolds devoted the following discourse to Thomas Gainsborough (1727–88), a portrait and landscape painter who had exhibited intermittently at Royal Academy exhibitions from 1769 until his death. Yet in many ways Gainsborough represented the antithesis of all that the Academy stood for. He had received no academic training, avoided history painting and had no sympathy with the grand style. Reynolds, however, admits that he is captivated by the way in which Gainsborough paints ordinary nature with a 'lightness of effect' and a 'painter's eye for colouring'. Even the president of the Academy was forced to acknowledge the existence of 'genius in a lower rank of art'.

GENTLEMEN, In the study of our Art, as in the study of all Arts, something is the result of *our own* observation of Nature, something, (and that is not little) the effect of the example of those who have studied the same nature before us, and who have cultivated before us the same Art, with diligence and success. The less we confine ourselves in the choice of those examples, the more advantage we shall derive from them; and the nearer we shall bring our performances to a correspondence with nature, and the great general rules of Art.[1] When we draw our examples, from remote and revered antiquity, (with some advantage undoubtedly in that selection) we subject ourselves to some inconveniences. We may suffer ourselves to be too much led away by great names, and be too much subdued by overbearing authority. Our learning, in that case, is not so much an exercise of our judgment as a proof of our docility. We find ourselves, perhaps, too much over-shadowed; and the character of our pursuits is rather distinguished by the tameness of the follower, than animated by the spirit of emulation. It is sometimes of service, that our examples should be *near* us; and such as raise a reverence, sufficient to induce us carefully to observe them, yet not so great as to prevent us from engaging with them in something like a generous contention.

We have lately lost Mr. Gainsborough, one of the greatest orna-ments of our Academy. It is not our business here, to make panegyrics on the living, or even on the dead, who were of our body. The praise of the former might bear the appearance of adulation; and the latter of untimely justice; perhaps of envy to those whom we have still the happiness to enjoy, by an oblique suggestion of invidious comparisons. In discoursing therefore on the talents of the late Mr. Gainsborough, my object is, not so much to praise or to blame him, as to draw from his excellencies and defects, matter of instruction to the Students in our Academy. If ever this nation should produce genius sufficient to acquire to us the honourable distinction of an English School; the name of Gainsborough will be transmitted to posterity, in the history of the Art, among the very first of that rising name. That our reputation in the Arts is now only rising, must be acknowledged; and we must expect our advances to be attended with old prejudices, as adversaries, and not as supporters; standing in this respect in a very different situation from the late artists of the Roman School, to whose reputation ancient prejudices have certainly contributed: the way was prepared for them, and they may be said rather to have lived in the reputation of their country, than to have contributed to it; whilst whatever celebrity is obtained by English Artists, can arise only from the operation of a fair and true comparison. And when they communicate to their country a share of their reputation, it is a portion of fame not borrowed from others, but solely acquired by their own labour and talents. As Italy has undoubtedly a prescriptive right to an admiration bordering on prejudice, as a soil peculiarly adapted, congenial, and, we may add, destined to the production of men of great genius in our Art, we may not unreasonably suspect that a portion of the great fame of some of their late artists has been owing to the general readiness and disposition of mankind, to acquiesce in their original prepossessions in favour of the productions of the Roman School.

On this ground, however unsafe, I will venture to prophecy, that two of the last distinguished Painters of that country, I mean Pompeio Battoni, and Rafaelle Mengs,[2] however great their names may at present sound in our ears, will very soon fall into the rank of Imperiale, Sebastian Concha, Placido Constanza, Massuccio,[3] and the rest of their immediate predecessors, whose names, though equally renowned in their lifetime, are now fallen into what is little short of total oblivion. I do not say that those painters were not superior to the artist I allude to, and whose loss we lament, in a certain routine of practice, which, to the eyes of common observers, has the air of a learned composition, and bears a sort of superficial resemblance to the manner of the great men who went before them. I know this perfectly well, but I know likewise, that a man, looking for real and lasting reputation, must unlearn much of the common-place method, so observable in the works of the artists whom I have named. For my own part, I confess, I take more interest in, and am more captivated with, the powerful impression of nature, which Gainsborough exhibited in his portraits, and in his landskips, and the interesting simplicity and elegance of his little ordinary beggar children, than with any of the works of that School, since the time of Andrea Sacchi,[4] or perhaps, we may say of Carlo Maratti,[5] two painters who may truly be said to be Ultimi Romanorum.[6]

I am well aware how much I lay myself open to the censure and ridicule of the academical professors of other nations, in preferring the humble attempts of Gainsborough to the works of those regular graduates in the great historical stile. But we have the sanction of all mankind in preferring genius in a lower rank of art, to feebleness and insipidity in the highest.

It would not be to the present purpose, even if I had the means and materials, which I have not, to enter into the private life of Mr. Gainsborough. The history of his gradual advancement, and the means by which he acquired such excellence in his art, would come nearer to our purpose and wishes, if it were by any means attainable; but the slow progress of advancement is in general, imperceptible to the man himself who makes it; it is the consequence of an accumulation of various ideas, which his mind has received, he does not, perhaps, know how or when. Sometimes indeed it happens, that he may be able to mark the time, when from the sight of a picture, a passage in an author, or a hint in conversation, he has received, as it were, some new and guiding light, something like inspiration, by which his mind has been expanded, and is morally sure that his whole life and conduct has been affected by that accidental circumstance. Such interesting accounts we may however sometimes obtain from a man, who has acquired an uncommon habit of self-examination, and has attended to the progress of his own improvement.

It may not be improper to make mention of some of the customs and habits of this extraordinary man; points which come more within the reach of an observer; I however mean such only as are connected with his art, and indeed were, as I apprehend, the causes of his arriving to that high degree of excellence, which we see and acknowledge in his works. Of these causes we must state, as the fundamental, the love which he had to his art; to which, indeed, his whole mind appears to have been devoted, and to which every thing he saw was referred; and this we may fairly conclude from various circumstances of his life which were known to his intimate friends. Among others he had a habit of continually remarking to those who happened to be about him, whatever peculiarity of countenance, whatever accidental combination of figures, or happy effects of light and shadow occurred in prospects, in the sky, in walking the streets, or in company. If, in his walks, he found a character that he liked, and whose attendance was to be obtained, he ordered him to his house; and from the fields he brought into his painting-room, stumps of trees, weeds, and animals of various kinds, and designed them, not from memory, but immediately from the objects. He even framed a kind of models of landskips, on his table, composed of broken stones, dryed herbs, and pieces of looking glass, which he magnified and improved into rocks, trees, and water. How far this latter practice may be useful in giving hints, the professors of landskip can best determine. Like every other technical practice, it seems to me wholly to depend on the general talent of him who uses it. Such methods may be nothing better than contemptible and mischievous trifling; or they may be aids. I think upon the whole, unless we constantly refer to real nature, that practice may be more likely to do harm than good. I mention it only, as it shews the solicitude and extreme activity which he had about every thing that related to his art; that he wished to have his objects embodied as it were, and distinctly before him, that he neglected nothing which could keep his faculties in exercise, and derived hints from every sort of combination.

We must not forget, whilst we are on this subject, to make some remarks on his custom of painting by night, which confirms what I have already mentioned, his great affection to his art; since he could not amuse himself in the evenings, by any other means so agreeable to himself. I am indeed much inclined to believe that it is a practice very advantageous and improving to an artist; by this means he will acquire a new and a higher perception of what is great and beautiful in Nature. By candle-light, objects not only appear more beautiful, but from their being in a greater breadth of light and shadow, as well as having a greater breadth and uniformity of colour, nature appears to me in a higher stile; and even the flesh seems to take a higher and richer tone of colour. Judgment is to direct us in the use to be made of this method of study; but the method itself is (I am very sure of it) advantageous. I have often imagined that the two great colourists, Titian and Corregio,[7] (though I do not know that they painted by night) formed their high ideas of colouring from the effects of objects by this artificial light: but I am more assured, that whoever attentively studies, the first and best manner of Guercino,[8] will be convinced that he either painted by this light, or formed his manner on this conception.

Another practice Gainsborough had, which is worth mentioning, as it is certainly worthy of imitation; I mean his manner of forming all the parts of his picture together; the whole going on at the same time, in the same manner as nature creates her works. Though this method is not uncommon to those who have been regularly educated, yet probably it was suggested to him, by his own natural sagacity. That this custom is not universal appears from the practice of the painter whom I just now mentioned, Pompeio Batoni, who finished his historical pictures.part after part; and in his portraits completely finished one feature before he proceeded to another. The consequence was, as might be expected; the countenance was never well expressed; and, as the painters say, the whole not well put together.

The first thing required to excel in our Art, or I believe in any art, is, not only a love for it, but even an enthusiastic ambition to excel in it. This never fails of success proportioned to the natural abilities with which the artist has been endowed by Providence. Of Gainsborough, we certainly know, that his passion was not the acquirement of riches, but excellence in his art; and to enjoy that honourable fame which is sure to attend it. – That *he felt this ruling passion strong in death*, I am myself a witness. A few days before he died he wrote me a letter, to express his acknowledgements for the good opinion I entertained of his abilities, and the manner in which (he had been informed) I always spoke of him, and desired he might see me, once more, before he died. I am aware how flattering it is to myself to be thus connected with the dying testimony which this excellent painter bore to his art. But I cannot prevail on myself to suppress that I was not connected with him by any habits of familiarity; if any little jealousies had subsisted between us they were forgotten, in those moments of sincerity; and he turned towards me as one, who was engrossed by the same pursuits, and who deserved his good opinion, by being sensible of his excellence. Without entering into a detail of what passed at this last interview, the impression of it upon my mind was, that his regret at losing life, was principally the regret of leaving his art; and more especially as he now began, he said, to see what his deficiencies were; which, he said, he flattered himself in his last works were supplied.

When such a man as Gainsborough arrives to great fame, without the assistance of an academical education, without travelling to Italy, or any of those preparatory studies which have been so often recommended, he is produced as an instance, how little such studies are necessary; since so great excellence may be acquired without them. This is an inference not warranted by the success of any individual; and I trust it will not be thought that I wish to make this use of it.

It must be remembered that the style and department of art which Gainsborough chose, and in which he so much excelled, did not require that he should go out of his own country for the objects of his study; they were every where about him; he found them in the streets, and in the fields; and from the models thus accidentally found, he selected with great judgment, such as suited his purpose. As his studies were directed to the living world principally, he did not pay a general attention to the works of the various masters, though they are, in my opinion, always of great use, even when the character of our subject requires us to depart from some of their principles. It cannot be denied that the department of the art which he professed may exist with great effect without them; that in such subjects, and in the manner that belongs to them, they are supplied, and more than supplied, by natural sagacity, and a minute observation of particular nature. If Gainsborough did not look at nature, with a poet's eye, it must be acknowledged that he saw her with the eye of a painter; and gave a faithful, if not a poetical representation of what he had before him.

Though he did not much attend to the works of the great historical painters of former ages, yet he was well aware, that the language of the art, the art of imitation, must be learned somewhere; and as he knew that he could not learn it in an equal degree from his cotemporaries, he very judiciously applied himself to the Flemish School;[9] who are undoubtedly the greatest masters of one necessary branch of art; and he did not need to go out of his own country for examples of that school: From that he learnt the harmony of colouring, the management and disposition of light and shadow, and every means which the masters of it practised to ornament, and give splendor to their works. And to satisfy himself as well as others, how well he knew the mechanism and artifice which they employed to bring out that tone of colour, which we so much admire in their works, he occasionally made copies from Rubens, Teniers, and Vandyck,[10] which it would be no disgrace to the most accurate connoisseur to mistake, at the first sight, for the Works of those masters. What he thus learned, he applied to the originals of nature, which he saw with his own eyes; and imitated, not in the manner of those masters, but in his own.

Whether he most excelled in portraits, landskips, or fancy pictures, it is difficult to determine: whether his portraits were most admirable for exact truth of resemblance, or his landskips for the portrait-like representation of nature, such as we see in the works of Rubens, Rysdale,[11] and others of those Schools. In his fancy pictures, when he had fixed on his object of imitation, whether it was the mean and vulgar form of a wood-cutter, or a child of an interesting character, as he did not attempt to raise the one, so neither did he lose any of the natural grace and elegance of the other; such a grace, and such an elegance as are more frequently found in cottages than in courts. This excellence was his own, the result of his particular observation and taste; for this he was certainly not indebted to the Flemish School; nor indeed to any School; for his grace was not academical, or antique, but selected by himself from the great school of nature; and there are yet a thousand modes of grace, which are neither theirs nor his, but lie open in the multiplied scenes and figures of life, to be brought out by skilful and faithful observers.

Upon the whole, we may justly say, that whatever he attempted he carried to a high degree of excellence. It is to the credit of his good sense and judgment that he never did attempt that stile of historical painting, for which his previous studies had made no preparation.

And here it naturally occurs to oppose the sensible conduct of Gainsborough in this respect, to that of our late excellent Hogarth, who, with all his extraordinary talents, was not blessed with this knowledge of his own deficiency; or of the bounds which were set to the extent of his own powers. After this admirable artist had spent the greatest part of his life, in an active, busy, and we may add, successful attention to the ridicule of life; after he had invented a new species of dramatic painting, in which probably he will never be equalled, and had stored his mind with such infinite materials to explain and illustrate the domestic and familiar scenes of common life, which were generally (and ought to have been always) the subject of his pencil; he very imprudently, or rather presumptuously, attempted the great historical style; for which his previous habits had by no means prepared him: he was indeed so entirely unacquainted with the principles of this style, that he was not even aware, that any artificial preparation was at all necessary. It is to be regretted, that any part of the life of such a genius should be fruitlessly employed. Let his failure teach us not to indulge ourselves in the vain imagination, that by a momentary resolution we can give either dexterity to the hand, or a new habit to the mind.

I have however little doubt, but that the same sagacity, which enabled those two extraordinary men, to discover the true object, and the peculiar excellence of that branch of art which they cultivated, would have been equally effectual in discovering the principles of the higher style; if they had investigated those principles with the same eager industry, which they exerted in their own department. As Gainsborough never attempted the heroic stile,[12] so neither did he destroy the character and uniformity of his own stile, by the idle affectation of introducing mythological learning in any of his pictures. Of this boyish folly, we see instances enough, even in the works of great painters. When the Dutch School[13] attempt this poetry of our art in their landskips, their performances are beneath criticism; they become only an object of laughter. This practice is hardly excuseable, even in Claude Lorrain,[14] who had shewn more discretion if he had never meddled with such subjects.

Our late ingenious acadamician Wilson,[15] has I fear, been guilty, like many of his predecessors, of introducing gods and goddesses, ideal beings, into scenes which were by no means prepared to receive such personages. His landskips were, in reality too near common nature to admit supernatural objects. In consequence of this mistake, in a very admirable picture of a storm, which I have seen of his hand, many figures are introduced in the fore ground, some in apparent distress, and some struck dead, as a spectator would naturally suppose, by the lightning; had not the painter, injudiciously (as I think) rather chosen that their death should be imputed to a little Apollo, who appears in the sky, with his bent bow, and that those figures should be considered as the children of Niobe.[16]

To manage a subject of this kind, a peculiar stile of art is required; and it can only be done without impropriety, or even without ridicule, when we adapt the character of the landskip, and that too, in all its parts, to the historical or poetical representation. This is a very difficult adventure, and it requires a mind, thrown back two thousand years, and as it were naturalized in antiquity, like that of Nicolo Poussin,[17] to atchieve it. In the picture alluded to, the first idea that presents itself, is that of Wonder, at seeing a figure in so uncommon a situation as that of the Apollo is placed, for the clouds on which he kneels, have not the appearance of being able to support him; they have neither the substance nor the form, fit for the receptacle of a human figure, and they do not possess in any respect that romantic character which is appropriated to such a subject, and which alone can harmonize with poetical stories.

It appears to me, that such conduct is no less absurd than if a plain man, giving a relation of a real distress, occasioned by an inundation, accompanied with thunder and lightening, should, instead of simply relating the event, take it into his head, in order to give a grace to his narration, to talk of Jupiter and his thunder-bolts, or any other figurative idea; an intermixture which (though in poetry, with its proper preparations and accompaniments, it might be managed with effect) yet in the instance before us would counteract the purpose of the narrator, and instead of being interesting, would be only ridiculous.

The Dutch and Flemish style of landskip, not even excepting those of Rubens, is unfit for poetical subjects; but to explain in what this inaptitude consists, or to point out all the circumstances that give nobleness, grandeur, and the poetic character to stile, in landskip, would require a long discourse of itself; and the end would be then perhaps but imperfectly attained. The painter who is ambitious of this perilous excellence, must catch his inspiration from those who have cultivated with success the poetry, as it may be called, of the art, and they are few indeed.

I cannot quit this subject without mentioning two examples which occur to me at present, in which the poetical stile of landskip may be seen happily executed; the one is Jacob's dream by Salvator Rosa,[18] and the other the journey of the arc, by Sebastian Bourdon.[19] With whatever dignity those histories are presented to us in the language of Scripture, this stile of painting possesses the same power of inspiring sentiments of grandeur and sublimity, and is able to communicate them to subjects which appear by no means adapted to receive them. – A ladder against the sky has no very promising appearance of possessing a capacity to excite any heroic ideas; and the arc, in the hands of a second-rate master, would have little more effect than a common waggon on the highway; yet those subjects are so poetically treated throughout, the parts have been such a correspondence with each other, and the whole and every part of the scene is so visionary, that it is impossible to look at them, without feeling, in some measure, the enthusiasm which seems to have inspired the painters.

By continual contemplation of such works, a sense of the higher excellencies of art will by degrees dawn on the imagination; at every review that sense will become more and more assured, until we come to enjoy a sober certainty of the real existence (if I may so express myself) of those almost ideal beauties; and the artist will then find no difficulty of fixing in his mind the principles by which the impression is produced; which he will feel and practice, though they are perhaps too delicate and refined, and too peculiar to the imitative art, to be conveyed to the mind by any other means.

To return to Gainsborough: the peculiarity of his manner, or stile, or we may call it the language in which he expressed his ideas, has been considered by many, as his greatest defect. But without altogether wishing to enter into the discussion whether a defect or not, intermixed as it was, with great beauties, of some of which it was probably the cause, it becomes a proper subject of criticism and discussion to a painter.

A NOVELTY and peculiarity of manner, as it is often a cause of our approbation, so likewise it is often a ground of censure; as being contrary to the practice of other painters, in whose manner we have been initiated, and in whose favour we have perhaps been prepossessed from our infancy; for, fond as we are of novelty, we are upon the whole creatures of habit. However, it is certain, that all those odd scratches and marks, which, on a close examination, are so observable in Gainsborough's pictures, and which even to experienced painters appear rather the effect of accident than design; this chaos, this uncouth and shapeless appearance, at a certain distance, by a kind of magic, assumes form; and all the parts seem to drop into their proper places; so that we can hardly refuse acknowledging the full effect of diligence, under the appearance of chance and hasty negligence. That Gainsborough himself considered this peculiarity in his manner and the power it possesses of exciting surprize, as a beauty in his works, I think may be inferred from the eager desire, which we know, he always expressed that his pictures, at the exhibition, should be seen near, as well as at a distance.

The slightness which we see in his best works, cannot always be imputed to negligence. However they may appear to superficial observers, painters know very well that a steady attention to the general effect, takes up more time, and is much more laborious to the mind, than any mode of high finishing or smoothness, without such attention. *His handling, the manner of leaving* the colours, or in other words, the methods he used for producing the effect, had very much the appearance of the work of an artist who had never learnt from others the usual and regular practice belonging to the art; but still like a man of strong intuitive perception of what was required, he found out a way of his own to accomplish his purpose.

It is no disgrace to the genius of Gainsborough, to compare him to such men as we sometimes meet with, whose natural eloquence appears even in speaking a language, which they can scarce be said to understand, and who, without knowing the appropriate expression of almost any one idea, contrive to communicate the lively and forcible impressions of an energetic mind.

I think some apology may reasonably be made for his manner, without violating truth, or running any risk of poisoning the minds of the younger students, by propagating false criticism, for the sake of raising the character of a favorite artist. It must be allowed that this hatching manner of Gainsborough, did very much contribute to the lightness of effect which is so eminent a beauty in his pictures; as on the contrary, much smoothness, and uniting the colours, is apt to produce heaviness. Every artist must have remarked, how often that lightness of hand, which was in his dead-colour,[20] or first painting, escaped in the finishing, when he had determined the parts with more precision; and another loss he often experiences, which is of greater consequence; whilst he is employed in the detail, the effect of the whole together, is either forgot or neglected. The likeness of a portrait, for instance, consists more in preserving the general effect of the countenance, than in the most minute finishing of the features, or any of the particular parts. Now Gainsborough's portraits were often little more, in regard to finishing, or determining the forms of the features, than what generally attends a dead colour; but as he was always attentive to the general effect, or whole together, I have often imagined that this unfinished manner, contributed even to that striking resemblance for which his portraits are so remarkable. Though this opinion may be considered as fanciful, yet I think a plausible reason may be given, why such a mode of painting should have such an effect. It is presupposed that in this undetermined manner, there is the general effect; enough to remind the spectator of the original; the imagination supplies the rest, and perhaps more satisfactory to himself if not more exactly than the artist, with all his care, could have possibly done. At the same time it must be acknowledged there is one evil attending this mode; that if the portrait were seen, previous to any knowledge of the original, different people would form different ideas, and all would be disappointed at not finding the original correspond to their own conception; under the great latitude which indistinctness gives to the imagination, to assume almost what character or form it pleases.

Every artist has some favorite part on which he fixes his attention, and which he pursues with such eagerness, that it absorbs every other consideration; and he often falls into the opposite error of that which he would avoid, which is always ready to receive him. Now Gainsborough having truly a painter's eye for colouring, cultivated those effects of the art which proceed from colours, and sometimes appears to be indifferent to or to neglect other excellencies. Whatever defects are acknowledged, let him still experience from us the same candour that we so freely give upon similar occasions to the ancient masters; let us not encourage that fastidious disposition, which is discontented with every thing short of perfection, and unreasonably require, as we sometimes do, a union of excellencies, not perhaps quite compatible with each other. – We may, on this ground, say even of the divine Raffaele, that he might have finished his picture as highly and as correctly as was his custom, without heaviness of manner; and that Poussin might have preserved all his precision without hardness or dryness.

To shew the difficulty of uniting solidity with lightness of manner, we may produce a picture of Rubens in the Church of S. Judule, at Brussels, as an example; the subject is, *Christ's charge to Peter*; which, as it is the highest, and smoothest, finished picture I remember to have seen of that master, so it is by far the heaviest; and if I had found it in any other place, I should have suspected it to be a copy; for painters know very well, that it is principally by this air of facility, or the want of it, that originals are distinguished from copies. – A lightness of effect, produced by colour, and that produced by facility of handling, are generally united; a copy may preserve something of the one, it is true, but hardly ever of the other; a connoisseur therefore finds it often necessary to look carefully into the picture before he determines on its originality.

GAINSBOROUGH possessed this quality of lightness of manner and effect, I think, to an unexampled excellence; but, it must be acknowledged, at the same time, that the sacrifice which he made to this ornament of our art, was too great; it was in reality, preferring the lesser excellencies to the greater. To conclude. However, we may apologize for the deficiencies of *Gainsborough*, (I mean particularly his want of precision and finishing) who so ingeniously contrived to cover his defects by his beauties; and who cultivated that department of art, where such defects are more easily excused; you are to remember, that no apology can be made for this deficiency, in that stile which this academy teaches, and which ought to be the object of your pursuit; it will be necessary for you, in the first place, never to lose sight of the great rules and principles of the art, as they are collected from the full body of the best general practices, and the most constant and uniform experience; this must be the ground work of all your studies; afterwards you may profit, as in this case I wish you to profit, by the peculiar experience, and personal talents of artists living and dead; you may derive lights, and catch hints from their practice; but the moment you turn them into models, you fall infinitely below them; you may be corrupted by excellencies, not so much belonging to the art as personal and appropriated to the artist, and you become bad copies of good painters, instead of excellent imitators of the great universal truth of things.

Notes

1   In his first discourse Reynolds advised 'that an implicit obedience to the Rules of Art, as established by the practice of the great Masters, should be exacted from the

young Students'. He was against copying from ordinary nature, believing that, in accordance with classical tradition, the artist should select from and improve upon nature.

2   Batoni, (1708–87): a painter who worked largely in Rome and an admirer of Raphael and the antique. He painted mostly portraits and altarpieces. Anton Raffael Mengs (1728–79): an influential Neoclassical painter. He was born in Germany but spent most of his career in Rome where he met and befriended the art theorist Winkelmann.

3   Gerolamo Imperiale (d. 1639?): a painter and engraver from Genoa and an imitator of Corregio.
Sebastiano Conca (1680–1764): a Baroque painter renowned for his church decorations.
Constanzi (1690–1759): a Roman painter who worked in the Baroque style. He was principal of the Roman Academy of St. Luke between 1758–9.
Agostino Massuci (1691–1758): a history and portrait painter and principal of the Academy of St. Luke in 1736–38.

4   Andrea Sacchi (1599–1661): a Roman painter in a style similar to that of the French Neoclassicist Nicolas Poussin.

5   Normally spelt Maratta (1625–1713): a pupil of Andrea Sacchi. Maratta painted mostly altarpieces in a Neoclassical style much influenced by Raphael.

6   The last of the Romans.

7   Titian (1487/90–1576): a leading High Renaissance Venetian painter, renowned for his sensitive use of light and colour. His work included official portraits and altarpieces. Antonio Correggio (1494–1534): renowned for his soft atmospheric style. He worked mostly in Parma.

8   Guercino (1591–1666): worked mostly in Bologna, painting in a style influenced by the strong chiaroscuro of Carravaggio.

9   The school of seventeenth-century Flemish painters became very popular in Britain during the eighteenth century. Reynolds goes on to mention three important members of the school: Rubens, Teniers and Van Dyck.

10   Sir Peter Paul Rubens (1577–1640): a leading Flemish painter who went to Italy in 1600 to work as court painter to the Duke of Mantua, but spent most of his later life in Antwerp. Usually categorized as a northern Baroque painter, his work became well known and much admired in eighteenth-century Britain.
David I. Teniers (1582–1649): was greatly influenced by Rubens and worked mostly in Antwerp and Brussels. Many of his subjects were peasant genre scenes.
Sir Anthony Van Dyck (1599–1641): worked as an assistant of Rubens and was employed at the court of Charles I of England from 1632 until his death. He is probably best known for his series of equestrian portraits of Charles I, and his style of portrait painting influenced both Reynolds and Gainsborough.

11   Jacob von Ruisdael (1628/9–82): a Dutch landscape painter whose works influenced Gainsborough's early landscape style.

12   The 'grand style'.

13   The seventeenth-century school of Dutch landscape and genre painters which included Jacob von Ruisdael, Johannes Wynants and Philips Wouwerman.

14   Claude Lorrain (1600–82): French painter of pseudo-classical landscapes which often include groups of figures from ancient mythology. Reynolds seems to think that these works would have been better without the addition of classical figures.

15   Richard Wilson (1713/14–82): an English landscape painter much influenced by the works of Claude Lorrain.

16   According to Greek mythology, Niobe was the proud daughter of Tantalus. She had seven sons and seven daughters, boasting that she was superior to Leto who only had two children. To punish her for her pride Apollo killed the boys with his arrows, and Artemis the girls.

17   Nicolas Poussin (1593/4–1665): a French painter of religious and mythological subjects, who worked in a Neoclassical style.

18   Salvator Rosa (1615–73): worked in Rome and his native Naples. He was renowned for his stormy landscapes inspired by the Neapolitan countryside.

These works were enormously popular in eighteenth-century England.

19   Sebastian Bourdon (1616–71): a French painter who worked in a Neoclassical style. He was influenced by the work of Claude Lorrain and Nicolas Poussin.

20   'The first or preparatory layer of colour in a painting' – *Shorter Oxford English Dictionary*.

DIDEROT

Salons of 1761, 1763, 1765, 1767, 1769, 1781

[The *Salons* were not published until after Diderot's death, appearing separately between 1795 and 1857.] First collected edition: *Diderot Oeuvres complètes*, Assézat et Tourneux, 1875–77. Reprinted from Denis Diderot, *Salons*, eds. J. Seznec and J. Adhémar, Oxford, 1956–68. Translation by Rosemary Smith.

Denis Diderot (1713–84) became an art critic when well into his forties. In 1759 he was invited by Friedrich-Melchior Grimm (1723–1807) to review the current Paris Salon for *La Correspondance Littéraire*; a private fortnightly journal with a small list of subscribers which included the Empress Catherine of Russia, the Queen of Sweden, the Grand-Duke of Tuscany and several German Princes. Providing the latest news of Parisian life and culture, the journal's private status meant that it escaped French royal censorship and the laws of libel. Diderot made full use of this freedom.

Each of the biennial salon exhibitions from 1759 to 1771 (and also those of 1775 and 1781) were reviewed by Diderot. Although these *Salons* were not published in France until 1795 he had extra copies made for his friends and thus ensured contemporary awareness of his writings. Diderot was not always consistent about his view of art but by any standards his art criticism is undoubtedly the greatest of the eighteenth century. He had little respect for reputations but relied on the freshness of his impressions and on a belief that art should not only be true to 'Nature' but also be morally instructive and elevating. A similar reliance on personal impression as a way of being 'true to Nature' can be found in Laugier (see p.10). The consequences of this were that Diderot's descriptions of paintings often read like descriptions of theatrical scenes and sometimes his distinctions between aesthetics and ethics were unclear. However, his morality was consistently secular.

As a social, literary or art historical source for scholars of the eighteenth century the *Salons* are very rich. For nineteenth-century art critics the great influences were Diderot's style and his emphasis on a moralized view of nature, on the social relevance of 'history painting' and on the emotional power of pictorial composition. For the importance of 'history painting' see La Font de St. Yenne (p. 58) and Reynolds (p. 90).

SALON DE 1761

M. CHARDIN

Chardin[1] has painted a *Bénédicité*,[2] *Animals*, *Lapwings*, and a few other pieces. He always imitates nature very faithfully, in the manner that is this artist's own; a rough and somewhat ready manner; a base, common domestic nature. It is a long time since this painter has finished anything; he does not trouble any more to paint hands and feet. He works like a man of the world who has talent and ease of expression, and who is content to sketch in his ideas with a few strokes of the brush. He now heads the list of careless painters, after having painted a great many canvasses which earned him a place of honour among artists of the first rank. Chardin is a witty man, and no one, perhaps, talks better than he does about painting. His *tableau de réception*[3] at the Academy proves that he has understood the magic of colours. He has filtered this magic into several other compositions, and, together with design,[4] invention and an extreme regard for truth, so many assembled qualities have made these pieces very valuable now. Chardin is original in his own field. This originality flows from his paintings to the engravings. When you have seen one of his canvasses, you can never mistake them; you recognize them everywhere. Look at his *Governess with her Children* and you have seen his *Bénédicite*.'[5]

SALON DE 1763

DESHAYS[6]

[. . .]Let anyone tell me, after this, that our mythology lends itself less well to painting than the mythology of the Ancients! Perhaps antique Fable offers more agreeable and gentle subjects; perhaps we have nothing comparable in its kind to the 'Judgement of Paris';[7] but the blood which the abominable cross[8] has caused to run on every side is a very different source of inspiration to the tragic artist. There is doubtless sublimity in a head of Jupiter; it took genius to invent such a character as the Eumenides[9] the Ancients have left us. But what are these isolated figures compared to those scenes where it is a question of depicting madness, or religious fervour, the atrocity of intolerance, incense smoking on an altar in front of an idol, a priest coldly sharpening his knives, a praetor deliberately tearing his fellow-man to pieces with a whip, a madman giving himself up with joy to all the tortures that are shown him and defying his executioners; a people in terror, children who hide their eyes and throw themselves on their mothers' bosom; lictors parting the crowd; in a word, all the occurrences inherent in these kinds of spectacles! The crimes which Christian fanaticism has committed and still causes to be committed are such very great dramas and of quite a different order to the difficulties of Orpheus's descent to the underworld, the charms of the Elysian fields, the torture of Tenarus or the delights of Paphos.[10] In another genre look at all that Raphael and other great masters have drawn from Moses, the prophets and the evangelists. Are Adam, Eve, her family, the posterity of Jacob and all the details of patriarchcal life sterile ground for a man of genius? As for our Paradise, I must confess that it is as dull as those who inhabit it and as the happiness they find therein. There is no comparison between our saints and apostles and our mournfully ecstatic virgins, and those Olympian banquets where vigorous Hercules, leaning on his club, looks amorously at dainty Hebe; where Apollo of the divine head and sweeping locks enchants his companions with his harmonies; where the king of the gods, growing drunk on nectar from a cup filled deep by a youth with ivory shoulders and thighs of alabaster, makes his jealous wife's heart swell with sorrow. Unquestionably I prefer seeing the rump, the bosom and the beautiful arms of Venus[11] to the mysterious triangle,[12] but where in all this is the tragic subject I am looking for? The talent of a Racine, a Corneille[13] or a Voltaire calls out for crimes. No religion has ever been so prolific in crimes as Christianity; from the murder of Abel to the torture of Calas,[14] there is not one line of its history which is not steeped in blood. Crime is a fine thing in both history and in poetry, on canvas and in marble. I am sketching, my friend, as my pen takes me; I am scattering seeds which I leave to the fertility of your mind to develop.

Here is an idea which I have had for a long time now, that if the Greek religion was more favourable to poetry, ours, on the other hand, is much worthier of the brush. The passions aroused by fanaticism and linked with fervency are the worthiest of a sublime artist, and our religion teems with such kinds of subjects. I do not share the opinion of the philosopher on the subjects furnished by the historical portions of our sacred books; and in this I find that the advantage is altogether on the side of Greek mythology. The details of patriarchal life may suggest some beautiful paintings of the countryside, but the *Idylls* of Theocritus and of Gessner[15] would inspire ones just as interesting. As for historical subjects drawn from the Old and New Testaments, I admit that they have a certain simplicity, and that nurses can make good enough stories of them to amuse the children; but they almost all lack nobility, poetry and grace, and have a ring of poverty and meanness which only force of habit disguises from us. What a difference between the story of the Virgin and that of the mother of Love! Now I am going to commit blasphemy myself about the painting *The Marriage of the Virgin*.[16] It comes way above the others, it is the first picture of the Salon. It is a large and beautiful work of genius; but it seems to me that I have seen some in this genre that are even more sublime. The Carracci, the Tintorettos, the Domenichinos[17] leave many French paintings much wanting when one calls them to mind. Deshays' Virgin is fine, very fine, but if I dared I would say that the good Joseph seems to be saying to her: 'Come now, don't be childish'; I would say that Saint Anne is so placed in the background that she doesn't seem to give the impression of being the mother at all, but of a very minor character; I would say that I could have wished that the great priest had manifested his enthusiasm by the look of his head rather than by his gestures. Besides, my pastor, M. Baer, chaplain to the Swedish Royal Chapel,[18] has made me notice some awful blunders in reproducing history in this picture. He has assured me that the Jews did not celebrate their marriages in front of an altar, and neither did they have candles lit as if a mass were about to be said; but it is only a heretic pastor who could pick out such mistakes, for the catholic priests are too ignorant to be shocked by them. However, that's enough, let the good Catholic Diderot continue his career.[. . .]

CHARDIN

Here is the real painter; here is the true colourist.

There are several small paintings by Chardin in the Salon; they almost all depict fruit surrounded by the accessories of a meal. There is nature itself; the objects stand out from the canvas and their very reality deceives the eye.

The one you see as you go up the staircase is especially worthy of attention. On a table the artist has placed an old Chinese porcelain vase, two biscuits, a jar of olives, a basket of fruit, two glasses half-full of wine, a Seville orange and some pâté.

To look at the paintings of other artists, I seem to need a new pair of eyes; to look at Chardin's, I need only keep those that nature has given me and use them well.

If I intended my child to be a painter, this is the painting I would buy. 'Copy this for me' I would say to him, 'copy this for me again'. But perhaps nature itself is not more difficult to copy.

The fact is, this porcelain vase is made of porcelain; those olives are really separated from the eye by the water in which they are immersed; one has only to take these biscuits to eat them, this orange to cut it and squeeze it, this glass of wine to drink it, these fruits to peel them, this pâté to put one's knife into it.

Here is the painter who truly understands the harmony of colours and reflections: Oh Chardin! It is not white, red and black you mix on your palette; it is the very substance of objects, it is the air and the light that you take on the tip of your brush and apply to the canvas.

After my child had copied and recopied this painting, I would set him to work on the *Raie Dépouillé* [*The Gutted Skate*][19] by the same master. The object itself is disgusting, but that scaling is the flesh of the fish, its skin, its blood; the very look of the thing would not affect one otherwise. Monsieur Pierre,[20] look carefully at this painting when you next go to the Academy, and learn if you can the secret of using your talent to keep certain natural beings from causing distaste.

This magic is beyond our understanding. Here are thick layers of colour laid one on top of the other, whose effect is to glow through from the first layer to the last. At other times, one would swear a vapour had been breathed on to the canvas; elsewhere, a light foam has been cast over it. Rubens, Berghem, Greuze, Loutherbourg[21] could explain this technique to you far better than I; all of them can make your eyes experience this same effect. When you draw near, everything becomes confused, flattened, and disappears; when you retreat, everything takes shape and is created once again.

I have been told that Greuze, on going up the stairs to the Salon and seeing the Chardin painting I have just described, looked at it and passed on, sighing deeply. This praise is briefer and more valuable than mine.

Who will pay for the paintings of Chardin, when this unusual man is no more? You should know, moreover, that this artist has sound good sense and can talk wonderfully about his art.

Ah! my friend, spit on the curtain of Apelles and on the grapes of Zeuxis.[22] An impatient artist is easily deceived and animals are bad judges of painting. Haven't we seen the birds in the Royal garden cracking their heads open on some of the worst perspective? But when he so wishes, it is you, it is me that Chardin will deceive.

BOUCHER[23]

There are two paintings by Boucher: the *Sommeil de l'enfant Jésus* [*The sleep of the infant Jesus*] and a *Bergerie* [*Sheepfold*].

This master still has the same fire, the same facility. the same fertile imagination, the same magic and the same faults which spoil a rare talent.

His infant Jesus is painted with relaxed limbs: he is sleeping well. His Virgin, whose draperies are badly executed, is without character. Her halo is very misty. The flying angel is altogether ethereal. It would be impossible to stir the emotions more grandly or to give a more handsome head to Joseph who is dozing behind the Virgin who is adoring her son . . . But the colour? As far as the colour goes, order your chemist to detonate or rather to make a combustion of copper with saltpetre for you and you will see colour as it is in Boucher's painting. It is the colour of good Limoges enamel. If you say to the painter: 'But Monsieur Boucher, where have you got these tints and these colours from?' he will say 'From my head.' – 'But they are false.' 'That's possible; moreover I don't worry about being truthful. I paint a story-tale event with a storyteller's brush. What do you really know about it? The light of Thabor or of paradise is perhaps like this. Have you ever been visited by angels in the night?' – 'No.' – 'No more have I: and that's why I try my hand as I please at a scene which has no model in nature.' 'Monsieur Boucher, you are not a good philosopher if you do not know that in whatever part of the world you go and men speak of God, they are talking of anything else but man himself.'

La Bergerie. In the background imagine a vase placed on its pedestal and crowned with an inverted bundle of branches; below it, a shepherd asleep on the lap of his shepherdess; next scatter around a shepherd's crook, a small hat filled with roses, a dog, some sheep, a small fragment of landscape and I know not how many other objects piled up one on top of the other; then paint it all in the most vivid colour, and you will have Boucher's *Bergerie*.

What misuse of talent! How much time has been wasted! With half the trouble, half as much effect again could have been obtained. Among so many details, all just as carefully contrived, the eye does not know where to alight; there is no air, no repose. And yet the shepherdess has the true countenance of one in her estate of life: and this bit of landscape which runs round the vase is of a surprising delicacy, freshness and charm. But what does this vase and its pedestal signify? What is the meaning of those heavy overhanging branches? When one is writing, must one write everything? When one is painting, must one paint everything? For pity's sake, leave something to my imagination... Say that, however, to a man corrupted by praise and stubbornly convinced of his talent, and he will shake his head disdainfully; he will let you speak on and we will leave him: Jussum se suaque solum amare.[24] It is a great pity, however.

This painter, when he was newly returned from Italy, did some very good things; his colour was strong and true; his composition was well considered though full of warmth; his manner of painting broad and large. I know a few of his first pieces which today he calls 'daubs' and would willingly buy them back in order to burn them.

[...] This man is the run of all young student painters. They barely know how to wield their brush or hold their palette before they torture themselves trying to knot childrens' garlands, paint chubby red backsides, and rush into all kinds of extravagances which remain unredeemed by the warmth, originality, charm or the magic of their model; they only have its shortcomings.

GREUZE[25]

Here is my kind of man, this Greuze fellow. [...] I will turn at once to his picture *Piété Filiale* which would have been better entitled *The Reward for Giving a Good Upbringing*.

In the first place, I like the genre; it is a painting with a moral. Just think! Hasn't the painter's brush been given over long enough, too long, to the portrayal of debauchery and vice? Ought we not to be satisfied to see it competing at last with dramatic poetry in moving us, teaching us, correcting us and encouraging us in virtue? Courage, Greuze my friend, teach morality in your paintings, and go on painting like this always! When the time comes for you to leave this life, there will not be one of your compositions you cannot recall without pleasure. Why were you not at the side of that young girl who, looking at the head of your *Paralytic*,[26] exclaimed with charming vivacity: 'Oh, heavens, how it moves me! But if I look at it any more, I am sure I shall cry . . . ! I wish this young girl had been my own daughter! I would have recognized her as such by this spontaneous emotion. Like her, as I looked at that eloquent and pathetic old man, I felt pity soften my heart and the tears brimming in my eyes. [. . .]

SALON DE 1765

TO MY FRIEND M. GRIMM[27]

Non fumum ex fulgore, sed ex fumo dare lucem cogitat[28]

If I have any well-founded opinions on painting or sculpture, it is to you, my friend, that I owe them; I would otherwise have followed the idle crowd to the Salon; like them, I would have thrown a superficial, absentminded glance at the production of our artists; in a word, I would have thrown a precious piece on the fire or praised a mediocre work to the skies, acclaiming or rejecting without seeking out the reasons for my infatuation or my disdain. It is the task that you suggested to me that has fixed my eyes on the canvas, and made me examine every side of the marble. I have given time to my impressions on arriving and entering. I have opened my mind to impressions. I have let myself be filled with them. I have gathered the old man's pronouncement, the child's thoughts, the judgement of a man of letters, the witticism of a man of the world, and the chatter of the people; and if I have perchance hurt the artist, it is often with the weapon he himself has sharpened. I have interrogated him and have come to know what delicacy of design and truth to nature could be. I have a concept of the magic of light and shade. I have understood colour. I have acquired a feeling for the rendering of flesh. Alone I have meditated on what I have seen and heard; and those terms in art, such as unity, variety, contrast, symmetry, arrangement, composition, characters and expression, so familiar to my mouth, so vague in my mind, have been defined and settled.

Oh my friend! these arts whose object it is to imitate nature, how long, hard and difficult they are; whether in speech, as with eloquence and poetry; whether in sound, as with music; whether with colours and the brush, as in painting; whether with the pencil, as in drawing;

109

whether with the chisel and soft clay, as in sculpture; with the etcher's needle, stone and metal, as in engraving; with the small cutting wheel, as in stone engraving; with the chasing-chisel, the matting tool and the graver, as in tooling.

Remember what Chardin used to say to us in the Salon: 'Gentlemen, gentlemen, softly. Look for the worst among the pictures here; and realise that at least two thousand unhappy wretches have broken their brushes between their teeth in despair of ever achieving even such mediocrity. Parrocel,[29] who is called a dauber, and who is indeed one if you compare him to Vernet; this man Parrocel, however, is outstanding in comparison to those who have abandoned the career they entered along with him. Le Moyne[30] said that thirty years were necessary in the profession before knowing how to preserve the value of a first sketch, and Le Moyne was no fool. If you listen to me, you will learn perhaps to be kind.' [...]

Chardin seemed to think that there could not be an education which was longer or harder than the painter's; the doctor's, the lawyer's and the doctor of Sorbonne included. 'They put a pencil-case into our hands at the age of seven or eight years. We begin to draw eyes, mouths, noses, ears, then feet and hands after a model. Our backs have been bent for a long time over our portfolios when they put us in front of Hercules or the torso;[31] and you have not witnessed the tears that this satyr, this gladiator, this Venus de' Medici, this Antaeus[32] have caused to flow. Rest assured that these Greek masterpieces would no longer excite the jealousy of the masters, if they had been given to plague the pupils. Having ground away by day and at night by lamplight at lifeless, static nature, suddenly we are presented with living nature; and suddenly all the work of the preceding years seem to be reduced to nothing: we are as self-conscious as the first time we took up the pencil. It is the eye that we must teach to look at nature; and how many have never seen it and will never see it! It is the torment of our lives. We were kept in front of a model for five or six years, and then suddenly we are left to exercise our own genius, if we have any. Talent does not appear overnight. One does not confess one's inability at the first try. How many attempts there are, sometimes happy, sometimes unhappy ones! Precious years pass by before the day of disgust, of disillusion, and of boredom arrives. The pupil is nineteen or twenty years old when, his palette falling from his hands, he is left without a profession, without resources and without morals; since it is not possible to have natural models constantly in front of one, and to remain young and virtuous.

What is to be done, what is he to become? He will have to throw himself into one of those lowly occupations which are so close to poverty, or die of hunger. He takes the first choice; and with the exception of some twenty painters who come here every two years[33] to be thrown to the wolves, the others, unknown and less unhappy, wear a breast-plate on their chest in a fencing-school, or a musket on their shoulder in some regiment, or a theatrical costume whilst treading the boards. This story I am telling you here is the story of Belcourt, of

LeKain and of Brisart, now poor players since they despaired of being mediocre painters.'

Chardin told us, if you remember, that one of his colleagues whose son was the drummer in a regiment, used to reply to those who asked for news of him, that he had left painting for music; then, becoming serious again, he added; 'All fathers of sons unequal to their careers and left without a calling do not take the thing so lightly. What you see here is the fruit of the labours of a small number who have battled on with more or less success. He who has not felt the difficulty of art, will never paint anything of worth; he who like my son[34] has felt it too soon, will not do anything at all. And believe me that most of the upper ranks of society would be empty, if people were admitted there only after as severe an examination as we have to undergo.'

'But', I said to him, 'Monsieur Chardin, you should not blame us if mediocribus esse poetis, non di, non homines, non concessere columnae;[35] and this man who angers the gods, men and bookstalls against mediocre imitators of nature would understand the difficulty of the craft.'

'Well,' he replied, 'it is better to think that he warned the young student of the dangers he runs, than to make him an apologist of the gods, of men and of bookstalls it is as if he said to him: "My friend, be careful, you do not know your judge. He knows nothing, and is none the less cruel because of that." Goodbye, gentlemen. Be gentle, be gentle.' [. . .]

BOUCHER

I don't know what to say about this painter. The degradation of his taste, his colours, his composition, his characters, his expression, his drawing has followed the depravity of his morals step by step. What do you expect an artist to put on his canvases? Whatever is in his imagination. And what can a man have in his imagination who spends his entire time with the lowest kind of prostitutes? The grace of his Shepherdesses is the grace of Favart in Rose et Colas;[36] that of his goddesses is borrowed from Deschamps.[37] I defy you to find in a whole reach of countryside one blade of grass like the ones in his pictures. And then, the confusion of objects heaped up on each other, so out of place, so ill-assorted that it is less the painting of a sensible man than a madman's fantasy. It is about him that these words are written:

... velut aegri somnia, vanae
Fingentur species: ut nec pes, nec caput ... [38]

I make bold to say that this man does not know what true grace is; that he has never known truth; that the ideas of delicacy, decency, innocence, simplicity have become almost total strangers to him; I dare to say that he has not for one instant looked at nature, not at least at that nature which is apt to stir my heart or yours or that of a well-born child, or of a sensitive woman. I make bold to say he has no taste. Among an infinity of proofs that I could give, one alone will suffice; in all the multitude of figures, both of men and women, that he has painted, I defy you to find four that would be suitable for a bas-relief, still less for a statue. There is too much grimacing, simpering and affection there for an art of any rigour. It is no good his showing me these women nude, I still see them wearing rouge, patches, pompoms, and all the trifles of the boudoir. Can you believe that anything in any way resembling this charming and decent picture of Petrarch's has ever passed through his mind?

E'l riso, e'l canto, e'l parlar dolce, humano.[39]

Those fine and subtle analogies which require the presence of certain objects on the canvas and tie them together with secret and imperceptible threads, by heaven I swear he doesn't even know they exist. All of his compositions have the visual effect of an unbearable uproar. He is the most deadly enemy of silence that I know; he is now at the stage of painting the prettiest little puppets in the world; he will end up by mere illustration. And yet, my friend, it is just at this very moment that Boucher has ceased to be an artist that he has been named principal painter to the king. Do not believe that he is the same in his field as Crébillon fils[40] in his. They indeed have nearly the same morals, but the writer has a quite different talent to the painter. The only advantage of the latter is an inexhaustible fecundity, an unbelievable facility, especially in the accessories of his pastorals. When he paints children, he groups them well; but I wish he had left them romping up there in the clouds. Among the whole of that innumerable family, you will not find one engaged in the real actions of life, learning lessons, reading, writing, beating hemp. They are imaginary, fanciful beings, little natural sons of Bacchus or Silenus.[41] Those children there would be well suited to frolicking around a sculpted vase of ancient Greece. They are fat, chubby, dimpled. If the artist knows how to work in marble, we'll see if I'm not right. In short take all the paintings of this man and there will hardly be one to which you could not say as Fontenelle[42] did to the sonata; 'Sonata, what do you want of me?' 'Painting, what do you want of me?' Was there not a time when he had a passion for painting virgins? And what were they, his virgins? Some nice little hussies. And his angels? Dissolute little satyrs. And then there is such a greyish colour in his landscapes and such uniformity of tone that you could mistake his canvas, from two feet away, for a piece of smooth lawn or a quartered parsley bed. He is no fool, however. He is a fake painter, in the same way as there are fake wits. He has no conception of art, only its conceits.

CHARDIN

You are just in time, Chardin, to revive my eyes so mortally afflicted by your colleague Challe.[43] So there you are again, great magician, with your mute symphonies! How eloquently they speak to the artist! How much they tell him about the imitation of nature, the science of colour, and the composition of harmony! How the air flows round these

Pl. V.

Plate 9   from *Encyclopédie*   Rococo Work by Silver and Goldsmiths

Élévation du côté de la Cheminée de la même pièce

Bénard Fecit

Echelle de 1 2 3 4 5 6 12 18 pieds

Architecture.

Plate 10   from *Encyclopédie*   Design (1760) for one of the
'new' rooms in the Palais Royal

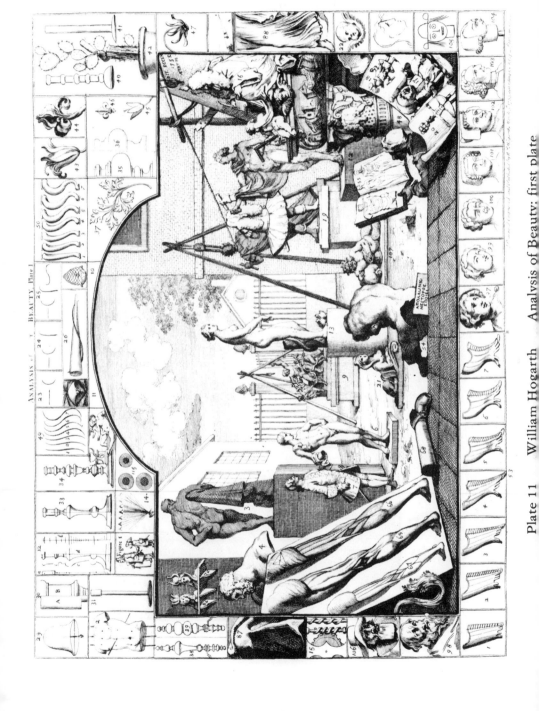

Plate 11   William Hogarth   Analysis of Beauty: first plate

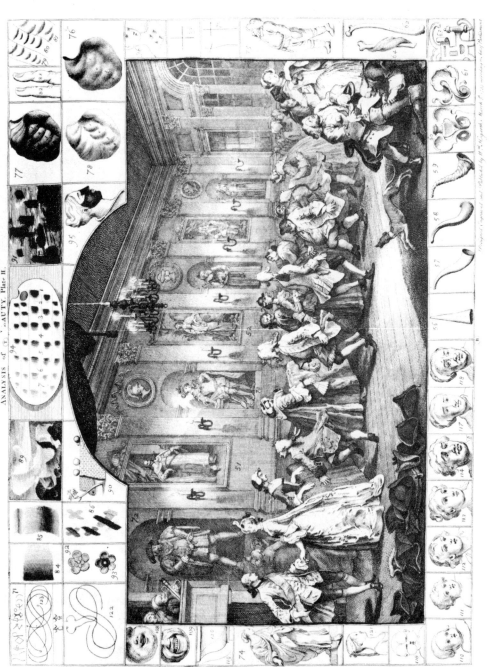

ANALYSIS of BEAUTY. Plate II.

Plate 12   William Hogarth   Analysis of Beauty: second plate

Plate 13   Joshua Reynolds   Mrs Siddons as the Tragic Muse

I. G. de Saint-Aubin. Le Salon de 1767

Plate 14   Gabriel de Saint-Aubin   Le Salon du Louvre en 1767

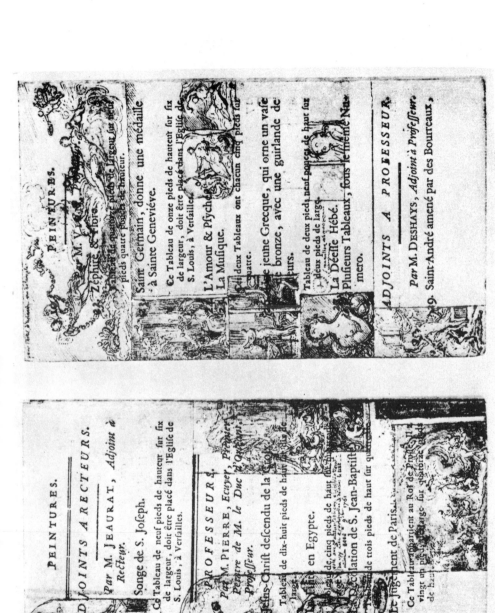

Plate 15 Gabriel de Saint-Aubin Sketches in a Salon Catalogue

Plate 16   Jean-Baptiste-Siméon Chardin   Le Bénédicité

Plate 17   Jean-Baptiste-Siméon Greuze   Le Paralytique ou La piété filiale

Plate 18   François Boucher   Angélique et Médor

Plate 19   François Boucher   Jupiter et Callisto

Plate 21   Joseph-Marie Vien   Saint Denis prêchant la foi en Gaule

Plate 22　François-Gabriel Doyen　Le Miracle des Ardents

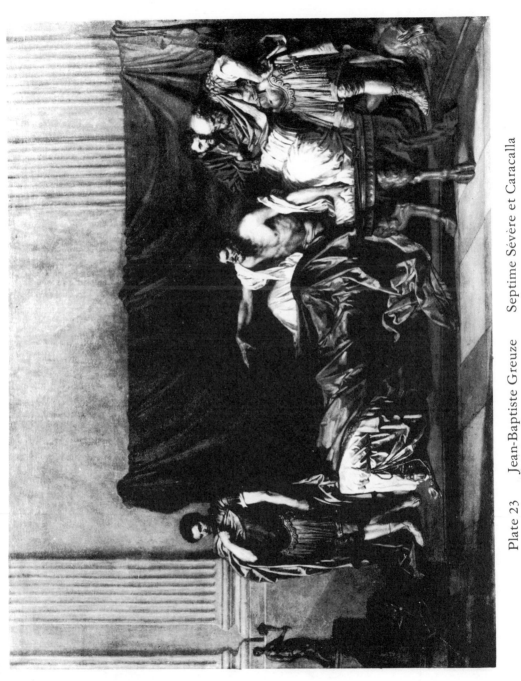

Plate 23   Jean-Baptiste Greuze   Septime Sévère et Caracalla

Plate 24   Jacques Louis David   Bélisaire

objects! Even sunlight cannot keep the disparate beings it illumines better from incongruity! This is the man who will not recognize that there are harmonious and inharmonious colours.

If it is true, as the philosophers say, that there is nothing real but our sensations; that neither the emptiness of space, nor the solidity of bodies is perhaps anything of the kind that we experience; then let them tell me, these philosophers, what difference there is, four feet away from your paintings, between the Creator and yourself.

Chardin is so true, so true, so harmonious, that even though there is nothing to be seen on his canvas but inanimate objects – vases, cups, bottles of wine, water, grapes, fruit, paté – he still holds his own and can perhaps draw you away from two of the most beautiful Vernets beside which he has had no hesitation in placing himself. This is just the way it is, my friend, in the world we live in, where the presence of a man, of a horse, or an animal in no way destroys the effect of a piece of rock, or a tree, or a brook. The brook, the tree, the piece of rock doubtless interest us less than the man, the woman, the horse or the animal; but they are equally true.

I must tell you, my friend, about an idea which has just occurred to me, and which may not come back to me later; it is this, that what we call 'genre' painting[44] should be the province of old painters or those who are born old. It demands only study and patience. No fire, very little genius, barely any poetry; a great deal of technique and truth; and that is all. And you know too that the time of life when we devote ourselves to what is commonly called the search for truth, for philosophy, is precisely that when our temples are becoming grey and when we should look rather foolish trying to write a love letter. [...]

This man is the principal colourist of the Salon, and perhaps one of the principal colourists in painting. I cannot forgive that impertinent Webb[45] for having written a treatise on art without having mentioned a single Frenchman. Nor do I forgive Hogarth either for having said that the French School did not possess even a mediocre colourist. You have lied, Mr. Hogarth; it is either sheer ignorance or a commonplace on your part. I know that your nation has taken to the habit of turning up your noses at an impartial author who dares to speak of us with praise; but do you have to curry favour with your fellow citizens so odiously at the expense of truth? Paint, and paint better if you can. Learn to draw, and keep off writing. We, the English and the French, have two very different obsessions. Ours is to overrate English works; theirs is to disparage French ones. [...]

VERNET[46]

A view of the port of Dieppe. The four quarters of the day. Two views of the outskirts of Nogent-sur-Seine. A shipwreck. A landscape. Another shipwreck. A seascape at sunset. Seven minor landscapes. Two other seascapes. A storm, and several other paintings under the same numbering.

Twenty-five paintings, my friend! Twenty-five paintings? And what paintings! He is like the creator for despatch; and like nature herself for truth. There is hardly one of these paintings on which another artist, using his time well, would not have spent the entire two years in which Vernet was able to complete them all. What unbelievable effects of light! What beautiful skies! What water! What composition! What a prodigious variety of scenes! Here a child who has escaped from a shipwreck is being carried on his father's shoulders; there a woman is lying stretched out dead on the shore while her husband is grieving. The sea roars, the winds whistle, the thunder growls, the dark glow of the pallied lightning breaks the clouds and now reveals, now conceals the scene. You can hear the groans from the side of a ship as it breaks up; its masts are leaning, its sails torn: some people on deck are raising their arms to the heavens; others have thrown themselves into the waters. The waves are carrying them along to dash them against the nearby rocks, where their blood mingles with the white foam of the crests. I see some who are floating; some who are about to disappear into the deeps; and some who are hastening to gain the shore on which they will be broken. The same variety of character, of action and of expression is shown among the spectators; some shudder and avert their gaze, others are running to help, and still others watch without a movement. Some have lit a fire beneath a rock; they are trying to revive a dying woman, and I hope they will succeed. But turn your eyes to another sea, and you will see it in calm weather with all its charms. The placid waters, smooth and laughing, stretch into the distance, imperceptibly losing their transparency, imperceptibly growing lighter on the surface from the shore out to the line where the horizon meets the sky. The ships are motionless; the sailors and the passengers are amusing themselves with all that can beguile their impatience. If it is morning, see what light mists filtering over all the objects of nature have revived and freshened them! If it is evening, see how the summits of the mountains turn to gold. With what delicate hues the skies are tinted! How the clouds are sailing across the sky, moving, coming to lay down their tribute of colours in the waters below. Go out into the countryside, raise your eyes to the vaults of heaven, observe well all that is to be seen there at that moment, and you will swear that a piece of the great luminous canvas that is lighted by the sun has been cut out and put on the artist's easel; or close your hand and make a tube of it which only lets you see a limited amount of that great canvas, and you will swear that it is a Vernet painting taken from its easel and carried up to the sky. Although he is the most prolific of all our painters, he gives me the least work of all. It is impossible to describe his compositions; they have to be seen. His nights are as touching as his days are beautiful; his ports are as beautiful as his imaginary pieces are full of interest. He is equally wonderful whether his captive brush becomes the servant of a scene already provided by nature or whether his muse, released from all constraints, is left free to follow her own devices; equally incomprehensible, whether he uses the star of the day or the star of the night, natural light or artificial lights to illumine his pictures; always harmonious, vigorous and wise, like those great poets, those rare men whose zeal is so well balanced by their judgement that they are never exaggerated or cold. His mills, his buildings, the clothing, the actions, the men, the animals – everything is true. From close to, his works are striking; from a distance, they are more striking still. Chardin and Vernet, my friend, are two great magicians. You could say of the latter that he begins by creating the country, and that he has men, women and children up his sleeve with whom he peoples his canvas, as one peoples a colony; then he gives them the weather, the sky, the season, the good or bad fortune that pleases him. He is Lucian's[47] Jupiter, who, tired of hearing woeful human cries, gets up from the table and says: 'Hail in Thrace'; and the trees are immediately stripped, the harvest ruined and thatch on the huts scattered; 'Plague in Asia'; and the doors of the houses are shut, the streets deserted, and men avoid each other; 'A volcano here'; and the earth trembles under one's feet, buildings crumble, animals grow wild and town-dwellers escape into the countryside; 'A war here'; and nations rush to arms and slaughter each other; 'A famine here', and the old labourer is dying of hunger on his doorstep. Jupiter calls all that governing the world, and he is wrong. Vernet calls all that painting pictures, and he is right.

GREUZE

The ungrateful son

I don't know how I'm going to manage with this one: still less with the one that follows. This Greuze fellow will be the ruin of you, my friend.

Imagine a room into which scarcely any light can enter except through the door, when it is open, or through a square opening above it when it is shut. Let your eyes wander around this melancholy room, and you will see nothing but poverty. There is, however, on the right, in one corner a bed which does not seem too bad; it is carefully made. In the foreground on the same side is a large grandfather-chair in black leather which may be fairly comfortable to sit on; seat the ungrateful son's father on that. Close to the door, place a low cupboard; and beside the decrepit old man a small table on which a bowl of soup has just been served.

In spite of the assistance that the eldest son of the house could be to his old father, to his mother and his brothers, he has enlisted. He will not go, however, without having extracted a financial contribution from these wretched people. He has come with an old soldier; he has made his demands. His father is outraged by this; he does not hesitate to use harsh words to this unnatural child who no longer recognizes father, mother, nor his duties, and who insults his father in return for his reproaches. We see him at the centre of the picture; he looks violent, insolent and fiery; his right arm is raised against his father, above the head of one of his sisters; he is standing upright, his hand threatening; he has his hat on and his gesture and expression are equally insolent. The good old man who has loved his children but never allowed any of them to show disrespect, is trying to rise from his chair; but one of his daughters, on her knees in front of him, is restraining him by his coat-tails. The young rake is surrounded by his eldest sister, his mother, and one of his little brothers. His mother holds her arms around him; he is trying to disengage himself brutally, and thrusts her aside with his foot. The mother looks overwhelmed and grief-stricken; the eldest sister has also come between her brother and her father; both the mother and the sister seem to be trying to hide the two men from each other, judging by their attitudes. The sister has seized her brother by his coat, and the way in which she is pulling at it says: 'Wretch, what are you doing? You are spurning your mother, you are threatening your father; fall on your knees and ask for forgiveness.' Meanwhile the little brother is weeping, covering his eyes with one hand; with his other he hangs on to his brother's right arm, trying to drag him out of the house. Behind the old man's armchair, the youngest son is standing with a frightened, bewildered look. At the opposite end of the scene, near the door, the old soldier who enlisted the ungrateful son and came back with him to his parent's home is leaving, his back turned on what is happening, his sabre under his arm, his head well down. I almost forgot that in the midst of this tumult, there is a dog in the foreground adding to the hubbub with his barking.

Everything in this sketch is intelligently worked out, well ordered, sharply characterized, clear; the grief, even the weakness of the mother for a child she has spoilt; the violence of the old man; the various actions of the sisters and young children; the insolence of the ungrateful son; the reticence of the old soldier, who cannot help but shrug his shoulders at what is going on; finally, this barking dog is one of those additions full of meaning, which Greuze can conjure up through his own particular talent. [. . .]

SALON DE 1767

VIEN[48]

Saint Denis preaching the faith in France. Picture 21 feet 3 inches high by 12 feet 4 inches wide. It is for one of the chapels in Saint-Roch.

The public has been torn between this painting by Vien, and the one by Doyen on the *Epidémie des Ardents* [*Plague of the Ardents*] and it is certain that these are two beautiful paintings; two great compositions. I will describe the first. You will find the description of the other in its place.

On the right there is an architectural structure, the facade of an ancient temple with its terrace in front. Above a few steps which lead to this terrace, near the temple door, we can see the apostle preaching to the Gauls. [. . .]

This composition is in complete contrast to Doyen's. All the qualities that are lacking in one of these artists are possessed by the other. Here there reigns the greatest harmony of colour, and a peace and silence which charm everyone. Here is all the secret magic of art, without affectation, without contrivance, without effort. This is praise one cannot withhold from Vien; however, when you look at Doyen and see how dark, vigorous, fervent and passionate he is, you must allow that it is only by a kind of superior weakness that anything in the *Prédication de Saint Denis'* [*Sermon of St. Denis*] makes itself felt at all. It is this weakness that Doyen's strength shows up; but this harmonious weakness in its turn shows up all the discordance in its adversary. Here are two great athletes who strike an exchange hit. Comparing the two compositions is like comparing the characters of the two men. Vien is large and wise like Domenichino. Here are beautiful heads, accurate drawing, beautiful feet, beautiful hands, well-draped folds, simple and natural expressions; there is nothing tortured here, nothing strained either in the details or in the composition. The most beautiful tranquillity reigns in his pictures. The more one looks, the more pleasure one gains from looking at him. He is at the same time of the school of Domenichino and of Le Sueur.[49] The group of women on the left is very handsome. All the features of their heads seem to have been derived from the first of these masters, while the group of young men on the right, of a good colour, is in the style of Le Sueur. Vien captivates you but leaves you all the time in the world to study him. Doyen, who has a more stimulating effect upon the eye, seems to hurry you for fear that with the impression of one object coming on top of the impression of another and destroying it before you have grasped the whole of the charm of this picture should disappear completely. Vien has all the qualities which characterize a great painter. Nothing is neglected in his work. There is a beautiful background here. This picture is an excellent source of studies for the young. If I were a teacher, I would say to the students: 'Go to Saint-Roch, look at the *Prédication de Saint Denis*. Immerse yourselves in it but pass quickly by the painting of the *Ardents*; that is a sublime stroke of genius which you are not yet capable of imitating. [. . .] Just notice that in spite of the high reputation of Vien's harmony, his paintings are grey; that there is no variety in the shades of his carnations, and that the flesh-tones of his men and of his women are nearly the same. Notice how, in spite of the greatest understanding of art, he is quite without an ideal, without zest, without poetry, without animation, without incidents, without interest. [. . .]

CHARDIN

[. . .] This painter is said to have a technique which is all his own and to use his thumb as much as his brush. I know nothing about this; what is certain is that I have never known anyone who has seen him working. Be that as it may, his paintings attract the ignorant and the connoisseur indiscriminately. Here is unbelievable strength of colour, general harmony, true and stimulating effects, beautiful forms, a manner of painting whose magic makes others despair, a mixture of diversity and order. Take your distance, come closer, there is the same illusion, but no confusion, nor any symmetry either, and no flitting about; the eye is always refreshed, because there is peace here and repose. One stops in front of a Chardin by instinct, as a traveller wearied of his journey goes almost without noticing it to sit down in that place which can offer him a seat on a grassy bank, silence, the sound of water, some shade, and cool breezes.

DOYEN[50]

Multaque in rebus acerbis
Acrius advertunt animos ad Relligionem. *Lucretius.*[51]
67. *Le Miracle des Ardens* [*The Miracle of the Ardents*]

A picture of 22 feet high by 12 feet wide, for the Chapel of the Ardens at St. Roch.

Here are the facts. In the year 1129, in the reign of Louis VI, fire from heaven fell on the city of Paris, which devoured peoples very guts, and they died a most cruel death. This plague stopped suddenly through the intercession of St. Geneviève.[52]

There are no circumstances in which men are more likely to pronounce the sophism 'post hoc, ergo propter hoc' [after this, therefore on account of this] than when long drawn-out disasters and the uselessness of human aid makes them have recourse to heaven.

[...] On the far left of the picture, on the bank at the foot of the staircase and of the mountain, there is a vigorous young man supporting a sick, naked man beneath his arms. This man has one knee on the earth, the other limb extended; his body is flung backwards, his appearance is one of suffering; his face is turned towards the heavens, and he is crying aloud and tearing his sides with his right hand. We see the youth who is succouring this sick man in convulsions only from behind and in profile. His neck is uncovered, his shoulders and head are naked. He is imploring help with his left hand and with his eyes.

On the bank once again, at the foot of the same mountain, a little further in the background than the last group, there is a dead woman, her feet stretched out at the side of the man in convulsions, her face turned towards the heavens, all the upper part of her body naked, her left arm extended on the ground and circled with a long string of beads; her hair is in disorder, her head rests against the mountain. She is lying on a feather bolster, some straw, a few draperies and a household implement. Further in the background, her child can be seen in profile, leaning towards her with his eyes fixed on his mother's face; he is numb with horror, his hair is standing straight up on his forehead, and he is trying to see if his mother is still living or if he is an orphan.

Beyond this woman the bank slopes, breaks, and then continues to descend to the lower right angle of the mountain, to the ditch and the cave where the two ends of a stretcher and the two legs of a dead man cast in there can be seen sticking out. [...]

At first sight, this large work is great, imposing, calls one imperiously, holds one before it, and could inspire pity and terror together. It inspires nothing but terror, and this is the fault of the artist, who has not had the genius to make the incidents he has imagined touch the spectator.

[...] It is nevertheless a noble idea, very poetic. [...] I know that some pusillanimous spectators have turned away from this canvas in horror, but what do I care [...] Where should I expect to find such scenes of horror, such frightening images, if not in a battle, a famine, a plague, an epidemic? If you consult those people with a petty refined taste who fear over-strong sensations, you will have painted out the frenzied who rush out from the hospital, the moribund man who tears his flesh at the foot of the building; then I shall burn the rest of your composition except however the woman of the rosary, who belongs to such taste.

DURAMEAU[53]

Le Triomphe de la Justice[54]

[...] If I had to compose a painting for a criminal court, that place of inquisition where a fearless, subtle, impudent crime sometimes escapes scot-free through the loop-holes of procedure, while at other times timid, frightened, startled innocence is sacrificed; instead of inciting men grown cruel through habit to increase their ferocity by the terrible spectacle of monsters that they must destroy, I would have leafed through history; and in default of history, I would have searched my imagination until I had brought forth deeds capable of inclining them to pity, to mistrust, of making them feel the weakness of man, the atrocity of capital punishment and the value of life. Ah! my friend, the evidence of only two men is enough to send someone to the gallows. Is it then so rare for two evil men to make up a story, or for two good men to make a mistake? Is there no fact that cannot be absurd, false, even though attested by a crowd who have not acted in concert? Are there no circumstances where the fact alone gives evidence and where so to speak there is no need for a witness? Indeed are there not others where the very great number of statements cannot offset the improbability of what they say?[55] The first step of criminal justice should be, should it not, to decide upon the nature of the action, on the number of witnesses necessary to establish the guilt of the accused? Should this number not be in proportion to the time, the place, the nature of the deed, the character of the accused, the character of the accusers? Would I not believe Cato more readily than half the Roman people? Calas! poor Calas! You would be living in honour surrounded by your family now if you had been judged by the rules; and yet you have perished and yet you were innocent, although you were innocent yet you were judged guilty both by your judges and by the majority of your countrymen. Oh judges! I call upon you and ask if the testimony of a catholic servant, who had converted one of the children in the house should not have weighed heavier in your scales than all the cries of a blind and fanatical people? Oh, judges! I ask you, did this father whom you accuse of the death of his son believe in a God, or did he not believe in Him? If he did not believe in Him, he certainly did not kill his son in the cause of religion. If he did believe in one, he was not able to call on this God in whom he believed to witness to his innocence at the last minute, or offer him his life in expiation of all other transgressions he had committed. That is neither the act of a man who believes, nor of a man who believes in nothing – nor of a fanatic who has to accuse himself of his crime and boast about it. And these people you listen to, when they make mistakes, when they are carried away by rage or by their prejudices, are they always just what they should be?

SALON DE 1769

CHARDIN

I should point out to you Chardin's pieces, and refer you to what I have said about this artist in previous Salons; but I like to repeat myself when I am singing someone's praises; I am going to give in to my natural inclination. Good generally affects me much more than evil. Evil makes me hit the roof in the first few moments; but it's an emotion that passes. The admiration of what is good remains with me. Chardin is no painter of history, but he is a great man. He is the master of all for harmony, that rare ingredient that everyone talks about and very few are acquainted with. Stop in front of a beautiful Teniers[56] or a superb Chardin for a long while; establish their effect in your imagination; then measure all that you afterwards see against this model, and without fail you will have discovered the secret of how to be scarcely ever satisfied. [...]

A woman returning from market

This cook who is returning from market is the repetition of a little piece which was painted forty years ago. This painting is indeed a pretty little thing. Since Chardin keeps to his particular style of painting, if he has a failing, you will find it everywhere; for the same reason, whatever he does perfectly will never alter. He is just as harmonious in this picture, there is the same understanding of the play of reflections, the same veracity of effect, which is uncommon, for it is easy to produce an effect when one takes some licence, when, for instance, a mass of shadows is built up without proper care for what produces it. To be passionate and to have principles, to be the slave of nature and a master of art, to have taste and to be rational at the same time is like the Devil going to confess himself. It is a pity that Chardin puts his mark on everything, and that his technique sometimes becomes heavy and ponderous going from one object to another. It is marvellously appropriate to the opaque, to all that is dull or lustreless, and to the solidity of inanimate objects; it clashes with living things, and the fragility of living beings. You can see this manner of painting in the stove, the rolls and other accessory objects; you must judge if this style does as well for the face and the arms of this servant, who incidentally seems to me rather vast in proportion and affected in her bearing.

Chardin is so exact an imitator of nature, so severe a judge of himself, that I have seen a painting of *Gibier* [*Game*] by him that he has never finished; because some little rabbits from which he was drawing were on the point of decay, he despaired of ever achieving the harmony he had conceived with any others. All of those brought to him were either too dark or too light. [...]

GREUZE

[...] I have promised, my friend, that I would talk to you about Greuze's *Morceau de réception*, and that I would talk about it impartially. I am going to keep my word.

You should know first that since the paintings of this artist have created the greatest sensation in society and in the Salon, the Academy has been woefully afflicted by the fact that such a clever man, so justly admired, only possessed the title of *Agréé*.[57] It wished him to be decorated on the spot with the title of Academician, and this desire and the letter that Cochin, the secretary, was instructed to write in consequence, were in high praise of Greuze. I have seen the letter, which is a model of courtesy and esteem; and I have seen Greuze's reply, which is a model of vanity and impertinence. He should have followed this up with a master-piece, but that is just what Greuze has not done.

Septimus Severus[58] is a low-born character, he has the tanned and swarthy skin of the convict; what he is doing is doubtful. He is badly drawn, and his wrist is broken. The length from his neck to the breast-bone is disproportionate, and the knee of the right thigh raising the coverlet is all out of place and disconnected.

Caracalla is even more base than his father, he is a vile, low rogue; the artist has not known the art of mingling wickedness with nobility. He is moreover a wooden figure, without motion and without suppleness. He is the *Antinous*[59] disguised in a Roman costume, and I am as certain of this as if the artist had told me.

'But', you will say to me, 'If this Caracalla is drawn after the *Antinous* he must be a handsome figure.' Reply. 'Have the *Antinous* drawn by a Raphael, and you will have a masterpiece; have the *Antinous* traced by an ignorant man, and you will have a cold, miserable drawing.' – 'But Greuze is not an ignorant man.' – 'The cleverest man in the world is an ignorant man when he tries his hand at something he has never done.' Greuze is out of his depth; as a scrupulous imitator of nature, he has been unable to rise to the kind of over-statement that is called for in historical painting. His Caracalla would fit marvellously into a rural, domestic scene. [. . .]

[. . .] Without this *Septimus Severus* Greuze would have had reason to be satisfied this year, but this accursed *Septimus* has spoilt everything. If we are not forced to point to our talent we will produce nothing with grace.

This tapissier[60] Chardin is a prankster of the first order; he is enchanting when he makes these clever mischiefs; it is true that they are all turned into the profit of artists and of the public; for the public they induce enlightenment by juxtaposing paintings for comparison; between artists they establish a contest altogether perilous. He has played this year an outrageous trick on Greuze by placing *The Young Child who Plays with and Caresses a Black Dog* between the *Young Girl who Prays to Love* and the *Young Girl who Blows a Kiss*; with a painting by the same artist he has found the means of killing two others. It is a good lesson, but a cruel one. [. . .]

SALON DE 1781

DAVID[61]

311. *Belisarius*[62] *recognized by a soldier who had served under him, just as a woman gives him alms.*

I look at him every day, and every day I believe I am seeing him for the first time. The grand manner shows through in the way he carried out his work, this young man has a soul, his heads are expressive without affectation, his characters' attitudes are noble and entirely natural, he can draw, he knows how to drape cloth and throw beautiful folds, his colour is handsome without being glossy. I would like less rigidity in the flesh he paints, however; his muscles do not have enough suppleness in some places. If you mentally tone down his architectural drawing, the effect will perhaps be better. If I talked of my admiration of the soldier, of the woman giving alms, of those folded arms, I would spoil my pleasure and embarrass the artist; but I would still have to say to him: 'Don't you think Belisarius is humiliated enough by receiving alms? Did you have to make him ask for them? Instead, make his arm upraised for charity encircle the child or point to the heavens in accusation of their severity.'

312. *St. Roch interceding with the Virgin for the lives of those stricken with the plague.*

A beautiful composition, with figures full of expression, a beautiful play of masses, beautiful draperies highlighting naked flesh, everything finely drawn. Perhaps there is something to be desired in the hands of the Saint, perhaps this huge terrifying man struck with the plague, and this tall St. Roch make the Virgin seem too small. Try to look long, if you can, at this sick youth whose reason has gone and who seems to be overcome with fury, and you will run from this painting in horror, but you will return before it through your love of art and your admiration for the artist.

Notes

1 Jean-Baptiste–Siméon Chardin (1699–1779).
2 *c.* 1740–46, see Plate 16. This was a copy, with additions, of the more famous *Bénédicité c.* 1739–40, owned by Louis XIV and now in the Louvre.
3 *Tableau* (or *morceau*) *de réception* was a painting on a given subject which an artist presented for consideration by the Academy in order to be *received* within its ranks.
4 Roughly the same as composition: the art of composing the parts of a painting into a harmonious whole.
5 The former painting is probably the 1739 *Governess* (now in Ottawa) which secured Chardin's reputation, the latter is in the Louvre *Bénédicité, c.* 1739–40.
6 Jean-Baptiste Deshays (1721–65).
7 The story of Paris' (the Trojan prince) award of the golden apple to Venus in a contest of beauty between her, Juno and Minerva was one of the most popular of mythological themes in art.
8 The cross of the crucifixion.
9 The avenging deities in Greek mythology, sometimes called the Erinyes or, in Latin, Furiae.
10 Elysian fields: the underworld of the noble dead in Greek and Latin mythology. Le Cap Ténare, now known as Cape Matapan, is the most southerly point of the Greek mainland. In Greek mythology a cave nearby which emitted sulphurous fumes was thought to be one of the entrances to the Infernal Regions. Paphos: a town on the west coast of Cyprus and centre of the cult of Aphrodite.
11 The Roman goddess of love and fertility.
12 The Trinity of God the Father, God the Son, and God the Holy Ghost; this has often been given a symbolic representation by the use of the triangle as a compositional device (particularly in Renaissance painting).
13 Jean Racine (1639–99), Piere Corneille (1606–84). The two outstanding writers of tragedy in seventeenth-century France.
14 Jean Calas whose trial and execution in 1762 amid the hysteria of Huguenot (French Protestant) and Catholic conflict caused Voltaire to lead a campaign for religious tolerance and the reform of the French criminal code.
15 Theocritus: Greek pastoral poet who lived in the third century B.C. S. Gessner (1730–88): Swiss painter and author of narrative idylls in verse.
16 By Deshays, exhibited in 1763 Salon.
17 Reference to the Bolognese Carracci (Ludovico 1555–1619, and his cousins

Agostino 1557–1602 and Annibale 1560–1609, who were brothers), the Venetian Tintoretto (1518–94) and Domenichino (1581–1641) from Bologna.

18   And therefore a Protestant.

19   The Louvre painting of 1727–28 which together with *Le Buffet* formed his *morceau de réception* to the Academy.

20   The painter Jean-Baptiste Pierre (1713–89) who became Premier Peintre to the King in 1770.

21   Nicholas Berghem, or Nicolaes Berchem (1620–83), Dutch pastoral scene painter much favoured by eighteenth-century French collectors. Philippe Jacques de Loutherbourg (1740–1812) Swiss-German painter and graphic artist.

22   Apelles (fourth century B.C.) and Zeuxis (second half of fifth century B.C.) were two of the most esteemed painters of Ancient Greece. None of their work survives.

23   François Boucher (1703–70).

24   Ordered to love only himself and his own things.

25   Jean-Baptiste Greuze (1725–1805).

26   A reference to the dying man in *Filial Piety*.

27   Most of Diderot's *Salons*, at least up to 1767, contained an introductory address to Baron de Grimm, literary critic and *philosophe*.

28   Horace, *Ars Poetica* 143–4: 'one with a flash begins, and ends in smoke,/The other out of smoke brings glorious light' Translation (published 1680) by the earl of Roscommon (1633?–85).

29   Charles Parrocel, painter (1688–1752).

30   François Le Moine (1688–1737).

31   These would normally have been casts of antique sculpture.

32   Reference to artists' subject matter derived from the antique. Antaeus was a giant who was finally defeated and killed by Hercules (Heracles).

33   The biennial Salon.

34   Pierre-Jean Chardin who, in 1754, was awarded the Grand Prix, the Academy's highest award for students. He subsequently produced little work and committed suicide in Venice.

35   Horace, *Ars Poetica* lines 372–3: 'Neither men nor gods nor booksellers ever forgive a poet for having a middling talent.'

36   Play (1764) by the French dramatist Michel-Jean Sedaine (1719–97).

37   A famous courtesan of the period.

38   Horace, *Ars Poetica*, lines 7–8. ' . . . that book is as ridiculous,/whose incoherent style (like sick men's dreams)/Varies all shapes, and mixes all extremes' Roscommon's translation.

39   Petrarch (1304–74) Italian poet and humanist.
'Her Laughter, her singing, and her sweet, kindly voice.'

40   Claude-Prosper Jolyot de Crébillon (1707–77), a novelist whose works give a licentious and satirical view of French eighteenth-century high society.

41   Bacchus, also known as Dionysus, god of fertility and wine in Greek and Latin mythology. Silenus, a satyr and attendant of Dionysus.

42   Bernard Le Bovier de Fontenelle (1657–1757) critic, popularizer of science and secretary of Académie des Sciences.

43   Michel-Ange Challe (1719–65) painter.

44   Genre painting: paintings depicting scenes from daily life. Diderot sometimes used the term to describe painters who had specialized in one kind (genre) of subject such as animals or, as in the case of Greuze, 'moral' subjects from middle-class life.

45   Daniel Webb (1719?–98) *An Inquiry into the beauties of Painting, and into the merit of the most celebrated Painters ancient and modern*, London, 1760.

46   Claude-Joseph Vernet (1714–89).

47   Lucian of Samosata (*c.*A.D. 115–*c.*A.D. 200), writer of satiric dialogues.

48   Joseph-Marie Vien (1716–1809).

49   Eustache Le Sueur, French painter (1616–55).

50   Francois-Gabriel Doyen (1726–1806).

51   Titus Lucretius Carus (*c.*99–55 B.C.). His major work was the philosophical poem

in six books *De Rerum Natura*. The quotation comes from Book III, lines 53–54 '. . . and in their bitter days their minds turn far more eagerly to religion'.

52 St. Geneviève (*c*.A.D. 422–*c*.A.D. 500) patron saint of Paris. The Mal des Ardents was a form of epidemic disease which occurred in parts of France, Germany, Spain and Sicily in the tenth, eleventh, twelfth and fourteenth centuries. It may have been one particular disease, some authorities have suggested Erysipelas (St. Anthony's Fire), but it is more likely that 'Ardents' was a general term covering the symptoms of such diseases as Erysipelas, Typhus and Bubonic plague.

53 Louis Durameau (1733–96).

54 Destined for the Chambre Criminelle of the Parlement de Rouen.

55 See David Hume's argument Vol. 1, p. 47 *et seq.*

56 David Teniers II (1610–90) active in Antwerp and Brussels.

57 Literally a painter 'approved' by the Academy.

58 Septimus Severus and Caracálla refer to the characters in the painting discussed by Diderot. The work was an attempt by Greuze to prove that he was worthy of being called a 'history painter'.

59 Antinous (*c*.A.D. 110–130), the favourite of the Emperor Hadrian, has often been used as the model of youthful male beauty.

60 The person responsible for hanging the exhibited paintings.

61 Jacques Louis David (1748–1825).

62 Belisarius (*c*.A.D. 505–565). Byzantine general. This painting depicts a period of disgrace for Byzantium's greatest military leader.

D'ALEMBERT

A History of the Sciences (1751)

Denis Diderot and Jean D'Alembert (editors), *Encyclopédie, ou Dictionnaire raisonné des sciences, des arts et des métiers, par une société de gens de lettres*. Mis en ordre et publié par M. Diderot, ... et à la partie mathématique, par M. D'Alembert, Chez Briasson, David, Le Breton, Durand, Paris, 1751–1780. [35 volumes]. Tome Premier (1751). Reprinted from D'Alembert, *Preliminary Discourse to the Encyclopedia*. Translation by R.N. Schwab, Bobbs-Merrill, 1963.

Between 1751 and 1780 there was published in France a great multi-volume illustrated encyclopaedia, under the general editorship of Diderot and D'Alembert and with contributions from other major *philosophes*, such as Voltaire, Montesquieu, Turgot and Rousseau, as well as many other lesser-known writers. It was sceptical, radical and subversive in its views and attitudes and had a very chequered publishing career, being more than once officially banned.

The *Encyclopédie* project had begun as a translation of Ephraim Chambers's *Encyclopaedia* and the original *Prospectus* of 1745 committed the editors to following the English encylopaedia to some extent. After Diderot had taken over the leadership of the project he wrote another *Prospectus* which explained the now more tenuous connection with the other encyclopaedia and details of such other matters as who had agreed to contribute on what topics. Subsequently, a revised version of the *Prospectus* formed part of the 'Preliminary Discourse of the Editors', following the contribution by D'Alembert, at the beginning of the first volume.

The task of D'Alembert (1717–83) was to explain the aims of the enterprise. His discourse falls into two parts, corresponding to the two main aims. The first part is concerned with the work as an encyclopaedia which sets forth as well as possible 'the order and connection of the parts of human knowledge'. Here D'Alembert provides what he calls a 'metaphysical analysis of the origin and connection of the sciences'.

The second part is intended to reflect the other aim of the

project, to produce a *Reasoned Dictionary of the Sciences, Arts, and Trades,* an aim which is reflected in the full title of the *Encyclopédie.* What D'Alembert produced, however, is not so much a rationale for a Reasoned Dictionary as a perspective on the history of the sciences and the arts.

The extract which follows is taken from this second part. Most of D'Alembert's remarks about 'the arts and belles-lettres' have been excluded, but most of his remarks about 'philosophy' and the natural sciences have been included here.

[. . .]We are now going to consider this work as a *Reasoned Dictionary of the Sciences and the Arts.* This object is all the more important, since it may possibly be of greater interest to the majority of our readers [than the object of the first part of this Discourse], and fulfilling it has required the most care and work. But before entering upon this subject in all the detail which may legitimately be required of us, it will be worth our while to examine at some length the present state of the sciences and the arts, and to show what series of steps have led us to it. Our metaphysical analysis of the origin and connection of the sciences has been of great utility in designing the encyclopedic tree;[1] an historical analysis of the order in which our knowledge has developed in successive steps will be no less useful in enlightening us concerning the way we ought to convey this knowledge to our readers. Moreover, the history of the sciences is naturally bound up with that of the small number of great geniuses whose works have helped to spread enlightenment[2] among men. And since these works have been helpful in a general way to our own, we ought to begin by speaking of them before giving account of the particular contributions and assistance that we have obtained. So as not to go back too far, let us turn our attention to the renaissance of letters.

When we consider the progress of the mind since that memorable epoch, we find that this progress was made in the sequence it should naturally have followed. It was begun with erudition, continued with belles-lettres, and completed with philosophy. This sequence differs, it is true, from that which a man would necessarily follow if left to his own intelligence or limited to exchanges with his contemporaries – a sequence that we analyzed[3] in the first part of this Discourse. For indeed we have demonstrated that a mind left in isolation would of necessity encounter philosophy before it arrived at belles-lettres; whereas the regeneration of ideas, if we can speak thus, must necessarily have been different from their original generation, as it involved moving out of a long interval of ignorance that had been preceded by centuries of enlightenment. We are going to try to demonstrate this.

The masterpieces that the ancients left us in almost all genres were forgotten for twelve centuries. The principles of the sciences and the arts were lost, because the beautiful and the true, which seem to show themselves everywhere to men, are hardly noticed unless men are already apprised of them. Not that these unfortunate times were less fertile than others in rare geniuses; Nature is always the same. But what could these great men do, scattered as they always are, from place to place, occupied with different purposes, and left to their solitary enlightenment with no cultivation of their abilities? Ideas which are acquired from reading and from association with others are the germ of almost all discoveries. It is like the air one breathes without thinking about it, to which one owes life; and the men of whom we are speaking were deprived of such sustenance. They were like the first creators of the sciences and the arts who have been forgotten because of their illustrious successors, and who, had they but come later, would themselves have caused the memory of the others to fade. The man who first discovered wheels and pinions would have invented watches in another century. Gerbert,[4] situated in the time of Archimedes,[5] would perhaps have equaled him.

Most of the superior intelligences of those dark times called themselves poets or philosophers. And indeed what did it cost them to usurp two titles with which people bedeck themselves at so little expense, ever flattering themselves that they can hardly owe them to borrowed wit? They thought it useless to seek models for poetry in the works of the Greeks and the Romans, whose language was no longer spoken; and they mistook for the true philosophy of the ancients a barbarous tradition which disfigured it. Poetry for them was reduced to a puerile mechanism. The careful examination of Nature and the grand study of mankind were replaced by a thousand frivolous questions concerning abstract and metaphysical beings – questions whose solution, good or bad, often required much subtlety, and consequently a great abuse of intelligence. Added to this confusion were the condition of slavery into which almost all of Europe was plunged and the ravages of superstition which is born of ignorance and which spawns it in turn. If one considers all these difficulties it will be plain that nothing was lacking to the obstacles that for a long time delayed the return of reason and taste. For liberty of action and thought alone is capable of producing great things, and liberty requires only enlightenment to preserve itself from excess.

And so one of those revolutions which make the world take on a new appearance was necessary to enable the human species to emerge from barbarism. The Greek empire was destroyed, and its ruin caused the small remainder of knowledge in the world to flow back into Europe.[6] The invention of printing and the patronage of the Medici[7] and of Francis I[8] revitalized minds, and enlightenment was reborn everywhere.

People turned first to the study of languages and history, which had perforce been abandoned during the centuries of ignorance. On emerging from barbarism, the human mind found itself in a sort of infancy. It was eager to accumulate ideas, but incapable at first of acquiring those of a higher order because of the kind of sluggishness in which the faculties of the soul had for so long a time been sunk. Of all these faculties, memory was the one which was cultivated first, because it is the easiest to satisfy and because the knowledge that is obtained with its help can be built up most easily. Thus they did not begin by studying Nature as the first men had had to do. They enjoyed an advantage which the earliest men lacked: they had the works of the ancients, which printing and the generosity of men of power and noble birth began to make common. They thought they needed only to read in order to become learned; and it is far easier to read than to understand. And so they devoured indiscriminately everything that the ancients left us in each genre. They translated them, commented on them, and out of a kind of gratitude began to worship them, although they were far from knowing their true worth.

These circumstances gave rise to that multitude of erudite men, immersed in the learned languages to the point of disdaining their own, who knew everything in the ancients except their grace and finesse, as a celebrated author has said, and whose vain show of erudition made them so arrogant because the cheapest advantages are rather often those whose vulgar display gives most satisfaction. They acted like great lords who do not resemble their forefathers in any real merit but who are excessively proud of their ancestry. Moreover, that vanity was not without some degree of plausibility. The realm of erudition and of facts is inexhaustible; the effortless acquisitions made in it lead one to think that one's substance is continually growing, so to speak. On the contrary, the realm of reason and of discoveries is rather small. Through study in that realm, men often succeed only in unlearning what they thought they knew, instead of learning what they did not know. That is why a scholar of most unequal merit must be much more vain than a philosopher or even perhaps a poet. For the inventive mind is always dissatisfied with its progress because it sees beyond, and for the greatest geniuses, even their self-esteem may harbor a secret but severe judge whom flattery may momentarily silence but never corrupt. Thus we should not be surprised that the scholars of whom we speak gloried so proudly in practising a science that was thorny, often ridiculous, and sometimes barbarous.[. . .]

While the arts and belles-lettres were held in honor, philosophy was far from making the same progress, at least in each nation taken as a whole; it reappeared only much later. It is not that to excel in belles-lettres is essentially easier than in philosophy; superiority in all genres is equally difficult to attain. But the reading of the ancients was to contribute more promptly to the advancement of belles-lettres and of good taste than to the progress of the natural sciences. Literary beauties do not have to be viewed for a long time in order to be felt; and as men feel before they think, for the same reason they judge their sensations before judging their thoughts. Moreover, as philosophers the ancients did not approach the perfection they achieved as writers [of literature], and indeed, though in the sequence of our ideas the first operations of

129

reason precede the first efforts of the imagination, the imagination moves much faster than reason once it has made its first steps. Imagination has the advantage of operating on objects which it produces itself, whereas reason all too often exhausts itself in fruitless investigations, since perforce it is limited to the ideas which lie before it, and forced to check itself at each instant. The universe and reflections [of the mind] are the first book of the true philosophers, and the ancients doubtless had studied it; thus men should have done what the ancients did. That study could not be replaced by a study of their works, most of which had been destroyed. The small number [that survived], mutilated by time, could give us only very uncertain and much corrupted ideas on so vast a matter.

Scholasticism, which constitutes the whole of so-called science of the centuries of ignorance, still was prejudicial to the progress of true philosophy in that first century of enlightenment. Since time immemorial, so to speak, men had been persuaded that they possessed the doctrine of Aristotle in all its purity,[9] [even though it had been] commented on by the Arabs[10] and corrupted by thousands of absurd or childish additions. So great was their respect for the ancients that they did not even think of ascertaining whether that barbarous philosophy was really the philosophy of this great man. It is in this fashion that many peoples, born and confirmed by education in their errors, believe in all sincerity that they are on the road to truth, because it has never even occurred to them to form the least doubt about it. And so, in the time when several writers were rivals of the Greek orators and poets, marching in the same rank as their models and perhaps even surpassing them, Greek philosophy, although very imperfect, was not even well known.

This multitude of prejudices, which was partially supported by blind admiration for antiquity, seemed to be strengthened further by the abuse which a few powerful theologians dared to make of the submission of peoples. I say a few, for I am far from extending an accusation that concerns only some of its members to an entire respectable and highly enlightened body. Poets were permitted to sing of the divinities of paganism, because men were rightly persuaded that using the names of these divinities could be no more than a game from which there was nothing to fear. If, on the one hand, the religion of the ancients, thinking of every object as being alive, opened a broad scope to the imagination of literary men, on the other hand its principles were so absurd that no one needed to worry about a revival of Jupiter or Pluto by some sect of innovators. But some people did fear, or appeared to fear, the blows which blind reason might deliver against Christianity. How did they fail to see that such a feeble attack was not of the slightest danger to them? Christianity was sent to men from heaven, and the promises of God himself assured forever that righteous and ancient veneration which people manifested towards it. Moreover, however absurd a religion might be (a reproach which only impiety can make of ours), it is never the philosophers who destroy it. Even when they teach truth, they are satisfied to demonstrate it without forcing recognition from anyone. Such a power belongs only to the Omnipotent Being. It is the inspired men who enlighten the people and the enthusiasts who lead them astray. The bridle that we are obliged to impose upon the license of the latter should in no way harm that liberty which is so necessary to true philosophy and from which religion can draw the greatest advantages. If Christianity brings to philosophy the enlightenment that it lacks and if grace alone can force the incredulous to submit, it is reserved for philosophy to reduce them to silence. To assure the triumph of faith, the theologians of whom we speak needed only to employ those weapons which were supposed to constitute a threat to it.

But some among these men had much more compelling reasons to oppose the advance of philosophy. Falsely persuaded that the faith of peoples becomes firmer as the different objects upon which it is exercised become more numerous, they were not content to require a legitimate submission to our mysteries. They tried to elevate their individual opinions into dogmas. And it was these opinions themselves, far more than the dogmas, which they wanted to make secure. They would by this means have inflicted the most terrible blow upon religion, had religion been the work of men. For there was a danger that once these opinions were recognized as false, the common people (who have no discernment) might treat the truths of religion and the false opinions with which some had wished to confound them in the same way.

Other theologians who were of better faith, but equally dangerous, joined with the first for different motives. Although religion is intended uniquely to regulate our mode of life and our faith, they believed it was to enlighten us also on the system of the world – in short, on matters which the All-Powerful has expressly left to our own disputations. They did not make the reflection that the sacred books and the works of the Fathers, which were created to teach the common people as well as the philosophers the requirements of practice and belief, would have spoken only the language of the common people when it came to indifferent questions. However, theological despotism or prejudice won out. A tribunal whose name still cannot be spoken without fear in France[11] became powerful in the south of Europe, in the Indies, and the New World. Faith in no way ordained belief in it, nor charity the approval of it. It condemned a celebrated astronomer[12] for having maintained that the earth moved and declared him a heretic, almost in the way that Pope Zachary had, some centuries before, condemned a bishop for not having thought as St. Augustine did concerning the antipodes, and for having guessed their existence six hundred years before Christopher Columbus discovered them. It was thus that the abuse of the spiritual authority, conjoined with the temporal, forced reason to silence; and they were not far from forbidding the human race to think.

While poorly instructed or badly intentioned adversaries made open

131

war on it, philosophy sought refuge, so to speak, in the works of a few great men. They had not the dangerous ambition of removing the blindfolds from their contemporaries' eyes; yet silently in the shadows they prepared from afar the light which gradually, by imperceptible degrees would illuminate the world.

The immortal Chancellor of England, Francis Bacon,[13] ought to be placed at the head of these illustrious personages. His works, so justly esteemed (and more esteemed, indeed, than they are known), merit our reading even more than our praises. One would be tempted to regard him as the greatest, the most universal, and the most eloquent of the philosophers, considering his sound and broad views, the multitude of objects to which his mind turned itself, and the boldness of his style, which everywhere joined the most sublime images with the most rigorous precision. Born in the depths of the most profound night, Bacon was aware that philosophy did not yet exist, although many men doubtless flattered themselves that they excelled in it (for the cruder a century is, the more it believes itself to be educated in all that can be known). Therefore, he began by considering generally the various objects of all the natural sciences. He divided these sciences into different branches, of which he made the most exact enumeration that was possible for him. He examined what was already known concerning each of these objects and made the immense catalogue of what remained to be discovered. This is the aim of his admirable book *The Advancement of Learning*. In his *Novum Organum*, he perfects the views that he had presented in the first book, carries them further, and makes known the necessity of experimental physics, of which no one was yet aware. Hostile to systems, he conceives of philosophy as being only that part of our knowledge which should contribute to making us better or happier, thus apparently confining it within the limits of the science of useful things, and everywhere he recommends the study of Nature. His other writings were produced on the same pattern. Everything, even their titles, proclaims the man of genius, the mind that sees things in the large view. He collects facts, he compares experiments and points out a large number to be made; he invites scholars to study and perfect the arts, which he regards as the most exalted and most essential part of human science; he sets forth with a noble simplicity his *Conjectures and Thoughts* on the different objects worthy of men's interest; and he would have been able to say, like that old man in Terence, that nothing which touches humanity was alien to him. Natural science, ethics, politics, economics, all seem to have been within the competence of that brilliant and profound mind. And we do not know which we ought to admire more, the riches he lavishes upon all the subjects he treats or the dignity with which he speaks of them. His writings can best be compared to those of Hippocrates[14] on medicine; and they would be no less admired, nor less read, if the culture of the mind were as dear to mankind as the conservation of health. But in every area only the works of those who head a school of disciples make a brilliant impression. Bacon was not of that number, and the form of this philosophy prevented it; it was too wise to astonish anyone. Scholasticism, which continued to dominate, could not be overthrown except by bold and new opinions. And apparently circumstances are not such that a philosopher who is content to say to men: "Here is the little that you have learned, there is what remains for you to find," is destined to cause much stir among his contemporaries. If we did not know with what discretion, and with what superstition almost, one ought to judge a genius so sublime, we might even dare reproach Chancellor Bacon for having perhaps been too timid. He asserted that the scholastics had enervated science by their petty questions, and that the mind ought to sacrifice the study of general beings for that of individual objects; nonetheless, he seems to have shown a little too much caution or deference to the dominant taste of his century in his frequent use of the terms of the scholastics, sometimes even of scholastic principles, and in the use of divisions and subdivisions, fashionable in his time. After having burst so many irons, this great man was still held by certain chains which he could not, or dared not, break.

We declare here that we owe principally to Chancellor Bacon the encyclopedic tree of which we have already spoken at length. We have stated this in several places in the *Prospectus*, we come back to it again, and we will not lose any opportunity to repeat it. However, we have not believed it necessary to follow on every point the great man whom we acknowledge here to be our master. If we have not put reason after imagination as he did, it is because we have followed the metaphysical order of the operations of the mind in the encyclopedic system rather than the historical order of its progress since the renaissance of letters. The illustrious Chancellor of England perhaps had this latter order in mind to some extent when he made what he called "the census" and the enumeration of the parts of human knowledge. Moreover, since the plan of Bacon is different from ours, and since the sciences have subsequently made great progress, it should not be surprising that we have sometimes taken a different route.[...]

Chancellor Bacon was followed by the illustrious Descartes.[15] That exceptional man, whose fortune has varied so much in less than a century, possessed all the qualities necessary for changing the face of philosophy: a strong imagination, a most logical mind, knowledge drawn from himself more than from books, great courage in battling the most generally accepted prejudices, and no form of dependence which forced him to spare them. Consequently, he experienced even in his own life what ordinarily happens to any man who has too marked an ascendancy over others. He had few enthusiasts and many enemies. Whether because he knew his country or only because he distrusted it, he took refuge in an entirely free land[16] in order to meditate with less possibility of disturbance. Though he was much less concerned with attracting disciples than with deserving them, persecution went to search him out in his retreat, and the secluded life he led could not protect him from it. In spite of all the sagacity that he had employed to prove God's existence, he was accused of denying it by some officials

133

who perhaps did not believe in it themselves. Tormented and slandered by foreigners, and rather poorly received by his compatriots, he went to die in Sweden, doubtless far from anticipating the brilliant success that his opinions would one day have.

One can view Descartes as a geometer or as a philosopher. Mathematics, which he seems to have considered lightly, nevertheless today constitutes the most solid and the least contested part of his glory. Algebra, which had been virtually created by the Italians and prodigiously augmented by our illustrious Viète,[17] received new acquisitions in the hands of Descartes. One of the most considerable is his method of indeterminates, a very ingenious and very subtle artifice, which we have since been able to apply to a large number of investigations. But above all what immortalized the name of this great man is the application he was able to make of algebra to geometry, one of the grandest and most fortunate ideas that the human mind has ever had. It will always be the key to the most profound investigations, not only in sublime geometry, but also in all the physico-mathematical sciences.

As a philosopher he was perhaps equally great, but he was not so fortunate. Geometry, which by the nature of its object always gains without losing ground, could not fail to make a progress that was most sensible and apparent for everyone when plied by so great a genius. Philosophy found itself in quite a different state. There everything remained to be done, and what do not the first steps in any branch of knowledge cost? One is excused from making larger steps by the merit of taking any at all. If Descartes, who opened the way for us, did not progress as far along it as his sectaries believe, nevertheless the sciences are far more indebted to him than his adversaries will allow; his method alone would have sufficed to render him immortal. His *Dioptrics* is the greatest and the most excellent application that has yet been made of geometry to physics. In a word, we see his inventive genius shining forth everywhere, even in those works which are least read now. If one judges impartially those vortices[18] which today seem almost ridiculous, it will be agreed, I daresay, that at that time nothing better could be imagined. The astronomical observations which served to destroy them were still imperfect or hardly established. Nothing was more natural than to postulate a fluid which carried the planets. Only a long sequence of phenomena, of reasonings, and of calculations, and consequently a long sequence of years, could cause such an attractive theory to be renounced. Moreover, it had the singular advantage of explaining gravitation of bodies by the centrifugal force of the vortex itself, and I am not afraid to assert that this explanation of weight is one of the finest and most ingenious hypotheses that philosophy has ever imagined. Thus, physicists had to be carried forward almost in spite of themselves by the theory of central forces and by experiments made much later before they would abandon it. Let us recognize, therefore, that Descartes, who was forced to create a completely new physics, could not have created it better; that it was necessary, so to speak, to pass by way of the vortices in order to arrive at the true system of the world; and that if he was mistaken concerning the laws of movement, he was the first, at least, to see that they must exist.

His metaphysics, as ingenious and new as his physics, suffered virtually the same fate. And it too can be justified by more or less the same reasons; for such is the fortune of that great man today, that after having had innumerable disciples, he is reduced to a handful of apologists. No doubt he was mistaken in admitting the existence of innate ideas. But had he retained that single truth taught by the Aristotelians concerning the origin of ideas through the senses, perhaps it would have been more difficult to uproot the errors that debased this truth by being alloyed with it. Descartes dared at least to show intelligent minds how to throw off the yoke of scholasticism, of opinion, of authority – in a word, of prejudices and barbarism. And by that revolt whose fruits we are reaping today, he rendered a service to philosophy perhaps more difficult to perform than all those contributed thereafter by his illustrious successors. He can be thought of as a leader of conspirators who, before anyone else, had the courage to arise against a despotic and arbitrary power and who, in preparing a resounding revolution, laid the foundations of a more just and happier government, which he himself was not able to see established. If he concluded by believing he could explain everything, he at least began by doubting everything, and the arms which we use to combat him belong to him no less because we turn them against him. Moreover, when absurd opinions are of long duration, one is sometimes forced to replace them by other errors, if one cannot do better, in order to disabuse the human race. The uncertainty and the vanity of the mind are such that it always needs an opinion to which to cleave. It is a child to whom one must offer a toy in order to take a dangerous weapon away from him. He will quit this toy by himself when he reaches the age of reason. In thus deceiving the philosophers, or those who believe themselves such, one teaches them at least to distrust their intelligence, and that frame of mind is the first step toward truth. Thus was Descartes persecuted in his own lifetime, as if he had come to bring truth to men.

Newton,[19] whose way had been prepared by Huyghens, appeared at last, and gave philosophy a form which apparently it is to keep. That great genius saw that it was time to banish conjectures and vague hypotheses from physics, or at least to present them only for what they were worth, and that this science was uniquely susceptible to the experiments of geometry. It was perhaps with this aim that he began by inventing calculus and the method of series, whose applications are so extensive in geometry itself and still more so in explaining the complicated effects that one observes in Nature, where everything seems to take place by various kinds of infinite progressions. The experiments on weight and the observations of Kepler[20] led the English philosopher to discover the force which holds the planets in their orbits. Simultaneously he showed how to distinguish the causes of their movements and how to calculate them with a precision such as one might reasonably expect only after several centuries of labor. Creator of an entirely new optics, he made the properties of light known to men by breaking it up into its constituent parts. Anything we could add to the praise of the great philosopher would fall far short of the universal testimonial that is given today to his almost innumerable discoveries and to his genius, which was at the same time far-reaching, exact, and profound. He had doubtless deserved all the recognition that has been given him for enriching philosophy with a large quantity of real assets. But perhaps he has done more by teaching philosophy to be judicious and to restrict within reasonable limits the sort of audacity which Descartes had been forced by circumstances to bestow upon it. His Theory of the World (for I do not mean his System) is today so generally accepted that men are beginning to dispute the author's claim to the honor of inventing it (because at the beginning great men are accused of being mistaken, and at the end they are treated as plagiarists). To the people who find everything in the works of the ancients I leave the pleasure of discovering gravitation of planets in those works, even if it is not there. But even supposing that the Greeks had had the idea of it, what was only a rash and romantic system with them became a demonstration in the hands of Newton. That demonstration, which belongs exclusively to him, constitutes the real merit of his discovery. Without such support, the theory of attraction would only be an hypothesis like so many others. If today some celebrated writer takes it into his head to predict without any proof that one day we will succeed in making gold, would our descendants be justified in trying on this pretext to deprive a chemist who actually achieved it of the glory of the great work? And does the invention of telescopes belong any less to its authors, even though some ancient might have thought it possible that we would one day extend the range of our vision?

Other scholars believe they are making a far better founded criticism of Newton by accusing him of reviving the "occult qualities"[21] of the scholastics and ancient philosophers in physics. But are the scholars of whom we are speaking quite sure that these two words were anything for the ancient philosophers but the modest expression of their ignorance? They were empty of sense among the scholastics, though intended to designate a being of which they thought they could conceive. Newton, who had studied Nature, did not flatter himself that he knew more than the ancients concerning the first cause which produces phenomena. But he refrained from employing the same language, in order not to offend some contemporaries who would have attached an idea to it other than what he intended. He contented himself with proving that the vortices of Descartes could not reasonably explain the movement of the planets, that phenomena and the laws of mechanics unite in overthrowing the vortices, that there is a force through which the planets tend toward one another, whose principle is entirely unknown to us. He did not reject impulsion; he limited himself to asking that it be employed more felicitously than it had been up to that time to explain the movement of the planets. His desires have not yet been fulfilled and perhaps will not be for a long time. After all, by giving us grounds to think that matter may have properties which we did not suspect and by disabusing us of our ridiculous confidence that we know everything, what harm could he have done to philosophy?

It appears that Newton had not entirely neglected metaphysics. He was too great a philosopher not to be aware that it constitutes the basis of our knowledge and that clear and exact notions about everything must be sought in metaphysics alone. Indeed, the works of this profound geometer make it apparent that he had succeeded in constructing such notions for himself concerning the principal objects that occupied him. However, he abstained almost totally from discussing his metaphysics in his best known writings, and we can hardly learn what he thought concerning the different objects of that discipline, except in the works of his followers. This may have been because he himself was somewhat dissatisfied with the progress he had made in metaphysics, or because he believed it difficult to give mankind sufficiently satisfactory and extensive enlightenment on a discipline too often uncertain and disputed. Or finally, it may have been because he feared that in the shadow of his authority people might abuse his metaphysics as they had abused Descartes', in order to support dangerous or erroneous opinions. Therefore, since he has not caused any revolution here, we will abstain from considering him from the standpoint of this subject.

Locke[22] undertook and successfully carried through what Newton had not dared to do, or perhaps would have found impossible. It can be said that he created metaphysics, almost as Newton had created physics. He understood that the abstractions and ridiculous questions which had been debated up to that time and which had seemed to constitute the substance of philosophy were the very part most necessary to proscribe. He sought the principal causes of our errors in those abstractions and in the abuse of signs,[23] and that is where he found them. In order to know our soul, its ideas, and its affections, he did not study books, because they would only have instructed him badly; he was content with probing deeply into himself, and after having contemplated himself, so to speak, for a long time, he did nothing more in his treatise, *Essay Concerning Human Understanding*, than to present mankind with the mirror in which he had looked at himself. In a word, he reduced metaphysics to what it really ought to be: the experimental physics of the soul–a very different kind of physics from that of bodies, not only in its object, but in its way of viewing that object. In the latter study we can, and often do, discover unknown phenomena. In the former, facts as ancient as the world exist equally in all men; so much the worse for whoever believes he is seeing something new. Reasonable metaphysics can only consist, as does experimental physics, in the careful assembling of all these facts, in reducing them to a corpus of information, in explaining some by others, and in distinguishing those which ought to hold the first rank and serve as the foundation. In brief, the principles of metaphysics, which are as simple as axioms, are the same for the philosophers as for the general run of people. But the meager progress that this science has made for such a long time shows how rarely these principles are applied felicitously, whether because of the difficulty that surrounds such an application, or perhaps also because of the natural temptations that prevent us from holding ourselves within bounds when we engage in metaphysical speculations. Nevertheless, the title of metaphysician, and even of great metaphysician, is still rather common in our century, for we love to squander everything. But how few persons are really worthy of that name! How many are there who earn it only by the unfortunate talent of obscuring clear ideas with a great deal of subtlety and of preferring their own extraordinary notions to true ones which are always simple? One should not be astonished, therefore, if the majority of those who are called metaphysicians have so little regard for one another. I have no doubt that this title will soon become an insult for our men of intelligence, as the name "sophist," degraded by those who bore it in Greece, was rejected by true philosophers, even though it means "a sage."

We may conclude from all this history that England is indebted to us for the origins of that philosophy which we have since received back from her. It is perhaps a greater distance from substantial forms[24] to vortices than from vortices to universal gravitation; just as perhaps a greater interval exists between pure algebra and the idea of applying it to geometry than between the small triangle of Barrow[25] and differential calculus.

Such are the principal geniuses that the human mind ought to regard as its masters. Greece would have raised statues to them, even if she had been obliged to tear down those of a few conquerors in order to give them room.

The limits of the Preliminary Discourse prevent us from speaking of several illustrious philosophers who, without proposing views as great as those which we have just mentioned, have contributed much to the advancement of the sciences through their works and lifted, so to speak, a corner of the veil that concealed truth from us. Among these are: Galileo, whose astronomical discoveries contributed so much to geography, as did his theory of acceleration to mechanics; Harvey[26], who will be immortalized by his discovery of the circulation of blood; Huyghens,[27] whom we have already named, and whose forceful and ingenious works have served geometry and physics so well; Pascal,[28] author of a treatise on the cycloid which ought to be regarded as a prodigy of wisdom and of penetration, and of a treatise on the equilibrium of liquids and the weight of air which has opened a new science to us – a sublime and universal genius whose talents could not be too much mourned by philosophy, if religion had not profited from them; Malebranche,[29] who unraveled the errors of the senses so well, and who knew the errors of the imagination— as if he had not often been misled by his own; Boyle, the father of experimental physics; and several others, among whom men like Vesalius, Sydenham, Boerhaave,[30] and an infinite number of celebrated anatomists and physical scientists ought to be counted with distinction.

Among these great men there is one whose philosophy, which is today both very well received and strongly opposed in the north of Europe, obliges us not to pass over him in silence. This is the illustrious Leibniz.[31] If he had had nothing more than the glory of sharing, or even the suspicion of sharing, the invention of differential calculus with Newton, he would deserve honourable mention on that score alone. But we wish to examine him principally for his metaphysics. Like Descartes, he seems to have recognized the inadequacy of all previous solutions to those lofty questions concerning the union of the body and the soul, Providence, and the nature of matter. He seems even to have had the advantage of setting forth the difficulties which can be raised on these questions more forcefully than anyone else. But, less judicious than Locke and Newton, he was not contented with formulating doubts; he tried to dissipate them, and in that respect he was perhaps no more fortunate than Descartes. His principle of *sufficient reason*,[32] excellent and very true in itself, does not seem very useful to beings so poorly enlightened, as we regarding the primary reasons of all things. His *monads*[33] at most prove that he understood better than anyone else our incapacity to form a clear idea of matter; but they do not appear to be such as to give us that clear idea. His *pre-established harmony*[34] seems only to add a further difficulty to the opinion of Descartes concerning the union of the body and the soul. Finally, his system of *Optimism*[35] is perhaps dangerous because of the alleged advantage that it has of explaining everything. This great man seems to have brought to metaphysics more sagacity than enlightenment, but however one thinks on this point, one cannot refuse him the admiration which he merits by the grandeur of his views of all kinds, the prodigious extent of his knowledge, and above all the philosophical spirit by which he was able to illuminate them.[36] [...]

But while intending to please, philosophy seems not to have forgotten that it is designed principally to instruct. For that reason the taste for systems[37] – more suited to flatter the imagination than to enlighten reason – is today almost entirely banished from works of merit. One of our best philosophers seems to have delivered the death blow to it.[38] The spirit of hypothesis and conjecture formerly was perhaps quite useful and even necessary for the renaissance of philosophy, because at that time judiciousness was less important than acquiring independence of thought. But times have changed, and a writer among us who praised systems would have come too late. The advantages now afforded by that spirit are too small to counterbalance the resulting disadvantages, and if the very small number of discoveries they once occasioned are claimed as proof of the usefulness of systems, one might just as well counsel our geometers to apply themselves to squaring the circle, because the efforts of several mathematicians to do so have given us a few theorems. The spirit of systems is in physics what metaphysics is in geometry. If it may sometimes be required in order to start us on the way, it is almost never capable by itself of leading us to truth. It can glimpse the causes of phenomena when enlightened by the observation of Nature; but it is for calculations to assure, so to speak, the existence of these causes by determining exactly the effects they can produce and by comparing these effects with those revealed to us by experience. Any hypothesis without such a support rarely acquires that degree of certitude which ought always to be sought in the natural sciences, and which is so seldom found in those frivolous conjectures honored by the name of "systems." If all he could have were conjectures of that kind, the principal merit of the physicist would be, properly speaking, to have the spirit of system but never to create one. Thousands of experiments prove how dangerous the use of systems is in the other sciences.

Physics is therefore confined solely to observations and to calculations; medicine to the history of the human body, of its maladies and their remedies; natural history to the detailed description of vegetables, animals, and minerals; chemistry to the composition and experimental decomposition of bodies. In a word, all the sciences are confined, as much as possible, to facts and to consequences deducted from them, and do not concede anything to opinion except when they are forced to. I do not speak of geometry, astronomy, and mechanics, which are destined by their nature always to be perfecting themselves.

Men abuse the best things. That philosophic spirit so much in fashion today which tries to comprehend everything and to take nothing for granted extends even into belles-lettres. Some claim that it is even harmful to their progress, and indeed it is difficult to conceal that fact. Our century, which is inclined toward combination and analysis, seems to desire to introduce frigid and didactic discussions into things of sentiment. It is not that the passions and tastes do not have their own sort of logic, but their logic has principles completely different from those of ordinary logic; these principles must be unraveled within us, and it must be confessed that ordinary philosophy is quite unsuited for the task. Totally immersed in the analysis of our perceptions, philosophy disentangles their nuances much more readily when the soul is in a state of tranquillity than when it is in the throes of passions or of the lively sentiments which affect us. In truth, how could it possibly be easy to analyze such feelings as these with precision? We must indeed surrender ourselves to them in order to know them, even though the moment in which the soul is affected by them is the very time when it is least capable of study. It must be admitted, however, that this spirit of discussion has contributed to freeing our literature from blind admiration for the ancients; it has taught us to value in them only the beauties that we would be compelled to admire in the moderns. But it is perhaps also to the same source that we owe that species of metaphysics of the heart which has seized hold of our theaters.[39] While we do not have to banish it entirely, still less are we obliged to let it thus hold sway. This "anatomy of the soul" has even slipped into our conversations; people make dissertations, they no longer converse; and our societies have lost their principal ornaments – warmth and gaiety.

Thus, let us not be astonished that our literary works are generally inferior to those of the preceding century. One can find the reason for this circumstance in the very efforts we make to surpass our predecessors. Taste and the art of writing make rapid progress in a short time, once the true route is open; hardly does a great genius glimpse the beautiful before he sees it in its entire extent, and imitation of *la belle Nature* seems restricted to certain limits which are reached in only a generation or two at the most, so that for the following generation imitation is all that remains. Yet this next generation is not content with this share: the riches that it has inherited authorize the desire to increase them. It strives to add to what it has received, and it misses the mark while trying to surpass it. Thus, we have at the same time more principles for good judgment, a larger fund of enlightenment, more good judges, and fewer good works. We do not say of a book that it is good, but that this is the book of a man of intelligence. In this manner did the century of Demetrius of Phalerum immediately follow that of Demosthenes, the century of Lucan and of Seneca that of Cicero and of Virgil, and our century that of Louis XIV. [. . .]

Notes

1. The encyclopaedic tree was intended to exhibit the relationships between different parts of human knowledge. Behind the 'tree' metaphor (as also behind talk of 'branches of knowledge') is an assumption about the *unity* of human knowledge.
2. Term used by the translator to cover such diverse phrases in the original as 'pour nous éclairer', 'à répandre la lumière' etc.
3. The sequence indicated by D'Alembert's 'metaphysical analysis' puts Reason and Imagination in the reverse order from that suggested by his 'historical analysis' in this section.
4. Gerbert of Aurillac (*c.* 940–1003), became Pope Sylvestre II. He was a scholar whose main interest was in mathematics and the physical sciences.
5. The great ancient Greek mathematician and inventor Archimedes (287–212 B.C.).
6. D'Alembert's reference here is to the destruction of the Byzantine Empire. In so far as there is a factual basis for this large claim it is that the Greek texts of Aristotle were not available to Western scholars until after the fall of Constantinople in 1453. That D'Alembert may have had Aristotle specifically in mind at this point is borne out by his remarks on p. 130.
7. The powerful Florentine family who, from the late fourteenth century, derived their fortune from banking and trade. Their patronage of the arts in the fifteenth and sixteenth centuries was a source of encouragement to the Italian Renaissance.
8. King of France from 1515–47. As a patron of the arts Francis contributed to the Renaissance in France.
9. D'Alembert's observation is correct. Much of Aristotle's philosophical thought is what he himself calls 'aporetic', that is, raising difficulties without solving them. It is therefore hardly surprising that the interpretation and re-interpretation of Aristotle's work has been very much part of the history of European philosophy, both inside and outside the Christian tradition.
10. One of the most famous of these commentaries is that by Averroës (1126–98).
11. A reference to the Inquisition: 'the ecclesiastical jurisdiction dealing in the Middle Ages and subsequently with the detection and punishment of heretics and offenders against Catholic orthodoxy'. (*Encyclopaedia Britannica*)
12. Galileo Galilei (1564–1642), experimental philosopher and astronomer. He was summoned by the Roman Inquisition in 1633 following the publication of his great *Dialogue on the Ptolemaic and Copernican Systems*, and obliged to abjure his 'heresies'.
13. (See also Vol. 1, p. 64 note 33.) In his Preface to *De Interpretatione Naturae* (1620), Bacon wrote of himself:

> Believing that I was born for the service of mankind, I set myself to consider what service I was myself best fitted to perform. Now if a man should succeed, not in striking out some new invention, but in kindling a light in nature – a light that should eventually disclose and bring into sight all that is most hidden and secret in the universe – that man (I thought) would be benefactor indeed of the human race . . . For myself I found that I was fitted for nothing so well as the study of truth,

141

as having a mind nimble and versatile enough to catch the resemblances of things (which is the chief point) and at the same time steady enough to fix and distinguish their subtler differences; as being gifted by nature with desire to seek, patience to doubt, fondness to meditate, slowness to assert, readiness to reconsider, carefulness to dispose and set in order; and as being a man that neither affects what is new nor admires what is old, and hates every kind of imposture. So I thought that my mind had a kind of familiarity and relationship with truth.

(*The Works of Francis Bacon*, ed. J. Spedding, Boston, 1863.)

D'Alembert's generous remarks about Bacon disguise the considerable intellectual distance between them: Bacon had much more of a disciple in Diderot himself. (See also Diderot, *Art*, p. 144.)

14 The Greek physician Hippocrates (*c*.460–*c*.375 B.C.), the 'Father of medicine'.

15 René Descartes (1596–1650) was one of the most outstanding and influential philosophers and mathematicians of all time. His works include *Discourse on Method* (published, together with the *Geometry*, the *Dioptrics* and the *Meteors*, in French in 1637), *Meditations on First Philosophy* (1641) and *Principles of Philosophy* (1644).

In the *Discourse on Method*, Descartes gives an account of four rules that, he says, he had found adequate to express his method:

The first of these was to accept nothing as true which I did not clearly recognize to be so: that is to say, carefully to avoid precipitation and prejudice in judgements, and to accept in them nothing more than was presented to my mind so clearly and distinctly that I could have no occasion to doubt it.

The second was to divide up each of the difficulties which I examined into as many parts as possible, and as seemed requisite for it to be resolved in the best manner possible.

The third was to carry on my reflections in due order, beginning with objects that were the most simple and easy to understand, in order to rise little by little, or by degrees, to knowledge of the most complex, assuming an order, even if a fictitious one, among those which do not follow a natural sequence relative to one another.

The last was in all cases to make enumerations so complete and reviews so general that I should be certain of having omitted nothing.

(*The Philosophical Works of Descartes* 1931–34.)

Descartes's disciples, referred to by D'Alembert as his 'sectaries', formed a centre of resistance to Newtonian ideas in France.

16 Descartes left France for Holland, where he spent most of his time from 1628 to 1649.

17 Francois Viète (1540–1603) made innovations in algebra which Descartes subsequently developed.

18 Descartes postulated vortices in order to explain the movement of the planets. (The much more adequate explanation offered by Newton is what made Descartes's account 'seem almost ridiculous'.)

19 The great English mathematician and physicist Isaac Newton (1642–1727) produced a 'Theory of the World' which had already become the established view in D'Alembert's time and was to remain so for more than a century later. The comparative rigour and precision of his *Mathematical Principles of Natural Philosophy* (1687) secured for it a far-reaching influence. It came to be regarded as a model of what science should be like. Those, like D'Alembert, who sought to propagate views about the form which natural philosophy should take, looked for them in Newton. (Subsequent scholarship has revealed that Newton was not as averse to speculation as D'Alembert would have his readers believe.)

20 Johannes Kepler (1571–1630), German mathematician and astronomer. His discovery of the three celebrated laws of planetary motion which bear his name, revolutionized astronomical calculation, though they were not proved until Newton's *Principia* appeared.

21 The allegation against Newton was that, in introducing the idea of universal 'attraction', he was introducing an idea which had no more explanatory value than

the scholastic appeal to a 'dormitive virtue' to explain the power certain drugs had of putting people to sleep.

22 John Locke (see also Vol. 1, p. 35, note 1) was not, as D'Alembert implies, a disciple of Newton. Though his *Essay Concerning Human Understanding* was not published until 1690, he wrote the first drafts of it in 1671. It was only later in life that the two men became associated. D'Alembert offers a highly simplified and retrospective view of Locke's achievement when he remarks that 'he created metaphysics, almost as Newton had created physics'. D'Alembert was by no means alone in pairing Locke with Newton. It is indeed a natural pairing in view of their broadly similar intellectual outlook.

23 Locke thought that a common cause of obscurity and confusion in men's thoughts was their failure to attach a clear idea to the signs they were using.

24 The scholastics used the 'substantial form' of a thing as an explanation of what made that thing a thing of the particular sort it was.

25 Isaac Barrow (1630–77) was Newton's Professor who had himself come close to discovering the differential calculus.

26 William Harvey (1578–1657), eminent English physician, physiologist and anatomist.

27 Christiaan Huyghens (1629–95) was a Dutch physicist, mathematician and astronomer. He perfected the telescope and made many other useful discoveries concerning optics and dynamics.

28 Blaise Pascal (1623–62) French philosopher and mathematician.

29 Nicholas Malebranche (1638–1715) devised a metaphysical system in which the interaction of spirit and matter was denied. Malebranche held that God arranged an exact correspondence between our notions of material objects and the motions of the objects themselves. This view, known as 'occasionalism', was the source of considerable controversy and stimulated the metaphysical system of Leibniz.

30 Boyle (1627–91), chemist and natural philosopher. Vesalius (1514–64), celebrated anatomist; Sydenham (1624–89), physician and clinician; Boerhaave (1668–1738), Dutch physician who applied Newton's experimental method to medicine and chemistry.

31 G. W. Leibniz (1646–1716) German philosopher and mathematician.

32 Leibniz himself, in his *Monadology*, states the principle as that 'by virtue of which we consider that no fact can be real or existing and no proposition can be true unless there is a sufficient reason, why it should be thus and not otherwise, even though in most cases these reasons cannot be known to us'. (§32)

33 A 'Monad' is a true indivisible unity. Leibniz reasoned that, if the essence of matter consisted in extension, as Descartes had maintained, there would be no true unities to be found in the world. There would be no individuals in any strict sense. D'Alembert here credits Leibniz with having seen a problem but evidently did not think that Leibniz's own solution to it was helpful.

34 Leibniz's monads could not interact with one another and therefore the causal transactions which we perceive in the world must, or so Leibniz argued, be the result of a harmony between the behaviours of the individual monads which was pre-established by God. For Leibniz, the world we see only provides us with regularities.

35 Leibniz's so-called 'optimism' is a consequence of his principle of sufficient reason together with his conclusion that the world was created by a perfect God. Since God must have been able to choose between creating any of an infinite number of possible universes, the existing universe must be the most perfect one possible.

36 This sentence was included in later editions of the *Preliminary Discourse*.

37 D'Alembert is criticizing the tendency, to be found in Descartes and Leibniz, to construct a deductive system in which scientific propositions will be derived from metaphysical propositions. D'Alembert's remarks about such systems show his hostility to such metaphysics.

38 Abbé Condillac (1714–80), a French disciple of Locke and perhaps in his own right the best philosopher of the philosophes. The 'death blow' referred to by D'Alembert is in a reference to Condillac's *Traité des Systèmes* (1746).

39 It has been suggested, by Richard M. Schwab, that D'Alembert is referring here to the minute analysis of various forms of love, usually the beginning stages of tender young love, by Marivaux (1688–1763) in his comedies of the 1720s and 1730s.

DIDEROT

Art (1751)

From Diderot, (ibid., Vol. 1, 1751) *Art*. Reprinted from *Encyclopedia, Selections*, translation by N. S. Hoyt and T. Cassirer, Bobbs-Merrill, 1965.

One of the chosen functions of the *Encyclopédie* was to provide detailed articles on trades and technical processes. There were doctrinaire implications in this, in that the culture of the court of Louis XIV had been predominantly literary, in a narrow sense. The courtier had been expected to have no special subject of knowledge, nor to use any specialized or technical words or phrases, these being felt to be 'low'. Even writings on technical and scientific matters tended to be couched in generalized and 'polite' language. Thus, the insistence in the *Encyclopédie* on technical detail, and on the social importance of the craftsman, and the artisan, was part of a general attack upon *ancien régime* values.

Diderot's article 'Art' was published in the periodical *Mercure de France* in advance of the first volume of the *Encyclopédie*, and was important in arousing interest in the forthcoming work. Diderot goes to some lengths in his opening paragraphs to define and explain the meaning of the word 'Art'; and the change of meaning in the word that has taken place both in France and Great Britain between his day and our own is very instructive and encapsulates a great deal of social history.

ABSTRACT METAPHYSICAL term. Men began by collecting observations on the nature, function, use and qualities of beings and their symbols. Then they gave the name of science or art to the center or focal point to which they linked the observations they had made, in order to create a system of instruments, or of rules which were all directed toward the same object. That is the most general meaning of art. To give an example: Men reflected on the usage and function of words and subsequently invented the word "grammar." Grammar is the name of a system of instruments and rules that relate to a specific object; this object is articulated sound. The same is true of the other arts and sciences.

Origin of the arts and sciences. In pursuit of his needs, luxury, amusement, satisfaction of curiosity, or other objectives, man applied his industriousness to the products of nature and thus created the arts and sciences. The focal points of our different reflections have been called "science" or "art" according to the nature of their "formal" objects, to use the language of logic. If the object leads to action, we give the name of "art" to the compendium of the rules governing its use and to their technical order. If the object is merely contemplated under different aspects, the compendium and technical order of the observations concerning this object are called "science." Thus metaphysics is a science and ethics is an art. The same is true of theology and pyrotechnics.

Speculative and practical aspects of an art. From the preceding it is evident that every art has its speculative and its practical aspect: the former consists in knowing the principles of an art, without their being applied, the latter in their habitual and unthinking application. It is difficult if not impossible to go far in the practice of an art without speculation, and, conversely, to have a thorough knowledge of the speculative aspects of an art without being versed in its practice. In every art there are many particulars concerning its material, its instruments, and its application which can only be learned through practice. It is the function of practice to present difficulties and phenomena, while speculation must explain the phenomena and solve the difficulties. Consequently, only an artist who can think logically can talk well about his art.

Division of the arts into liberal and mechanical arts. When men examined the products of the arts, they realized that some were primarily created by the mind, others by the hands. This is *part* of the cause for the pre-eminence that some arts have been accorded over others, and of the distinction between liberal and mechanical arts. This distinction, although it is quite justified, has led to bad consequences because it has given a low name to people who are very worthy and useful, and encouraged us in a certain natural laziness. We are all too inclined to believe that it is beneath the dignity of the human spirit to apply oneself diligently and continuously to specific and concrete experiments and objects, and that our mind forfeits its dignity when it descends to the study, let alone the practice, of the mechanical arts; the mind here stoops to questions in which research is laborious, reflection inglorious, and exposition difficult; such questions are dishonorable to deal with, countless in number, and of scarcely any value. *Minui majestatem mentis humanae, si in experimentis et rebus particularibus,*[1] etc. (Bacon, *Novum Organum*). This prejudice has tended to fill the cities with useless spectators and with proud men engaged in idle speculation, and the countryside with petty tyrants who are ignorant, lazy, and disdainful. Such was not the thinking of Bacon, one of the foremost geniuses of England, nor of Colbert,[2] one of the greatest ministers of France, nor, in

145

a word, of the right-thinking and sensible men of all times. Bacon considered the history of the mechanical arts the most important branch of true philosophy; therefore he certainly did not scorn its practice. Colbert considered the industry of the people and the founding of manufactures the most reliable resource of a kingdom. In the opinion of those who today can discern true worth, the state benefited no less from a man who filled France with engravers, painters, sculptors, and artists of all types, who wrested from the English the secret of the machine for producing hosiery, from the Genoese their velvet, from the Venetians their mirrors, than it benefited from those who vanquished the enemies of France and took their fortresses. In the eyes of a philosopher a sovereign may deserve more praise if he has encouraged men like Le Brun, Le Sueur, and Audran,[3] if he has had the battles of Alexander painted and engraved, and the victories of our generals represented in tapestry, than he would for having gained those victories. Place on one side of the scales the actual advantages of the most sublime sciences and the most honored arts, and on the other side the advantages of the mechanical arts, and you will find that esteem has not been accorded to the one and to the other in just proportion to the benefits they bring. You will discover that far more praise has been heaped on those men who spend their time making us believe that we are happy, than on those who actually bring us happiness. How strangely we judge! We expect everyone to pass his time in a useful manner, and we disdain useful men.

General purpose of the arts. Man is only the minister or interpreter of nature: he can only understand or act insofar as he has knowledge of the beings that surround him, either by means of experiment or reflection. His bare hand can only achieve a small number of effects, however robust, tireless, and supple it may be; it succeeds in great enterprises only with the help of instruments and rules. The same is true of the understanding. It is as if instruments and rules provided additional muscles for the arms, and additional energy for the mind. The general purpose of any art, or of any system of instruments and rules concurring toward the same end, is to impress specific forms onto the basic element provided by nature. This element can be either matter, or spirit, or some function of the soul, or some product of nature. However, I shall devote most of my attention to the mechanical arts, particularly because other authors have written little about them. In these arts *man's power is limited to moving natural objects closer or farther away. Man is capable of everything or nothing, depending on whether it is or is not possible to bring objects closer or move them farther away* (see Bacon, *Novum Organum*).

A project for a general treatise on the mechanical arts. Often we do not know the origin of a mechanical art or have only vague information on its progress. That is the natural consequence of the scorn in which those who engage in these arts have been held at all times and in every learned or warlike nation. In such a situation we must have recourse to philosophic suppositions, begin from some probable hypothesis, from some first fortuitous event, and proceed from there until we reach the point to which the art has advanced. I shall explain this by an example, and I prefer to take it from the mechanical arts, which are not so well known, rather than from the liberal arts which have been described in a thousand different ways. If the origin and progress of glassmaking or papermaking were unknown, what would a philosopher do if he intended to write the history of these arts? He would suppose that a piece of cloth had accidentally fallen into a container filled with water and had remained in it long enough to dissolve, so that when the container was emptied it was found to have in it, instead of a piece of cloth, only a kind of sediment. It would have been difficult to determine the nature of that sediment, had it not been for a few remaining filaments which indicated that the original matter of the sediment had been cloth. As far as glassmaking is concerned, he would suppose that the first solid dwellings built by men were made of baked clay or brick. Now it is impossible to burn brick in a strong fire without some part of it vitrifying, and it is in this form that glass first occurred. But how far removed this dirty greenish shard is from the pure, transparent matter used in windows, etc.! Yet this or a similar fortuitous happening is the starting point from which the philosopher will proceed to the present state of glassmaking.

Advantages of this method. By this procedure the progress of an art would be presented in a clearer and more instructive manner than by its true history, if that were known. The difficulties that had to be overcome to improve the art would occur in an entirely natural order, the synthetic explanation of its successive steps would render it comprehensible even for very average minds, and this would divert artists onto the path leading to perfection.

The order that would have to be followed in such a treatise. As for the order that would have to be followed in such a treatise, I believe that it would be most advantageous to link the arts to the products of nature. An exact enumeration of these products would give rise to many arts that are as yet unknown. A detailed examination of the different aspects from which the same product can be studied would lead to the discovery of still other arts. The first of these possibilities demands a very extensive knowledge of natural history and the second, great dialectical ability. Consequently, a treatise on the arts, as I envisage it, cannot be the work of an ordinary man. Let no one imagine that I am engaged in idle speculation and that the discoveries I promise are mere figments of my imagination. I have already pointed out that the history of nature is incomplete without the history of the arts, and here I echo a philosopher [Bacon] whom I never tire of praising because I never tire of reading him. I have already suggested to the naturalists that they perfect their studies of the vegetable, mineral, and animal kingdoms by including the experiments of the mechanical arts, a branch of knowledge much more important for true philosophy. Now I shall dare to add with him: *Ergo rem quam ago, non opinionem, sed opus esse; eamque non sectae alicujus, aut placiti, sed utilitatis esse et amplitudinis immensae fundamenta.*[4] We are not dealing here with a philosphical system nor with the whims of one man, but with the decrees of experience and of reason and the foundation of an immense edifice. Whoever thinks otherwise seeks to limit the sphere of our knowledge and to discourage men's minds. We owe to chance very important discoveries we did not actively seek. Should we assume that we will not find anything if we add our efforts to the whims of chance and introduce order and method into our research? If we now possess secrets that men formerly did not hope to uncover, and if we may conjecture from the experience of the past, why should the future not hold riches for us that we can scarcely count on today? If, a few centuries ago, anyone had said to those people who measure possibilities by the reach of their genius and who do not imagine anything beyond what they already know, that there exists a dust that breaks rocks and overthrows the thickest walls from an unbelievable distance, that a few pounds of this dust, enclosed in the depths of the earth, shake the earth, make their way through the enormous mass that covers them, and open up an abyss large enough to contain an entire city, these people would certainly have compared such effects to the action of wheels, pulleys, levers, counterweights, and other known machines; they would have declared that such a dust is a mere figment of the imagination and that only lightning, or the cause that produces earthquakes by means of an inimitable mechanism, can produce such fearful prodigies. Thus we may conclude that the great philosopher spoke to his century and to all the centuries to come. We may ask, as he would have done, how much erroneous speculation would have been occasioned by the project of raising water by fire,[5] as was carried out for the first time in London, especially if the inventor of the machine would have modestly presented himself as a man little versed in mechanics? If this were the only attitude toward inventions nothing either great or small would be produced. Men who render hasty judgments upon inventions that do not deviate from established practice and sometimes are merely slight modifications of familiar machines, requiring at most a skillful worker to carry them out, men, I repeat, who are so narrow-minded that they judge these inventions to be impossible, should know that they themselves are not learned enough to formulate appropriate aspirations. The chancellor Bacon tells them so: *Qui sumpta*, or what is even more inexcusable, *qui neglecta ex his quae praesto sunt conjectura, ea aut impossibilia, aut minus verisimilia, putet; eum scire debere se non satis doctum, ne ad optandum quidem commode et apposite esse.*[6]

Another reason for carrying on research. We ought also to be encouraged in our research and prompted to look attentively around us, since so many centuries have gone by without men becoming aware of important things which they had, so to speak, right before their eyes, such as the arts of printing and engraving. How strange is the condition of the human mind! *During the act of discovery it mistrusts its strength, it becomes entangled in self-created difficulties and what it seeks seems impossible to find. Once the discovery is made, the mind no longer conceives why it was necessary to seek so long, and feels sorry for its inadequacy.*

Remarkable differences between machines. Having now set forth my ideas concerning a philosophic treatise on the arts in general, I am going to continue with some useful remarks on the manner of treating certain mechanical arts individually. Sometimes we use a very complex machine to produce an effect that appears quite simple; at other times a machine that is really very simple produces by itself a very complex action. In the first case one must begin by stating the effect to be produced, since it is easily grasped and will not burden one's memory with knowledge nor confuse one's mind. The description of the machine will then follow. In the second case, on the contrary, it is more to the point to go from the description of the machine to knowledge of its effect. The effect of a clock is to divide time into equal parts with the aid of a needle that moves evenly and very slowly on a marked surface. If then I show a clock to someone who does not know this machine, I will first explain its effects and will then deal with its mechanism. I shall certainly not proceed in the same manner with someone who asks me what a stocking-stitch is, or cloth, or drugget, or velvet, or satin. Here I would begin with a detailed description of the frames on which these materials are produced. If the construction of the machine is clear, its effect is grasped all at once, something that might be impossible without this preliminary explanation. Anyone who would like to convince himself of the truth of these remarks should try to define exactly what gauze is, without presupposing any knowledge of the machine of the gauze-maker.

Of the geometry of the arts. Everyone will readily agree that there are few artists who can dispense with the elements of mathematics. Yet here we have a paradox, although its truth is not immediately obvious: in many situations knowledge of these elements would actually hamper an artist if, in practice, the precepts of mathematics were not corrected by an extensive knowledge of physical circumstances; such as location, position, irregular figures, materials and their qualities, elasticity, rigidity, friction, consistency, duration, as well as the effects of air, water, cold, heat, dryness, and so forth. It is clear that the elements of academic geometry constitute only the simplest and least complex elements of workshop geometry. There exists not one lever in nature that is the same as the one which Varignon[7] presupposes in his propositions; there exists not one lever in nature whose factors can all be calculated. Among these factors we find a great number, some of them very essential in practice, which cannot even be subjected to the mathematical operations by which we determine the slightest discernible differences of quantity. Hence a man who knows only theoretical geometry is usually not skilful, and an artist who knows only experimental geometry is very limited as a worker. But, in my opinion, experience shows us that it is easier for an artist to get along without theoretical geometry than for any man to get along without some experimental geometry. In spite of calculus the entire subject of friction has remained the province of experimental and practical mathematics. It is remarkable how far we can go with only this mathematics. How many bad machines are suggested every day by men who imagine that levers, wheels, pulleys, and cables perform in a machine as they do on paper! Because they have not taken part in practical work, they have never learned the difference between the effects of the machine itself and of its section. We will add a second observation since the subject suggests it: there are machines that are successful on a small scale but not on a large scale. Of some others the opposite is true. I believe that the latter should include all the machines whose effect depends principally on the considerable weight of their component parts, on the force of reaction in a fluid, or on a great volume of elastic matter upon which these machines have to act. If one constructs them on a small scale, the weight of the parts is reduced to nothing, the reaction of the fluid is almost nonexistent, the forces on which one has counted disappear and the machine is ineffective. However, just as there is a point, if we may use the term, a limit that stands in relation to the size of the machine, where it ceases to be effective, there is another below or beyond which the potential of its mechanism does not produce its maximum effect. Every machine has, in the language of geometry, a *maximum* size. When we consider each part in relation to its most perfect functioning, it has a size that is determined by the other parts. Similarly, from the point of view of its most perfect functioning, the whole has a size determined by the machine, by its intended use, and by an infinity of other matters. But where, you will ask, is the limit in the dimensions of a machine, beyond or below which it is either too large or too small? Which is the actual and absolute size of an excellent watch, a perfect mill, or a ship of the best possible construction? To give us an approximate solution to these problems, we need the experimental and practical geometry of several centuries, assisted by the most subtle theoretical geometry, I am convinced that it is impossible to obtain any satisfactory result when these types of geometry are kept separate, and that it is very difficult to do so even when they are combined.

Of the language of the arts. I have found the language of the arts to be very imperfect for two reasons: the scarcity of proper nomenclature and the frequency of synonyms. Some tools have several different names while others have only the generic name "engine" or "machine," without any additional name to distinguish them. At times an insignificant difference is enough to make artists invent specific names to substitute for the generic name. At other times a tool that is distinctive because of its form and use either has no name or is given the name of another tool with which it has nothing in common. One would wish for more attention to analogy of form and use. Geometers do not have as many names as they have figures, but in the arts a hammer, a pair of tongs, a bucket, a shovel, etc., have almost as many names as there are arts. A good part of the language changes from manufacture to manufacture. Yet I am convinced that the most unusual operations and the most complex machines could be explained by a rather small number of familiar, well-known terms, if it were decided to use technical terms only when they communicate a distinctive idea. What I am saying must carry conviction for anyone who considers that complex machines are only combinations of simple machines, that there are few simple machines, and that in the description of any operation all the movements can be reduced, without any significant error, to rectilinear and circular movements. It would be desirable if a good logician, well versed in the arts, undertook to describe the elements of a "grammar of the arts." For a first step he would have to determine the value of the correlatives "big," "large," "average," "thin," "thick," "slight," "small," "light," "heavy," etc. For this purpose one must seek a constant measure in nature or evaluate the height, width, and average force of man, and relate to it all indeterminate expressions of quantity, or at the least set up tables to which artists would be asked to make their language conform. The second step would be to decide on the differences and similarities between the form and the use of one instrument and another, between one operation and another, in order to determine when these should keep the same name and when they should be given different names. I do not doubt that anyone who undertakes this task will find it necessary to eliminate synonyms rather than to introduce new terms. I am also sure that it is more difficult to give a good definition of common terms, such as "elegance" in painting, "knot" in trimming, "hollow" in several arts, than it is to explain the most complicated machines. It is the lack of precise definitions and the great number, not the diversity, of movements in various operations that makes it difficult to speak clearly about the arts. The only remedy for the second problem is to familiarize oneself with the objects: they are well worth the trouble whether we think of the advantages they bring us or of the fact that they do honor to the human mind. In what physical or metaphysical system do we find more intelligence, discernment, and consistency than in the machines for drawing gold or making stockings, and in the frames of the braid-makers, the gauze-makers, the drapers, or the silk workers? What mathematical demonstration is more complicated than the mechanism of certain clocks or the different operations to which we submit the fiber of hemp or the chrysalis of the silkworm before obtaining a thread with which we can weave? What projection is more beautiful, more subtle, and more unusual than the projection of a design onto the threads of a simple[8] and from there onto the threads of a warp? What can conceivably be more subtle than the art of shadowing velvet? I could never enumerate all the marvels that amaze anyone who looks at factories, unless his eyes are closed by prejudice or stupidity.

I shall follow the example of the English philosopher and mention three inventions that were unknown to the ancients. It is to the shame of modern history and poetry that the names of their inventors are scarcely known. I am speaking of the art of printing, the discovery of gunpowder, and the properties of the magnetic needle. What a revolution these discoveries have brought about in the republic of letters, in military art, and in seafaring! The magnetic needle has led our

151

ships to the most remote regions, typographic characters have created enlightened communication between learned men of all countries and all future time, and gunpowder has occasioned all the architectural masterpieces that defend our frontiers as well as those of our enemies; these three arts have almost transformed the face of the earth.

Let us finally render artists the justice that is their due. The liberal arts have sung their own praise long enough; they should now raise their voice in praise of the mechanical arts. The liberal arts must free the mechanical arts from the degradation in which these have so long been held by prejudice, while royal protection must save them from the indigent state in which they still languish. The artisans have thought they deserved disdain because they were in fact disdained; let us teach them to think better of themselves, only then can we obtain more perfect products from them! We would wish that from the halls of the academies there would emerge a man who would go into the workshops, record everything noteworthy about the arts, and set it forth in a work that would induce the artists to read, the philosophers to think usefully, and the nobles to begin exercising their authority and their munificence in a useful manner.

If we may give some advice to learned men, we would suggest that they practice what they teach, namely not to judge too hastily nor to condemn an invention as useless because in its early stages it does not bring all the advantages that could be expected of it. If Montaigne, who in other ways was so much of a philosopher, returned among us, he would blush to have written that "firearms are so little effective, except in deafening our ears – to which everyone has become accustomed" that he hopes they will drop out of use.[9] Would he not have shown greater wisdom if he had encouraged the harquebusiers of his time to replace the match and wheel-lock by some machine activated by gunpowder? And would he not have shown more perspicacity if he had predicted that one day such a machine would be invented? Imagine Bacon in the place of Montaigne: you would see him study the nature of the agent and prophesy, if I may say so – grenades, mines, cannons, bombs, and the entire apparatus of military pyrotechnics. However, Montaigne is not the only philosopher who decided too hastily whether a machine is possible or impossible. Descartes, that extraordinary genius who was born both to confuse and to lead men, and many others, who were certainly the equals of the author of the *Essais*, maintained that the mirror of Archimedes[10] was a fiction. Yet this mirror is exhibited in the *Jardin du Roi* for all learned men to see. M. Buffon, who rediscovered it, is using it so successfully that we can no longer doubt the results which Archimedes is supposed to have achieved with it, on the walls of Syracuse. Such great examples suffice to render us circumspect.

On the other hand we invite the artists to take counsel with learned men and not to allow their discoveries to perish with them. The artists should know that to lock up a useful secret is to render oneself guilty of theft from society. It is just as despicable to prefer the interest of one individual to the common welfare in this case as in a hundred others where the artists themselves would not hesitate to decide for the common good. If they communicate their discoveries they will be freed of several preconceptions and especially of the illusion, which almost all of them hold, that their art has reached its ultimate perfection. Because they have so little learning they are often inclined to blame the nature of things for a defect that exists only in themselves. Obstacles seem insuperable to them whenever they do not know the means of overcoming them. Let them carry out experiments and let everyone make his contribution to these experiments: the artist should contribute his work, the academician his knowledge and advice, the rich man the cost of materials, labor, and time; soon our arts and our manufactures will be as superior as we could wish to those of other countries.

Of the superiority of one process of manufacture over another. But the superiority of one process over another will depend primarily on the quality of the materials used, together with the speed of work and the perfection of workmanship. The quality of the materials must be assured by inspection. As for the speed of work and the perfection of workmanship, they depend only on the number of workers brought together. When a process of manufacture employs many workers, each operation will be the responsibility of a different man. A particular workman will spend his lifetime performing one single operation; hence each operation is carried out quickly and well, and moreover the best-made product is also the cheapest. It is also true that when a great number of workers are assembled, taste and workmanship necessarily improve because there will be some who are able to reflect, put facts together, and discover the only way to surpass their fellow workers: they must economize on materials, make better use of time, or excel in inventiveness. This they can do by introducing either a new machine or a more practical process. If foreign industry does not surpass our manufacture in Lyon, it is not because our processes are unknown elsewhere; everywhere we find the same looms, the same silks, and more or less the same practices, but only in Lyon are there thirty thousand workers assembled, all working on the manufacture of the same material.

We could make this article even longer, but what we have already said suffices for those readers who know how to think, and we could never write an article long enough for the others. Perhaps in some places people will find our metaphysics too daring, but that was inevitable. We had to speak of art in general and, consequently, had to deal in generalizations. Good sense tells us, however, that the more general a proposition the more abstract it is, since abstraction consists in extending a truth by eliminating from its statement terms that particularize it. If only we could have spared the reader these thorny passages, we would have spared ourselves a great deal of work.

Notes

1   Diderot is quoting from Francis Bacon's Latin work *Novum Organum* (1620), which discusses, in a series of aphorisms, the methods of acquiring knowledge. In the aphorism here quoted (Book I, Aphorism LXXXIII) Bacon is quoting the common view that 'the dignity of the human mind is lowered by long and frequent intercourse with experiments and particulars'.

2   Jean-Baptiste Colbert (1619–83), Minister of Finance to Louis XIV, did a great deal to encourage French industry and technology and was instrumental in founding the French Academy of Sciences in 1666.

3   Charles le Brun (1619–90) and Eustache Le Sueur (1616–55) were painters; Gerard Audran (1640–1703) was an engraver who engraved many of their paintings.

4   'Therefore I am not dealing with opinion but with actual performance, and this provides the foundations, not of any sect or school, but rather of utility in general and huge possibilities of future development' (*Cogitata et Visa*, in *The Works of Francis Bacon*, ed. J. Spedding (Boston, 1863) VII, 140).

5   The steam engine was patented by Captain Thomas Savery in 1698.

6   The Latin is paraphrased by Diderot in the preceding sentence. It is from *Cogitata et Visa*, VII, 135.

7   Pierre Varignon (1654–1722), French mathematician, author of *Nouvelle mécanique et statique* (1725).

8   'One of a number of lines or cords attached to the warp in a draw-loom' *OED*.

9   Michel de Montaigne (1533–92), the great French essayist and humanist, made this remark in an essay entitled 'Des destries' (Of War-horses).

10   Archimedes (287–212 B.C.) of Syracuse was said to have constructed a burning mirror with which he destroyed Roman ships besieging his native city. The naturalist Buffon reconstructed the mirror in 1747 in the Royal Botanical Garden in Paris.

DIDEROT

The Stocking Machine (1751)

From Diderot, 'Bas' (ibid., Vol. 2, 1751). Reprinted from *Oeuvres complètes*, eds. J. Lough and J. Proust, Paris, 8 vols., 1975–77, Vol. 6. Translation by P. N. Furbank, 1978.

Diderot took a particular interest in the stocking-making machine and had a model of it which he could take apart and re-assemble, in his own study. His remark about the machine being 'one single and prolonged act of reason' of which the final product, the stocking, is the logical conclusion, resembles his comment in the article 'Art' comparing a complex machine to a philosophical system.

The complete article is enormously long, occupying some sixteen double-column folio pages and accompanied by many pages of illustration. Diderot, who had an extremely fertile and inventive mind, has evidently had the notion of constructing his article as though it were itself a machine – a very characteristic flight of fancy.

Stocking [. . .] The part of our clothing, which covers the legs; it is made of wool, leather, linen, cloth, cotton, floss-silk, silk. It is knitted with knitting-needle, or on a loom (for the first, see *Knitting*).

Here follows the description of stockings made on the loom [. . .]

The stocking-loom is one of the most complicated and the most rational and ingenious of all machines; one can regard it as one single and prolonged act of reason, of which the manufactured article is the logical conclusion; there is also such an interdependence between its parts that to remove a single one of them, or to change the shape of even the least apparently important of them, would be to wreck the whole mechanism.

It sprang from its inventor's hands[1] practically in its present state of perfection, and since this is a fact which adds to our amazement and admiration, I have decided to deal with it in its original form rather than its modern one, merely mentioning the minor differences between them as occasion demands.

It will be obvious, from what I have said about the interdependence of the parts of the stocking-loom, that one can hope for no understanding of the machine as a whole without going into minute detail of its parts; but these are so numerous that it might seem we should have to go beyond all practical limits, both in number of words and of plates. Besides how would one ever begin the description, or design the plates? The interdependence of the machine's various parts would seem to require one to talk about them, and illustrate them, all at the same time; and that is impossible – both in prose description, which has to be sequential (i.e. a matter of one thing after another), and in the plates, in which one working part will inevitably obscure the view of another.

These are apparently the difficulties which decided the useful and talented author of *The Spectacle of Nature*[2] not to include this admirable machine among those he described; he felt that he needed to say *all* about it or nothing; that it was not a machine that you could give any clear idea of without an enormous apparatus of plates and explanation; and so he has left us without any help on the subject.

I would like the reader, instead of being amazed at the length of the present article, to believe that we have spared no pains to make it as short as possible – as I hope he will realize when he considers that, within the space of a few pages, we have crammed a description not only of the working parts of the machine, but also of the function of its operator. These functions amount to very little; the machine does practically everything itself; which is a tribute to the perfection and delicacy of its mechanism. But there is no hope of understanding the mechanism without a thorough knowledge of its parts; and I dare affirm that, in a loom of the type that the workers call a 'Forty-two', there are at least two thousand five hundred parts. Of these, many would be similar; and whereas these are less of a problem for the mind, since they perform the same operation, they are very inconvenient to illustrate, since one inevitably masks another.

To overcome these obstacles we have decided to pursue a kind of analysis or dissection, dividing the machine up into a number of separate assemblages, showing beneath the picture of each assemblage the parts which are not clearly seen in it, combining these assemblages progressively, and thus building up the complete machine. In this manner one passes from a simple assemblage to a compound one, and from that to a more compound one, so arriving finally, without obscurity or fatigue, at a very complicated whole.

With this in view, we divide the stocking-loom into two parts: the frame or the wooden parts which support the loom, and which feature in the worker's operations; and the loom proper, or the metal parts and others which make it up.

We shall treat each of these parts separately. But before going into detail, we will quote the opinion expressed about this machine by a man who well knows how to value our modern inventions. Here is how M. Perrault[3] speaks of it in a book which pleases us in proportion to our lack of prejudices. 'Those who have the capacity, not to invent such things, but merely to understand them fall into amazement at the sight of the almost innumerable working parts of which the stocking-loom is composed, and the number of their different and extraordinary movements. When one watches someone knitting a stocking, one is impressed by the suppleness and dexterity of his hands, though he is only making a single stitch at a time. What is one to think when one beholds a machine which makes hundreds of stitches at once – that is to say, which performs in a minute all the various movements that human hands can only perform in many hours? What a number of little springs pull the silk towards themselves, then release it, in order to take hold of it a second time, and make it pass from one stitch to another in a manner quite inexplicable? And all this, without the workman himself understanding, or knowing, or even having the remotest picture of, what is happening. In which one might compare it to the most perfect machine that God ever made . . . '

Notes
1   It is not certain to whom the article is referring here; possibly William Lee, a curate of Calverton, near Nottingham, who in 1589 invented a mechanical knitting-machine or 'stocking-frame' which he introduced into France (and which was re-introduced there under Colbert later) and which has been described as the 'ancestor' of the stocking-loom of the eighteenth century.
     Stockings, only invented in the sixteenth century, and for some time an expensive luxury, became the rage in the eighteenth century, and both mechanical and hand-knitting became a large-scale industry.
2   *Le Spectacle de la Nature* (1732) by Abbé Noël Antoine Pluche.
3   Presumably Claude Perrault (1613–88), physician, architect and designer of the colonnade of the Louvre. He published a useful *Recueil de Machines*.

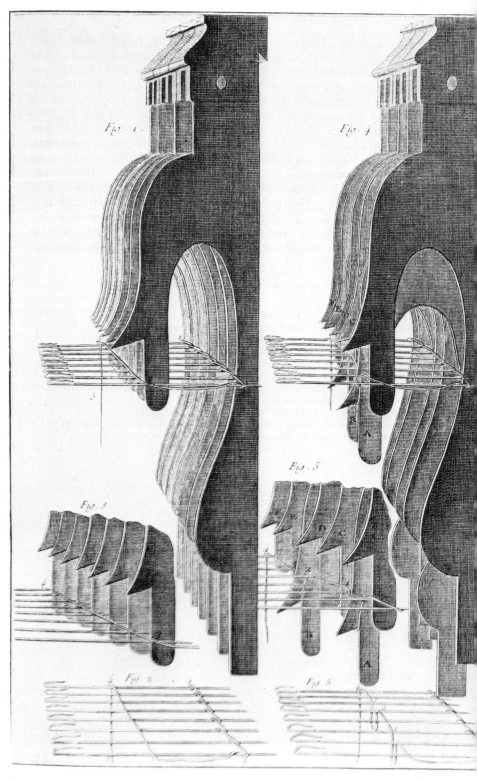

Plate 25   from *Encyclopédie*   The Stocking Machine

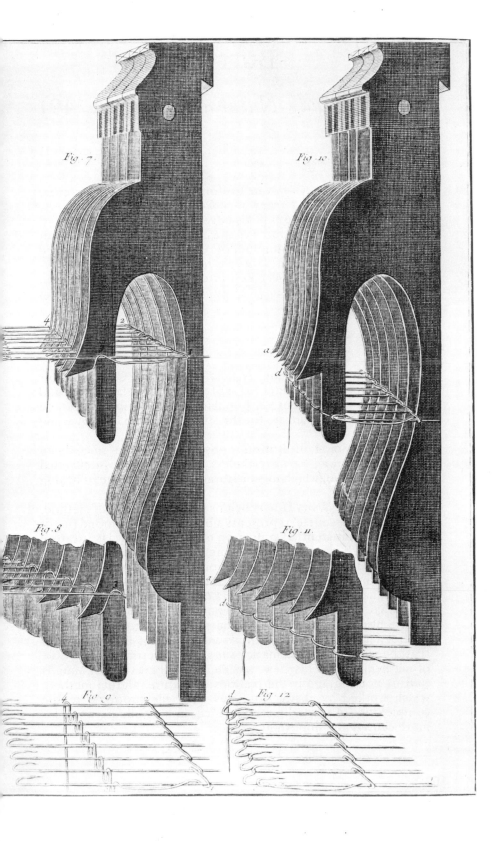

BUFFON

How to Study Natural History (1749)

From G. L. Leclerc, Comte de Buffon, *Histoire naturelle, générale et particulière, avec la description du cabinet du roi*, de L'imprimerie Royale, à Paris, 1749–67. [This covers the first fifteen volumes. The publication of the full work, which finally ran to forty-four volumes and involved a number of other writers, was completed in 1803.] *Premier Discours: De la manière d'étudier et de traiter l'Histoire naturelle* (ibid., Vol. 1, 1749). Reprinted from a translation by John Lyon in *Journal of the History of Biology*, Vol. 9, no. 1; D. Reidel 1976.

The great, many-volume *Natural History* of Georges-Louis Leclerc, Comte de Buffon (1701–88) presented the facts of natural history in a comprehensive, popular and intelligible form, and successfully created a taste for the study of Nature in France and elsewhere.

Although some of Buffon's observations have since been proved inaccurate, he nevertheless established the intellectual framework within which most naturalists worked in the following century.

How to Study Natural History begins with a discussion of method. This 'Initial Discourse' represents a brilliant and profound (if not altogether consistent) examination of the nature of classificatory systems. Such systems are fundamental to the study of natural history, and much of Buffon's discourse is devoted to attacking what he considered the hopeless inadequacies of the system of the Swedish naturalist Carl Linnaeus (1707–78). (Posterity has been somewhat kinder to Linnaeus's reputation than Buffon was.)

The discourse also gives strong expression to what may be regarded as the heart of Buffon's scientific message, which was that the science of mathematics was grossly overrated. The whole of mathematics, in his view, was an artificial creation of Man. It told us nothing about the realities of Nature, and its method, which worked by abstraction, was quite inappropriate to the complexities of natural history, which, in his opinion, was a far more central and important science.

Natural history, taken in its fullest extent, is an immense subject. It embraces all objects which the universe displays to us. This prodigious multitude of quadrupeds, birds, fishes, insects, plants, minerals, etc., offers to the curiosity of the human mind a vast spectacle, the totality of which is so grand that it appears, and indeed is, inexhaustible in its details. A single division of natural history, such as the history of insects, or the history of plants, is vast enough to occupy the attention of many men. The objects which these particular branches of natural history present are so multitudinous that the most capable observers, after many years' work, have given only very imperfect rough outlines of those branches to which they have been singly devoted. However, they have done all that they were capable of doing. And, far from blaming these observers for the trifling advancement of the science to which their work has been devoted, one could not give them too much praise for their assiduity and patience. It is impossible to deny that they possess the very highest qualities, for it takes a peculiar kind of genius and courage of spirit to be able to envisage nature in the innumerable multitude of its productions without losing one's orientation, and to believe oneself capable of understanding and comparing such productions. It takes a particular predilection to love these things, a predilection beyond that which has as its goal only particular objects. For it can be said that the love of the study of nature supposes two qualities of mind which are apparently in opposition to each other: the grand view of the ardent genius who takes in everything at a glance, and the detailed attention of an instinct which concentrates laboriously on a single minute detail.

The first obstacle encountered in the study of natural history comes from this great multiplicity of objects. But the variety of these same objects, and the difficulty of bringing together the various productions of different climates, is another apparently insurmountable obstacle to the advancement of our understanding, an obstacle which in fact work alone is unable to surmount. It is only by dint of time, care, expenditure of money, and often by lucky accidents, that one is able to obtain well-preserved specimens of each species of animal, plant, or mineral, and thus form a well-ordered collection of all the works of nature.

But when specimens of everything that inhabits the earth have been collected; when, after much difficulty, examples of all things that are found scattered so profusely on the earth have been brought together in one location; and when for the first time this storehouse filled with things diverse, new, and strange is viewed, the first sensation that results is bewilderment, mixed with admiration. And the initial reflection that follows is a humbling return to oneself. It seems unimaginable that, even with time, one could come to the point of distinguishing all these different objects, or that one could succeed not only in distinguishing them by their form, but further by knowing all that pertains to the birth, the generation, the organization, the habits – in a word, all that pertains to the history of each thing in particular.

161

However, as these objects become familiar, after they have been seen often and, so to speak, without any plan, they slowly create lasting impressions, which are soon bound together in our mind by fixed and invariable relationships. And, despite ourselves, we construct more general views by which we are able to embrace at one and the same time many different objects. And it is thus that we find ourselves in a position to undertake disciplined study, to reflect fruitfully, and to open up for ourselves routes by which we may arrive at useful discoveries.

Thus, a beginning should be made by observing things often and by frequently re-examining them. However necessary attention to the whole may be, here, at the beginning, one may dispense with this responsibility: I mean that scrupulous attention which is always useful when a great number of things are undertaken, and often detrimental to those who are beginning to learn natural history. The essential thing is to fill the heads of such beginners with ideas and facts, and thus prevent them, if possible, from prematurely establishing schemata. For it always happens that through ignorance of certain facts and through a limited stock of ideas, such neophytes use up their energy in false combinations, and load their memories with vague consequences and results contrary to truth, which form in the sequel preconceptions that are difficult to erase.

In order to avoid such shortsightedness, I have said that it is necessary to begin the study of nature by very broad observation. And it is also necessary that this observation be almost at random. For if you have resolved to consider things only from a certain point of view, or in a certain order, or in a certain system, although you may have taken the best road, you will never arrive at the same breadth of knowledge to which you might lay claim if, at the outset, you allowed your mind to follow its own lead, to get to know itself, to acquire a degree of certainty without extraneous assistance, and to fashion by itself the first chain of connections which depicts the order of its ideas.

This is true without exception for all persons of mature mind and disciplined intellect. Young people, on the contrary, ought to be guided and advised in these matters. It is even necessary to encourage them by means of that which is most stimulating in science, by calling their attention to the most remarkable things without giving to such things any precise explication. For the mysterious, at that age, excites curiosity, whereas at a mature age it would only inspire aversion. The young easily lose interest in things which they have already seen. They review things with indifference unless they are presented with these same things from other points of view. And instead of simply repeating to them what has already been said, it is better to add other details, even strange or useless ones. Less is lost by deceiving them than by disgusting them.

After having seen and reviewed things many times, the young will begin to describe such things in a comprehensive way, and of them-selves make divisions and perceive general distinctions. At this point the taste for science may be born, and one should step in and assist the birth. This enthusiasm, so necessary for all things yet so hard to come by, cannot be supplied by precepts. In vain would education wish to provide it; in vain do parents compel their children to learn it. Such efforts will lead only to that end common to all men, that is, to that degree of intelligence and memory which suffices for social life or ordinary affairs. But it is to nature that one ought to ascribe that initial spark of genius, that first hint of interest, of which we speak, which subsequently develops in various directions contingent upon various circumstances and purposes. In addition, the minds of young people ought to be presented with things of all kinds, with all manner of studies, and with objects of all sorts, so that they might be able to recognize the type toward which their mind tends with greater inclination, or to which they would devote themselves with greater pleasure. For its part, natural history ought to be presented to them precisely at that time when their reason is beginning to develop, or at that age when they might begin to think that they already know quite a bit. Nothing is more apt to lessen their conceit and make them feel how much there is that they are ignorant of. And, independently of this initial result, which cannot but be useful, even a slight study of natural history will elevate their ideas and give them a knowledge of an infinity of things of which the common man is ignorant and which are often encountered in the course of life.

But let us return to the man who would apply himself seriously to the study of nature, and take up again a consideration of the subject at the point at which we let it drop, namely, at the point at which the adept begins to generalize ideas and to form for himself a method of arrangement and systems of explication. It is at this point that he should consult those who are proficient in the field, read solid authors, examine their various methods, and borrow insights wherever he comes upon them. But since it ordinarily happens that one is easily carried away at this point by his affection and taste for certain authors, or for a certain method, and that often, without a sufficiently mature examination, it is easy to adopt a system which is sometimes ill-conceived, it is proper that we give here several preliminary notions about the methods that have been devised in order to facilitate a knowledge of natural history. These methods are very useful, when applied with appropriate restrictions. They shorten the work, assist the memory, and offer to the mind a series of ideas composed indeed of objects which differ among themselves but which nevertheless have certain common relations. These common relations then form stronger impressions than would be the case with discrete objects which have no connection among themselves. Therein lies the utility of the various methods. But the disadvantage here is the tendency to overextend or to unduly constrict the chain of connections, to wish to subject the laws of nature to arbitrary laws, to wish to divide this chain where it is not divisible, and to wish to measure its strength by means of our weak imagination. Another drawback which is no less serious, and which is the contrary of the one just described, is the temptation to restrict oneself to a regime of overly-detailed methods, and thus to wish to judge of the whole by a single instance, to reduce nature to the status of petty systems which are foreign to her, and, from her immense works, to fashion arbitrarily just as many unconnected assemblages of data as there are petty systems. The final disadvantage of such methods is that, in multiplying names and systems, they make the language of science more difficult than science itself.

We are naturally led to imagine that there is a kind of order and uniformity throughout nature. And when the works of nature are only cursorily examined, it appears at first that she has always worked upon the same plan. Since we ourselves know only one way of arriving at a conclusion, we persuade ourselves that nature creates and carries out everything by the same means and by similar operations. This manner of thinking causes us to invent an infinity of false connections between the things nature produces. Plants have been compared with animals, and minerals have been supposedly observed to vegetate. Their quite different organization and their quite distinct means of operation have often been reduced to the same form. The common matrix of these things so unlike each other lies less in nature than in the narrow mind of those who have poorly conceived her, and who know as little about appraising the strength of a fact as they do about the proper limits of comparative analogy. For example, since blood circulates, must it be asserted that the sap of plants circulates also? Or should it be concluded that there is a growth in minerals like that known in plants? Is it proper to proceed from the movement of the blood to that of the sap, and from that to the movement of the petrifying juice?[1] Isn't what we are doing in these cases only bringing the abstractions of our limited mind to bear upon the reality of the works of the Creator, and granting to him, so to speak, only such ideas as we possess on the matter? Nevertheless, such poorly founded statements have been made and are repeated every day. Systems are constructed upon uncertain facts which have never been examined, and which only go to show the penchant men have for wishing to find resemblances between most disparate objects, regularity where variety reigns, and order among those things which they perceive only in a confused manner.

For, when not stopping at superficial knowledge – which only gives us incomplete ideas of the productions and methods of nature – we wish to penetrate further and examine more meticulously the form and behavior of nature's works, it is surprising what variety of design, and what a multiplicity of means we see. The number of the productions of nature, however prodigious, is only the least of our astonishment. Nature's mechanism, art, resources, even its confusion, fill us with admiration. Dwarfed before that immensity, overwhelmed by the number of wonders, the human mind staggers. It appears that all that might be, actually is. The hand of the Creater does not appear to be opened in order to give existence to a certain limited number of species. Rather, it appears as if it might have cast into existence all at once a world of beings some of whom are related to each other, and some not; a world of infinite combinations, some harmonious and some opposed; a world of perpetual destruction and renewal. What an impression of power this spectacle offers us! What sentiments of respect this view of the universe inspires in us for its Author! And what would be the case in this regard if the weak light which guides us became sufficiently keen to allow us to perceive the general order of causes and of the dependence of effects? But the greatest mind, the most powerful genius, will never lift itself to such a pinnacle of knowledge. The first causes of things will remain ever hidden from us, and the general results of these causes will remain as difficult for us to know as the causes themselves. All that is given to us is to perceive certain particular effects, to compare these with each other, to combine them, and, finally, to recognize therein more of an order appropriate to *our* own nature than one pertaining to the existence of the things which we are considering.

But seeing that this is the only route open to us, and since we have no other means of arriving at a knowledge of the things of nature, it is necessary to follow that route as far as it can lead us. We must gather together all the objects, compare them, study them, and extract from the totality of their connections all the insights which may be able to assist us to see them clearly and to know them better.

The first truth which issues from this serious examination of nature is a truth which perhaps humbles man. This truth is that he ought to classify himself with the animals, to whom he bears resemblance by everything he has that is material. The instinct of animals will perhaps appear to man even more certain than his own reason, and their industry more admirable than his arts. Then, examining successively and by order the various objects which compose the universe, and placing himself at the head of all created beings, man will see with astonishment that it is possible to descend by almost imperceptible degrees[2] from the most perfect of creatures to the most formless matter, from the most perfectly formed animal to the most amorphous mineral. He will recognize that these imperceptible nuances are the great work of nature, and will find them not only in the size and shape of things, but in the changes, productions, and successions of the whole species.

In thoroughly studying this idea, one sees clearly that it is impossible to establish one general system, one perfect method, not only for the whole of natural history, but even for one of its branches. For in order to make a system, an arrangement – in a word, a general method – it is necessary that everything be taken in by it. It is necessary to divide the whole under consideration into different classes,[3] apportion these classes into genera, subdivide these genera into species, and to do all this following a principle of arrangement in which there is of necessity an element of arbitrariness. But nature proceeds by unknown gradations, and, consequently, it is impossible to describe her with full accuracy by such divisions, since she passes from one species to another, and often from one genus to another, by imperceptible nuances. As a result, one finds a great number of intermediate species and mixed objects which it is impossible to categorize and which necessarily upset the project of a general system. This truth is too important for me not to insist on whatever makes it clear and evident.

Take botany, for example, that admirable part of natural history which, by virtue of its utility, has deserved at all times to be the most cultivated. Let us call to mind the principles of all methods which botanists have given us. We shall see with some surprise that they have always had in view the aim of comprehending in their methods generally all species of plants, and that none of them have been completely successful. It always turns out that, in each of these methods, a certain number of plants must be considered anomalous, their species falling between two genera; and it has been impossible to categorize them, because there is no more reason to ascribe them to the one genus than to the other. Indeed, to propose to devise a perfect system is to propose an impossibility. It would necessitate a work which would represent exactly all the works of nature. But, contrary to such hopes, it always happens that, despite all known methods and despite any assistance which can be had from the most enlightened system of botany, species are constantly being discovered which it is not possible to assimilate to any of the genera posited by such systems. Experience accords with reason on this point, and one ought to be convinced that it is not possible to design a general and perfect system in botany. However, it appears that the search for such a general system may be the search for a kind of "philosopher's stone"[4] for botanists, a search which they have pursued with infinite pains and infinite labor. Some have taken forty years, and some fifty, in the creation of their systems, and what has happened in botany is the same as what has happened in chemistry, namely, that in the pursuit of the philosopher's stone – which has not been found – an infinite number of useful things have been discovered. Thus, from wishing to design a general and perfect system in botany, plants and their usages have been studied in more detail and have come to be better known. In this respect it is true that men need an imaginary goal in order to sustain them in their work. For if they had been persuaded that they would do only what in effect they are capable of doing, they would do nothing at all.

This proclivity which botanists have for establishing general systems with pretensions of perfection and methodological rigor is thus poorly founded. Consequently, their labors deliver to us only defective systems which have been successively destroyed, the one by the other, and have undergone the common fate of all systems founded on arbitrary principles. And what has contributed the most to this process of successive destruction is the freedom which botanists have allowed themselves of choosing arbitrarily a single feature of plants as a distinguishing characteristic. Some have established their method on the basis of the configuration of leaves; others on their position; others on the form of the flowers; some on the number of flower petals; others, finally, on the basis of the number of stamens. I would never finish if I wished to report in detail all the systems which have been imagined. But at the present time I wish to speak only of those systems which have had a good reception and have been followed, each in its turn, without sufficient attention having been given to that erroneous principle which all these systems share, namely, the desire to judge a whole or a combination of many wholes on the basis of a single part, and by comparing the differences of such single parts. For to desire to discern the differences of plants using solely the configurations of their leaves or their flowers as criteria is as if one set out to discern the differences between animals by means of the variations in their skins or generative organs. For who does not see that whatever proceeds in such a manner cannot be considered a science. It is at the very most only a convention, an arbitrary language, a means of mutual understanding. But no real cognizance of things can result from it.

Might I be permitted to speak my mind upon the origin of these various systems and upon the causes which have multiplied them to the point that botany itself is actually easier to apprehend than the nomenclature which is merely its language? May I be permitted to say that it would be preferable for a man to have engraved in his memory the forms of all plants and have clear ideas of them, which is what botany really is, than to memorize all the names which the various systems give to these plants, as a result of which scientific terminology has become more difficult than science itself? Here, then, is how it appears to me that this state of affairs has arisen. In the first place, the members of the plant kingdom were divided according to their various sizes. There are, after this fashion, large trees, small trees, shrubby trees, bushes, large plants, small plants, and herbs. This is the foundation of a classification which itself has subsequently been divided and subdivided according to other relations of size and form in order to give each species a particular character. After classification according to this plan, some people come along who have examined such a distribution, and who say that this method based on the relative size of plants cannot be maintained, for there are within the same species, such as that of the oaks, great variation in sizes. There are some kinds of oak which rise a hundred feet in height, and others which never grow more than two feet tall. The same is true, allowance being made, of chestnuts, pines, aloes, and of an infinity of other kinds of plants. Thus it is said that the genus of plants ought not be determined by their size, since this distinction is equivocal and uncertain. And, with reason, this method is then abandoned. Next, others have appeared on the scene who, believing they can do better, have said that in order to know plants it is necessary to stick to the most obvious parts of them. And, since the leaves are the most obvious feature, one should arrange plants according to the form, size, and position of the leaves. Thus one becomes familiar with another scheme or method, and follows it for a while. But then it becomes evident that the leaves of almost all plants vary prodigiously with age and terrain, that their form is no more constant than their size, and that their position is still more uncertain. Thus this method proves no more

167

satisfactory than the preceding one. Finally, someone imagined –
Gesner,[5] I believe – that the Creator had put in the structure of plants a
certain number of different and unvariable characters, and that it was
on this assumption that one ought to try to create a system. And, since
this idea turns out to be true, up to a point, in that the organs of
generation of plants are found to have some unique features more
constantly than all the other organs of the plant taken separately, there
have suddenly arisen many systems of botany, each founded nearly
upon the same principle. Among these methods that of M. de
Tournefort[6] is the most remarkable, the most ingenious, and the most
complete. This illustrious botanist was aware of the shortcomings of a
system which would be purely arbitrary. As a man of intellect, he
avoided the absurdities which are found in most of the other systems of
his contemporaries, and he made his allocations and his exceptions
with boundless knowledge and skill. In a word, he had put botany in a
position to do without other methods, and he had made it capable of a
certain degree of perfection. But there arose another methodologist[7]
who, after having praised de Tournefort's system, tried to destroy it in
order to establish his own. This same person, having adopted with M. de
Tournefort the distinguishing characteristics drawn from fructi-
fication, then employed all the organs of generation of plants, and
above all the stamens, for the purpose of dividing his genera. Holding in
contempt the wise concern of M. de Tournefort not to push nature to
the point of confusing, for the sake of his system, the most various
objects – like trees and herbs – he put together in the same class the
mulberry and the nettle, the tulip and the barberry, the elm and the
carrot, the rose and the strawberry, the oak and the bloodwort. Now,
isn't this to make sport of nature and of those who study her? And if all
that classification were not given with a certain appearance of mysterious order and wrapped up in Greek and botanical erudition, would
one be long in perceiving the ridiculousness of such a system, or rather
in pointing out the confusion which results from such a bizarre
assemblage? But that is not all; and I am going to persist in this
assertion, because it is proper to preserve for M. de Tournefort the
glory which he merited by his sensitive and persistent labor, and
because it is not necessary that those who have learned botany
according to de Tournefort's system should waste their time studying
that new system wherein everything is changed, even to the names and
surnames of plants. I say, then, that this recent method which brings
together in the same class genera of plants which are entirely dissimilar,
has, furthermore, independently of its incongruities, essential shortcomings and drawbacks greater than all the methods which have
preceded it. As the characters of the genera come to be set by
distinctions almost infinitely small, it becomes necessary to proceed to
the identification of a tree or plant with a microscope in one's hand. The
size, the form, the external appearance, the leaves, all the obvious
features are useless for purposes of identification. Nothing is important
except the stamens, and if one is unable to see the stamens, one can do

nothing, one has seen nothing of significance. This large tree which you see is perhaps only a bloodwort. It is necessary to count its stamens in order to know what it is, and, since its stamens are often so small that they escape the naked eye or the magnifying glass, one must have a microscope. But unfortunately for this system there are plants which do not have stamens. There are also plants in which the number of stamens varies, and therein lies the shortcoming of this method of classification, just as in the others, in spite of the magnifying glass and microscope.[1]

After this frank exposition of the bases upon which the various systems of botany have been constructed, it is easy to see that the great shortcoming here is a metaphysical error in the very principle of such systems. This error involves disregarding the progression of nature, which is always a matter of nuances, and wishing to judge the whole by a single part. This is a manifest error, and one that it is astonishing to find so widespread. For almost all who have systematically named things have employed only a single feature, such as the teeth, the claws, or the spurs, as a means of classifying animals, and the leaves or the flowers in classifying plants, rather than making use of all parts of the organism, and searching out the differences and similarities of complete individual specimens. To refuse to make use of all the features of objects which we are considering is to voluntarily renounce the greatest number of advantages which nature offers us as a means of knowing her. And even if one were assured of finding constant and invariable characters in the several parts taken by themselves, it would not be necessary to restrict thus the knowledge of the productions of nature to a knowledge of these constant characters, which only give particular and very imperfect ideas of the whole organism. And it appears to me that the sole means of constructing an instructive and natural system is to put together whatever is similar and to separate those things which differ. If the individual entities resemble each other exactly, or if the differences between them are so small that they can be perceived only with difficulty, such individuals will be of the same species. If the differences begin to be perceptible, while at the same time there are always many more similarities than differences, such individuals will be of different species, but of the same genus. And if the differences are even more marked, without however exceeding the resemblances, then such individuals will be not only of another species, but even of another genus than the first and the second instances, but of the same class, for they resemble each other more than they differ. But if, on the contrary, the differences exceed the similarities, such individuals are not even of the same class. This is the systematic order which ought to be followed in arranging the productions of nature. Certainly the similarities and

---

1 This system, indeed, namely Linnaeus's, is not only far more vile and inferior to the already known systems, but is further exceedingly forced, slippery, and fallacious; indeed, I would consider it childish, for it only brings after itself enormous confusion with regard to the division and denomination of plants, but it is also to be feared that from this would come an almost complete clouding and disruption of the more solid botanical systems.

differences will be taken not only from one feature but from the whole organism. And likewise this method of inspection will be brought to bear on form, size, external bearing, upon the various parts, upon their number and position, even upon the substance of the thing. Similarly, these elements will be used in large or small number as the occasion necessitates. And these principles will be applied in such a way that if an individual specimen, whatever its nature may be, is so singular as to be always recognizable at first sight, it will be given but one name. But if this specimen has a form in common with another, and differs constantly from it in size, color, substance, or by any other obviously sensible quality, then it is given the same name as the other, to which is added an adjective to mark the difference. And thus one proceeds, putting in as many adjectives as there are differences. By this means one will be certain to express the various attributes of each species, and there need be no fear of falling into the inconveniences of the too restricted methods of which we have spoken, and about which we have discoursed at length. This is so because of a common shortcoming of all systems of botany and natural history and because the systems which have been devised for animals are even more defective than the systems of botany. For, as we have already hinted, there has been a desire to pronounce on the resemblance and difference of animals by employing in such proceedings only the number of fingers or claws, of teeth and breasts – a project which greatly resembles that of recognition by stamens, and which is in effect of the same author.

It follows from all that we have just set forth that, in the study of natural history, there are two equally dangerous positions: the first is to have no system at all, and the second is to try to convert everything to a restricted system. In the great number of persons who currently apply themselves to this science there could be found striking examples of these two approaches, so opposed to each other and yet both equally vicious. Most of those who, without any prior study of natural history, wish to have collections of this sort are people of leisure with little to occupy their time otherwise, who are looking for amusement, and regard being placed in the ranks of the curious as an achievement. Such persons start out by purchasing indiscriminately everything that catches their eye. They appear to passionately desire whatever they have been told is rare and extraordinary. They esteem the things they have acquired in terms of the price which they paid for them. They arrange their collection with smugness, or stack things up confusedly; and they soon end by being sick of the whole thing. Those who take the other approach, however (and these are more erudite), after having filled their heads with names, phrases, and restricted systems, come finally to adopt one of these methods, or else busy themselves with creating a new one. They thus labor all their life upon one particular approach and in a false direction, and, desiring to bring everything to their particular point of view, they restrict their minds, cease to see things as they really are, and end by embarrassing science and loading it with the burden of ideas which have nothing to do with science.

Thus, one ought not regard as fundamental to science the methods that these authors have given us concerning natural history in general or those designed for one of its parts. Such methods should be used only as systems of artificial signs which are agreed upon for purposes of mutual understanding. Actually, they are only arbitrary connections and differing points of view under which the objects of nature have been considered. Only making use of such methods in this spirit is it possible to draw from them some usefulness. For although it may not appear very necessary, it might be good if one knew all species of plants whose leaves resemble each other, all those whose flowers look alike, all those which may nourish certain kinds of insects, all those which have a given number of stamens, and all those which have certain excretory glands. The same is true of animals: there might be a point in knowing all animals which have a given number of digits. To speak precisely, each of these methods is only a dictionary in which one may find names arranged according to an order derived from a certain idea, and, consequently, arranged as arbitrarily as the alphabetical. But the advantage which may be had from such arrangements is that, in comparing all the results, one may finally come across the true method, which involves the complete description and exact history of each particular thing.

Here is the principal goal which must be kept in mind: A pre-fabricated method can be used as a convenience for studying, but it should be regarded as a means of mutual understanding. The sole true means of advancing natural science is to labor at the description and history of the various things which are its objects.

Things, in themselves, have no existence for us; nor does giving them a name call them into existence. But they begin to exist for us when we become acquainted with their relations to each other and their properties. Yet even by means of their relations we are unable to give things a definition. Now, a definition such as we can construct verbally is still no more than a very imperfect representation of the thing, and we are never able adequately to define a thing without describing it exactly. This difficulty of forming an adequate definition is found constantly in all systems and in all the epitomes which have been attempted in order to relieve the burden on the memory. It must also be said that in the things of nature nothing is well-defined but that which is exactly described. Now, in order to describe exactly, it is necessary to have seen, reviewed, examined, and compared the thing which one wishes to describe. And it is necessary to do all this without prejudging things and without an eye to systematization. Otherwise the description would not have the character of truth, which is the only characteristic called for. Even the style of the description ought to be simple, clear, and measured. The nature of the enterprise does not allow of grandeur of style, of charm, even less of digressions, pleasantries, or equivocation. The sole adornment permitted is nobility of expression, of choice, and of propriety in the use of terms.

Of the great number of authors who have written on natural history, very few have written well. To depict things simply and clearly, without changing or oversimplifying them, and without adding anything to them from one's imagination, is a talent all the more praiseworthy the less it is paraded about; a talent which is only to be felt in a small number of persons who are capable of the particular attention necessary in order to pursue things in their finest details. Nothing is more common than works encumbered with numerous and desiccated nomenclature or with tedious and hardly natural methods which such authors think will bring them renown. Nothing is so rare as to discover exactitude in descriptions, novelty in details, and subtlety in observations.

Aldrovandi,[8] the most hard-working and knowledgeable of all naturalists, after sixty years of labor has left behind his immense volumes on natural history, which have been printed successively, most of them after his death. They could be reduced to one tenth their present size if all those things which are useless and foreign to the subject were removed. Except for this prolixity (which, I confess, is overwhelming), his books ought to be considered the best contribution to the whole spectrum of natural history that there is. The plan of his work is good, his distributions show discretion, the divisions are well demarcated, and his descriptions are quite exact – monotonous, to be sure, but accurate. Historically he is less adequate, often mixing in the fabulous and giving evidence of quite a penchant for credulity.

In going over Aldrovandi's works I have been struck by a fault, or rather an excess, which is almost always found in books printed one or two hundred years ago, and which still characterizes the German scholar today. I refer to the vast amount of useless erudition with which they purposively stuff their works, such that the subject which they treat is drowned in an ocean of foreign matter over which they argue with such self-satisfaction and carry on with so little consideration for the readers that they appear to have forgotten what it was they had to say to you, telling you only what others have said on the matter. It appears to me that a man like Aldrovandi, having once conceived the plan of outlining the whole of natural history, sits in his library and reads one after the other the Ancients, the Moderns, the philosophers, the theologians, the jurists, the historians, the explorers, and the poets; and he reads them without any other end than that of seizing upon all the words and phrases which are directly or distantly related to his object. He himself copies and has others copy down all these remarks, arranges them alphabetically, and, after having filled several portfolios with notes of all kinds – often taken without scrutiny or discretion – he begins to work on a particular subject, wishing to let nothing that he has gathered go unused. Thus, when writing a natural history of cocks or oxen, he tells you everything that has ever been said about cocks or oxen, everything the Ancients have thought about them, everything that has been imagined about their qualities, their character, their courage; all the things they have been used for; all the old wives' tales about them; all the miracles attributed to them in various religions; all the superstitious stories they have occasioned; all the comparisons poets have drawn from them; all the attributes which certain people have ascribed to them; all the representations of them found in hieroglyphics or on coats-of-arms – in a word, all the stories and all the fables which have ever been noticed about cocks or oxen. How much natural history can one expect to find in this hodge-podge of writing? Indeed, if the author had not put natural history into some articles separated from others, the natural history would not be discoverable, or at least not worth the pain of searching for.

This particular failing has been completely eliminated in this century. The order and precision which characterizes present writing has made the sciences more pleasant and easy to come by, and I am persuaded that this difference of style contributes perhaps as much to their advancement as the spirit of research which reigns today. For our predecessors searched as we do, but they gathered everything that they happened upon, whereas we reject that which appears to us to have little value. And we prefer a closely reasoned brief work to a huge volume of miscellaneous scholarship. One thing is to be feared in this connection, however, and this is that, coming to distrust erudition, we may also come to imagine that the mind is able to provide everything and that science is only an empty name.

Sensible people will nevertheless always feel that the sole true science is the knowledge of facts. The mind itself is unable to provide this, and facts are in the sciences what experience is in ordinary life. The sciences might thus be divided into two principal classes which would contain all that is suitable for man to know. The first class encompasses the history of man in society, and the second, natural history. Both are founded upon facts which it is often important and always pleasant to know. The first is the study of statesmen, and the second that of philosophers. And although the usefulness of the latter may not be as immediate as that of the former, it is certain that natural history is the source of the other physical sciences and the mother of all the arts. How many excellent medical remedies have been taken from certain productions of nature previously unknown! Furthermore, all the ideas of the arts have their models in the productions of nature. God created, and man imitates. All the inventions of men, whether they be necessities or conveniences, are only grossly executed imitations of that which nature makes with the utmost finesse.

But without insisting at further length on the utility that may be drawn from natural history, whether in connection with other sciences or in connection with the arts, let us return to our main object, the manner of studying and expounding natural history. The precise description and the accurate history of each thing is, as we have said, the sole end which ought to be proposed initially. So far as the description is concerned, one ought to show form, size, weight, colors, positions of rest and of movement, location of organs, their connections, their shape, their action, and all external functions. If there could be joined to all this an exposition of internal organs, the description would be all the more complete. But care must be taken against losing one's way in such a number of petty details or dwelling too long on some organs of minor importance, while considering too lightly the main and essential things. The history ought to follow the description, and it ought to treat only relations which the things of nature have among themselves and with us. The history of an animal ought to be not only the history of the individual, but that of the entire species. It ought to include their conception, the time of gestation, their birth, the number of young, the care shown by the parents, their sort of education, their instinct, the places where they live, their nourishment and their manner of procuring it, their customs, their instinctual cleverness, their hunting, and, finally, the services which they can render to us and all the uses which we can make of them. And when any of the internal organs of an animal are worthy of note, whether because of their striking configuration or because of the uses to which they might be put, they ought to be added either to the description or to the history of the species. But it would be foreign to the purposes of natural history to enter into a very circumstantial anatomical examination. At least, this is not its principal object. These details should be reserved for some memoirs on comparative anatomy.

This general plan ought to be followed and completed with all possible exactness. And in order to avoid falling into monotonous repetitions the form of descriptions ought to be varied and the thread of history changed as it appears necessary. And, likewise, for the sake of making descriptions less dry, it is wise to blend into them facts, comparisons, and reflections upon the uses of various organs – in a word, to write so that you can be read without boredom as well as without contention.

With regard to the general order and the method of distribution of the various subjects of natural history, this could be considered purely arbitrary. Consequently, one is certainly free to choose what seems either the most convenient or the most commonly accepted. But before giving reasons which would lead to the adoption of one system rather than another, it is still necessary to make a few reflections by means of which we shall try to make the reader aware of how far the divisions which we have made of natural productions correspond to reality.

In order to recognize this we must dismantle our prejudices for a moment and even abstract from our ideas. Let us imagine a man who indeed has forgotten everything, or who awakens to completely strange surroundings. Let us set this man in a field where animals, birds, fishes, plants, and stones appear successively to his eyes. This man, upon first perceiving them, would distinguish nothing and confound everything. But allow his ideas to become gradually more settled by means of repeated sensations from the same objects, and soon he will form a general idea of animated matter which he will easily distinguish from inanimate matter. And shortly thereafter he will distinguish quite accurately between animated matter and vegetative matter, and he will naturally arrive at that first great division, *Animal*, *Vegetable*, and *Mineral*.

And since at the same time he will have come to a clear idea of those great and quite diverse objects, *Earth*, *Air*, and *Water*, he will come shortly to form a particular idea of the animals who inhabit the earth, of those who live in the water, and of those who take to the air. And, consequently, he will easily make that second division between *Four-footed Animals*, *Birds*, and *Fishes*. Likewise, in the vegetable kingdom he will distinguish trees and plants with facility, whether it be by their size, their substance, or their shape. This is what simple observation must necessarily show him, and what with the very least attention he could not fail to recognize. That is what we also must recognize as real, what we must respect as a division given by nature herself. Next, let us put ourselves in the place of that man, or let us suppose that he may have acquired as much knowledge and experience as we have on this matter. He will come to judge the objects of natural history by the connections which they have with his own life. Those which are the most necessary or useful to him will hold the first rank – for example, he will give preference in the order of animals to the horse, the dog, oxen, etc., and he will always know more about those which are most familiar to him. Next, he will occupy himself with those which, without being familiar, nevertheless inhabit the same places and climates as he does – such as deer, hares, and all the wild animals. And only after acquiring all these details will his curiosity lead him to inquire into what the animals of strange climates may be like – those such as elephants, dromedaries, etc. The case will be the same with fishes, birds, insects, shellfish, plants, minerals, and all the other productions of nature. He will study them in proportion to their usefulness; he will consider them to the extent that they are familiar to him, and he will rank them in his mind relative to the order of his acquaintance with them, because that is indeed the order according to which he experienced them and according to which it is important to him to preserve them.

This order, the most natural of all, is what we believe ought to be followed. Our method of distribution is no more mysterious than that which we have just observed. We start from general divisions such as we have just indicated, divisions which are incontestable. Next we take those objects which interest us the most owing to the connections which they have with us. From this point we pass little by little to those which are most distant, and which are strange to us. And we believe that this simple and natural manner of considering things is preferable to more recondite and complex methods because there is not one of them, whether of those which have been constructed, or of all those which might be constructed, which would not have more of an arbitrary element in them than our method. From every point of view, it is easier, more agreeable, and more useful to consider things in relation to us rather than from another point of view.

I foresee that two objections could be made to this. The first is that these great divisions which we regard as real are perhaps not exact, that, for example, we are not sure that it is possible to draw a line of separation between the animal kingdom and the vegetable kingdom, or indeed between the vegetable kingdom and the mineral, and that in nature it is possible to find things which partake equally in the properties of the one and the other, and which, consequently, one cannot register in either one or the other of these divisions.

To that I reply that if there exist things which are exactly half animal and half plant, or half plant and half mineral, etc., such things are presently unknown to us, so that in fact the division is complete and precise. And it is evident that the more general the divisions are, the less risk there will be of coming across mixed objects which might partake of the nature of the two things included in these divisions. In this manner, that same objection which we have used with advantage against particular distributions has no place when there is a question of divisions as general as this one is, particularly if these divisions are not made exclusive, and if there is no pretension of thereby including without exception not only all known beings but, further, all those which might be discovered in the future. Moreover, if the matter is considered carefully, it will surely appear that our general ideas are only composed of particular ideas. They are relative to a continuous chain of objects. It is only the central area of each link of this chain which we perceive clearly, while the two extremes continually evade our efforts to delineate them. In this manner, the more we pursue them the more they escape us, in such a way that we never seize anything except the general outlines of things. And, consequently, we ought not believe that our ideas, however general they may be, will ever encompass the detailed conception of all existing and possible things.

The second objection which will doubtless be made to us is that by following in our work the order that we have indicated we shall fall into the error of placing together objects which are quite different. For example, in the study of animals, if we begin with those which are the most useful and familiar to us, we shall be obliged to give the history of the dog after or before that of the horse, and this does not appear to be natural, since these animals are so different in other respects that they appear in no way made to be placed so close to each other in a treatise on natural history. And it will perhaps be added that there would be more value in following the former method of dividing animals into *Solipedes*,[9] *Fissipeds*,[10] and *those with cloven hoofs*, or else the new method of dividing animals on the basis of their teeth, or their mammary glands, etc.

This objection, which might appear attractive at first, disappears upon examination. Is it not better to arrange objects, not only in a treatise on natural history, but even in a scientific display, or anywhere else, in the order and position that they ordinarily occupy, rather than to force them together on the basis of a supposition? Isn't it better to have the horse, which is soliped, followed by the dog, which is fissiped, and which indeed customarily follows it, than by the zebra, which is little known to us, and which perhaps has no other connection with the horse than being soliped? Moreover, isn't there the same disadvantage in the latter arrangements as in ours? Doesn't a lion, because it is fissiped, resemble a rat, which is also fissiped, more than a horse resembles a dog? Doesn't a soliped elephant also resemble more closely a soliped donkey than does a deer, which is split-hoofed? If one wishes to make use of the new method in which the teeth and mammary glands are the specifying characters, and upon which the divisions and distributions are based, won't it be found that a lion more closely resembles a bat than a horse resembles a dog? Or, indeed, in order to make our comparison more exact, doesn't a horse resemble a pig more than a dog, or a dog resemble a mole more than a horse?[2] And since there are more disadvantages and just as great differences in these methods of arrangement as there are in ours, and since, besides, these methods do not have the same advantages as ours, and since they are much more distant from the ordinary and natural manner of considering things, we believe we have had sufficient reason for giving the preference to our method. Our divisions are based solely upon the relations which things seem to have with us.

We shall not examine in detail all the artificial methods which have been devised for the purpose of dividing animals. They are all more or less subject to the disadvantages of which we have spoken in connection with the systems of botany. It seems to us that an examination of only one of these systems suffices in order to discover the faults of the others. Consequently, we shall limit ourselves here to the examination of that system of M. Linnaeus, which is the newest of such methods, so that the reader might be in a position to judge whether or not we have been right to reject this system and to hold fast only to the natural order in which all men have customarily viewed and considered things.

M. Linnaeus divides all animals into six classes: namely, *Quadrupeds, Birds, Amphibians, Fishes, Insects,* and *Worms*. This initial division is, as anyone can see, quite arbitrary and very incomplete, for it gives us no idea of certain kinds of animals which are, however, quite numerous and very widespread – snakes, for example, and shellfish, and crustaceans. It appears at first glance that they have been overlooked. For one would not at first imagine that snakes might be amphibians, crustaceans insects, and shellfish worms. Instead of making only six classes, if this author had made twelve or more of them, and if he had spoken of quadrupeds, birds, reptiles, amphibians, cetacean fish, oviparous fish, dipnoan fish, crustaceans, shellfish, land insects of the sea, freshwater insects, etc., he would have spoken more clearly, and his divisions would have been more accurate and less arbitrary. For, in general, the more one augments the number of divisions of the productions of nature, the more one approaches the truth, since in nature only individuals exist, while genera, orders, and classes only exist in our imagination.

If the general characters which M. Linnaeus employs and the manner in which he makes his particular divisions are examined, even more essential shortcomings will appear. For example, a general character such as the mammary glands, which is taken for purposes of identifying

2 See Linnaeus, *Systema naturae* (1735).

the quadrupeds, should at least belong to all the quadrupeds. However, it has been known since Aristotle that the horse has no mammary glands whatsoever.

M. Linnaeus divides the class of quadrupeds into five orders: the first, *Anthropomorpha*; the second, *Ferae*; the third, *Glires*; the fourth, *Jumenta*; and the fifth, *Pecora*. And, according to him, these five orders comprise all four-footed animals. It will become evident by the exposition, and even by the enumeration, of these five orders that his division not only is arbitrary, but, further, is quite poorly thought out. For the author places in the first order man, the ape, sloths, and scaly lizards. One must indeed have a mania for classification in order to put together beings as different as man and the sloths, or the ape and scaly lizards. Passing to the second order which he calls *Ferae*, the savage beasts, he indeed begins with the lion and the tiger, but he then continues with the cat, the weasel, the otter, the seal, the dog, the bear, the badger, and ends with the hedgehog, the mole, and the bat. Would one ever have believed that the appellation of *Ferae* (in Latin), savage or ferocious beasts (in French), was applicable to the bat, the mole, or the hedgehog? Or that domestic animals such as the dog and the cat might be savage beasts? Isn't that just as careless a use of ideas as it is of the words that represent them? But let us pass to the third order, *Glires*, the mice: these mice of M. Linnaeus are the porcupine, the hare, the squirrel, the beaver, and the rats. I confess that of all these I see only one species of rat which might indeed be a mouse. The fourth order is that of the *Jumenta*, or beasts of burden. These beasts of burden are the elephant, the hippopotamus, the shrew-mouse, the horse, and the pig – another assemblage, as it appears, which is so gratuitous and bizarre that it appears the author had designed it with just these ends in mind. Finally we have the fifth order, *Pecora*, or the cattle, which includes the camel, the deer, the goat, the sheep, and the bullock. But isn't there quite a difference between a camel and a sheep, or between a deer and a goat? And what reason can there be for claiming that these are animals of the same order, except that, if one wishes at all costs to create orders, and only a small number of them at that, it becomes quite necessary to cram beasts of all kinds into such categories? After examining the last division of animals into particular species, one finds that the lynx is only a species of cat, the fox and the wolf species of dog, the civet cat but a species of badger, the guinea pig but a species of hare, the water rat a species of beaver, the rhinoceros a species of elephant, the ass a species of horse, etc. And all that because there are some small resemblances between the number of mammary glands and teeth of these animals, or some slight resemblance in the form of their horns.

There is, however, a means of limiting this system of nature for the quadrupeds that suffers no omissions. Wouldn't it be more simple, more natural, and more true to call an ass an ass, a cat a cat, than to wish, without knowing why, that an ass might be a horse, and a cat a lynx?

The rest of the system can be judged by this example. Serpents, according to this author, are amphibians, crayfish are insects – and not

178

only insects, but insects of the same order as lice and fleas, and all shellfish, crustaceans, and dipnoan fish are worms. Oysters, mussels, sea urchins, starfish, squid, and so forth, are, according to this author, only worms. Is it necessary to go any further to make it apparent that all these divisions are arbitrary and this method is not justifiable?

We reproach the Ancients for not having constructed systems, and the Moderns believe themselves to be quite a bit above them because they have constructed a great number of these methodological arrangements and these lists of classified objects of which we have just spoken. They have convinced themselves that that alone is sufficient to prove that the Ancients did not have nearly the knowledge of natural history that we have. However, the complete opposite of this is the case, and we shall have a thousand occasions in the continuation of this work to show that the Ancients were far more advanced and knowledgeable than we are, not in physics, but in the natural history of animals and minerals, and that the facts of that history were far more familiar to them than they are to us who should have profited from their discoveries and comments. Until such time as we see detailed examples of this, we shall be content with indicating here the general reasons which should be sufficient to make us think this to be the case, even should we not have particular proofs of it.

The Greek language is one of the most ancient of languages, and the one that has been in use for the longest time. Before and after Homer,[11] Greek was written and spoken until the thirteenth or fourteenth centuries. And even today Greek corrupted by foreign idioms does not differ as much from ancient Greek as Italian does from Latin. This language, which may be regarded as the most perfect and the richest of all, as early as the time of Homer had been brought to a high degree of perfection, which of necessity supposes a considerable antiquity for it even before the century in which that great poet wrote. For one can judge of the ancient or recent origin of a language by the greater or lesser quantity of words in use, and the more or less subtle variety of its constructions. Now we have in this language the names of a very great number of things which have no name in either Latin or French. The rarest of animals, certain species of birds or fish or minerals which one comes across only with great difficulty and quite rarely, have names, and in fact established names, in Greek. This obviously shows that these objects of natural history were known, and that the Greeks not only knew them, but even had a precise idea of what they were, which they would not have been able to acquire except by a study of these same objects – a study which necessarily supposes observations and formal comments. They even have names of varieties, and what we are only able to represent by a phrase is identified in that language by a single substantive. This abundance of words, this treasury of clear and precise expressions, does it not suppose the same abundance of ideas and knowledge? Isn't it obvious that peoples who have named far more things than we consequently knew far more about them? However, the Greeks did not create systems and arbitrary arrangements as we do.

179

They thought that true science consisted in knowledge of facts. In order to acquire this knowledge, it was necessary to become familiar with the productions of nature; to give each thing its name in order to make it recognizable, in order to be able to talk about such things, in order to describe to oneself more often ideas of rare and singular things, and thus to multiply knowledge, which without this process would perhaps have disappeared, nothing being more subject to oblivion than that which has no name. Whatever is not in common usage can only be sustained by the aid of representations.

Moreover, the Ancients who have written on natural history were great men, men who did not restrict themselves to the field of study alone. They had a lofty spirit, broad and thorough knowledge, and comprehensive views. And if it seems to us at first glance that they were somewhat imprecise in certain details, it is easy to recognize, in reading them with reflection, that they did not think that minute details merited as great attention as is given to them today. And whatever reproach the Moderns are able to lay at the doorstep of the Ancients, it seems to me that Aristotle,[12] Theophrastus,[13] and Pliny,[14] who were the first naturalists, are also the greatest in certain respects. Aristotle's history of animals is perhaps still today the best that we have of this genre, and it is greatly to be desired that he had left us something as complete on vegetables and minerals. But the two books of plants which some authors attribute to him do not resemble his other works, and are indeed not his. It is true that botany was not in great honor in his time. The Greeks and even the Romans did not regard it as a science which ought to exist in its own right, and which ought to be made a particular object of investigation. They considered it only in connection with agriculture, gardening, medicine, and the arts. And although Theophrastus, a disciple of Aristotle, knew more than five hundred kinds of plants, and although Pliny cites more than a thousand of them, they speak of them only so that we might know how to grow them, or in order to tell us that some are involved in the composition of drugs, that others are useful in the arts, that still others may serve to decorate our gardens, etc. In a word, they only considered plants according to the use which might be made of them, and they did not bother to describe them with any precision.

The history of animals was better known to them than that of plants. Alexander[15] gave orders and made quite considerable expenditures in order to gather specimens of animals, caused them to be brought from all lands, and placed Aristotle in a position to be able to observe them well. It appears from the latter's work that he perhaps knew them better and viewed them under more adequate categories than is the case today. Finally, although the Moderns have added their discoveries to those of the Ancients, I do not see that we have many works in natural history which can be placed above those of Aristotle and Pliny. But since the natural prepossession which one has for his own century might persuade one that what I have said is proposed rashly, I shall say a few words in exposition of the plan of their works.

Aristotle begins his history of animals by establishing the general differences and resemblances between various kinds of animals. Instead of dividing them on the basis of small special characteristics such as the Moderns do, he gathers historically all the facts and all the observations which bear on the general resemblances and the sensible characteristics. He draws these characteristics from the form, color, size, and all the exterior qualities of the whole animal, as well as from the number and position of its organs, from the size, movement, and form of its limbs, and from the likenesses or dissimilarities which are found in a comparison of these same parts. And he everywhere gives examples in order to make himself better understood. He also considers among animals in their style of life, their actions and their habits, their places of habitation, etc. He speaks of organs which are common to all animals and essential to them, and of those which they may lack and which are indeed missing in many kinds of animals. The sense of touch, he says, is the only thing which ought to be regarded as necessary, and which cannot be absent in any animal. And since this sense is common to all animals, it is impossible to give a name to that part of their bodies wherein the faculty of sensation resides. The most essential organs are those by which the animal secures its nourishment, those which receive and digest this food, and those by which it rids itself of what remains. He next examines the various methods of generation among animals and the variety of their different organs which are used for purposes of motion and for their natural functions. These general preliminary observations form a picture all the parts of which are interesting. And this great philosopher also tells us that he has presented such observations in this manner in order to give a foretaste of what is to follow and to stimulate the attention which the particular history of each animal, or rather of each thing, requires.

He begins with man, and describes him first, rather because he is the best-known animal than because he is the most perfect. And in order to make his description less dry and more piquant, he tries to draw ethical considerations while going over the physical connections of the human body. He indicates the characteristics of men by means of their facial traits. To be well versed in physiognomy would indeed be a useful knowledge for whoever acquired it. But can this be gained from natural history? After this he describes man by means of all his parts, interior and exterior, and this description is the only one which can be considered to be complete. Rather than describing each animal in particular, he presents animals in terms of the connection which all the parts of their bodies have with those of man's body. When he describes the human head, for example, he compares the head of various species of animals with it, and does the same with all the other parts of the body. In the description of the lung of man, he brings in historically everything that is known about the lungs of animals, and he notes the history of those species which lack lungs. He does the same with the organs of generation. He draws upon all the varieties of animals according to their manner of copulating, generating, bearing and

181

giving birth, etc. So far as blood is concerned, he gives the history of animals which are without it. And so, following out this plan of comparison in which, as we see, man serves as the model, and giving only the differences which separate animals from man, he purposively eliminates all particular description. He avoids thus all repetition, he gathers facts, and he writes down not one useless word. Thus there is comprised in a small volume an almost limitless number of different facts, and I do not believe that it would be possible to put in fewer words all that he has had to say about that material, which appears so little susceptible to such precision that it takes a genius like Aristotle to thus maintain in it both order and clarity at the same time. This work of Aristotle's appears to me like a table of materials which might have been extended with the greatest care for many thousands of volumes filled with descriptions and observations of all kinds. It is the most learned abridgment that has ever been made, if science is, indeed, the history of facts. And even if one were to suppose that Aristotle had drawn from all the books of his time that which he put into his own, the plan of the work, its distribution, the choice of examples, the exactness of the comparisons, a certain form in the ideas, which I shall gladly describe as philosophic in character, all this does not leave one in doubt for even an instant that he was himself far richer than those from whom he supposedly borrowed.

Pliny worked on an even greater project, one that was, perhaps, too vast. He wished to encompass everything, and he appears to have taken the measure of nature and to have found her still too small for the scope of his spirit. His *Natural History* takes in, exclusive of the history of animals, plants, and minerals, the history of heaven and earth, medicine, commerce, navigation, the history of the liberal and mechanical arts, the origin of customs, and finally all the natural sciences and all the skills of man. And what is astonishing is that in each part of the work Pliny is equally great. The elevation of thought, the nobility of style further reveal his profound erudition. Not only was he familiar with everything that it was possible to know in his time, but he had that facility for comprehensive thought which causes science to grow. He had the acuity of reflection upon which elegance and taste depend, and he transmits to his readers a certain freedom of spirit, a boldness of thought, which is the germ of philosophy. His work, which matches nature in its variety, always shows nature in its best light. His work is, if you prefer, a compilation of everything that was written on the subject before him, a copy of everything that had been done before him which was excellent and useful to know. But this copy is drawn with such broad strokes, this compilation contains things arranged in so novel a manner, that it is preferable to most of the original works which consider the same material.

We have said that the faithful history and the exact description of each thing were the two sole objects which one ought to set oneself initially in the study of natural history. The Ancients have fulfilled the first well, and are perhaps as much superior to the Moderns in this respect as they are inferior to them in the second. For the Ancients have treated quite adequately the history of the life and habits of animals, the culture and uses of plants, the properties and uses of minerals, and at the same time they appear to have consciously neglected the description of each thing. It is not that they were not capable of doing so quite well. They obviously scorned to write about things which they regarded as useless. This fashion of thinking emphasized comprehensive views, and was not as unreasonable as one might think it to be. And, at the same time, authors such as Pliny were scarcely even capable of thinking otherwise. In the first place, they put a premium on brevity, and put in their works only those facts which were essential and useful, for they did not have the facility for multiplying and enlarging books that we do. In the second place, their concern with all the sciences always revolved around their usefulness, and they were much less devoted to vain curiosity than we are. Anything that was not of interest to society, or of use for health, or for the arts, they neglected. They related everything to the ethical side of man, and did not believe that things which had hardly any use were worth bothering with. A useless insect whose maneuvers our observers admire, a plant without healing qualities whose stamens our botanists consider, were for them merely an insect and a plant. One could cite, for example, the twenty-seventh book of Pliny's *Reliqua herbarum genera*,[16] where he puts together all the plants on which he places no high value, and which he is content to mention alphabetically, indicating only some of their general characteristics and their uses for medicine. All this shows what little taste the ancients had for natural science. Or to speak more exactly, it shows that they had no idea of what we call particular and experimental natural science. They did not think that any advantage could be had from the scrupulous examination and exact description of all the parts of a plant or of a small animal, and they did not see the connections which that process might have with the explication of the phenomena of nature.

However, this object is the most important, and it is not necessary to imagine even today that, in the study of natural history, one ought to limit oneself solely to the making of exact descriptions and the ascertaining of particular facts. This is, in truth, and as has been pointed out, the essential end which ought to be proposed at the outset. But we must try to raise ourselves to something greater and still more worthy of our efforts, namely: the combination of observations, the generalization of facts, linking them together by the power of analogies, and the effort to arrive at a high degree of knowledge. From this level we can judge that particular effects depend upon more general ones; we can compare nature with herself in her vast operations; and, finally, we are able to open new routes for the further perfection of the various branches of natural science. A vast memory, assiduity, and attention suffice to arrive at the first end. But more is needed here. General views, a steady eye, and a process of reasoning informed more by reflection than by study are what is called for. Finally, that quality of spirit is needed which makes us capable of grasping distant relationships, bringing them together, and making out of them a body of reasoned ideas after having precisely determined their nearness to truth and weighted their probabilities.

Here there is need for a methodical approach to guide the mind, not for that artificial method of which we have spoken, for that only serves to arrange words arbitrarily, but for that method which sustains the very order of things, guides our reasoning, enlightens our views, extends them, and prevents us from being led astray.

The greatest philosophers have felt the need for such a method, and they have indeed attempted to give us principles and outlines of it. But some of them have left us only the history of their thoughts, while others have left only the story of their imagination. And if some have risen to the elevated stations of metaphysics from which the principles, connections, and totality of the sciences can be viewed, none of them have communicated their ideas to us on these subjects or given us any advice concerning them; and the manner of properly conducting one's mind in the sciences is yet to be found. In the absence of precepts, examples have been substituted; in place of principles, definitions have been used; instead of authenticated facts, dangerous suppositions have been supplied by guesswork.

Even in our own century, when the sciences seem to be cultivated with care, I believe that it is easy to perceive that philosophy is neglected, perhaps more so than in any other century. The skills which one would like to call scientific have taken its place. The methods of calculus and geometry, those of botany and natural history – formulas, in a word, and dictionaries – occupy almost everyone. We think that we know more because we have increased the number of symbolic expressions and learned phrases. We pay hardly any attention to the fact that all these skills are only the scaffolding of science, and not science itself. We ought to use them only when we cannot do without them, and we ought always to be careful lest they happen to fail us when we wish to apply them to the edifice of science itself.

Truth, that metaphysical entity of which everyone believes himself to have a clear idea, seems to me to be confounded with such a great number of strange objects to which its name is applied that I am not at all surprised that it is hard to recognize. Prejudices and false applications are multiplied in proportion as our hypotheses have become more learned, more abstract, and more perfected. It is thus more difficult than ever to recognize what we can know, and to distinguish clearly what we ought to ignore. The following reflections will serve at least as advice on this important subject.

The word *truth* gives rise to only a vague idea; it never has had a precise definition. And the definition itself, taken in a general and absolute sense, is but an abstraction which exists only by virtue of some supposition. Instead of trying to form a definition of truth, let us rather try to make an enumeration of truths. Let us look closely at what are commonly called truths and try to form clear ideas of them.

There are many kinds of truths, and customarily placed in the first order are those of mathematics, which are, however, only truths of definition. These definitions are concerned with simple but abstract suppositions, and all the truths of this sort are nothing more than the worked-out and always abstract consequences of these definitions. We have made the suppositions, and we have combined them in all sorts of ways. The body of combinations that results is the science of mathematics. There is, then, no more in that science than what we have put into it, and the truths which are drawn from it can only be different expressions under which the suppositions which we have used are presented. Thus, mathematical truths are only the exact repetitions of definitions or suppositions. The last consequence is true only because it is identical with that which preceded it, and this latter in its turn with its antecedent. Thus one may proceed backward right to the first presupposition. And since definitions are the sole principles upon which everything is established, and since they are arbitrary and relative, all the consequences which can be deduced from them are equally arbitrary and relative. Hence, that which we call mathematical truth is thus reduced to the identity of ideas, and has nothing of the real about it. We make suppositions, we reason on the basis of our suppositions, we draw the consequences of them, we come to conclusions. The conclusion, or the last consequence, is a proposition which is true in proportion as our supposition was true. But the truth of this proposition cannot exceed that of the supposition itself. This is hardly the place to discourse on the methods of the science of mathematics, or on the abuse of such methods. It is sufficient for our purposes to have proved that mathematical truths are only truths of definition or, if you prefer, different expressions of the same thing, and that they are only truths in relation to the very definitions with which we started. It is for this reason that they have the advantage of always being precise and conclusive, but abstract, intellectual, and arbitrary.

The truths of the physical sciences, on the other hand, are in no way arbitrary, and in no way depend on us; instead of being founded on suppositions which we have made, they depend only on facts. A sequence of similar facts or, if you prefer, a frequent repetition and an uninterrupted succession of the same occurrences constitute the essence of this sort of truth. What is called "truth" in physical sciences is thus only a probability, but a probability so great that it is equivalent to certitude. In mathematics, one supposes. In the physical sciences, one sets down a claim and establishes it. There, one has definitions; here, there are facts. One goes from definition to definition in the abstract sciences, but one proceeds from observation to observation in the factual sciences. In the first case one arrives at evidence, while in the latter the result is certitude. The word "truth" is used for both, and consequently corresponds to two different ideas. Its signification is vague and complicated, and it thus has not been possible to define the term in a general way. It has been necessary, as we have just seen, to distinguish the kinds of truth in order to form a clear idea of it.

I shall not speak of other orders of truths: those of the moral order, for example, which are in part actual and in part arbitrary, would demand a lengthy discussion which would take us away from our goal, and that more especially because they have as object and end only decorum and probabilities.

Mathematical evidence and physical certitude are thus the only two aspects under which we ought to consider truth.[17] As soon as it withdraws from one or another of these, it is no more than appearance and probability. Let us then examine what we can know through evident or certain science, after which we shall see what we can come to know only by conjecture; and finally we shall see what we ought to ignore.

We know, or we can know, in evident science, all the characteristics or, rather, all the relationships of numbers, lines, surfaces, and of all the other abstract quantities. We shall be able to know them in a more complete manner to the extent that we train ourselves to solve new problems, and more surely to the extent that we search out the causes of the difficulties which arise. Since we are the creators of this sort of knowledge, and since it takes under consideration absolutely nothing except what we ourselves have already imagined, it is impossible to have therein either obscurities or paradoxes which may be actual or impossible of resolution. A solution will always be found for these apparent difficulties through a careful examination of the premises, and by following all the steps which have been taken to arrive at the solution. Since the combination of these principles and the ways in which they can be used are innumerable, there is in mathematics a vast field of acquired knowledge to be gained of which we shall always be the masters, cultivating it when we wish, and from which we shall always garner the same abundance of truths.

But these truths would have been perpetually matters of pure speculation, of simple curiosity, and entirely useless if the means had not been found of conjoining them to the truths of the physical sciences. Before considering the advantages of that union, let us see what we could hope to know in this area.

The phenomena which offer themselves daily to our eyes, which follow one another and repeat themselves without interruption and uniformly, are the foundation of our physical knowledge. It is enough that a thing always happens in the same way for it to become a certainty or a truth for us. All the facts of nature which we have observed, or which we could observe, are just so many truths. And thus we are able to increase the number as much as we please by multiplying our observations. Our science is limited in this case only by the dimensions of the universe.

But when, after having determined the facts through repeated observations, when, after having established new truths through precise experiments, we wish to search out the reasons for these same occurrences, the causes of these effects, we find ourselves suddenly baffled, reduced to trying to deduce effects from more general effects, and obliged to admit that causes are and always will be unknown to us, because our senses, themselves being the effects of causes of which we have no knowledge, can give us ideas only of effects and never of causes. Thus we must be content to call cause a general effect, and must forego hope of knowing anything beyond that.

These general effects are for us the true laws of nature. All the phenomena that we recognize as holding to these laws and depending on them will be so many accountable facts, so many truths understood. Those phenomena which we are unable to associate with these general effects will be simple "occurrences" which we must keep in reserve until such time as a greater number of observations and a more extended experience make us aware of other facts and bring to light their physical cause, that is to say, the general effect from which these particular effects derive. It is here that the union of the two sciences of mathematics and physics might result in great advantages. The one gives the "how many," the other the "how" of things. And since it is a question here of combining and estimating probabilities in order to judge whether an effect depends more on one cause than on another, when you have imagined by physics the *how*, that is to say, when you have seen that such and such an effect might well depend upon such and such a cause, you then apply mathematics in order to assure yourself as to *how often* this effect happens in conjunction with its cause. And if you find that the result accords with the observations, the probability that you have guessed correctly is so increased that it becomes a certainty. But in the absence of such corroboration, the relation would have remained a simple probability.

It is true that this union of mathematics and physics can be accomplished only for a very small number of subjects. In order for this to take place it is necessary that the phenomena that we are concerned with explaining be susceptible to being considered in an abstract manner and that their nature be stripped of almost all physical qualities. For mathematics is unapplicable to the extent that such subjects are not simple abstractions. The most beautiful and felicitous use to which this method has ever been applied is to the system of the world. We must admit that if Newton had only given us the physical conform-ations of his system without having supported them by precise mathematical evaluations they would not have had nearly the same force. But at the same time one ought to be aware that there are very few subjects as simple as this, that is to say, as stripped of physical qualities as the Newtonian universe. For the distance of the planets is so great that it is possible to consider them in reference to each other as being no more than points. And it is possible simultaneously, without being mistaken, to abstract from all the physical qualities of the planets and take into consideration only their force of attraction. Their movements are, moreover, the most regular that we know, and suffer no retardation from resistance. All of this combines to render the explanation of the system of the world a problem in mathematics, for the realization of which fortunately there was needed only one well-conceived physical idea, that idea being to have thought that the force which makes bodies fall to the surfaces of the earth might well be the same as that which holds the moon in its orbit.

But, I repeat: there are very few subjects in physics in which the abstract sciences can be applied so advantageously. And I scarcely see anything but astronomy and optics to which they might be of any great service: astronomy, for the reasons which we have just explained; and optics because light being a body almost infinitely small, whose effects operate in straight lines with almost infinite speed, its properties approximate those of mathematics, which allows one to apply to optics with some success arithmetic and geometric measurement. I shall not speak of mechanics, for *rational* mechanics is itself a mathematical and abstract science from which practical mechanics, or the art of making and designing machines, borrows only one single principle, by which one is able to judge all the effects by abstracting from friction and other physical qualities. Also, it has always appeared to me that there was a sort of abuse in the manner in which experimental physics is taught, the object of that science being by no means the one ordinarily attributed to it. Mechanical effects – such as the power of levers and, pulleys, the equilibrium of solids and fluids, the effect of inclined planes, of centrifugal forces, etc. – belonging entirely as they do to mathematics, and capable of being grasped by the mind with the least evidence, it seems to me superfluous to represent demonstration of these effects to the senses. The true goal of experimental physics is, on the contrary, to experiment with all the things which we are not able to measure by mathematics, all the effects of which we do not yet know the causes, and all properties whose circumstances we do not know. That alone can lead us to new discoveries, whereas the demonstration of mathematical effects will never show us anything except what we already know.

But this abuse is as nothing in comparison with the inconveniences into which one stumbles when one wishes to apply geometry and arithmetic to quite complicated subjects of physics, to objects whose properties we know too little about to allow us to measure them. One is obliged in all such cases to make suppositions which are always contrary to nature, to strip the subject of most of its qualities, and to make of it an abstract entity which has no resemblance to the actual being. And after long reasoning and calculation on the connections and the properties of this abstract entity, and after having arrived at a conclusion equally abstract, it appears that something real has been found, and the ideal result is transferred back upon the real subject. This process produces an infinity of false consequences and errors.

Here then is the most delicate and the most important point in the study of the sciences: to know how to distinguish what is really in a subject from what we arbitrarily put there in considering it, to recognize clearly the properties which belong to it and those which we give to it. This appears to me to be the foundation of the true method of leading one's mind in the way of the sciences. And if this principle were always kept in mind, a false step would never be taken. One might thus avoid falling into learned errors which at times are taken as truths. Paradoxes and insoluble problems in the abstract sciences would begin to disappear. The prejudices and the doubts which we ourselves bring to the sciences of the actual would become apparent, and agreement would be reached on the metaphysics of sciences. Disputes would cease, and all would unite to advance along the same path in the pursuit of experience. Finally, we would arrive at the knowledge of all the truths which are within the competence of the human mind.

When the subjects are too complicated to allow the advantageous application of calculation and measurement, as is almost always the case with natural history and the physics of the particular, it seems to me that the true method of guiding one's mind in such research is to have recourse to observations, to gather these together, and from them to make new observations in sufficient number to assure the truth of the principal facts, and to use mathematics only for the purpose of estimating the probabilities of the consequences which may be drawn from these facts. Above all, it is necessary to try to generalize these facts and to distinguish well those which are essential from those which are only accessories to the subject under consideration. It is then necessary to tie such facts together by analogies, confirm or destroy certain equivocal points by means of experiment, form one's plan of explication on the basis of the combination of all these connections, and present them in the most natural order. This order can be established in two ways: the first is to ascend from particular effects to more general ones, and the other is to descend from the general to the particular. Both ways are good, and the choice of one or the other depends more on the bent of the author than on the nature of things, which always allows of being treated equally well by either method. We are going to give trial to this proposition in the discourses which follow, of the "Theory of the Earth," of the "Formation of Planets," and of the "Generation of Animals."

Notes
1   The idea of a 'juice' in minerals was still entertained by some.
2   The traditional theory of the 'Great Chain of Being', that is, the idea that the productions of Nature were continuously linked one to the other, from the simple to the complex (see also Vol. 1, p. 94 note 2).
3   Present-day botany divides plants in descending order into Divisions, Classes, Orders, Families, Tribes, Genera, Species and Varieties.
4   The hypothetical substance which, according to the alchemists, would convert all baser metals into gold.
5   Konrad von Gesner of Zurich (1516–65), polymath and naturalist, who left an encyclopaedic work on plants, animals and fossils uncompleted at his death.
6   J. de Tournefort (1656–1708), was a distinguished French botanist who made extensive collections of plants, in the course of wide travels.
7   Carl Linnaeus (see introduction).
8   Ulysses Aldrovandi (1522–1605) was Director of the botanic garden at the University of Bologna.
9   Animals with whole and uncloven feet.
10   Animals with divided toes.

11 Epic poet (date of birth variously placed between 1050 and 850 B.C.) author of the *Iliad* and the *Odyssey*.
12 Aristotle (384–322 B.C.) left a *History of Animals*.
13 The Greek philosopher Theophrastus (*c.* 370–*c.* 286 B.C.) wrote a *History of Plants* and *The Causes of Plants*.
14 Pliny the Elder (A.D. 23–79) was a Roman writer who wrote on many subjects, his sole surviving work being a *Natural History*.
15 Alexander the Great (356– 323 B.C.).
16 'The remaining kinds of plants'.
17 Compare the last paragraph of Hume's *An Enquiry Concerning Human Understanding*: 'If we take in our hand any volume; of divinity or school metaphysics, for instance; let us ask, Does it contain any abstract reasoning concerning quantity or number? No. Does it contain any experimental reasoning concerning matter of fact and existence? No. Commit it then to the flames; for it can contain nothing but sophistry and illusion.' (*Enquiries*, op. cit., XII, 165).

BUFFON

History and Theory of the Earth (1749)

From *Histoire naturelle* (ibid., Vol. 1, 1749) 'Second Discours: Histoire et théorie de la terre'. Reprinted from *Natural History, General and Particular*. [From the translation by William Smellie first published London, 1781] edited by William Wood, Printed for T. Cadell and W. Davies..., Strand, 1812. [20 volumes,] Vol. 1.

The 'Initial Discourse' on method was followed by a 'Second Discourse', on 'The History[1] and Theory of the Earth', designed to illustrate the method. The translated extract shows how Buffon described the earth as the setting for life. For him this was an indispensable preliminary to any satisfactory account of the life and habits of the animals and plants which dwell on the earth's surface. The article is remarkable for its treatment of geology in terms of slow, uniform action. Such an explanation deprived the Biblical story of the Flood of any significance from a geological point of view, and Buffon was probably rather more of a sceptic in regard to orthodox religion than his cautious (and occasionally ambiguous) language on such matters conveys.

The figure of the earth, its motions, or the external relations which subsist between it and the other parts of the universe, belong not to our present inquiry. It is the internal structure of the globe, its form and manner of existence, which we here propose to examine. The general history of the earth ought to precede that of its productions. Details of particular facts, relating to the economy[2] and manners of animals, or to the culture and vegetation of plants, are not, perhaps, so much the objects of natural history, as general deductions from the observations that have been made upon the different materials of which the earth itself is composed; as its heights, depths, and inequalities; the motions of the sea, the direction of mountains, the situation of rocks and quarries, the rapidity and effects of currents in the ocean, &c. This is the history of Nature at large, and of her principal operations, by which every other inferior or less general effect is produced. The theory of these effects constitutes what may be called the primary science, upon which a precise knowledge of particular appearances, as well as of terrestrial substances, solely depends. This species of science may be considered as appertaining to physics; but, is not all physical knowledge, where system is excluded,[3] a part of the history of Nature?

In subjects of an extensive kind, the relations of which it is difficult to trace, where some facts are but partially known, and others obscure, it is more easy to form a fanciful system, than to establish a rational theory. Thus the theory of the earth has never hitherto been treated but in a vague and hypothetical manner. I shall, therefore, exhibit a cursory view only of the notions of some authors who have written upon this subject.

The first hypothesis I shall mention is more conspicuous for its ingenuity than solidity. It is the production of an English astronomer,[4] who was an enthusiastic admirer of Sir Isaac Newton's system of philosophy. Convinced that every possible event depends upon the motions and direction of the stars, he endeavours to prove, by means of mathematical calculations, that all the changes this earth has undergone have been produced by the tail of a comet.

For another hypothesis we are indebted to a heterodox divine,[5] whose brain was so fully impregnated with poetical illusions, that he imagined he had seen the universe created. After telling us the state of the earth when it first sprung from nothing, what changes have been introduced by the deluge, what the earth has been, and what it now is, he assumes the prophetic style, and predicts what will be its condition after the destruction of the human kind.

A third writer,[6] a man of more extensive observation than the two former, but equally crude and confused in his ideas, explains the principal appearances of the globe by the aid of an immense abyss in the bowels of the earth, which, in his estimation, is nothing but a thin crust inclosing this vast ocean of fluid matter.

These hypotheses are all constructed on tottering foundations. The ideas they contain are indistinct, the facts are confounded, and the whole is a motley jumble of physics and fable. They, accordingly, have never been adopted but by men who embrace opinions without examination, and who, incapable of distinguishing the degrees of probability, are more deeply impressed with marvellous chimeras than with the genuine force of truth.

My ideas on this subject will be less extraordinary, and may even appear unimportant, when compared with the grand systems of such hypothetical writers. But it should not be forgotten, that it is the business of an historian to describe, not to invent; that no gratuitous suppositions are to be admitted in subjects which depend upon fact and observation; and that, in historical compositions, the imagination cannot be employed, except for the purpose of combining observations, of rendering facts more general, and of forming a connected whole, which presents to the mind clear ideas and probable conjectures: I say, probable; for it is impossible to give demonstrative evidence on this subject. Demonstration is confined to the mathematical sciences. Our knowledge in physics and natural history depends entirely on experience, and is limited to the method of reasoning by induction.[7]

With regard to the history of the earth, therefore, we shall begin with such facts as have been universally acknowledged in all ages, not omitting those additional truths which have fallen within our own observation.

The surface of this immense globe exhibits to our observation heights, depths, plains, seas, marshes, rivers, caverns, gulfs, volcanos; and, on a cursory view, we can discover, in the disposition of these objects, neither order nor regularity. If we penetrate into the bowels of the earth, we find metals, minerals, stones, bitumens, sands, earths, waters, and matter of every kind, seemingly placed by mere accident, and without any apparent design. Upon a nearer and more attentive inspection, we discover sunk mountains, caverns filled up, shattered rocks, whole countries swallowed up, new islands emerged from the ocean, heavy substances placed above light ones, hard bodies inclosed within soft bodies; in a word, we find matter in every form, dry and humid, warm and cold, solid and brittle, blended in a chaos of confusion, which can be compared to nothing but a heap of rubbish, or the ruins of a world.

These ruins, however, we inhabit with perfect security. The different generations of men, of animals, and of plants, succeed one another without interruption: the productions of the earth are sufficient for their sustenance; the motions of the sea, and the currents of the air, are regulated by fixed laws; the returns of the seasons are uniform, and the rigours of winter invariably give place to the verdure of the spring. With regard to us, every thing has the appearance of order: the earth, formerly a chaos, is now a tranquil, an harmonious, a delightful habitation, where all is animated and governed by such amazing displays of power and intelligence, as fill us with admiration, and elevate our minds to the contemplation of the great Creator.

But let us not decide precipitantly concerning the irregularities on the surface of the earth, and the apparent disorder in its bowels: we shall soon perceive the utility, and even the necessity of this arrangement. With a little attention, we shall perhaps discover an order of which we had no conception, and general relations that cannot be apprehended by a slight examination. Our knowledge, indeed, with regard to this subject, must always be limited. We are entirely unacquainted with many parts of the surface of this globe, and have partial ideas only concerning the bottom of the ocean, which, in many places, has never been sounded. We can only penetrate the rind of the earth. The greatest caverns, the deepest mines, descend not above the eight thousandth part of its diameter. Our judgement is therefore confined to the upper stratum, or mere superficial part. We know, indeed, that, bulk for bulk, the earth is four times heavier than the sun: we likewise know the proportion its weight bears to that of the other planets. But still this estimation is only relative. We have no standard. Of the real weight of the materials we are so ignorant, that the internal part of the globe may be either a void space, or it may be composed of matter a thousand times heavier than gold. Neither is there any method of making farther discoveries on this subject. It is even with difficulty that rational conjectures can be formed.

We must therefore confine ourselves to an accurate examination and description of the surface of the earth, and of such inconsiderable depths as we have been able to penetrate. The first object which attracts attention, is that immense collection of waters with which the greatest part of the globe is covered. These waters occupy the lowest grounds; their surface is always level; and, notwithstanding their uniform tendency to equilibrium and rest, they are kept in perpetual agitation by a powerful agent, which counteracts their natural tranquility, which communicates to them a regular periodic motion, alternately elevating and depressing their waves, and which produces a concussion or vibration in the whole mass, even to the most profound depths. This motion of the waters is coëval with time, and will endure as long as the sun and moon, by which it is produced.

In examining the bottom of the sea, we perceive it to be equally irregular as the surface of the dry land. We discover hills and valleys, plains and hollows, rocks and earths of every kind: We discover, likewise, that islands are nothing but the summits of vast mountains, whose foundations are buried in the ocean; we find other mountains whose tops are nearly on a level with the surface of the water; and rapid currents which run contrary to the general movement. These currents sometimes run in the same direction; at other times their motion is retrograde; but they never exceed their natural limits, which seem to be as immutable as those which bound the efforts of land-rivers. On one hand, we meet with tempestuous regions, where the winds blow with irresistible fury, where the heavens and the ocean, equally convulsed, are mixed and confounded in the general shock; violent intestine motions, tumultuous swellings, water spouts, and strange agitations, produced by volcanos, whose mouths, though many fathoms below the surface, vomit forth torrents of fire, and push, even to the clouds, a thick vapour, composed of water, sulphur, and bitumen; and dreadful gulfs or whirlpools[1] which seem to attract vessels for no other purpose than to swallow them up. On the other hand, we discover vast regions of an opposite nature, always smooth and calm, but equally dangerous to the mariner.[2] Here the winds never exert their force; the nautical art is of no utility; the becalmed voyagers must remain immoveably fixed, till death relieve them from misery. To conclude, directing our eyes toward the southern or northern extremities of the globe, we discover huge masses of ice, which, detaching themselves from the polar regions,

1 The Malestroom in the Norwegian Sea.
2 The calms and tornados in the Aethiopian Sea.

advance, like floating mountains, to the more temperate climates, where they dissolve and vanish from our view.

Beside these grand objects, the ocean presents us with myriads of animated beings, almost infinite in variety: some, clothed in light scales, swim with amazing swiftness; others, loaded with thick shells, trail heavily along, leaving their traces in the sand: to others, Nature has given fins resembling wings, with which they support themselves in the air, and fly before their enemies to considerable distances. Lastly, the sea gives birth to other animals, which, totally deprived of motion, live and die immoveably fixed to the same rocks: all, however, find abundance of food in this fluid element. The bottom of the ocean, and the shelving sides of rocks, produce plentiful crops of plants of many different species; its soil is composed of sand, gravel, rocks, and shells; in some places, it is a fine clay, in others, a compact earth; and, in general, the bottom of the sea has an exact resemblance to the dry land which we inhabit.

Let us next take a view of the land: what prodigious differences take place in different climates! What a variety of soils! What inequalities in the surface! But, upon a more attentive observation, we shall perceive, that the great chains of mountains lie nearer the equator than the poles; that, in the Old Continent, their direction is more from east to west than from south to north; and that, on the contrary, in the New Continent, they extend more from north to south than from east to west. But, what is still more remarkable, the figure and direction of these mountains, which have a most irregular appearance, correspond so wonderfully, that the *prominent* angles of one mountain are constantly opposite to the *concave* [3] angles of the neighbouring mountain, and of equal dimensions, whether they be separated by an extensive plain or a small valley. I have farther remarked, that opposite hills are always nearly of the same height; and that mountains generally occupy the middle of continents, islands, and promontories, dividing them by their greatest lengths. I have likewise traced the courses of the principal rivers, and find that their direction is nearly perpendicular to the sea-coasts into which they empty themselves; and that, during the greatest part of their courses, they follow the direction of the mountains from which they derive their origin. The sea-coasts are generally bordered with rocks of marble and other hard stones, or rather with earth and sand accumulated by the waters of the sea, or brought down and deposited by rivers. In opposite coasts, separated only by small arms of the sea, the different strata or beds of earth are of the same materials. I find that volcanos never exist but in high mountains; that a great number of them are entirely extinguished; that some are connected with others by subterranean passages, and their eruptions not unfrequently happen at the same time. There are similar communications between certain lakes and seas. Some rivers suddenly disappear and seem to precipitate themselves into the bowels of the earth. We likewise find certain mediterranean or inland seas, which constantly

3 *Saliant* and *re-entering* angles; Muller's Fortification.

receive, from many and great rivers, prodigious quantities of water, without any augmentation of their bounds, probably discharging, by subterraneous passages, all these extraneous supplies. It is likewise easy to distinguish lands which have been long inhabited, from those new countries where the earth appears in a rude state, where the rivers are full of cataracts, where the land is either nearly overflowed with water, or burnt up with drought, and where every place capable of producing trees is totally covered with wood.

Proceeding in our examination, we discover that the upper stratum of the earth is universally the same substance; that this substance, from which all animals and vegetables derive their growth and nourishment, is nothing but a composition of the decayed parts of animal and vegetable bodies, reduced into such small particles that their former organic state is not distinguishable. Penetrating a little deeper, we find the real earth, beds of sand, lime-stone, clay, shells, marble, gravel, chalk, &c. These beds are always parallel to each other, and of the same thickness through their whole extent. In neighbouring hills, beds or strata of the same materials are uniformly found at the same levels, though the hills be separated by deep and large valleys. Strata of every kind, even of the most solid rocks, are uniformly divided by perpendicular fissures. Shells, skeletons of fishes, marine plants, &c., are often found in the bowels of the earth, and on the tops of mountains, even at the greatest distances from the sea. These shells, fishes, and plants, are exactly similar to those which exist in the ocean. Petrified shells are to be met with, almost every where, in prodigious quantities: they are not only inclosed in rocks of marble and lime-stone, as well as in earths and clays, but are actually incorporated and filled with the very substances in which they are inclosed. In fine, I am convinced, by repeated observation, that marbles, lime-stones, chalks, marls, clays, sand, and almost all terrestrial substances, wherever situated, are full of shells and other spoils of the ocean.

Having enumerated these facts, let us try what conclusions can be drawn from them.

The changes which the earth has undergone during the last two or three thousand years are inconsiderable, when compared with the great revolutions which must have happened in those ages that immediately succeeded the creation. For, as terrestrial substances could only acquire solidity by the continued action of gravity, it is easy to demonstrate, that the surface of the earth was at first much softer than it is now; and, consequently, that the same causes, which at present produce but slight and almost imperceptible alterations during the course of many centuries, were then capable of producing very great revolutions in a few years. It appears, indeed, to be an incontrovertible fact, that the dry land which we now inhabit, and even the summits of the highest mountains, were formerly covered with the waters of the sea; for shells, and other marine bodies, are still found upon the very tops of mountains. It likewise appears, that the waters of the sea have remained for a long track of years upon the surface of the earth;

because, in many places, such immense banks of shells have been discovered, that it is impossible so great a multititude of animals could exist at the same time. This circumstance seems likewise to prove, that, although the materials on the surface of the earth were then soft, and, of course, easily disunited, moved, and transported, by the waters; yet these transportations could not be suddenly effected. They must have been gradual and successive, as sea-bodies are sometimes found more than one thousand feet below the surface. Such a thickness of earth or of stone could not be accumulated in a short period. Although it should be supposed, that, at the deluge, all the shells were transported from the bottom of the ocean, and deposited upon the dry land; yet, beside the difficulty of establishing this supposition, it is clear, that, as shells are found incorporated in marble and in the rocks of the highest mountains, we must likewise suppose, that all these marbles and rocks were formed at the same time, and at the very instant when the deluge took place; and that, before this grand revolution, there were neither mountains, nor marbles, nor rocks, nor clays, nor matter of any kind, similar to what we are now acquainted with, as they all, with few exceptions, contain shells, and other productions of the ocean. Besides, at the time of the universal deluge, the earth must have acquired a considerable degree of solidity, by the action of gravity for more than sixteen centuries. During the short time the deluge lasted, therefore, it is impossible that the waters should have overturned and dissolved the whole surface of the earth, to the greatest depths that mankind have been able to penetrate.

But, not to insist longer on this point, which shall afterwards be more fully canvassed, I shall confine myself to known and established facts. It is certain, that the waters of the sea have, at some period or other, remained for a succession of ages upon what we now know to be dry land; and, consequently, that the vast continents of Asia, Europe, Africa, and America, were then the bottom of an immense ocean, replete with every thing which the present ocean produces.

It is likewise certain, that the different strata of the earth are horizontal, and parallel to each other. This parallel situation must, therefore, be owing to the operation of the waters, which have gradually accumulated the different materials, and given them the same position that water itself invariably assumes. The horizontal position of strata is almost universal: In plains, the strata are exactly horizontal. It is only in the mountains that they are inclined to the horizon; because they have originally been formed by sediments deposited upon an inclined base. Now, I maintain, that these strata must have been gradually formed, and that they are not the effect of any sudden revolution; because nothing is more frequent than strata composed of heavy materials placed above light ones, which never could have happened, if, according to some authors, the whole had been blended and dissolved by the deluge, and afterwards precipitated. On this supposition every thing should have had a different aspect from what now appears. The heaviest bodies should have descended first, and every stratum should have had a situation corresponding to its specific gravity. In this case we should not have seen solid rocks or metals placed above light sand, nor clay under coal.

The beds of calcarious matters are not only horizontal in the plains, but likewise in all mountains which have not been disturbed by earthquakes or other accidental causes: and, when the strata are inclined, the whole mountain is likewise inclined, and has been forced into that position by a subterraneous explosion, or by the sinking of a part of the earth, which had served it as a basis. We may therefore conclude, in general, that all strata formed by the sediments of water are horizontal, like the water itself, except those which have been formed on an inclined base, as is the case with the most part of coal-mines.

The most external part of the earth, whether in plains or mountains, is solely composed of vegetable earth, which owes its origin to sediments of the air, of vapours, and of dews, and to the successive destruction of herbs, leaves, and other parts of decomposed plants. This first stratum every where follows the declivities and curvatures of the earth, and is more or less thick, according to particular local circumstances.[4] The vegetable stratum is commonly much thicker in valleys than on hills; and its formation is posterior to that of the primitive strata of the globe, the most ancient and most internal of which have been formed by fire, and the newest and most external have derived their origin from matters transported and deposited in the form of sediments by the motion of the waters. These, in general, are horizontal; and it is only by the action of particular causes that they sometimes appear inclined. The beds of calcarious stones are commonly horizontal, or slightly inclined; and, of all calcarious substances, the beds of chalk preserve their horizontal position most exactly. As chalk is only the dust of decayed calcarious bodies, it has been deposited by waters whose movements were tranquil, and their oscillations regular; whilst the matters which were only broken into large masses, have been transported by currents, and deposited by the removal of the waters; which is the reason why their strata are not so perfectly horizontal as those of chalk. The high coasts of Normandy are composed of horizontal strata of chalk so regularly perpendicular, that, at a distance, they have the appearance of fortified walls. Between the strata of chalk there are small beds of black flint, which give rise to the black veins in white marble.

Beside the calcarious shells, the strata of which are slightly inclined, and whose position has never been changed, there are many others which have been deranged by different accidents, and which are all

4 On the tops of some mountains, the surface is absolutely naked, and presents nothing to the view but pure rock, or granite, without any vegetation, except in the small fissures, where the wind has transported sand, and collected the particles of earth which float in the air. At some distance from the last branch of the Nile, there is a mountain composed of granite, of porphyry, and of jasper, which extends more than twenty leagues in length by perhaps an equal number in breadth. The surface of the summit of this enormous quarry, we are assured, is absolutely devoid of vegetables, and forms a vast desert, where neither quadrupeds, nor birds, nor even insects, can exist. But exceptions of this kind, which are particular and local, merit no consideration.

much inclined. Of these there are many examples in various parts of the Pyrennees, some of which are inclined forty-five, fifty, and even sixty degrees below the horizontal line. This circumstance seems to prove, that great changes have been produced in these mountains by the sinking of subterraneous caverns, which had formerly supported them.

Another circumstance demands our attention. No cause but the motion and sediments of water could possibly produce the regular position of the various strata of which the superficial part of this earth is composed. The highest mountains consist of parallel strata, as well as the lowest valleys. Of course, the formation of mountains cannot be imputed to the shocks of earthquakes, or to the eruptions of volcanos. Such small eminences as have been raised by volcanos or convulsions of the earth, instead of being composed of parallel strata, are mere masses of weighty materials, blended together in the utmost confusion. But this parallel and horizontal position of strata must necessarily be the operation of a uniform and constant cause.

We are, therefore, authorized to conclude, from repeated and incontrovertible facts and observations, that the dry and habitable part of the earth has for a long time remained under the waters of the sea, and must have undergone the same changes which are at present going on at the bottom of the ocean. To discover what has formerly happened to the dry land, let us examine what passes in the bottom of the sea; and we shall soon be enabled to make some rational conclusions with regard to the external figure and internal constitution of the earth.

The ocean, from the creation of the solar system, has been constantly subject to a regular flux and reflux. These motions, which happen twice in twenty-four hours, are principally occasioned by the action of the moon, and are greater in the equatorial regions than in other climates. The earth likewise performs a rapid motion round its axis, and, consequently, has a centrifugal force, which is also greatest at the equator. This last circumstance, independent of actual observations, proves, that the earth is not a perfect sphere, but that it must be more elevated under the equator than at the poles. From these two combined causes, the tides, and the motion of the earth, it may be fairly concluded, that, although this globe had been originally a perfect sphere, its diurnal motion, and the ebbing and flowing of the tides, must necessarily, in a succession of time, have elevated the equatorial parts, by gradually carrying mud, earth, sand, shells, &c. from other climates, and depositing them at the equator. On this supposition, the greatest inequalities on the surface of the earth ought to be, and, in fact, are found, in the neighbourhood of the equator. Besides, as the alternate motion of the tides has been constant and regular since the existence of the world, is it not evident, that, at each tide, the water carries from one place to another a small quantity of matter, which falls to the bottom as a sediment, and forms those horizontal and parallel strata that every where appear? The motion of the waters, in the flux and reflux, being always horizontal, the matter transported by them must necessarily take the same parallel direction after it is deposited.

To this reasoning, it may be objected, that, as the flux is equal to, and regularly succeeded by, the reflux, the two motions will balance each other; or, that the matter brought by the flux will be carried back by the reflux; and, consequently, that this cause of the formation of strata must be chimerical, as the bottom of the ocean can never be affected by a uniform, alternate motion of the waters; far less could this motion change its original structure, by creating heights, and other inequalities.

But, in the first place, the alternate motion of the waters is by no means equal; for the sea has a continual motion from east to west: besides, the agitations occasioned by the winds produce great inequalities in the tides. It will likewise be acknowledged, that, by every motion in the sea, particles of earth, and other materials, must be carried from one place, and deposited in another; and that these collections of matter must assume the form of parallel and horizontal strata. Farther, a well known fact will entirely obviate this objection. On all coasts, where the ebbing and flowing are discernible, numberless materials are brought in by the flux, which are not carried back by the reflux. The sea gradually increases on some places, and recedes from others, narrowing its limits, by depositing earth, sand, shells, &c. which naturally take a horizontal position. These materials, when accumulated and elevated to a certain degree, gradually shut out the water, and remain for ever in the form of dry land.

But to remove every doubt concerning this important point, let us examine more closely the practicability of a mountain's being formed at the bottom of the sea, by the motion and sediments of the water. On a high coast which the sea washes with violence during the flow, some part of the earth must be carried off by every stroke of the waves. Even where the sea is bounded by rock, it is a known fact, that the stone is gradually wasted by the water, and consequently, that small particles are carried off by the retreat of every wave. Those particles of earth or stone are necessarily transported to some distance. Whenever the agitation of the water is abated, the particles are precipitated in the form of a sediment, and lay the foundation of a first stratum, which is either horizontal, or inclined, according to the situation of the surface upon which they fall. This stratum will soon be succeeded by a similar one, produced by the same cause; and thus a considerable quantity of matter will be gradually amassed, and disposed in parallel beds. In process of time, this gradually accumulating mass will become a mountain in the bottom of the sea, exactly resembling, both in external and internal structure, those mountains which we see on the dry land. If there happened to be shells in that part of the bottom of the sea where we have supposed the sediments to be deposited, they would be covered, filled, and incorporated with the deposited matter, and form a part of the general mass. These shells would be lodged in different parts of the mountains, corresponding to the times they were deposited. Those which lay at the bottom, before the first stratum was formed, would occupy the lowest station; and those which were afterwards deposited, would be found in the more elevated parts.

In the same manner, when the bottom of the sea, at particular places, is troubled by the agitation of the waters, earth, clay, shells, and other matter, must necessarily be removed from these parts, and deposited elsewhere. For we are assured by divers, that the bottom of the sea, at the greatest depths to which they descend, is so strongly affected by the agitation of the water, that earth, clay, and shells, are removed to great distances. Transportations of this kind must, therefore, be constantly going on in every part of the ocean; and the matters transported, after subsiding, must uniformly raise eminences similar, in every respect, to the composition and structure of our mountains. Thus the motions produced by the flux and reflux, by winds and currents, must uniformly create inequalities in the bottom of the ocean.

Farther, we must not imagine that these matters cannot be carried to great distances, since we daily find grain, and other productions of the East and West Indies, arriving on our coasts.[5] These bodies are, indeed, specifically lighter than water; and the other substances are specifically heavier. Still, however, as they are reduced to an impalpable powder, they may be kept long suspended in the water, and, of course, transported to any distance.

It has been conceived, that the agitation produced by the winds and tides is only superficial, and affects not the bottom, especially when it is very deep. But it ought to be remembered, that, whatever be the depth, the whole mass is put in motion by the tides at the same time; and that, in a fluid globe, this motion would be communicated even to the centre. The power which occasions the flux and reflux is penetrating; it acts equally upon every particle of the mass. Hence the quantity of its force, at different depths, may be determined by calculation. Indeed, this point is so certain, that it admits not of dispute.

We cannot, therefore, hesitate in pronouncing, that the tides, the winds, and every other cause of motion in the sea, must produce heights and inequalities in its bottom; and that these eminences must uniformly be composed of regular strata, either horizontal or inclined. These heights will gradually augment; like the waves which formed them, they will mutually respect each other; and, if the extent of the base be great, in a series of years they will form a vast chain of mountains. Whenever eminences are formed, they interrupt· the uniform motion of the waters, and produce new motions, known by the name of currents. Between two neighbouring heights in the bottom of the ocean, there must be a current, which will follow their common direction, and, like a river, cut a channel, the angles of which will be alternately opposite through the whole extent of its course. These heights must continually· increase; for, during the flow, the water will deposit its ordinary sediment upon their ridges, and the waters which are impelled by the current will force along, from great distances, quantities of matter, which will subside between the hills, and, at the same time, scoop out a valley with corresponding angles at their foundation. Now, by means of

5 Particularly on the coasts of Scotland and of Ireland.

these different motions and sediments, the bottom of the ocean, though formerly smooth, must soon be furrowed, and interspersed with hills and chains of mountains, as we actually find it at present. The soft materials of which the eminences were originally composed, would gradually harden by their own gravity. Such of them as consisted of sandy and crystalline particles, would produce those enormous masses of rock and flint in which we find crystals and other precious stones. Others composed of stony particles mixed with shells, give rise to those beds of lime-stone and marble, in which vast quantities of sea shells are still found incorporated. Lastly, all our beds of marble and chalk have derived their origin from particles of shells mixed with a pure earth, collected and deposited at particular places in the bottom of the sea. All these substances are disposed in regular strata; they all contain heterogeneous matter, and vast quantities of sea-bodies situated nearly in proportion to their specific gravities. The lighter shells are found in chalk; the heavier in clay and lime-stone. These shells are uniformly filled with the matter in which they are found, whether it be stone or earth. This is an incontestible proof, that they have been transported along with the matter that fills and surrounds them, and that this matter was then in the form of an impalpable powder. In a word, all those substances, the horizontal situation of which has arisen from the waters of the sea, invariably preserve their original position.

It may here be objected, that most hills, the summits of which consist of solid rocks, or of marble, are founded upon small eminences, composed of less heavy materials, such as clay or light sand, the strata of which commonly extend over the neighbouring plains. If the above theory be just, what could bring about an arrangement so singular, so contrary to the laws of gravity? But this phenomenon admits of a natural and easy explication. The waters would operate first upon the upper stratum, either of coasts or the bottom of the sea: this upper stratum consists generally of clay or sand; and these light substances, being carried off and deposited previous to the more dense and solid, they would of course form small eminences, and become foundations for the more heavy particles to rest upon. After the light, superficial substances were removed, the harder and more ponderous would next be subjected to the attrition of the water, reduced to a fine powder, and carried off and deposited above the hillocks of sand or clay. These small stony particles would, in a succession of ages, form those solid rocks which we now find on the tops of hills and mountains. As particles of stone are heavier than sand or clay, it is probable that they were originally covered and pressed by superior strata of considerable depth; but that they now occupy the highest stations, because they were last transported by the waves.

To confirm this reasoning, let us investigate more minutely the situation of those materials which compose the superficial part of the globe, the only part of which we have any adequate knowledge. The different strata of stones in quarries are almost all horizontal, or regularly inclined. Those founded upon hard clay, or other solid matter, are evidently horizontal, especially in plains. The disposition of quarries, where flint or brownish free-stone are found in detached portions, is indeed less regular. But even here the uniformity of nature is not interrupted; for the horizontal or regularly inclining position of the strata is apparent in granite and brown free-stone, wherever they exist in large connected masses. This position is universal, except in flint and brown free-stone in small detached portions, substances the formation of which we shall demonstrate to have been posterior to those just now mentioned. The strata of granite, vitrifiable sand, clays, marbles, calcareous stones, chalk, and marls, are always parallel or equally inclined. In these the original formation is easily discoverable; for the strata are exactly horizontal, and very thin, being placed above each other like the leaves of a book. Beds of sand, of soft and hard clay, of chalk, and of shells, are likewise either horizontal or uniformly inclined. Strata of every kind preserve the same thickness through their whole extent, which is often many leagues, and might, by proper observations, be traced still farther. In a word, the disposition of strata, as deep as mankind have hitherto penetrated, is the same.

Those beds of sand and gravel which are washed down from mountains, must, in some measure, be excepted from the general rule. They are sometimes of a considerable extent in valleys, and are situated immediately under the soil or first stratum. In plains, they are level, like the more ancient and interior strata. But near the bottom, or upon the ridges of hills, they have an inclination corresponding to that of the ground upon which they have been deposited. As these beds of sand and gravel are formed by rivers and brooks, which, especially in the valleys, often change their channels, it is not surprising that such beds should be so frequent. A small rivulet is sufficient, in a course of time, to spread a bed of sand or gravel over a very large valley. In a champaign country,[8] surrounded with hills, whose bases, as well as the upper stratum of the plain, consisted of a hard clay, I have often observed, that, above the origin of the brooks or rivers, the clay was situated immediately under the vegetable stratum; but, in the low grounds, there was a stratum of sand, about a foot thick, above the clay, and extending to a great distance from the banks of the rivers. The strata formed by rivers are not very ancient; they are easily distinguished by their frequent interruptions, and the inequality of their thickness. But the ancient strata uniformly preserve the same dimensions through their whole extent. Besides, these modern strata may be distinguished, with certainty, by the form of the stones and gravel they contain, which bear evident marks of having been rolled, smoothed, and rounded by the motion of water. The same observation may be made with regard to those beds of turf, and corrupted vegetables, which are found in marshy grounds, immediately below the soil: They have no claim to antiquity, but have derived their existence from successive accumulations of decayed trees, and other plants. The strata of slime, or mud, which occur in many places, are also recent productions, formed by stagnating waters, or the inundations of rivers. They are not so exactly horizontal, nor so uniformly inclined, as the more ancient strata, produced by the regular motions of the sea. In strata formed by rivers, we meet with river, but seldom with sea-shells; and the few which occur are broken, detached, and placed without order. But, in the ancient strata, there are no river-shells; the sea-shells are numerous, well preserved, and all placed in the same manner, having been transported and deposited at the same time, and by the same cause. From whence could this beautiful regularity proceed? Instead of regular strata, why do we not find the matters composing the earth huddled together without order? Why are not rocks, marbles, clays, marls, &c. scattered promiscuously, or joined by irregular or vertical strata? Why are not heavy bodies uniformly found in a lower situation than light ones? It is easy to perceive, that this uniformity of nature, this species of organization, this union of different materials by parallel strata, without regard to their weights, could only proceed from a cause equally powerful and uniform as the motions of the sea, produced by regular winds, by the tides, &c.

These causes act with superior force under the equator than in other climates; for there the tides are higher, and the winds more uniform. The most extensive chains of mountains are likewise in the neighbourhood of the equator. The mountains of Africa and Peru are the highest in the world, often extending through whole continents, and stretching to great distances under the waters of the ocean. The mountains of Europe and Asia, which extend from Spain to China, are not so elevated as those of Africa and South America. According to the relations of voyagers, the mountains of the north are but small hills, when compared with the mountains of the equatorial regions. Besides, in the northern seas, there are few islands; but, in the Torrid Zone, they are innumerable. Now, as islands are only the summits of mountains, it is apparent, that there are more inequalities on the surface of the earth near the equator, than in northerly climates.

Those prodigious chains of mountains which run from west to east in the Old Continent, and from north to south in the New, must have been formed by the general motion of the tides. But the origin of the less considerable mountains and hills must be ascribed to particular motions, occasioned by winds, currents, and other irregular agitations of the sea: their formation may, indeed, be owing to a combination of all these motions, which are capable of infinite variations; for the winds, and the situation of different islands and coasts, constantly change the natural course of the tides, and oblige them to run in every possible direction. It is not, therefore, surprising to see considerable eminences which have no determined direction in their courses. But, for our present purpose, it is sufficient to have shown, that mountains have not been produced by earthquakes, or other accidental causes, but that they are effects equally resulting from the general laws of nature, as well as their peculiar structure, and the situation of the materials of which they are composed.

But how has it happened, that this earth, which we and our ancestors have inhabited for ages, which, from time immemorial, has been an immense continent, dry, compact, and removed from the reach of the water, should, if formerly the bottom of an ocean, be now exalted to such a height above the waters, and so completely separated from them? Since the waters remained so long upon the earth, why have they now deserted it? What accident, what cause, could introduce a change so great? Is it possible to conceive a cause possessed of power sufficient to operate such an amazing effect?

These are difficult questions. But, as the facts are incontrovertible, the precise manner in which they have happened may remain a secret, without prejudice to the conclusions that ought to be drawn from them. A little reflection, however, will furnish us at least with plausible solutions. We daily observe the sea gaining ground on certain coasts, and losing it on others. We know, that the ocean has a general and uniform motion from east to west; that it makes violent efforts against the rocks and the low grounds which encircle it; that there are whole provinces which human industry can hardly defend from the fury of the waves; and that there are instances of islands which have but lately emerged from the waters, and of regular inundations. History informs us of inundations and deluges of a more extensive nature. Should not all these circumstances convince us, that the surface of the earth has experienced very great revolutions, and that the sea may have actually given up possession of the greatest part of the ground which it formerly occupied? For example, let us suppose, that the Old and New worlds were formerly but one continent, and that, by a violent earthquake, the ancient Atalantis of Plato[9] was sunk. What would be the consequence of such a mighty revolution? The sea would necessarily rush in from all quarters, and from what is now called the Atlantic Ocean; and vast continents, perhaps those which we now inhabit, would, of course, be left dry. This great revolution might be effected by the sudden failure of some immense cavern in the interior part of the globe, and an universal deluge would infalliby succeed. I should rather incline to think, that such a revolution would not be suddenly accomplished, but that it would require a very long period. However these conjectures stand, it is certain, that such a revolution has happened, and I even believe that it happened naturally; for, if a judgment of the future is to be formed from the past, we have only to attend carefully to what daily passes before our eyes. It is a fact, established by the repeated observation of voyagers, that the ocean has a constant motion from east to west. This motion, like the trade-winds, is not only perceived between the tropics, but through the whole temperate climates, and as near the poles as navigators have been able to approach. As a necessary consequence of this motion, the Pacific Ocean must make continual efforts against the coasts of Tartary, China, and India; the Indian Ocean must act against the east coast of Africa; and the Atlantic must act in a similar manner against all the eastern coasts of America. Hence the sea must have gained, and will always continue to gain, on the east, and to lose on the west. This circumstance alone would be sufficient to prove the possibility of the change of sea into land, and of land into sea. If such is the natural effect of the sea's motion from east to west, may it not reasonably be supposed, that Asia, and all the eastern continent, is the most antient country in the world? and that Europe, and part of Africa, especially the west parts of these continents, as Britain, France, Spain, &c., are countries of a more recent date? Both history and physics concur in establishing this hypothesis.

But, beside the constant motion of the sea from east to west, other causes concur in producing the effect just mentioned. There are many lands lower than the level of the sea, and are defended by a narrow isthmus of rock only, or by banks of still weaker materials. The action of the waters must gradually destroy these barriers; and, consequently, such lands must then become part of the ocean. Besides, the mountains are daily diminishing, part of them being constantly carried down to the valleys by rains. It is likewise well known, that every little brook carries earth, and other matters, from the high grounds into the rivers, by which they are at last transported to the ocean. By these means the bottom of the sea is gradually filling up, the surface of the earth is approaching to a level, and nothing but time is wanting for the sea's successively changing places with the land.

I speak not here of causes removed beyond the sphere of our knowledge, of those convulsions of nature, the slightest effort of which would be fatal to the globe. The near approach of a comet, the absence of the moon, or the introduction of a new planet into the system, &c. are suppositions upon which the imagination may rove at large. Causes of this kind will produce any effect we choose. From a single hypothesis of this nature, a thousand physical romances might be composed, and their authors might dignify them with the title of *Theory of the Earth*. As an historian, I reject these vain speculations: They depend upon mere possibilities, which, if called into action, necessarily imply such a devastation in the universe, that our globe, like a fugitive particle of matter, escapes observation, and is no longer worthy of our attention. But, to give consistency to our ideas, we must take the earth as it is, examine its different parts with minuteness, and, by induction, judge of the future, from what at present exists. We ought not to be affected by causes which seldom act, and whose action is always sudden and violent. These have no place in the ordinary course of nature. But operations uniformly repeated, motions which succeed one another without interruption, are the causes which alone ought to be the foundation of our reasoning.

Some examples shall be given: We shall combine particular effects with general causes, and give a detail of facts, which will illustrate and explain the different alterations that the earth has undergone, whether by irruptions of the sea upon the land, or by the sea's retiring from lands which it formerly covered.[...]

Perpendicular fissures vary greatly as to the extent of their openings. Some are about half an inch, or an inch, others a foot, or two feet; some extend several fathoms, and give rise to those vast precipices which so frequently occur between opposite parts of the same rocks in the Alps and other high mountains. It is plain, that the fissures, the openings of which are small, have been occasioned solely by drying. But those which extend several feet are partly owing to another cause; namely, the sinking of the foundation upon one side, while that of the other remained firm. If the base sinks but a line or two, when the height of the rock is considerable, an opening of several feet, or even fathoms, will be the consequence. When rocks are founded on clay or sand, they sometimes slip a little to a side; and the fissures are of course augmented by this motion. I have not hitherto mentioned those large openings, those prodigious cuts, which are to be met with in rocks and mountains: These could not be produced by any other means than the sinking of immense subterraneous caverns which were unable longer to sustain their incumbent load. But these cuts or intervals in mountains are not of the same nature with perpendicular fissures: They appear to have been ports opened by the hand of nature for the communication of nations. This seems to be the intention of all large openings in chains of mountains, and of those straits by which different parts of the ocean are connected; as the Straits of Thermopylae, of Gibraltar, &c; the gaps or ports in Mount Caucasus, the Cordeliers, &c. A simple separation, by the drying of the matter, could not produce this effect: Large portions of earth must have been sunk, swallowed up, or thrown down.

These great sinkings, though occasioned by accidental and secondary causes, are leading facts in the history of the earth, and have contributed greatly in changing the appearance of its surface. Most of them have been produced by subterraneous fires, the explosions of which give rise to earthquakes and volcanos. The force of inflamed matter, shut up in the bowels of the earth, is irresistible. By the action of subterraneous fires, whole cities have been swallowed up, mountains, and large tracts of country, have been overturned and rendered unfit for the habitation of men. But, though this force be great, though its effects appear to be prodigious, we cannot assent to the opinions of some authors, who suppose that these subterraneous fires are only branches of an immense abyss of flame in the centre of the earth. Neither do we credit the common notion, that these fires have their seat at a great depth below the surface; for matter cannot begin to burn, or at least the inflammation cannot be supported, without air.[. . .]

From these facts it is easy to perceive how much subterraneous fires have contributed to change both the surface and internal part of the globe. This cause has power sufficient to produce very great effects. But it is difficult to conceive how any sensible alterations upon the land can be introduced by the winds. Their dominion would appear to be confined to the sea. Indeed, next to the tides, nothing has such a powerful influence upon the waters; the flux and reflux proceed with an uniform pace; their operations are always the same; but the action of the winds is capricious and violent. They rush on with irresistible fury, and excite such impetuous commotions, that the ocean, from a smooth and tranquil plain, in an instant is furrowed with waves, which emulate the height of mountains, and dash themselves in pieces against the shores. The surface of the ocean is subject to constant alterations from the winds. But ought not the surface of the land, which has so solid an appearance, ever to remain uninfluenced by a cause of this kind? It is consonant to experience, however, that the winds raise mountains of sand in Arabia and Africa; that they overwhelm large plains with it; and that they frequently carry these sands many leagues into the sea, where they accumulate in such quantities as to form banks, downs, and even islands. It is also well known, that hurricanes are the scourge of the Antilles, of Madagascar, and of other countries, where their impetuosity is so great, that they sweep away trees, plants, and animals, together with the soil which nourished them. They drive back, they annihilate rivers, and produce new ones; they overthrow rocks and mountains; they scoop out holes and gulfs in the earth, and totally change the face of those unhappy countries which give birth to them. Happily, few climates are exposed to the violence of those dreadful agitations of the air.

But the greatest changes upon the surface of the earth are occasioned by rains, rivers, and torrents from the mountains. These derive their origin from vapours raised by the sun from the surface of the ocean, and are transported by the winds through every climate. The progress of these vapours, which are supported by the air, and transported at the pleasure of the winds, is interrupted by the tops of the mountains, where they accumulate into clouds, and fall down in the form of rain, dew, or snow. At first, these waters descended into the plains without any fixed course; but they gradually hollowed out proper channels for themselves. By the power of gravity, they ran to the bottom of the mountains, and, penetrating or dissolving the lower grounds, they carried along with them sand and gravel, cut deep furrows in the plains, and thus opened passages to the sea, which always receives as much water by rivers as it loses by evaporation. The windings in the channels of rivers have uniformly corresponding angles on their opposite banks; and as mountains and hills, which may be regarded as the banks of the valleys by which they are separated, have likewise sinuosities with corresponding angles, this circumstance seems to demonstrate, that the valleys have been gradually formed by currents of the ocean, in the same manner as the channels of rivers have been produced. [. . .]

Notes

1   Buffon is using the word 'History' in a sense not restricted to the recording of the past – in the sense, that is to say, which it bears in the phrase 'Natural history', i.e. the systematic description of the works of nature.

2   'Organization, internal constitution, apportionment of functions'. OED.

3   That is, arbitrary and metaphysical systems, based not on observation but on a theoretical assumption.

4   William Whiston, (1667-1762) author of *A New Theory of the Earth, from the Original to the Consummation of All Things. Wherein the Creation of the World in Six Days, the Universal Deluge, and the General Conflagration, as laid down in the Holy Scriptures, are shown to be perfectly agreeable to Reason and Philosophy* (1696).

5   Thomas Burnet (*c.* 1635–1715) writer, author of the extraordinary visionary

work *Sacred Theory of the Earth*. First Latin edition 1680–89. English edition 1684–90.

6   John Woodward (1665–1728), a physician and Fellow of the Royal Society, author of *Essay Towards a Natural History of the Earth* (1695).

7   The logical method by which one proceeds from particular observations to a general principle (i.e. the opposite of deduction).

8   Level, open country.

9   Plato (*c.* 427–*c.* 347 B.C.) in his *Timaeus* and his *Critias* refers to a mythical island named Atlantis in the Atlantic ocean which was supposedly a powerful kingdom until engulfed by the sea.

BUFFON

An Examination of Some Other Theories of the Earth (1749)

From *Histoire naturelle* (ibid., Vol. 1, 1749), 'Preuves de la Théorie de la Terre.' Article V. 'Exposition de quelques autres systèmes'. Reprinted from *Natural History* (ibid., Vol. 1, 1812) 'Proofs of the Theory of the Earth, Article V.

The 'History and theory of the earth' was followed by 'Proofs of the theory of the earth', in the same volume. Here Buffon concentrates on naturalists who mixed physics with theology.

The three hypotheses formerly animadverted upon[1] have many things in common: they all agree in this, that, at the time of the deluge, both the external and internal form of the earth was changed. But none of these theorists considered that the earth, before the deluge, was inhabited by the same species of men and animals; and, consequently, that it must have been nearly the same, both in figure and structure, as it is at present. We are informed by the sacred writings, that, before the deluge, there were rivers, seas, mountains, and forests; that most of these mountains and rivers remained nearly in their former situation; the Tigris and Euphrates, for example, ran through Paradise; that the Armenian mountain on which the ark rested, was, at the deluge, one of the highest mountains of the earth, as it is at this day; and that the same plants and the same animals, which inhabited the earth before the deluge, continue still to exist; for we are told of the serpent, of the crow, and of the pigeon that carried the olive-branch into the ark. Tournefort[2] indeed alleges, that there are no olives within 400 leagues of Mount Araret, and affects to be witty on this head. It is, however, indisputable, that there were olives in the neighbourhood of this mountain at the time of the deluge; for Moses assures us of the fact in the most express manner. Besides, it is not surprising, that, in the course of 4,000 years, the olives should be extirpated in these provinces, and multiplied in others. It is, therefore, contrary both to scripture and reason, that these authors have supposed the earth, before the deluge, to have been totally different from what it is now; and this opposition between their hypotheses and the sacred writings, as well as sound philosophy, is sufficient to discredit their systems, although they should correspond with some phænomena. Burnet, who wrote first, gives neither facts nor observations in support of his system. Woodward's book is only a short essay, in which he promises much more than he was able to perform; it is only a project, without any degree of execution. He makes use of two general remarks: 1. That the earth is every where composed of materials which had formerly been in a state of fluidity, and which had been deposited by the waters in horizontal beds. 2. That, in the bowels of many parts of the earth, there are an infinite number of sea bodies. To account for these facts, he has recourse to the universal deluge; or rather, he appears to employ these as proofs of the deluge. But, like Burnet, he falls into evident contradictions; for it is absurd to suppose, with these authors, that, before the deluge, there were no mountains, since we are expressly told, that the waters rose fifteen cubits above the tops of the highest mountains. On the other hand, it is not said that the waters destroyed or dissolved the mountains. In place of this extraordinary dissolution, the mountains remained firm in their original situations, and the ark rested upon the one which was first deserted by the waters. Besides, it is impossible to imagine, that, during the short time the deluge continued, the waters could dissolve the mountains, and the whole fabric of the earth. Is it not absurd to suppose, that, in the space of forty days, the hardest rocks and minerals were dissolved by simple water? Is it not a manifest contradiction to admit this total dissolution, and yet to maintain that shells, bones, and other productions of the sea, were able to resist a menstruum to which the most solid materials had yielded? Upon the whole, I cannot hesitate in pronouncing, that Woodward, though furnished with excellent facts and observations, has produced but a weak and inconsistent theory.

Whiston, who wrote last, has greatly improved upon the other two; and, though he has given loose reins to his imagination, it cannot be said that he falls into contradiction. He advances many things which are incredible; but they are neither absolutely nor apparently impossible. As we are ignorant of what materials the centre of the earth is composed, he thinks himself entitled to suppose it a solid nucleus, surrounded with a ring of heavy fluid matter, and then follows a ring of water, upon which the external crust is supported. In this ring of water, the different parts of the crust sunk more or less in proportion to their gravities, and gave rise to mountains and inequalities on the surface of the earth. But our astronomer here commits a blunder in mechanics. He considered not, that the earth, on this supposition, must have formed one uniform arch; and, consequently, that it could not be supported by the water, and far less could any part of this arch sink deeper than another. If this be excepted, I doubt whether he has fallen into any other physical blunder: he has, however, committed many errors both in metaphysics and theology. In fine, it cannot be denied absolutely, that the earth, in meeting with the tail of a comet, would be deluged, especially if it be allowed to the author, that the tails of comets contain watery vapours. Neither is it absolutely impossible, that the tail of a comet, in returning from its perihelion, should burn the earth, if we suppose, with Mr. Whiston, that the comet passed very near the sun's body. The same observations may be made upon the rest of his system. But though his notions be not absolutely impossible, when taken separately, they are so exceedingly improbable, that the whole assemblage may be regarded as exceeding the bounds of human credulity.

These three are not the only books which have been written upon the theory of the earth. In 1729, M. Bourguet[3] published, along with his *Philosophical Letters on the Formation of Salts,* &c. a memoir, in which he gives a specimen of a system which he had projected; but the execution of it was prevented by the death of the author. It must be acknowledged, that no man was more industrious and acute in making observations, and in collecting facts. To him we are indebted for remarking the correspondence between the angles of mountains,[4] which is the chief key to the theory of the earth. He arranges the materials he had collected in the best order. But, with all these advantages, it is probable, that he would not have succeeded in giving a physical history of the changes which have happened in the earth; and he appears not to have discovered the causes of those effects which he relates. To be convinced of this remark, we have only to take a view of the propositions he deduces from those phænomena which must have been the foundation of his theory. He says, that the earth was formed at once, and not successively; that its figure and disposition demonstrate that it was formerly in a fluid state; that the present condition of the earth is very different from what it was some ages after its first formation; that the matter of the globe was originally more soft than after its surface was changed; that the condensation of its solid parts diminished gradually with its velocity; so that, after a certain number of revolutions round its own axis, and round the sun, its original structure was suddenly dissolved; that this happened at the vernal equinox; that the sea shells insinuated themselves into the dissolved matters; that the earth, after this dissolution, assumed its present form; and that, as soon as the fire or heat operated upon it, its consumption gradually began, and, at some future period, it will be blown up with a dreadful explosion, accompanied with a general conflagration, which will augment the atmosphere, and diminish the diameter of the globe; and then the earth, in place of strata of sand or clay, will consist only of beds of calcined materials, and mountains composed of amalgams of different metals.

This is a sufficient view of the system which M. Bourguet designed to compose. To guess at the past, and to predict the future, nearly in the same manner as others have guessed and predicted, requires but a small effort of genius. This author had more erudition than sound and general ideas. He appears not to have had the capacity of forming enlarged views, or of comprehending the chain of causes and effects.

In the Leipsic Transactions, the celebrated Leibnitz published a sketch of an opposite system, under the title of Protogæa.[5] The earth, according to Bourguet and others, was to be consumed by fire. But Leibnitz maintains, that it originated from fire, and that it has undergone innumerable changes and revolutions. At the time that Moses tells us the light was divided from the darkness, the greatest part of the earth was in flames. The planets, as well as the earth, were originally fixed and luminous stars. After burning for many ages, he alleges, that they were extinguished from a deficiency of combustible matter, and that they became opaque bodies. The fire, by melting the matter, produced a vitrified crust; and the basis of all terrestrial bodies is glass, of which sand and gravel are only the fragments. The other species of earth resulted from a mixture of sand with water and fixed salts; and, when the crust had cooled, the moist particles, which had been elevated in the form of vapour, fell down, and formed the ocean. These waters at first covered the whole surface, and even overtopped the highest mountains. In the estimation of this author, the shells, and other spoils of the ocean, which every where abound, are indelible proofs that the earth was formerly covered with the sea; and the great quantity of fixed salts, of sand, and of other melted and calcined matters shut up in the bowels of the earth, demonstrate, that the conflagration had been general, and that it had preceded the existence of the ocean. These ideas, though destitute of evidence, are elevated, and bear conspicuous marks of ingenuity. The thoughts have a connexion, the hypotheses are not impossible, and the consequences which might be drawn from them are not contradictory. But the great defect of this theory is, that it applies not to the present state of the earth. It only explains what passed in ages so remote, that few vestiges remain; a man may, therefore, affirm what he pleases, and what he says will be accompanied with more or less probability, in proportion to the extent of his talents. To maintain, with Whiston, that the earth was originally a comet, or with Leibnitz, that it was a sun, is to assert what is equally possible or impossible; it would, therefore, be ridiculous to investigate either by the laws of probability. The instantaneous creation of the world destroys the notion of the globe's being covered with the ocean, and of that being the reason why sea shells are so much diffused through different parts of the earth; for, if that had been the case, it must of necessity be allowed, that shells, and other productions of the ocean, which are still found in the bowels of the earth, were created long prior to man, and other land animals. Now, independent of scripture authority, is it not reasonable to think that the origin of all kinds of animals and vegetables is equally ancient?

M. Scheutzer,[6] in a dissertation addressed to the Academy of Sciences in 1708, attributes, like Woodward, the change, or rather new creation of the globe, to the deluge. To account for the formation of mountains, he tells us, that God, when he ordered the waters to return to their subterraneous abodes, broke, with his Almighty hand, many of the horizontal strata, and elevated them above the surface of the earth, which was originally level. The whole dissertation was composed with a view to support this ridiculous notion. As it was necessary that these eminences should be of a solid consistence, M. Scheutzer remarks, that God only raised them from places which abounded in stones. Hence, says he, those countries, like Switzerland, which are very stoney, are likewise mountainous; and those, like Flanders, Holland, Hungary, and Poland, which are mostly composed of sand and clay to great depths, have few or no mountains.

This author, like Woodward, blends physics and theology; and, though he has made some good observations, the systematic part of his work is weaker and more puerile than that of any of his predecessors. He has even descended to declamation, and absurd pleasantries. The reader, if he desires to see them, may consult his *Piscium Querelae*, &c., not to mention his *Physica Sacra*, consisting of several volumes in folio, a weak performance, fitter for the amusement of children than the instruction of men.

Steno,[7] and some others, have attributed the origin of mountains, and other inequalities upon the surface of the earth, to particular inundations, earthquakes, &c. But the effects of these secondary causes could produce nothing but slight changes. These causes may co-operate with the first cause, namely, the tides, and the motion of the sea from east to west. Besides, Steno has given no theory nor even any general facts, upon this subject.

Ray[8] alleges, that all mountains have been produced by earthquakes, and has written a treatise to prove the point. When we come to the article of volcanos, we shall examine the foundation of this opinion.

We cannot omit observing here, that Burnet, Whiston, Woodward, and most other authors, have fallen into an error which deserves to be rectified. They uniformly regard the deluge as an effect within the compass of natural causes, although the scripture represents it as an immediate operation of the Deity. It is beyond the power of any natural cause to produce on the surface of the earth a quantity of water sufficient to cover the highest mountains: and, although a cause could be imagined adequate to this effect, it would still be impossible to find another cause capable of making the waters disappear. Granting that Whiston's waters proceeded from the tail of a comet, we deny that any of them could issue from the abyss, or that the whole could return into it; for the abyss, according to him, was so environed and pressed on all sides by the terrestrial crust, that it was impossible the comet's attraction could produce the least motion in the fluid it contained, far less any motion resembling the tides: hence, not a single drop could either proceed from, or enter into, the great abyss. Unless, therefore, it is supposed, that the waters which fell from the comet were annihilated by a miracle, they would for ever have remained on the surface, and covered the tops of the highest mountains. The impossibility of explaining any effect by natural causes, is the most essential character of a miracle. Our authors have made several vain efforts to account for the deluge. Their errors in physics, and in the secondary causes they employ, prove the truth of the fact, as related in scripture, and demonstrate, that the universal deluge could not be accomplished by any other cause than the will of the Deity.

Besides, it is apparent, that it was not at one time, nor by the sudden effect of a deluge, that the sea left uncovered those continents which we inhabit; it is certain, from the authority of scripture, that the terrestrial Paradise was in Asia, and that Asia was inhabited before the deluge; consequently, the waters, at that period, covered not this large portion of the globe. The earth before the deluge, was nearly the same as now. This enormous quantity of water, poured out by Divine justice upon guilty men, destroyed every living creature; but it produced no change on the surface of the earth; it destroyed not even the plants; for the pigeon returned to the ark with an *olive branch* in her bill.

Why then should we suppose, with many naturalists, that the waters of the deluge totally changed the surface of the globe, even to the depth of two thousand feet? Why imagine that the deluge transported those shells, which are found at the depth of seven or eight hundred feet, immersed in rocks and in marble? Why refer to this event the formation of hills and mountains? And how is it possible to imagine, that the waters of the deluge transported banks of shells of 100 leagues in length! I perceive not how they can persist in this opinion, unless they admit a double miracle, one to create water, and another to transport shells. But as the first only is supported by holy writ, I see no reason for making the second an article of faith.

On the other hand, if the waters of the deluge had retired suddenly, they would have carried off such immense quantities of mud and soil, as would have rendered the land unfit for culture, till many ages after this inundation. In the inundation which happened in Greece, the country that was covered remained barren for three centuries. Thus the deluge ought to be regarded as a supernatural mode of chastising the wickedness of men, not as an effect proceeding from any natural cause. The universal deluge was a miracle, both in its cause and in its effects. It appears from the sacred text, that the sole design of the deluge was the destruction of men and other animals, and that it changed not in any manner the surface of the earth; for, after the retreat of the waters, the mountains and even the trees, kept their former stations, and the land was suited for the culture of vines and other fruits of the earth. It might be asked, if the earth was dissolved in the waters, or, if the waters were so much agitated as to transport the shells of India into Europe, how the fishes, which entered not into the ark, were preserved?

The notion that the shells were transported and left upon the land by the deluge, is the general opinion, or rather superstition, of naturalists. Woodward, Scheutzer, and others, call petrified shells the remains of the deluge; they regard them as medals or monuments left us by God of this dreadful catastrophe, that the memorial of it might never be effaced among men. Lastly, they have embraced this hypothesis with so blind a veneration, that their only anxiety is to reconcile it with holy writ; and, in place of deriving any light from observation and experience, they wrap themselves up in the dark clouds of physical theology, the obscurity and littleness of which derogate from the simplicity and dignity of religion, and present to the sceptic nothing but a ridiculous medley of human conceits and divine truths. To attempt an explanation of the universal deluge and of its physical causes; to pretend to give a detail of what passed during this great revolution; to conjecture what effects have resulted from it; to add facts to the sacred writings, and to draw consequences from these interpolations: is not this a presumptuous desire of scanning the power of the Almighty? The natural wonders wrought by his beneficent hand, in a uniform and regular manner, are altogether incomprehensible; his extraordinary operations, or his miracles, ought, therefore, to impress us with an awful astonishment, and a silent respect.

It may still be urged, that, as the universal deluge is an established fact, is it not lawful to reason upon its consequences? True. But you must commence with acknowledging, that the deluge could not possibly be the effect of any physical cause; you must regard it as an immediate operation of the Deity; you must content yourself with what is recorded in scripture; and you must, above all, avoid blending bad philosophy with the purity of divine truth. After taking these precautions, which a respect for the counsels of the Almighty requires, what remains for examination upon the subject of the deluge? Do the sacred writings tell us that the mountains were formed by the deluge? They tell us the reverse. Do they inform us that the agitation of the waters was so great, as to raise the shells from the bottom of the ocean, and to disperse them over the face of the earth? No: the ark moved gently on the surface of the waters. Do they tell us, that the earth suffered a total dissolution? By no means. The narration of the sacred historian is simple and true; that of naturalists is complicated and fabulous.

Notes

1   Those of Burnet, Woodward and Whiston.
2   Joseph Pitton de Tournefort (1656–1708), French botanist.
3   The French scientist Louis Bourguet who published a *Treatise on Petrifactions* (1742).
4   See *History and Theory of the Earth*, p. 195.
5   Leibniz wrote this work in 1691, his theory being the fruit of some years' work as a mining engineer, but it was not published in book form until 1749.
6   J. J. Scheutzer (1672–1733); Swiss naturalist, author of *Helvetiae Stoicheiographia*.
7   The Danish anatomist Niels Stensen, known as Steno (1648–86). He studied rock-formations in Tuscany and recognized the organic origin of fossils.
8   John Ray (1627–1705), botanist and zoologist.

BUFFON

The Ass (1753)

From *Histoire naturelle des quadrupèdes* (ibid., Vol. IV, 1753), 'L'Asne'. Reprinted from *History of Man and the Quadrupeds* (ibid., Vol. IV, 1812).

From 1753 to 1767, Buffon produced Vols. IV–XV of the *Natural History*, on the subject of quadrupeds.

The first of the following two extracts comes from Vol. IV. Here he attacks Linnaeus's classification 'family' as having no existence in Nature. For Buffon, the only notion that corresponds to reality is the idea of species, to which he gives a purely biological explanation: 'It is neither... the number nor the collection of similar individuals, but the constant succession and renovation of these individuals, which constitute the species' (see p. 222). Nevertheless, he does not rule out 'common variations of Nature' – those effected by the influence of climate and food – within a species.

This animal, even when examined with minute attention, has the appearance of a degenerated horse. The exact similarity in the structure of the brain, lungs, stomach, intestinal canal, heart, liver, and other viscera, and the great resemblance of the body, legs, feet, and whole skeleton, seem to support this opinion. The slight differences which take place between these two animals may be attributed to the long continued influence of climate and food, and to a fortuitous succession of many generations of small wild horses, who, by gradually degenerating, at last produced a new and permanent species, or rather a race of similar individuals, all marked with the same defects, and differing so widely from the genuine horse, as to be regarded as constituting a new species. The greater variety of the colour of horses than of asses appears to favour this idea: this circumstance shows that the former have been longer in a domestic state; for the colour of all domestic animals varies much more than that of wild ones of the same species. Besides, the wild horses mentioned by travellers are generally small, and have, like the

217

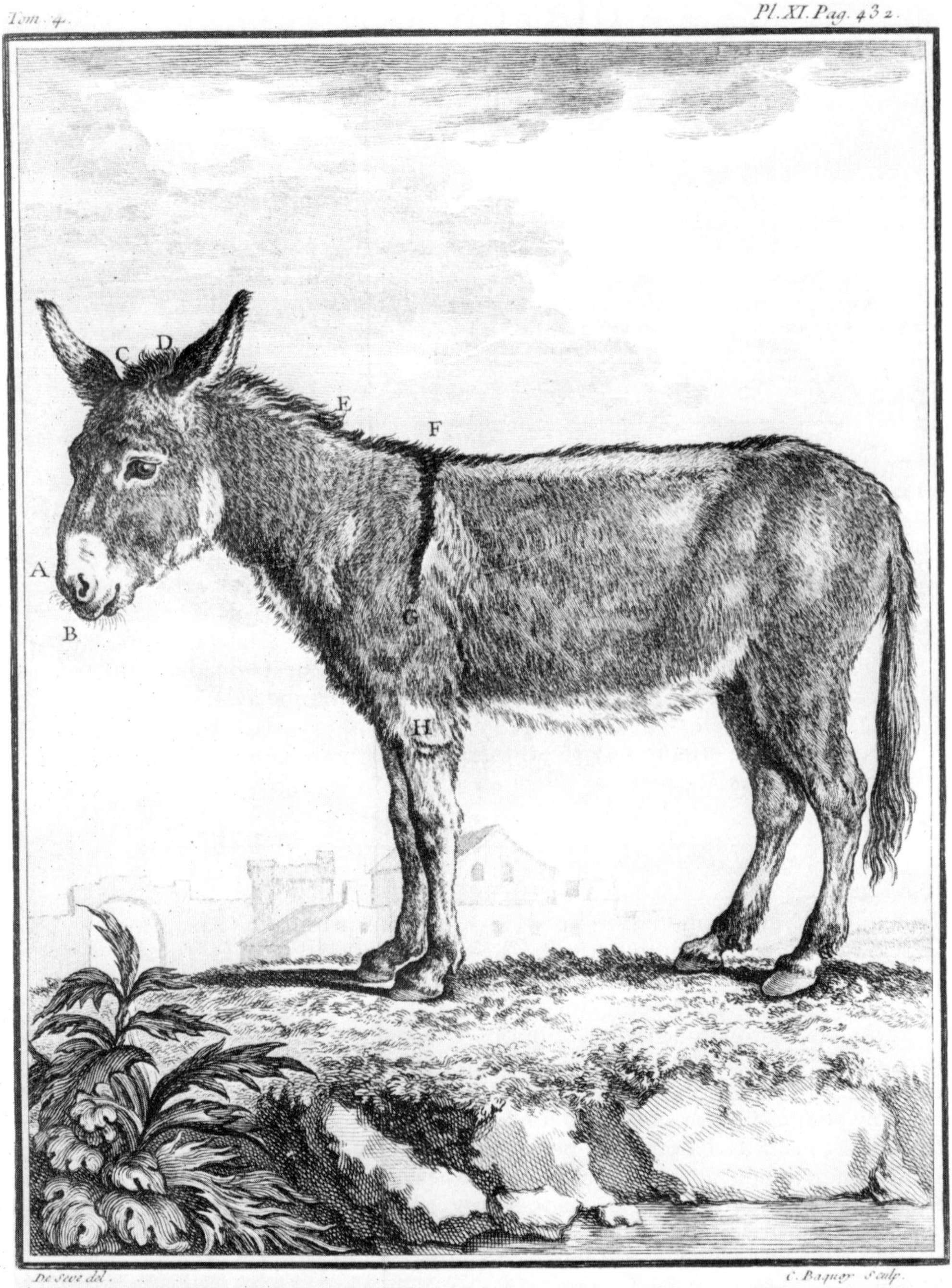
Tom. 4.
Pl. XI. Pag. 432.
C
D
E
F
A
B
G
H
De Seve del.
C. Baquoy Sculp.

Plate 26 from *Histoire naturelle* The Ass

Pl. XIII Pag. 432

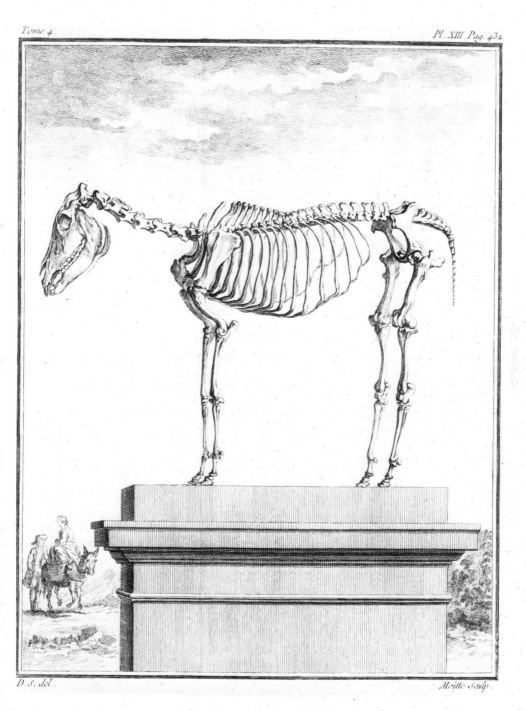

D.S. del. Moitte Sculp.

Plate 27   from *Histoire naturelle*   Skeleton of the Ass

ass, gray hair, and a naked tail, tufted at the extremity. Some wild, as well as domestic horses, have likewise a black line on the back, and other characters which make them nearly approach to the ass.

On the other hand, if we attend to the differences of temperament, dispositions, manners, and, in a word, of the general result of the organization of these two animals, particularly the impossibility of their commixture, so as to form a common, or even an intermediate species, capable of procreating, the opinion, that they were originally distinct species, equally removed from each other as at present, will appear to be the most probable. The ass, besides, differs materially from the horse, in smallness of stature, thickness of the head, length of the ears, hardness of the skin, nakedness of the tail, the form of the buttocks and the dimensions of the adjacent parts, the voice, the appetite, the manner of drinking, &c. Is it possible that animals so essentially different, should spring from the same original stock? Are they, to use the language of nomenclators, of the same family? Or rather, are they not, and have they not always been, distinct animals?

Philosophers will perceive the extent, the difficulties, and the importance of this question, which we shall here discuss, only because it for the first time occurs. It relates to the production of beings, and, for its illustration, requires that we should consider Nature under a new point of view. If, from the immense number of animated beings which people the universe, we select a single animal, or even the human body, as a standard, and compare all other organized beings with it, we shall find that each enjoys an independent existence, and that the whole are distinguished by an almost infinite variety of gradations. There exists, at the same time, a primitive and general design, which may be traced to a great distance, and whose degradations are still slower than those of figure or other external relations: for, not to mention the organs of digestion, of circulation, or of generation, without which animals could neither subsist nor reproduce, there is, even among the parts that contribute most to variety in external form, such an amazing resemblance, as necessarily conveys the idea of an original plan upon which the whole has been conceived and executed. When, for example, the parts constituting the body of a horse, which seem to differ so widely from that of man, are compared in detail with the human frame, instead of being struck with the difference, we are astonished at the singular and almost perfect resemblance. In a word, take the skeleton of a man, incline the bones of the pelvis, shorten those of the thighs, legs, and arms, lengthen the bones of the feet and hands, join the phalanges of the fingers and toes, lengthen the jaws by shortening the frontal bone, and, lastly, extend the spine of the back: this skeleton would no longer represent that of a man, but would be the skeleton of a horse; for, by lengthening the back-bone and the jaws, the number of vertebrae, ribs, and teeth, would likewise be augmented; and it is only by the number of these bones, which may be regarded as accessory, and by the prolonging, contracting, or junction of others, that the skeleton of a horse differs from the skeleton of a man. But, to trace these relations more minutely, let us examine separately some parts which are essential to the figure of animals, as the ribs: these we find in man, in all quadrupeds, in birds, in fishes, and the vestiges of them are apparent even in the shell of the turtle: let us next consider, that the foot of a horse, so seemingly different from the hand of a man, is, however, composed of the same bones, and that, at the extremity of each finger, we have the same small bone, resembling a horse-shoe, which bounds the foot of that animal. From these facts we may judge, whether this hidden resemblance is not more wonderful than the apparent differences; whether this constant uniformity of design, to be traced from men to quadrupeds, from quadrupeds to the cetaceous animals, from the cetaceous animals to birds, from birds to reptiles, from reptiles to fishes, &c., in which the essential parts, as the heart, the intestines, the spine, the senses, &c., are always included, does not indicate, that the Supreme Being, in creating animals, employed only one idea, and, at the same time, diversified it in every possible manner, to give men an opportunity of admiring equally the magnificence of the execution and the simplicity of the design?

In this view, not only the horse and ass, but man, monkeys, quadrupeds, and every species of animal, may be considered as one family. But from this are we warranted to conclude, that, in this great and numerous family, which were brought into existence by the Almighty alone, there are lesser families conceived by Nature, and produced by time, of which some should only consist of two individuals, as the horse and ass, others of several individuals, as the weasel, the ferret, the martin, the pole-cat, &c.; and, at the same time, that, among vegetables, there are families consisting of ten, twenty, thirty &c., plants? If these families really existed, they could only be produced by the mixture and successive variation and degeneration of the primary species: and if it be once admitted, that there are families among plants and animals, that the ass belongs to the family of the horse, and differs from him only by degeneration; with equal propriety may it be concluded, that the monkey belongs to the family of man; that the monkey is a man degenerated; that man and the monkey have sprung from a common stock, like the horse and ass; that each family, either among animals or vegetables, has been derived from the same origin; and even that all animated beings have proceeded from a single species, which, in the course of ages, has produced, by improving and degenerating, all the different races that now exist.

Those naturalists[1] who, on such slight foundations, have established families among animals and vegetables, seem not to have considered, that, if their doctrine were true, it would reduce the product of the creation to any assignable number of individuals, however small:[2] for, if it were proved, that animals and vegetables were really distributed into families, or even that a single species was ever produced by the degeneration of another, that the ass, for instance, was only a degenerated horse, no bounds could be fixed to the powers of Nature: she might, with equal reason, be supposed to have been able, in the course

221

of time, to produce, from a single individual, all the organized bodies in the universe.

But this is by no means a proper representation of Nature. We are assured, by the authority of revelation, that all animals have participated equally of the favours of creation; that the two first of each species were formed by the hands of the Almighty: and we ought to believe that they were then nearly what their descandants are at present. Besides, since Nature was observed with attention, since the days of Aristotle to those of our own, no new species have appeared, notwithstanding the rapid movements which break down and dissipate the parts of matter, notwithstanding the infinite variety of combinations which must have taken place during these twenty centuries, notwithstanding those fortuitous or forced commixtures between animals of different species, from which nothing is produced but barren and vitiated individuals, totally incapable of transmitting their monstrous kinds to posterity. Were the external or internal resemblances of particular animals, therefore, still greater than they are between the horse and ass, they should not lead us to confound these animals, or to assign them a common origin. For, if they actually proceeded from the same stock, we should be enabled to bring them back to their primitive state, and thus, with time, destroy the supposed operations of time.

It should likewise be considered, that, though Nature proceeds with gradual, and often imperceptible steps; yet the intervals or marks of distinction are not always equal. The more dignified the species, they are always the less numerous, and separated by more conspicuous shades. The diminutive species, on the contrary, are very numerous, and make nearer approaches towards each other. For this reason, we are often tempted to erect them into families. But it should never be forgotten, that these families are of our own creation; that we have contrived them to ease our memories, and to aid our imagination; that, if we cannot comprehend the real relations of all beings, it is our own fault, not that of Nature, who knows none of those spurious families, and contains, in fact, nothing but individuals.

An individual is a solitary, a detached being, and has nothing in common with other beings, except that it resembles, or rather differs from them. All the similar individuals which exist on the surface of the earth, are regarded as composing the species of these individuals. It is neither, however, the number nor the collection of similar individuals, but the constant succession and renovation of these individuals, which constitute the species. A being, whose duration was perpetual, would not make a species. Species, then, is an abstract and general term, the meaning of which can only be apprehended by considering Nature in the succession of time, and in the constant destruction and renovation of beings. It is by comparing present individuals with those which are past, that we acquire a clear idea of species; for a comparison of the number or similarity of individuals is an accessory idea only, and often independent of the first: the ass resembles the horse more than the spaniel does the greyhound; and yet the latter are of the same species, because they produce fertile individuals; but, as the horse and ass produce only unfertile and vitiated individuals, they are evidently of different species.

It is in the characteristic diversities of species, therefore, that the intervals in the shades of Nature are most conspicuously marked. We may even affirm, that these invervals between different species are the most equal and constant since we can draw a line of separation between two species, that is, between two successions of individuals who reproduce, but cannot mix; and since we cannot also unite into one species two successions of individuals who reproduce by mixing. This is the most fixed and determined point in the history of Nature. All other similarities and differences which can be found in the comparison of beings, are neither so real nor so constant. These intervals are the only lines of separation which shall be followed in this work. We shall introduce no artificial or arbitrary divisions. Every species, every succession of individuals, who reproduce and cannot mix, shall be considered and treated separately; and we shall employ no other families, genera, orders, and classes, than what are exhibited by Nature herself.

Species being thus limited to a constant succession of individuals endowed with the power of reproduction, it is obvious that this term ought never to be extended beyond animals and vegetables, and that those nomenclators who have employed it to distinguish the different kinds of minerals, have abused terms and confounded ideas. We should not, therefore, consider iron as one species, and lead as another species; they ought only to be regarded as two different metals, and should be distinguished by lines of separation very different from those employed in the distinctions of animals or vegetables.

But to return to the degeneration of beings, and particularly to that of animals. Let us examine more closely the proceedings of Nature in the varieties she offers to our consideration: and, as we are best acquainted with the human species, let us observe how far the varieties of it extend. Among men, all the gradations of colour, from black to white, are exhibited: they likewise differ, by one half, in height of stature, thickness, strength, swiftness, &c. But their mind is always the same. This latter quality, however, belongs not to matter, and ought not to be treated of in this place. The others are the common variations of Nature effected by the influence of climate and of food. But these differences in colour and dimensions prevent not the Negro and White, the Laplander and Patagonian, the giant and dwarf, from mixing together and producing fertile individuals; and, consequently, these men, so different in appearance, are all of one species, because this uniform reproduction is the very circumstance which constitutes distinct species. Beside these general varieties, there are others of a more particular nature, and yet fail not to be perpetuated; as the enormous legs of *the race of St. Thomas*[3] in the island of Ceylon; the red eyes and white hair of the Dariens and Chacrelas; the six fingers and

toes peculiar to certain families, &c. These singular varieties are accidental redundancies or defects, which, originating from some individuals, are propagated from generation to generation, like hereditary diseases. But they ought not to be regarded as constituting particular species; since these uncommon races of men with gross limbs, or with six fingers, are capable of mixing and of producing fertile individuals: the same remark is applicable to all other deformities which are communicated from parents to children.

Thus far only the errors of Nature and the varieties among men extend. If there are individuals who degenerate still farther, they produce nothing and change not the constancy and unity of the species. Hence man constitutes but one and the same species; and, though this species be, perhaps, the most numerous, capricious, and irregular in its actions; yet all the diversities in movement, food, climate, and other combinations which may be conceived, have not produced beings so different from each other as to constitute new species, and, at the same time, so similar to ourselves, as to be considered as belonging to us.

If the Negro and the White could not propagate, or if their productions remained barren, they would form two distinct species; the Negro would be to man what the ass is to the horse; or, rather, if the White were man, the Negro would be a separate animal, like the monkey; and we would be entitled to pronounce that the White and the Negro had not a common origin. But this supposition is contradicted by experience; for, as all the varieties of men are capable of mixing together, and of transmitting the kind, they must necessarily have sprung from the same stock or family.

A slight disparity of temperament, or some accidental defect in the organs of generation, will render two individuals of the same species barren. A certain degree of conformity in the structure of the body and in the organs of generation, will enable two animals, of different species, to produce individuals, similar to none of the parents, resembling nothing fixed or permanent; and, therefore, incapable of producing. But, what an amazing number of combinations are included in the supposition, that two animals, a male and a female, of a particular species, should degenerate so much as to form a new species, and to lose the faculty of producing with any other of the kind but themselves? It is still more incredible that the offspring of such degenerated creatures should follow exactly the same laws which are observed in the procreation of perfect animals: for a degenerated animal is a vitiated production; and how should an origin that is vitiated, depraved, and defective, constitute a new stock, and not only give rise to a succession of permanent and distinct beings, but even to produce them in the same manner, and according to the same laws which regulate the propagation of animals whose race is pure and uncorrupted?

Though, therefore, we cannot demonstrate, that the formation of a new species, by means of degeneration, exceeds the powers of Nature; yet the number of improbabilities attending such a supposition, renders it totally incredible: for, if one species could be produced by the degeneration of another, if the ass actually originated from the horse, this metamorphosis could only have been effected by a long succession of almost imperceptible degrees. Between the horse and ass, there must have been many intermediate animals, the first of which would gradually recede from the nature and qualities of the horse, and the last would make equal advances to those of the ass. What is become of these intermediate beings? Why are their representatives and descendants now extinguished? Why should the two extremes alone exist?

We may, therefore, without hesitation, pronounce the ass to be an *Ass*, and not a degenerated horse, a horse with a naked tail. The ass is not a marvellous production. He is neither an intruder nor a bastard. Like all other animals, his family, his species, and his rank, are ascertained and peculiar to himself. His blood is pure and untainted: and, though his race be less noble and illustrious, it is equally unalloyed, and as ancient as that of the horse. Why, then, should an animal so good, so patient, so temperate, and so useful, be treated with the most sovereign contempt? Do men despise, even in the brute creation, those who serve them best, and at the least expense? The horse we educate with great care; we dress, attend, instruct, and exercise him: while the poor ass, abandoned to the brutality of the meanest servants, or to the malicious abuse of children, instead of acquiring, is rendered more stupid and indocile, by the education he receives. If he had not a great stock of good qualities, they would necessarily be obliterated by the manner in which he is treated. He is the sport and pastime of rustics, who conduct him with a rod, who beat, overload, and abuse him, without precaution or management. We consider not, that, if the horse had no existence, the ass, both in himself and with regard to us, would be the first, handsomest, most beautiful, and most distinguished animal in the creation. He holds, however, only the second, instead of the first rank; and, for that reason, he is neglected and despised. It is comparison alone that degrades him. We view and judge of him, not as he is, but in comparison with the horse. We forget that he is an ass, that he has all the qualities and endowments peculiar to his species; and we contemplate the figure and qualities of the horse, which the ass neither has nor ought to possess.

In his disposition, the ass is equally humble, patient, and tranquil, as the horse is proud, ardent, and impetuous. Chastisement and blows he endures with constancy, and perhaps with courage.[1] He is temperate both as to the quantity and quality of his food. He eats contentedly the hardest and most disagreeable herbage, which the horse and other animals pass by and disdain. With regard to water, he is extremely nice.[4]

---

1 We ought not, in justice to the ass, to omit an excellent quality in him, which will plead very forcibly in his favour. It is his strong attachment to his master, notwithstanding the harsh treatment he so frequently experiences: the ass will scent him from afar, and distinguish him from all other men. He also recollects the places where he has formerly stopped, and the ways which he has been accustomed to frequent. Huzard saw an ass, who, after having remained six years in a village several leagues from Paris, to which he travelled twice a week, was sold and sent to a distance. Returning by chance to Paris about four years after, he effected his escape, found the way to his former dwelling, entered into the house where he had been so frequently received, and stopped at the door of his old stable.

He drinks only from the clearest brooks he can find. In drinking, he is equally moderate as in eating. He never sinks his nose in the water, being afraid, as has been alleged, of the shadow of his ears. As nobody takes the trouble of combing him, he often rolls on the grass, among thistles or ferns. Without paying any regard to the load he carries, he lies down and rolls as often as he can, seemingly with a view to reproach the neglect of his master; for he never wallows, like the horse, in the mire or in water. He is even afraid of wetting his feet, and turns off the road to avoid a puddle. His legs are also drier and cleaner than those of the horse. He is so susceptible of education, as to be sometimes exhibited in public shows.[. . .]

Notes
1   A reference to Linnaeus.
2   This rather obscure passage would be better translated: 'it would reduce the immediate production of the Creation to any desired number of individuals'.
3   Here Buffon repeats a traveller's tale: the alleged existence in Ceylon of men with giant limbs, supposedly descendants of St. Thomas.
4   i.e. particular and fastidious.

BUFFON

Of Animals Common to both Continents (1761)

From *Histoire naturelle des quadrupèdes* (ibid., Vol. IX, 1761),
'Animaux communs aux deux continens.' Reprinted from *History
of Man and the Quadrupeds* (ibid., Vol. VI, 1812).

As a result of his exhaustive research for the volumes on quadrupeds, Buffon revised his view on species even further; and an
instance of this can be seen from the following extract, from
Vol. IX.

His attempt to explain the puzzling peculiarities of American
fauna was one of his most important contributions to science: the
study of the geographical distribution of species, an approach
fully in keeping with his preference for the grand view of Nature.

From the preceding enumeration, it appears, that not only the
quadrupeds in the warmest climates of Africa and Asia, but most of
those in the temperate regions of Europe, are wanting in America. But
several of our animals, which can endure cold, and multiply in the
northern climates, are found in North America: and, though they differ
considerably, we are obliged to acknowledge them to be the same, and
to believe that they formerly passed from the one continent to the
other by lands, which are still unknown, or rather have long since been
swallowed up by the ocean. This proof, drawn from natural history, is a
stronger demonstration of the almost continued contiguity of these
two continents, than all the conjectures of speculative geographers.

The bears of the Ilionois, of Louisiana, &c., appear to be the same
with ours; only the former are smaller and blacker.

The stag of Canada, though less than ours, differs from him only by
the greater height of his horns, more numerous antlers, and a longer
tail.

The roebuck, which is found in the south of Canada and in Louisiana, is likewise smaller, and has a longer tail than the European kind. The original is the same animal with the elk, though it is not equally large.

The rein-deer of Lapland, the fallow-deer of Greenland, and the caribou of Canada, appear to be the same animal. The fallow-deer or stag of Greenland, described and painted by Edwards,[1] has too great a resemblance to the reindeer to be regarded as a different species. As to the caribou, though there is no exact description of it; yet, from the marks we have been able to collect, it seems to be the same animal with the rein-deer. M. Brisson[2] has made the caribou a different species, and refers it to the *cervus Burgundicus* of Johnston.[3] But this *cervus Burgundicus* is an unknown animal, and certainly never existed either in Burgundy or in Europe: it is a simple name that has been given to some uncommon horns of the stag or fallow-deer; or rather, M. Brisson may have seen the head of the caribou, whose horns consisted of one straight stem on each side, about ten inches long, with an antler or branch near the base, turned forwards; or the head of a female rein-deer; or a head of the first or second year; for the female rein-deer bears horns as well as the male, though much smaller, and, in both, the direction of the first antlers is forward; and, lastly, in this animal, as well as in all others of the deer kind, the ramifications of the horns are exactly proportioned to the number of years they have lived.

The hares, the squirrels, the hedgehogs, the otters, the marmots, the rats, the shrew-mice, and the moles, are also species common to the two continents, though, in all these kinds, there is not an American species perfectly similar to those of Europe; and it is extremely difficult, if not impossible, to pronounce with certainty whether they are really different species, or only varieties of the same, changed by the influence of the climate.

The beavers of Europe appear to be the same with those of Canada. Though these animals prefer cold countries, they can subsist, and even multiply, in temperate climates. There are still some of them in France, upon the islands of the Rhone. Their number was formerly much greater; and they seem to avoid populous countries more than very warm climates. They never establish their societies but in deserts remote from the habitations of men: and, even in Canada, which may be considered as a vast desert, they have retired far from any of our settlements.

The wolf and fox are also common to both continents. They are found, but with some varieties, in all parts of North America, where there are black foxes and wolves; but all of them are smaller than those of Europe, which is the case with every animal, whether native or transported.

Though the weesel and ermine frequent the cold countries of Europe, they are at least very rare in America; but the pine-weesel, the martin, and the polecat, are more numerous.

The pine-weesel of North America appears to be the same with ours. The vison, or pekan weesel of Canada, has a great resemblance to the martin; and the striped polecat of North America is perhaps only a variety of the European kind.

The American lynx seems to be the same with the European. He prefers cold countries; but he likewise lives and multiplies in temperate climates, and generally frequents the forests and high mountains.

The seal, or sea-calf, seems to be confined to northern countries, and is found equally on the coasts of Europe and of North America.

These are nearly all the animals which are common to the Old and New Worlds; and from this number, which is not considerable, we ought, perhaps, to retrench more than a third part, whose species, though apparently the same, may be different in reality. But, admitting the identity of all these species with those of Europe, the number common to the two continents is very small, when compared with that of the species peculiar to each. It is farther apparent, that, of all these animals, it is those only which frequent the northern countries that are common to both continents; and that none of those which cannot multiply but in warm or temperate climates are found in both worlds.

It is, therefore, no longer a doubtful point, that the two continents either are, or have formerly been, contiguous towards the north, and that the animals common to both have passed from the one to the other by lands with which we have now no acquaintance. We are led to believe, especially since the discoveries made by the Russians to the north of Kamtschatka, that the lands of Asia are contiguous to those of America; for the north of Europe seems to have been always separated from the New World by seas too considerable to permit the passage of any quadruped. These animals, however, of North America, are not precisely the same with those of the north of Asia; but have a stronger resemblance to the quadrupeds of the north of Europe. It is the same with the animals which belong to the temperate climates. The argali, or Siberian goat, the sable, the Siberian mole, and the Chinese musk, appear not in Hudson's Bay, nor in any other north-west part of the New Continent; but, on the contrary, we find, in the north-east parts of it, not only the animals common to the north of Europe and Asia, but likewise those which appear to be peculiar to Europe, as the elk, the rein-deer, &c. It must, however, be acknowledged, that the north-east parts of Asia are so little known, that we can have no certainty whether the animals of the north of Europe exist there or not.

We formerly remarked, as a singular phænomenon, that the animals in the southern provinces of the New Continent are small in proportion to those in the warm regions of the Old. There is no comparison between the size of the elephant, the rhinoceros, the hippopotamus, the camelopard, the camel, the lion, the tiger, &c., and the tapir, the cabiai, the ant-eater, the lama, the puma, the jaguar, &c., which are the largest quadrupeds of the New World: the former are four, six, eight, and ten times larger than the latter. Another observation brings additional strength to this general fact: all the animals which have been transported from Europe to America, as the horse, the ass, the ox, the sheep, the goat, the hog, the dog, &c., have become smaller; and those which were not transported, but went thither spontaneously, those, in a word, which are common to both continents, as the wolf, the fox, the stag, the roebuck, the elk, &c., are also considerably less than those of Europe.

In this New World, therefore, there is some combination of elements and other physical causes, something that opposes the amplification of animated Nature: there are obstacles to the development, and perhaps to the formation of large germs.[4] Even those which, from the kindly influences of another climate, have acquired their complete form and expansion, shrink and diminish under a niggardly sky and an unprolific land, thinly peopled with wandering savages, who, instead of using this territory as a master, had no property or empire; and, having subjected neither the animals nor the elements, nor conquered the seas, nor directed the motions of rivers, nor cultivated the earth, held only the first rank among animated beings, and existed as creatures of no consideration in Nature, a kind of weak automatons, incapable of improving or seconding her intentions. She treated them rather like a step-mother than a parent, by denying them the invigorating sentiment of love, and the strong desire of multiplying their species. For, though the American savage be nearly of the same stature with men in polished societies, yet this is not a sufficient exception to the general contraction of animated Nature throughout the whole continent. In the savage, the organs of generation are small and feeble. He has no hair, no beard, no ardour for the female. Though nimbler than the European, because more accustomed to running, his strength is not so great. His sensations are less acute; and yet he is more timid and cowardly. He has no vivacity, no activity of mind. The activity of the body is not so much an exercise or spontaneous motion, as a necessary action produced by want. Destroy his appetite for victuals and drink, and you will at once annihilate the active principle of all his movements; he remains, in stupid repose, on his limbs or couch for whole days. It is easy to discover the cause of the scattered life of savages, and of their estrangement from society. They have been refused the most precious spark of Nature's fire. They have no ardour for women, and, of course, no love to mankind. Unacquainted with the most lively and most tender of all attachments, their other sensations of this nature are cold and languid. Their love to parents and children is extremely weak. The bonds of the most intimate of all societies, that of the same family, are feeble; and one family has no attachment to another. Hence no union, no republic, no social state, can take place among them. The physical cause of love gives rise to the morality of their manners. Their heart is frozen, their society cold, and their empire cruel. They regard their females as servants destined to labour, or as beasts of burden, whom they load unmercifully with the produce of their hunting, and oblige, without pity or gratitude, to perform labours which often exceed their strength. They have few children, and pay little attention to them. Every thing must be referred to the first cause: they are indifferent, because they are weak; and this indifference to the sex is the original stain which disgraces Nature, prevents her from expanding, and, by destroying the germs of life, cuts the root of society.

Hence man makes no exception to what has been advanced. Nature, by denying him the faculty of love, has abused and contracted him more than any other animal. But, before examining the causes of this general effect, it must be allowed, that, if Nature has diminished all the quadrupeds in the New World, she seems to have cherished the reptile, and enlarged the insect tribes; for, though at Senegal there are longer serpents and larger lizards than in South America, yet the difference between these animals is not near so great as that which subsists between the quadrupeds. The largest serpent of Senegal is not double the size of the Cayenne serpent. But the elephant is perhaps ten times the bulk of the tapir, which is the largest quadruped of South America. With regard, however, to insects, they are no where so large as in South America. The largest spiders, beetles, caterpillars, and butterflies, are found in Cayenne and other neighbouring provinces: here almost all insects exceed those of the Old World, not in size only, but in richness of colouring, delicacy of shades, variety of forms, number of species, and the prodigious multiplication of individuals. The toads, the frogs, and other animals of this kind, are likewise very large in America. We shall take no notice of birds and fishes; because, as Nature has enabled them to pass from the one continent to the other, it is hardly possible to distinguish those which are proper to each. But reptiles and insects, like the quadrupeds, are confined to their respective continents.

Let us now examine why the reptiles and insects are so large, the quadrupeds so small, and the men so cold, in the New World. These effects must be referred to the quality of the earth and atmosphere, to the degree of heat and moisture, to the situation and height of mountains, to the quantity of running and stagnant waters, to the extent of forests, and, above all, to the inert condition of Nature in that country. In this part of the globe, the heat in general is much less, and the humidity much greater. If we compare the heat and cold of every degree of latitude, we shall find very considerable differences: at Quebec, for example, which is under the same degree of latitude with Paris, the rivers freeze every year some feet thick; a coat of snow still thicker covers the land for several months; the air is so cold that the birds fly off and disappear during the winter, &c. This difference of heat, under the same latitude in the Temperate Zone, though very considerable, is perhaps still less than the difference of heat under the Torrid Zone. In Senegal, the sun is perfectly scorching; while in Peru, which lies under the same line, an agreeable temperature prevails. The same remark applies to all the other latitudes. The continent of America is so formed and situated, that every circumstance concurs in diminishing the action of heat. America contains the highest mountains, and, of course, the largest rivers of the world. These mountains form a chain which seems to bound the continent towards the west, through its whole extent. The plains and low grounds are all situated on this side of the mountains, and run from their bottoms to the sea, which separates the continents on this side. Thus the east wind, which blows perpetually between the Tropics, arrives not in America, till it has traversed a vast ocean, by which it is greatly cooled. Hence this wind is much cooler in Brasil, Cayenne, &c., than at Senegal, Guinea, &c., where it arrives impregnated with the accumulated heat acquired from all the lands and burning sands in its passage through Asia and Africa. Let us recollect what was remarked concerning the different colours of men, and particularly of the Negroes. It seemed to be demonstrated, that the greater or less degree of a tawny, brown, or black colour, depends entirely on the situation of the climate; that the Negroes of Nigritia, and those of the west coast of Africa, are blackest, because their countries are situated in such a manner, that the heat is always greater than in any other part of the globe, the east wind before its arrival having traversed vast tracts of land; that, on the contrary, the American Indians under the Line, are only tawny, and the Brasilians brown, though under the same latitude with the Negroes; because the heat of their climate is neither so great nor so constant, the east wind arriving not till after being cooled by the waters, and loaded with moist vapours. The clouds which intercept the light and heat of the sun, and the rains which refresh the air and the surface of the earth, are periodic, and continue several months in Cayenne, and other regions of South America. This first cause renders all the east coasts of America much more temperate than Africa or Asia: and, after the east wind has arrived in a cool state, in traversing the plains of America, it begins to assume a greater degree of heat, when it is suddenly stopped and cooled by that enormous chain of mountains of which the western part of the New Continent is composed; so that it is still colder under the Line at Peru, than at Brasil, Cayenne, &c., on account of the prodigious elevation of the land. Hence the natives of Peru, Chili, &c., are less brown, red, or tawny, than those of Brasil. If these mountains were reduced to a level with the adjacent plains, the heat on the western coasts would become excessive, and we would soon find Negroes at Peru and Chili, as well as upon the west coasts of Africa.

Thus, from the situation of the land alone in the New Continent, the heat must be greatly inferior to that of the Old; and I shall now show, that there is likewise a greater degree of moisture in America. The mountains, which are the highest upon the globe, and are opposed to the direction of the east wind, stop and condense all the aerial vapours, and, of course, give rise to an infinite number of springs, which, by uniting, soon form the greatest rivers in the world. Hence in the New Continent, there are more running waters, in proportion to the extent of territory, than in the old; and this quantity of water is greatly increased for want of proper drains or outlets. The natives having neither stopped the torrents, nor directed the rivers, nor drained the marshes, the stagnating waters cover immense tracts of land, augment the moisture of the air, and diminish its heat. Besides, as the earth is every where covered with trees, shrubs, and gross herbage, it never dries. The transpiration of so many vegetables, pressed close together, produces immense quantities of moist and noxious exhalations. In these melancholy regions, Nature remains concealed under her old garments, and never exhibits herself in fresh attire; being neither cherished nor cultivated by man, she never opens her fruitful and beneficent womb. Here the Earth never saw her surface adorned with those rich crops, which demonstrate her fecundity, and constitute the opulence of polished nations. In this abandoned condition, every thing languishes, corrupts, and proves abortive. The air and the earth, overloaded with humid and noxious vapours, are unable either to purify themselves, or to profit by the influences of the sun, who darts in vain his most enlivening rays upon this frigid mass, which is not in a condition to make suitable returns to his ardour. Its powers are limited to the production of moist plants, reptiles, and insects, and can afford nourishment only to cold men and feeble animals.

The scarcity of men, therefore, in America, and most of them living like the brutes, is the chief cause why the earth remains in a frigid state, and is incapable of producing the active principles of Nature. To expand the germs of the largest quadrupeds, and to enable them to grow and multiply, requires all the activity which the sun can give to a fertile earth. It is for the opposite reason, that insects, reptiles, and all the animals which wallow in the mire, whose blood is watery, and which multiply in corruption, are larger and more numerous in the low, moist, and marshy lands of the New Continent.

When we reflect on these remarkable differences between the Old and New World, we are inclined to believe that the latter is actually more recent, and has continued longer than the rest of the globe under the waters of the ocean; for, if we except the enormous western mountains, which appear to be monuments of the highest antiquity which this globe affords, all the low parts of this continent seem to be new lands, elevated and formed by the sediments of waters. In many places, immediately under the vegetable stratum, we find sea shells and madrepores already forming large masses of lime-stone, but which are commonly softer than our free-stone. If this continent be really as ancient as the other, why was it so thinly peopled? Why were almost its whole inhabitants wandering savages? Why did the Peruvians and Mexicans, who had united into society, reckon only two or three hundred years since the existence of the first man who taught them to associate? Why are they still ignorant of the art of transmitting facts to posterity by permanent signs, since they had already discovered a method of conveying their ideas at a distance by tying knots upon cords? Why did they not reduce the lama, the pacos, and other animals into a domestic state? Their arts, like their society, were in embryo; their talents were imperfect, their ideas locked up, their organs rude, and their language barbarous. Below is a list of animals, whose names are so difficult to pronounce, that it is surprising how the Europeans could submit to the trouble of writing them.

Pelon ichiatl oquitli. The lama.

Tapiierete in Brasil, *maypoury* or *manipouris* in Guiana. The tapir.

Tamandua-guacu in Brasil, *ouariri* in Guiana. The great ant-eater.

Ouatiriouaou in Guiana. The little ant-eater.

Ouaikarè in Guiana, *ai* or *hai* in Brasil. The sloth.

Aiotochili in Mexico, *tatu* or *tatupeba* in Brasil, *chirquinchum*, in New Spain. The armadillo.

Tatu-ete in Brasil, *tatou-kabassou* in Guiana. The eight banded armadillo.

Macatlchichiltic temamacama. The antelope of New Spain.

Jiya or *carigueibeju*. The Brasilian otter.

Quauhtla coymatl or *quapizotl*, in Mexico, or *caaigoara* in Brasil. The Mexican hog.

Tlacoozclotl or *tlalocelotl*. The mountain cat.

Cabionara, or *capybara*. The cabiai, or thick-nosed tapir.

Tlatlauhqui occlotl in Mexico, *janowara* or *jaguara* in Brasil. The jaguar, or Brasilian cat.

Cuguacu arana, or *cuguacu ara, cougouacou ara*. The cuguar, or brown cat.

Tlaquatzin in Mexico, *aouarè* in Guiana, *carigueya* in Brasil. The opossum.

Hoitzlaquatzin. The porcupine of New Spain.

Cuandu or *gouandou*. The Brasilian porcupine.

Tape-maxtlaton in Mexico, *maraguae* or *maracaia* in Brasil, The Cayenne cat.

Quauhtec hallotl thliltic or *tlilocotequillin*. The black squirrel.

Quimichpatlan or *assapanick*. An animal resembling the flying squirrel, and is perhaps the same.

Yzquiepatl. The mouffette, or stifling weesel.

Xoloitzcuintli or *cuctlachtli*. The Mexican wolf.

Hence every circumstance indicates that the Americans are new men, or rather men who had been so long separated from their original country, that they had lost every idea of the part of the world from which they had issued; that the greatest part of the continent of America was new land, still untouched by the hand of man, and in which Nature had not time sufficient to accomplish her plans, or to unfold the whole extent of her productions; that the men are cold and the animals small, because the ardour of the former, and the magnitude of the latter, depend upon the salubrity and heat of the air; and that some centuries hence, when the lands are cultivated, the forests cut down, the courses of the rivers properly directed, and the marshes drained, this same country will become the most fertile, the most wholesome, and the richest in the whole world, as it is already in all the parts which have experienced the industry and skill of man. We mean not, however, to conclude, that large animals would then be produced. The tapir and cabiai will never acquire the magnitude of the elephant or hippopotamus. But the animals transported thither will no longer diminish as they have formerly done. Man will gradually fill up the vacuities in these immense territories, which were perfect deserts when first discovered.

From what has been advanced, the following general conclusions may be drawn: that man is the only animated being on whom Nature has bestowed sufficient strength, genius, and ductility, to enable him to subsist and to multiply in every climate of the earth. No other animal, it is evident, has obtained this great privilege; for, instead of multiplying everywhere, most of them are limited to certain climates, and even to particular countries. Man is totally a production of heaven: but the animals, in many respects, are creatures of the earth only. Those of one continent are not found in another; or, if there are a few exceptions, the animals are so changed and contracted that they are hardly to be recognised. Is any farther argument necessary to convince us, that the model of their form is not unalterable; that their nature, less fixed than that of man, may be varied, and even absolutely changed in a succession of ages; that, for the same reason, the least perfect, the least active, and the worst defended, as well as the most delicate and heavy species, have already, or will soon disappear; for their very existence depends on the form which man gives or allows to the surface of the earth? The prodigious *mammouth*, whose enormous bones I have often viewed with astonishment, and which were, at least, six times larger than those of the largest elephant, has now no existence; yet the remains of him have been found in many places remote from each other, as in Ireland, Siberia, Louisiana, &c. This species was unquestionably the largest and strongest of all quadrupeds, and, since it has disappeared, how many smaller, weaker, and less remarkable species must likewise have perished without leaving any evidence of their past existence? How many others have undergone such changes, either from degeneration or improvement, occasioned by the great vicissitudes of the earth and waters, the neglect or cultivation of Nature, the continued influence of favourable or hostile climates, that they are now no longer the same creatures? Yet the quadrupeds, next to man, are beings whose nature and form are the most permanent. Birds and fishes are subject to greater variations: the insect tribes are liable to still greater vicissitudes: and, if we descend to vegetables, which ought not to be excluded from animated Nature, our wonder will be excited by the quickness and facility with which they assume new forms.

Hence, it is not impossible, that, without inverting the order of Nature, all the animals of the New World were originally the same with those of the Old, from whom they derived their existence; but that, being afterwards separated by immense seas, or impassable lands, they would, in the progress of time, suffer all the effects of a climate that had become new to them, and must have had its qualities changed by the very causes which produced the separation, and, consequently, degenerate, &c. But these circumstances should not prevent them from being now regarded as different species of animals. From whatever cause these changes, produced by the operation of time and the influence of climate, have originated, and though we should date them from the creation itself, they are not the less real. Nature, I allow, is in a perpetual state of fluctuation: but it is enough for man to seize her in his own age, and to look backward and forward, in order to discover her former condition, and what future appearances she may probably assume.

Notes

1   George Edwards (1694–1773), the author of a *History of Birds* in several volumes (1743–51).
2   M.J. Brisson (1723–1806), French zoologist and physicist.
3   The Scottish naturalist John Johnstone or Johnston (1603–75).
4   'That portion of an organic being which is capable of development into a new individual' (OED).

D'ALEMBERT

On Men of Letters (1753)

From Jean D'Alembert, 'Essai sur les gens de lettres', published in his *Mélanges de litterature, d'histoire, et de philosophie*, à Berlin, 1753, 2 volumes. [Revised 1759 in 4 volumes]. Translation by P.N. Furbank from *Mélanges . . .*, Nouvelle Edition, chez Zacherie & Fils, Amsterdam, 1773.

This exhortation to men of letters to take more care of their own dignity and to show less sycophancy towards so-called 'great' patrons was very characteristic of D'Alembert and was aimed at, among others, Voltaire, whom D'Alembert considered as too prone to flattery of the 'great'.

[. . .] The sort of Great Man that *philosophes* are most eager to cultivate is the kind that, without devoting himself entirely to the profession of letters, cultivates it up to a certain point, but does not dream of letting either his prestige or his fortune depend upon his talents. Such men being engaged in so different a career, there is no danger of their criticisms being too penetrating; the *philosophe* finds in them precisely the degree of enlightenment that is no threat to his own vanity. Nevertheless, since even this species of 'semi-connoisseurs' is still fairly rare among the Great, the *philosophe* does not restrict himself to angling for the praises of the most enlightened; he is flattered to swallow the praises of any, in the hope that the praisers, being so much in the public eye, will bring in their train a further crowd of adulators. The favourable opinion of this inferior class of patrons would not be worth much on its own; but, by bathing in the reflected ray of the opinions that really do matter, it does not merely swell the number of praises, it acquires a certain value in itself. Those whose self-esteem is most avid of fame try to annex among the Great those who command most of such obedient "echoes"; a less sensitive vanity contents itself with placing one or two great names of any kind in the list of its supporters.

    [. . .] Three things, above all, lend distinction to men: intellectual talents, high birth and a fortune. The reader must not be surprised that I begin with talents. It is in them alone that the true difference in men lies. However, if one were to adjudicate between these three things, according to which contributes most to happiness, or gives us most independence of other people and does most to make others dependent on us, in a word which brings us the most (seeming) friends and the fewest confessed enemies, then the first place must be awarded to fortune. Why, then, do talents enjoy a higher reputation? It is because they have the precious advantage of being a sure and certain resource that can never be taken away and which misfortune makes even surer and more effective; it is because it is to talents that a Nation principally owes the esteem of foreigners and her own good fortune in attracting so many jealous and admiring neighbours to her soil.

But if talents take precedence over birth and fortune in the true order of esteem, by contrast they lag a long way behind either when it comes to public prestige. And this fact, strange and probably quite unjust as it is, is nevertheless based on certain reasons; for men would scarcely assent to a scheme of values so prejudicial to the great majority without some at least plausible shadow of good reason. And here is my own explanation.

Since all men cannot be equal, it is necessary, so that the difference between one man and another can be clearly and uncontroversially defined, that it should be based upon advantages which no-one can dispute or deny; now, that is precisely what you have in birth and fortune. To estimate these, all you need is to understand genealogies and title-deeds, a far simpler business than deciding the relative value of different talents. The difference of rank between talents is something there will never be unanimous agreement about – above all among the parties concerned. It has thus been agreed that birth and fortune should be the most accepted mark of difference between men – for the same reason as companies decide matters by majority vote, for all that the majority view may well not be the right one.

It is for this reason that reputation and actual public acclaim do not necessarily go hand-in-hand. A Man of Letters full of integrity and talent is incomparably more esteemed (he has a higher reputation) than a government Minister unworthy of his place, or some dishonourable great lord; nevertheless, put them in the same room, and all attention of the company will be on rank and social grandeur; and the Man of Letters, ignored by the guests, will have to fall back on saying, like Philopoemon,[1] 'That is the price you pay for looking like me.' It is no use for you to remind me of the honours paid to Corneille,[2] who, so they say, had his own private seat in the theatre and, as soon as he appeared there, was hailed and cheered by the whole audience. My reply to this is that, either people have exaggerated, or that society forgot to show this great man in private what it was willing to grant him in public.

It is so much the fact that public prestige derives more from rank than from talents, that, even between two Men of Letters, the stupider but richer one usually enjoys the greater prestige. If men of talent are shocked by this injustice, they only have themselves to blame; they should stop lavishing their homage upon people who imagine they are honouring them by their attention and who seem to be conveying by their very graciousness that this graciousness is more a matter of condescension than of justice. They should stop pursuing the society of Great Men regardless of the public or private snubs that they receive there; they should no longer forget the advantages which superiority in genius gives them over others and no longer kneel before those who ought to be at their own feet.

Notes

1   Greek soldier and statesman, born *c.* 252 B.C., who became general of the Achaean League. There is a life of him by Plutarch.
2   Pierre Corneille (1606–84), French dramatist.

SAMUEL JOHNSON

Letter to Lord Chesterfield (1755)

From James Boswell (ed.) *The Celebrated Letter from Samuel Johnson, LL.D. to Philip Dormer Stanhope, Earl of Chesterfield*; now first published, with notes, Printed by Henry Baldwin; for Charles Dilly, in the Poultry, London, 1790. [Actually published 12 May 1791.] Reprinted from James Boswell *The Life of Samuel Johnson*, Oxford Standard Authors, OUP, 1966.

This celebrated rebuke by Johnson to his unhelpful patron Lord Chesterfield, to whom he had addressed the Plan of his *Dictionary* in 1747, eight years before its eventual publication, was provoked by two articles published by Chesterfield in the periodical *The World* recommending Johnson's work. James Boswell (1740–95) records in his *Life of Johnson* (1791) that Johnson, in revising his poem *The Vanity of Human Wishes*, altered the couplet 'Yet think what ills the scholar's life assail,/ Toil, envy, want, the garret, and the jail' to read '. . . Toil, envy, want, the *Patron*, and the jail'. Johnson was throughout his career an energetic champion of the dignity of the independent man of letters.

True to his own advice Chesterfield bore the criticism bravely. Boswell quotes Robert Dodsley, one of the publishers of the *Dictionary*, reporting on a visit to Chesterfield: '. . . it [the letter] lay upon his table, where anybody might see it. He read it to me; said "this man has great powers," pointed out the severest passages, and observed how well they were expressed.'

To THE RIGHT HONOURABLE THE EARL OF CHESTERFIELD

MY LORD,   February 1755

I have been lately informed, by the proprietor of *The World*, that two papers, in which my Dictionary is recommended to the publick, were written by your Lordship. To be so distinguished, is an honour, which, being very little accustomed to favours from the great, I know not well how to receive, or in what terms to acknowledge.

When, upon some slight encouragement, I first visited your Lordship, I was overpowered, like the rest of mankind, by the enchantment of your address; and could not forbear to wish that I might boast myself *Le vainqueur du vainqueur de la terre*;[1] – that I might obtain that regard for which I saw the world contending; but I found my attendance so little encouraged, that neither pride nor modesty would suffer me to continue it. When I had once addressed your Lordship in publick, I had exhausted all the art of pleasing which a retired and uncourtly scholar can possess. I had done all that I could; and no man is well pleased to have his all neglected, be it ever so little.

Seven years, my Lord, have now past, since I waited in your outward rooms, or was repulsed from your door; during which time I have been pushing on my work through difficulties, of which it is useless to complain, and have brought it, at last, to the verge of publication, without one act of assistance, one word of encouragement, or one smile of favour. Such treatment I did not expect, for I never had a Patron before.

The shepherd in Virgil grew at last acquainted with Love, and found him a native of the rocks.[2]

Is not a Patron, my Lord, one who looks with unconcern on a man struggling for life in the water, and, when he has reached ground, encumbers him with help? The notice which you have been pleased to take of my labours, had it been early, had been kind; but it has been delayed till I am indifferent, and cannot enjoy it; till I am solitary, and cannot impart it,[3] till I am known, and do not want it. I hope it is no very cynical asperity not to confess obligations where no benefit has been received, or to be unwilling that the Publick should consider me as owing that to a Patron, which Providence has enabled me to do for myself.

Having carried on my work thus far with so little obligation to any favourer of learning, I shall not be disappointed though I should conclude it, if less be possible, with less; for I have been long wakened from that dream of hope, in which I once boasted myself with so much exaltation, my Lord, your Lordship's most humble, most obedient servant,

SAM. JOHNSON.

Notes

1   'The conqueror of the conqueror of the earth.'

2   A reference to Dryden's translation of Virgil's *Eclogues*. The relevant line comes in Eclogue VIII, 43.

    'I know thee, Love; in Desarts thou wast bred.'

3   Johnson here is referring to the death of his wife which had occurred in 1752.

BEAUMARCHAIS

The Marriage of Figaro (1784)
Opening Scene

From Pierre-Augustin Caron de Beaumarchais, *La Folle Journée, ou Le Mariage de Figaro*, au Palais-Royal, Chez Ruault, Libraire, près le Théâtre, 1785. Reprinted from the translation by John Wood in *The Barber of Seville and the Marriage of Figaro*, Penguin Books, London, 1964.

These two short extracts are from the play *The Marriage of Figaro* by Caron de Beaumarchais (1732–99). Beaumarchais wrote it towards the end of the 1770s but it was initially prohibited by Louis XV, its earliest performances being private productions in the salons. It was first publicly performed in 1784.

It was on this play that Mozart based his four-act *opera buffa*, *Le Nozze di Figaro*. The opera (Libretto by Lorenzo da Ponte) was first performed on 1 May 1786. There are some interesting comparisons that can be drawn from a consideration of both pieces.

The first extract is from the beginning of the play: here the situation is established. *Figaro* is valet and major-domo to *Count Almaviva*, Governor of Andalusia. *Suzanne* is maid to the countess, and betrothed to *Figaro*. The action takes place in and around the castle of Aguas-Frescas, three leagues from Seville.

SCENE: *A bedroom partly stripped of furniture; a large high-backed chair in the middle.*

[FIGARO *with a six-foot rule is measuring the floor.* SUZANNE *is trying on a wreath of orange blossom in front of the glass.*]

FIGARO: Nineteen feet by twenty-six.

SUZANNE: Look, Figaro. My wreath of orange blossom. Do you like it better so?

FIGARO [*taking her hands*]: Splendid, my darling! Oh! How precious in an adoring bridegroom's eyes is the charming virginal wreath that adorns the head of his beloved on her wedding morning.

SUZANNE: And what are you measuring there, my dear?

FIGARO: I'm just thinking about this fine bed which His Lordship is giving us. The question is – will it go here?

SUZANNE: In this room?

FIGARO: This is the one he's letting us have.

SUZANNE: Well *I* don't want it.

FIGARO: Why?

SUZANNE: I just don't.

FIGARO: But why not?

SUZANNE: I don't like it.

FIGARO: You might give a reason?

SUZANNE: Suppose I don't want to?

FIGARO: Ay! Once they are sure of us . . .

SUZANNE: Giving a reason for being right amounts to admitting I could be wrong. Are you my humble servitor or aren't you?

FIGARO: Why take a prejudice against the room? It's the most convenient one in the castle, and it's in between the two suites of rooms. Suppose My Lady wants something in the night – she rings from her side – Hey presto! A couple of steps and you are in her room. On the other hand, should His Lordship want anything he need only give a tinkle and lo and behold! A hop and a skip and I'm there.

SUZANNE: Very nice too! But suppose he has given a tinkle in the morning and sent you off on some lengthy task – Hey presto! A couple of steps and he's at my door. Then lo and behold! A hop and a skip . . .

FIGARO: Whatever *are* you talking about?

SUZANNE: Why don't you listen?

FIGARO: But good Lord! What is it all about?

SUZANNE: This is what it's about, my dear boy – My Lord the Count, tired of cultivating rustic beauties, has a mind to return to the castle but not to his wife: it's yours he has cast his eye on, understand, and he thinks that this room might well prove quite convenient; so the ever-loyal Bazile, faithful agent of his master's pleasures and my esteemed singing teacher, daily suggests to me as he gives me my lesson.

FIGARO: Ah! Friend Bazile! If a good stout cudgel properly applied to anyone's back and shoulders could . . .

SUZANNE: You didn't think, silly boy, that this dowry I am to receive was a tribute to your own outstanding merits?

FIGARO: I have done sufficient to hope so.

SUZANNE: How stupid clever men can be!

FIGARO: So they say.

SUZANNE: Yes, but some people are unwilling to believe it.

FIGARO: That's where you are wrong.

SUZANNE: Let me tell you – he means to use it some time when he gets me alone for a few minutes to exact an ancient *Droit de Seigneur*[1] . . . you know what that means.

FIGARO: So much so that if His Lordship hadn't abolished the infamous privilege when he got married himself I would never have married

243

you within his domains.

SUZANNE: Very well! He may have abolished it, but now he wishes he hadn't and it's with your bride-to-be that he means to revive it today.

FIGARO [*rubbing his forehead*]: I'm quite dizzy with the shock – and my forehead is sprouting . . . already . . .

SUZANNE: Don't rub it then.

FIGARO: There's no danger, is there?

SUZANNE: If there were to be the slightest little swelling . . . superstitious people . . .

FIGARO: You are laughing at me, you witch! Ah! If only there were some means of catching out this arch-deceiver, of leading him into a trap and pocketing his money.

SUZANNE: Intrigue and money – you are in your element now.

FIGARO: It isn't any sense of shame that restrains me.

SUZANNE: What is it, then, fear?

FIGARO: There's nothing in taking risks, but to take risks and at the same time turn them to your advantage – that's something! To enter some fellow's house at night, do him down with his wife, and to get a good hiding for your pains – nothing easier: a thousand blundering boobies have done it but . . .

[*Bell within.*]

SUZANNE: That means Her Ladyship is awake. She asked me to be the first person to speak to her on my wedding morning.

FIGARO: Has that some significance as well?

SUZANNE: There's an old saying that it brings luck to neglected wives. Good-bye, dear Fi-Fi-Figaro! Think about our little problem.

FIGARO: What about a kiss to encourage me?

SUZANNE: From my lover of today? I should think not! What will my husband say about it tomorrow?

[FIGARO *kisses her.*]

SUZANNE: There! There!

FIGARO: You just have no idea how I love you.

SUZANNE [disengaging herself]: When are you going to give up telling me so from morning to night, stupid?

FIGARO: When I can prove it from night until morning.

[*A second ring.*]

SUZANNE [*finger-tips to her lips*]: There's your kiss back, Sir. I want nothing more of you now.

FIGARO [*running after her*]: But you didn't say that when I gave it you.

[*Exit* SUZANNE.]

FIGARO: Dear charming girl! For ever laughing, blooming, full of gaiety and wit, loving and wholly delightful! And yet prudent. [*Walks up and down rubbing his forehead.*] And so, Your Lordship, you would do me down, would you! I wondered why, having put me in charge of the household, he wanted to take me with him on his embassy and make me his courier. I have got the idea, Your Highness! It's a triple promotion! You – Minister Plenipotentiary, me – the breakneck postilion, Suzie – lady of the back stairs and pocket ambassadress!

And then, off you go, courier! While I'm galloping in one direction you'll be progressing nicely in another – with my little wife! I shall be fighting my way through rain and mud for the greater glory of your family while you are condescending to cooperate in the increase of mine. A pretty sort of reciprocity! But it's going too far, My Lord! To be doing both your master's job and your valet's at the same time, representing the King – and myself – at a foreign court is overdoing it. It's too much by half! As for you, Bazile, you dirty old dog, I'll teach you to run with the hounds, I'll – no, we shall have to dissimulate if we are to use one against the other. Look to the day's work, Master Figaro! First bring forward the hour of your wedding to make sure of the ceremony taking place, head off Marceline who's so deucedly fond of you, pocket the money and the presents, thwart His Lordship's little game, give Master Bazile a good thrashing[. . .]

Notes

1   'Droit da seigneur' or 'jus primae noctis' ('right of first night'), was said to be the feudal right of the lord to share the bed of the bride of any one of his vassals, on the wedding night. 'Although it seems possible that such a custom may have existed at a very early date in parts of France and Italy, it certainly never existed elsewhere. A considerable number of feudal rights related to the vassal's marriage . . . but those are almost invariably known only in the form of a money payment, or "avail", for redemption.' *Encyclopaedia Britannica*.

BEAUMARCHAIS

The Marriage of Figaro (1784)
Figaro's Soliloquy

The second extract is from Act V of Beaumarchais's play; and provides an indication of how fully developed a career and character Beaumarchais's Figaro had, including that of journalist and man of letters, compared with Mozart/Da Ponte's.

SCENE: *A chestnut grove in a park; pavilions, kiosks, or garden temples are on either side; upstage is a clearing between two hedges; a garden seat downstage. It is dark.*

[*All go out.*]

FIGARO [*gloomily walking up and down in the dark*]: Oh, woman, woman, woman, feeble creature that you are! No living thing can fail to be true to its nature. Is it yours to deceive? After stubbornly refusing when I urged her to it in the presence of her mistress – at the very moment of her plighting her word to me, in the very midst of the ceremony . . . and he smiled while he read it, the scoundrel! And I standing by like a blockhead! No, My Lord Count, you shan't have her, you shall not have her! Because you are a great nobleman you think you are a great genius. . . . Nobility, fortune, rank, position! How proud they make a man feel! What have *you* done to deserve such advantages? Put yourself to the trouble of being born – nothing more! For the rest – a very ordinary man! Whereas I, lost among the obscure crowd, have had to deploy more knowledge, more calculation and skill merely to survive than has sufficed to rule all the provinces of Spain for a century! Yet you would measure yourself against me. . . . Somebody's coming – it's she! No, it's nobody at all. The night's as dark as the very devil and here am I plying the stupid trade of husband though I'm still only half married. [*Sits down.*] Could anything be stranger than a fate like mine? Son of goodness knows whom, stolen by bandits, brought up to their way of life, I become disgusted with it and yearn for an honest profession – only to find myself repulsed everywhere. I study Chemistry, Pharmacy, Surgery, and all the prestige of a great nobleman can barely secure me the handling of a horse-doctor's probe! Weary of making sick animals worse and determined to do something different, I throw myself headlong into the theatre. Alas, I might as well have put a stone round my neck! I fudge up a play about the manners of the Seraglio: a Spanish author, I imagined, could attack Mahomet without scruple, but, immediately, some envoy from goodness-knows-where complains that some of my lines offend the Sublime Porte, Persia, some part or other of the East Indies, the whole of Egypt, and the Kingdoms of Cyrenaica, Tripoli, Tunis, Algiers, and Morocco. Behold my play scuppered to please a set of Mohammedan princes – not one of whom I believe can read – who habitually beat a tatoo on our shoulders to the tune of 'Down with the Christian dogs!' Unable to break my spirit they decided to take it out of my body. My cheeks grew furrowed: my time was out. I saw in the distance the approach of the fell sergeant, his quill stuck into his wig: trembling I summoned all my resources. Economic matters were under discussion. Since one can talk about things even though one doesn't possess them – and though in fact I hadn't a penny, I wrote a treatise on the Theory of Value and its relation to the net product of national wealth. Whereupon I found myself looking from the depths of a hired carriage at the drawbridge of a castle, lowered for my reception, and abandoned all hope of liberty. [*Rises.*] How I would like to have hold of one of those Jacks in office – so indifferent to the evils that they cause – when disaster had extinguished his pride! I'd tell him that stupidities that appear in print acquire importance only in so far as their circulation is restricted, that unless there is liberty to criticize, praise has no value, and that only trivial minds are apprehensive of trivial scribbling. [*He sits again.*] Tiring of housing an obscure pensioner, they put me into the street eventually, and, since a man must eat even though he isn't in jail, I sharpen my quill again, inquire how things are going, and am told that during my economic retreat there had been established in Madrid a system of free sale of commodities which extended even to the products of the press, and that, provided I made no reference in my articles to the authorities or to religion, or to politics, or to morals, or to high officials, or to influential organizations, or the Opera, or to any theatrical productions, or to anybody of any standing whatsoever, I could freely print anything I liked – subject to the approval of two or three censors! In order to profit from this very acceptable freedom I announce a new periodical which, not wishing to tread on anyone else's toes, I call the *Good for Nothing Journal*. Phew! A thousand miserable scribblers are immediately up in arms against me: my paper is suppressed and there I am out of work once again! I was on the point of giving up in despair when it occurred to someone to offer me a job. Unfortunately I had some qualification for it – it needed a knowledge of figures – but it was a dancer who got it! Nothing was left to me but stealing, so I set up as a banker at Faro. Now notice what happens! I dine out in style, and so-called fashionable people throw open their houses to me – keeping three-quarters of the profits for themselves. I could well have restored my fortunes: I even began to understand that in making money *savoir-faire* is more important than true knowledge. But since everybody was involved in some form of swindle and at the same time demanding honesty from me, I inevitably went under again. This time I renounced the world, and twenty fathoms of water might have divided me from it when a beneficent Providence recalled me to my original estate. I picked up my bundle and my leather strop and, leaving illusions to the fools who can live by them and my pride in the middle of the road as too heavy a burden for a pedestrian, I set out with my razor from town to town, and lived henceforward carefree. A great nobleman comes to Seville and he recognizes me. I get him safely married, and as a reward for my trouble in helping him to a wife he now wants to intercept mine! Intrigue! Plots – stormy interludes! I'm on the point of falling into an abyss and marrying my own mother when, lo and behold, my parents turn up one after the other! [*He rises.*] Debate and discussion. It's you, it's him, it's me, it's thee, no, it isn't any of us, no, who is it then? [*Falls into his seat again.*] Oh! Fantastic series of events! Why should they happen to me? Why these things and not others? Who made me responsible? Obliged to follow a road I set out on, all unknowing, and one I shall come to the end of, willy nilly, I have strewn it with such flowers as my high spirits have permitted: I say my high spirits without knowing whether they are any more mine than the rest or who is this 'me' that I'm worrying about: a formless aggregation of unidentified parts, then a puny stupid being, a frisky little animal, a young man ardent in the pursuits of pleasure with every taste for enjoyment, plying all sorts of trades in order to live – now master, now servant, as fortune pleases, ambitious from vanity, industrious from necessity, but lazy from inclination! Orator in emergency, poet for relaxation, musician when occasion demands, in love by mad fits and starts. I've seen everything, done everything, been everything. At last all illusions destroyed – disabused – all too much disabused – Oh, Suzie, Suzie, Suzie, what torture you put upon me! I hear someone coming. This is the moment of decision!

[*Withdraws off-stage – right.*]

KANT

Answer to the Question: What is 'Enlightening'? (1784)

From Immanuel Kant, 'Was ist Aufklärung?' first published in
Berlinische Monatsschrift, IV, 12 December 1784. Reprinted from
Essays and Treatises on Moral, Political, and Various Philosophical Subjects
[translation by A.F.M. Willich], Printed for the translator and sold
by William Richardson, Royal Exchange, 1798–99, 2 volumes,
Vol. I.

In 1783 there was founded in Berlin a secret society called the
Berliner Mittwochsgesellschaft or 'Wednesday Society' (also known as
the *Freunde der Aufklärung*, or 'Friends of the Enlightenment'), and
in a monthly periodical the *Berlinische Monatsschrift*, founded in the
same year, one of their members, J.F. Zöllner, happened to ask, in
a footnote to an article: 'What is Enlightenment? This question,
which is almost as important as the question what is truth, would
seem to require an answer before one engages in enlightening
activity.' His question provoked a long debate in the Wednesday
Society, conducted within guidelines drawn up by the liberal
Jewish philosopher Moses Mendelssohn (1729–86); who said that two
questions were of especial importance. (1) Whether, in the past,
'Enlightenment' or unrestricted liberty had done actual harm to
the public weal? (2) If it was true (as he himself took for granted)
that 'certain prejudices and superstitions shared by a whole nation
must be spared and not trampled upon by all honest people, then
ought these necessary limits set on "Enlightenment" activities to
be prescribed by law, or fixed by censors, or merely left to the
discretion of individuals?' (He himself favoured the last.) The
discussion lasted from January to May 1784, and meanwhile
Zöllner's question had also stimulated the great philosopher
Immanuel Kant (1724–1804), who had no connection with the
Wednesday Society, to write his notable affirmation of faith:
'Answer to the Question: What is Enlightenment?' It will be seen
that he attached enormous importance to the rôle of Man of
Letters. (The word 'rôle' is used advisedly, because he is not
merely thinking of the full-time professional man of letters but of
the sense in which anyone, when he writes for the world at large, is
adopting a rôle with its own special rights and duties.)

We have printed Kant's article in an eighteenth-century translation, to give a sense of how it would have appeared to its first English readers. It is interesting to see that the term 'Enlightenment' (and by implication the concept also) had not yet become current in Britain, and the translator resorts to the awkward translation 'Enlightening'.

Enlightening is, Man's quitting the nonage[1] *occasioned by himself. Nonage* or minority is the inability of making use of one's own understanding without the guidance of another. This nonage is *occasioned by one's self*, when the cause of it is not from want of understanding, but of resolution and courage to use one's own understanding without the guidance of another. *Sapere aude!*[2] Have courage to make use of thy own understanding! is therefore the *dictum* of enlightening.

Laziness and cowardice are the causes, why so great a part of mankind, after nature has long freed them from the guidance of others (*naturaliter majorennes*),[3] willingly remain minors as long as they live; and why it is so easy for others, to set themselves up as their guardians. It is convenient to be a minor. If I have a book, which has understanding for me, a curate, who has conscience for me, a physician, who judges of diet for me, etc. I need not give myself any trouble. I have no occasion to think, if I can but pay; others will save me the trouble of that irksome business. Those guardians, who have graciously undertaken the super-intendence of mankind, take sufficient care, that by far the greater part of them (and all the fair) shall hold the step to majority, besides the trouble attending it, very dangerous. After these superintendents have first made them as stupid as their domestic animals, and carefully prevented those peaceable creatures from daring to venture a single step beyond the go-cart, in which they are inclosed; they point out to them the danger that threatens them, if they should try to go alone. Indeed this danger is not so very great, for, at the expence of a few falls, they would learn to walk at last; but an example of this sort renders timid, and commonly discourages from all further attempts. It is therefore difficult for every single man to extricate himself from the nonage, which is almost become natural to him. Nay, it is even become agreeable to him, and he is for the present actually incapable of using his own understanding, because he never was allowed to make the trial. Ordinances and formules, the mechanical instruments of a rational use, or rather misuse, of his gifts of nature, are the fetters of an everlasting minority. Whoever shook them off, would take but an uncertain leap over the smallest ditch even, because he is not accustomed to such a free motion. Hence there are but few, who have succeeded to emanci-pate themselves from nonage by their own labour, and yet to walk firmly.

But it is sooner possible for a nation to enlighten itself; nay, when it has the liberty, it is almost infallible. For a few who think for themselves will always be found, even among the installed guardians of the multitude, who, after they themselves have thrown off the yoke of nonage, will spread about them the spirit of a rational estimation of the proper value and of the vocation of every man to think for himself. It is singular in this, that the public, which was formerly brought under this yoke by them, afterwards compels them themselves to remain under it, when this public is thereto stirred up by some of its guardians, who are themselves totally incapable of enlightening; so pernicious is it to fill with prejudices; as they are revenged at last on those themselves who, or whose predecessors, were their authors. Hence a nation can attain enlightening but slowly. A deliverance from personal despotism, and interested and tyrannical oppression, may perhaps be obtained by a revolution, but never a true reform of the cast of mind, new prejudices will serve, just as well as the old, for leading-strings to the thoughtless multitude.

To this enlightening however nothing is required but LIBERTY; and indeed the most harmless of all that may be named liberty, to wit, that, to make a *public use* of one's reason in every point. But I hear exclaimed from all sides: *don't reason!* The officer says: don't reason, but exercise! The financier: don't reason, but pay! The clergyman: don't reason, but believe! (Only one master in the world[4] says: *reason*, as much as you please, and on what you please, *but obey!*) Here is everywhere restriction of liberty. But what restriction is a hindrance to enlightening? what not, but even favourable to it? – My answer is this: the *public* use of one's reason must always be free, and that only can bring about enlightening among men; but the *private use* of it may often be very strictly limited, without much hindering the progress of enlightening. By the public use of one's own reason however I understand that, which every one *as a man of letters* makes of it in the eyes of the whole reading world. I name the private use that, which he may make of his reason in a certain *civil post*, or office, intrusted to him. There is necessary to many businesses, which run in with the interest of the commonwealth, a certain mechanism, by means of which some members of the commonwealth must conduct themselves passively merely, in order, by an artificial unison directed by the government to public ends, to be withholden at least from the destruction of these ends. Here indeed it is not allowed to reason; but one must obey. But so far as this part of the machine considers itself at the same time as a member of the whole common-wealth, nay, even of the cosmopolitical society, consequently in the character of a man of letters, who addresses himself by writings to the public in the proper sense; he may by all means reason, without doing any injury thereby to the business, to which he is appointed, partly as a passive member. It would be very hurtful, if an officer, to whom his superior gives an order, should in actual service reason loudly on the conformity-to-end, or expediency of this order; he must obey. But he, as a man of letters, cannot in justice be hindered from making his observations on the faults of the military service, and from submitting these to the judgement of the public. The citizen cannot refuse to pay the taxes imposed on him; even a forward censure[5] of such taxes, when they are to be paid by him, may be punished as a scandal (which might occasion universal opposition). The very same person, notwithstanding that, does not act contrary to the duty of a citizen, when he, as a man of letters, publishes his thoughts on the unfitness or even the injustice of such imposts.[6] In like manner is a clergyman bound, to deliver himself to his congregation in all points according to the symbol of the church, which he serves; for he was ordained on this condition. But as a man of letters he has full liberty, nay, it is his call, to communicate to the public all his carefully proved and well-meant thoughts on what is faulty in that symbol, and to make his proposals for the better regulation of the affairs of religion and of the church. There is nothing in this, which can be burdensome to the conscience. For, what he teaches pursuant to his office, as agent of the church, he represents as something, in respect of which he has not a free power to teach according to his own sentiments, but he is ordered to propound that according to precept and in the name of another. He may say: our church inculcates this, or that doctrine; these are the arguments it makes use of. He then draws all, practical profit to his congregation from ordinances, to which he himself would not subscribe, perhaps with full conviction, to whose propounding however he can bind himself, because it is not quite impossible that truth may lie therein concealed, but at all events nothing is found in them inconsistent at least with the internal religion. For, did he believe to find in them anything repugnant to this, he could not administer his office with a safe conscience; he must resign it. The use, therefore, which an established teacher or pastor makes of his reason before his hearers, is a *private use* merely; as this is never but a domestic congregation, though ever so great, and in regard to which he, as *a priest*, is not free, and dare not be so, because he executes the commission of another. Whereas, as a man of letters, who speaks by writings to the proper public, namely, the world, consequently the ecclesiastic, in the *public use* of his reason, enjoys an unlimited liberty, to use his own reason and to speak in his own person. For it is an absurdity, which tends to the perpetuating of absurdities, that the guardians of the people (in spiritual things) shall themselves be again in a state of nonage.

But should not a society of clergymen, for instance, a church-assembly, or a reverend class (as the Dutch clergy name themselves) be intitled to bind one another by oath to a certain unalterable symbol, in order to exercise an incessant supreme guardianship over every one of their members and by their means over the people, and even to eternize this? I maintain that that is totally impossible. Such a contract, entered into for the purpose of withholding forever all farther enlightening from the human species, is absolutely void; and should it be confirmed by the chief power even, by diets[7] of the empire, and by the most solemn treaties of peace. An age cannot league itself, and by oath too, to put the following age into a state, wherein it must be impossible for it to enlarge its knowledge (especially a knowledge so very important), to purge away errors, and in general to make progress in enlightening. That were a crime against human nature, whose original destination consists directly in this progression; and posterity is therefore completely entitled to reject those resolutions, as at once incompetently and presumptuously formed. The test of all that can be finally determined with regard to a nation, lies in the question, Whether a nation itself could institute such a law? This would, as it were, in the expectation of a better, be possible for a determinate short time, with a view to introduce a better order; if at the same time all the citizens, principally the clergy, had the liberty, in the character of men of letters, to make their observations publicly, that is, by writings, on that which is faulty of the present economy,[8] but the established order might still continue, till the insight into the nature of these things attained such a degree, that they (the citizens) by uniting their voices (though not of all) could make a proposal to the throne, to take under its protection those congregations, which had united themselves in an altered economy of religion according to their conceptions of a better introspection, without however molesting those, who rather choose to continue with the old. But to unite one's self in a permanent constitution of religion, to be questioned by nobody publicly, even but during the life-time of one man, and thereby, as it were, annihilate a period in the progression of humanity to amendment, to render it fruitless and by that means even detrimental to posterity, is absolutely not allowed. A man may indeed, as to his own person, defer, and even then but for a time, the enlightening in that, which is incumbent on him to know; but to renounce it, let it be for his own person, but still more for posterity, is to violate and to trample on the sacred rights of humanity. But what a nation cannot finally determine with regard to themselves, still less can the monarch determine that finally with regard to the nation; for his legislative dignity rests upon his uniting in his own will the common will of the nation. If he but takes care, that all true or opiniative[9] improvement be consistent with the civil order; as for the rest, he may let his subjects themselves do what they find necessary to be done for the sake of the welfare of their own souls; that does not concern him, but it concerns him to take care that the one shall not violently prevent the other from labouring with all his strength at the determination and furtherance of that welfare. He derogates from his own majesty, when he interferes with the writings, by which his subjects endeavour to perfectionate their insights, and thinks them worthy of the inspection of his government, as well as when he does this from his own profound introspection, where he exposes himself to the exprobration,[10] *Caesar non est supra grammaticos*,[11] as also, and still more, when he humbles his supreme power so far, as to support the ecclesiastic despotism of a few tyrants in his state against his other subjects.

If it is now enquired, do we live at present in an *enlightened* age? The answer is, No, but by all means in an age of *enlightening*. There is still a great deal wanting to men, as things are at present, on the whole, to be in a state, or to be but able to be put in a state, to make a safe and a good use of their own understanding in affairs of religion without the guidance of another. But we have distinct proofs, that the field is now opened for them to labour in freely, and the hinderances of universal enlightening, or of quitting the nonage occasioned by themselves, become by degrees fewer. In this respect the present age is the age of enlightening, or FREDERICK'S century.

A prince, who does not think it unworthy of himself to say, that he holds it *duty*, not to prescribe any thing to men in matters of religion, but to allow them full liberty therein, who declines, even the lofty *name of being tolerating*, is himself enlightened, and merits to be esteemed as such by the grateful world and by posterity, a prince, who first freed the human species from nonage, at least on the part of government, and gave them liberty, in all that is an affair of conscience, to use their own reason. Under him could respectable clergymen, in the character of men of letters, without prejudice to the duty of their office, freely expose to the world to be proved their judgments and insights, here and there deviating from the received symbol; and still more every other person, who is limited by no duty of office. This spirit of liberty diffuses itself outwardly also, even where it has to struggle with external impediments of a government misunderstanding itself. For it gives an example to that government, that it needs not, on account of liberty, be under the smallest solicitude for the tranquillity, and union of the commonwealth. Men naturally extricate themselves insensibly from the state of rudeness and barbarity, when invention is not purposely plied to keep them in it.

The stress of the principal point of enlightening, that of men's quitting the nonage occasioned by themselves, I have laid upon *matters of religion* chiefly; because, with regard to arts and sciences, our rulers have no interest in playing the guardian over their subjects; besides, that state of nonage is not only the most pernicious, but the most dishonourable of any. But the way of thinking of a head of the state, who favours enlightening penetrates farther and perspects.[12] That even in regard of his *legislation* there is no danger in allowing his subjects to make a *public* use of their reason, and to lay before the world their thoughts on a better constitution, and even a free and honest criticism of the present; we have an eminent example of this, in which no monarch ever surpassed him, whom we honour.

But only he, who, enlightened himself, is not only not afraid of his shadow, but has at hand a well-disciplined numerous army as a security for the public tranquillity, can say, what a free state dares not risk: *reason as much as you please, and on what you please, but obey!* Thus a strange unexpected course of human affairs presents itself here; so that, when it is contemplated in the gross, almost every thing is paradoxical in it. A greater degree of civil liberty seems advantageous to the liberty of the *spirit of the nation*, and yet places insuperable barriers to it; whereas a degree less of that gives this full scope to extend itself to the utmost of its faculty. When nature has then unfolded under this rough rind the germe,[13] of which she takes the most tender care, namely, the propensity and the call to *thinking freely;* this gradually reacts on the minds of the people (whereby they become by degrees more capable *of the liberty of acting*), and finally, even on the principles of the government, which finds it profitable for itself to treat man, who is now more than a mere *machine*, conformably to his dignity.

Notes

1   Period of infancy or immaturity.
2   (Latin) 'Dare to know!' or 'Dare to be wise!'; a tag from Horace, *Epodes*, I, 2, 40.
3   (Latin) Those who have come of age by virtue of nature.
4   Kant is referring to his own king, Frederick the Great of Prussia (1712–86).
5   Presumptuous criticism.
6   Taxes.
7   Parliaments.
8   System of national organization.
9   Opiniative – relating to opinion.
10   Exprobration – reproachful language.
11   (Latin) 'Even Caesar is not above the grammarians' (i.e. the rules of grammar apply even to dictators).
12   Foresees.
13   Seed.

INDEX

Figures followed by an asterisk* refer to the notes following each extract

Académie française 104, 121, 123*,
    125*
Académie des Sciences 124*, 154*,
    213
Academy of St Luke, Rome 101*
Adam, Robert 24, 39
Alberti, Leon Battista 36, 38*
Aldrovandi, Ulysses 172, 189*
Alexander the Great 180, 190*
Ammanati, Bartolommeo 34, 37*
anatomy 67–8, 73–4, 174
Antinous 122, 125*
Apelles 41*, 107, 124*
Apulian work 37*
Arabic/Moorish
    architecture 12, 20
    scholarship 130
Ararat, Mt 210
Archimedes 128, 140*, 152, 154*
architecture, generally
    effect on the soul 12
    essential beauties 10, 14
    experiment in 35
    general principles 13–15, 43
    importance of study 1–2
    and national magnificence 43
    need for theoretical principles 9
    origins 8, 12, 14
    qualities of the architect 28–34
Argyll, third duke 84, 88*
Aristotle 130, 134, 140*, 178,
    180–2, 190*, 222
art
    definition 144–5
    language of 150–1
    liberal 145
    mechanical 145–6, 147–53
    origins 145
    purposes 146
    speculative and practical aspects
        145
ass, qualities of 225–6
astronomy 131, 133, 137, 142*,
    188, 192
Atlantis 205, 209*

attic storeys 51, 52*
Audran, Gérard 146, 154*
Augustine, St 131
Augustus, Roman emperor 37*
Averroës 140*

Bacon, Francis 132, 140–1*,
        145–6, 147, 148, 152, 154*
Baldovinetti, Alesso 81*
Barbaro 36, 38*
baroque
    architecture 23*, 37*
    painting 37*, 63*, 101*
    sculpture 47*
Barrow, Isaac 137, 142*
Batoni, Pompeio 92, 94, 101*
Beaumarchais, Pierre Augustin
        Caron de, *Le Mariage de Figaro*
        xiv, xv, 242, 246
beauty
    attempts to define 65
    essential 10, 14, 58
    existence of principles 66
    lines of 69–74
    nature and 64
Bedford, fourth duke 88*
Belcourt 110
Belisarius 122–3, 125*
Berghem, Nicholas 107
Berliner Mittwochsgesellschaft
    249
Bernini, Gian Lorenzo 31, 34, 37*
Blenheim Palace 44, 47*
Blondel, J.-F. xiv, 8, 24, 55
Boerhaave 137, 142*
Boffrand, Germain 23*
Boileau-Despréaux, Nicolas 58,
    63*
Borromini, Francesco 87, 88*
Boswell, James 240
Bouchardon, Edmé 44, 47*
Boucher, François 107–8, 111–2,
    124*
Bourdon, Sebastian 97, 101*
Bourguet, Louis 212–13, 216*

Boyle, Robert 137, 142*
Bramante, Donato 12, 34, 37*
Bridgeman, Charles 82, 88*
Brisart 110
Brisson, M.J. 228, 236*
Brosse, Salomon de 23*
Buffin 42
Buffon, Comte Georges de xii,
    xiv, 152, 160, 191, 210, 217
Buonarotti, Michelangelo *see*
    Michelangelo
Burleigh, Lord 87
Burlington, third earl 44, 46*, 75*
Burnet, Thomas 192, 208*, 211,
    214
Butler, Joseph xiii
Byzantine empire, destruction
    128, 140*

Calas, Jean 120, 123*
Campbell, Colin (Vitruvius
    Britannicus) 46*
Campo Vaccino, Rome 36, 38*
Caracci cousins 59, 106, 123–4*
Caravaggio, Michelangelo da 101*
Carlton House, Pall Mall 84
carving, French 49–50
Cataneo 36,38*
Catherine, empress of Russia 103
Caylus, Comte de 46*, 54, 54*
ceilings, decoration of 61
censorship 103, 126, 242, 247, 253
Challe, Michel-Ange 112, 124*
Chambers, Ephraim, *Encyclopaedia*,
    126
Chambers, William xiv, 22*, 24, 55
Chapel of the Ardens, St Roch 118
Chardin, Jean-Baptiste 48, 104,
    106–7, 110–11, 112–13,
    115, 117–18, 120–1, 122,
    123*
Chardin, Pierre-Jean 111, 124*
Charles I, king of England 101*
chemistry 166
Chesterfield, fourth earl 240
chinoiserie 1, 46, 55, 56*, 88, 89*
Christianity, and philosophy
    130–1
churches
  building of 8
  columns in 19
  gothic 12
Cicero, Marcus Tullius 140

civil architecture, defined 2, 37*
Claremont house 85
classical architecture 8, 12, 24,
    39–41
  Classical Orders 1, 2, 12, 19–20,
    34–5
  enrichment 21–2
Cochin, Charles-Nicolas xiv, 42,
    48, 53, 54*, 121
Colbert, Jean-Baptiste 63*, 145–6,
    154*, 157*
colour
  in architecture 21
  Boucher and 107–8
  Chardin and 104, 106, 113
  in Flemish painting 95
  Gainsborough and 99
Columbus, Christopher 131
columns
  defects 16–19
  essentialness of 14, 17
  orders of 2
  principles of use 15, 19, 35–6
comets 192, 212, 213, 214
Composite Order 20, 35–6
Conca, Sebastiano 92, 101*
Condillac, Abbé 143*
Constanzi, Placido 92, 101*
copying, as learning method 77–8,
    100, 106–7
Cordemoy, Jean Louis de 9, 16,
    22*, 39, 41*
Corinthian Order 12, 20, 34–6
Corneille, Pierre 105, 123*, 238
Correggio, Antonio da 93, 101*
Correspondance Littéraire, La 103
Cortona, Pietro da 34, 37*, 59,
    63*
Coventry, Frances 88*
Coypel, Antoine 59
craftsman/technician, social
    importance 144
Crébillon, C.-P. J. de 112, 124*
criticism
  Diderot's influence 103–4
  freedom of 247
  by non-specialists 13, 42, 57,
    58, 67
  by patrons 237
  respectability 57

D'Alembert, Jean xiv, 126–7,
    140–3*, 237

David, Jacques Louis 122, 125*
Delorme, Philibert 18, 20, 23*, 36, 38*
Demosthenes 140
Descartes, René 22*, 132–4, 135–6, 138, 141*, 143*, 152
Deschamps, Mme 111
Desgodetz, Antoine 40, 41*
Deshayes, Jean-Baptiste 104–6, 123*
design 31, 32, 44, 67, 78
Diderot, Denis xiii, xiv, 46*, 48, 103–4, 124*, 126, 141*, 155
Dodsley, Robert 240
Domenichino 59, 106, 117, 124*
Doric Order 12, 20, 34–6, 40
Dormer, General 84, 88*
Doyen, François Gabriel 116–17, 118–19, 124*
droit de seigneur 245*
Dryden, John 241*
Durameau, Louis 119, 125*
Dutch painting 96, 97

East India Co 24
École des Arts, Paris 24
Edwards, George 228, 236*
Egyptians 31
    Pyramids 43
empiricism 64
Encyclopédie, L' xiii, xiv, 55, 126, 144
encyclopédistes xiv, 8, 126
Englefield, Sir Henry Charles 87, 88*
English
    architecture 1, 43–4
    fashion 43–4, 85–6
    literature 58
    painting 91
    philosophy 137
engraving 48, 78, 148
enlightenment (Kant) 249–55
entablatures
    essentialness of 14
    principles of use 35–6
entasis 23*
erudition, perils of 129, 168, 172–3
Esher Lodge 85, 88*
essential beauty 10, 14, 58
Etrurian work 32, 37*
Etruscans 37*

existence, defined 171
Eyre, P.E. 82, 88*

faces, and character 74–5, 181
fashion
    in England 43–4, 85–6
    in France 45–6, 53
    genius and 49
Fielding, Henry xii, xiii, 64
Figaro 242, 246
fitness, and beauty 67–8
Flemish painting 57, 95, 97, 101*
Fontenelle, Bernard Le Bovier de 112, 124*
fountains 83, 86
Francis I, king of France 128, 140*
Frederick the Great, king of Prussia 52*, 254, 255*
French
    architecture 12, 19–20, 24, 44–5, 50–2, 53–4
    fashion 45–6, 53
    literature 58–9, 63*
    painting 57, 59–62, 113
    Revolution 47*
    sculpture 47*
Freunde der Aufklärung 249
furniture
    English 44
    French 45

Gainsborough, Thomas 24, 90–100, 101*
Galileo Galilei 131, 137, 140*
gardens
    design 8, 33, 45, 82–8
    landscape gardeners 1, 82–3, 86–7
    trees, new 84
    water in 83
Garrick, David 48
Geneviève, St 118, 125*
genius 10, 11, 12, 20, 44, 92, 129
    development 163
    and discipline 30
    and fashion 49
    and instinct 29–30
    and isolation 128
genre painting 113, 124*
Geoffrin, Mme 42
geography 137
    Europe/Asia formerly joined to America 226, 228

258

of natural history 227–35
relative climate, Old/New
World 231–3
geology 191, 193–208
action of water 196–206, 208
earth and the Flood 191,
197–8, 210–16
earthquakes 207,214
earth's fitness to bear life 191,
195
theories of earth's formation
192, 196–7, 210–16
George III, king of England 24
George, prince of Wales 84, 88*
Gerbert of Aurillac 128, 140*
Gesner, Konrad von 168, 189*
Gessner, S. 105, 123*
Ghezzi, Pier Leone 66, 75–6*
Gibbon, Edward xii, xiii, xiv, xv,
22*, 42
Glicon 68
Gobelins 61, 63*
Godrans, Collège des 42
Goethe xi
gothic architecture 12, 20, 24, 42,
45
Gothic Orders 1
grace 65, 69, 72, 95
Greeks 31
architecture 12, 19–20, 24,
39–41, see also classical
architecture
Greek flood 215
language 179
literature 58, 130
natural history 179–82
painting 41, 41*
philosophy 130
sculpture 41, 41*, 68, 90
Greenwich Hospital 81*
Greuze, Jean-Baptiste 107, 108–9,
115–16, 121–2, 124–5*
Grimm, Friedrich-Melchior 103,
109, 124*
grottoes 86
Guercino, Giovanni 94, 101*
gunpowder 148, 151–2

Hadrian, Roman emperor 125*
Hamilton, Charles 86
Hamlet xiii
Hampson, Norman xi
Harvey, William 137, 142*

Hawksmoor, Nicholas 47*
Hippocrates 141*
history, study of 128–9
history painting 57, 58–9, 61, 90,
96, 104, 122
Hogarth, William xiv, 39, 64, 76*,
77, 81*, 96, 113
Homer 58, 179
Horace 45, 255*
Ars Poetica 58, 63*, 81*, 124*
Houghton Hall, Norfolk 82, 88*
Hume, David xii, xiii, xiv 125,
190*
Huygens, Christian 134, 137, 142*

imagination 130, 132, 140*, 192
Imperiale, Gerolamo 92, 101*
Inquisition, The 131, 140*
inspiration 92
instinct 29–30
interior decoration 49–50, 55–6,
59–60, 61
see also furniture
intricacy, and beauty 68
Invalides, chapel at 18, 23*
Ionic Order 12, 20, 34–6, 40
Ireland, John 79, 81*
Italian
architecture 12, 34–5, 43
literature 58
painting 57, 91–2

Johnson, Samuel xii, xiii, xiv, 30,
239
Dictionary 240–1
Johnston(e), John 228, 236*
Jones, Inigo 44
Joseph Andrews xiii
Julian, Roman emperor 88*
justice, criminal 119–20, 123*

Kant, Immanuel xiv, 249–50
Kensington Gardens 85
Kent, William 76*, 83–6, 88*
Kepler, Johannes 134, 142*

La Font de Saint Yenne xiv, 23*,
42, 57, 90, 104
landscape painting 90, 93–4,
96–7, 101–2*
Lanfranco 63*
Langley, Batty xiv, 1
language

Greek 179
study of 128–9
technical 144, 150–1
Largillière, N. 63*
Latin Orders 34–5
Laugier, Marc-Antoine xiv, 8,
22–3*, 24, 28, 37, 38*, 39,
42, 64
Le Bas 48
Le Blanc, Jean-Bernard xiv, 8, 42,
48, 54*, 82
Le Brun, Charles 46*, 59, 75, 76*,
146, 154*
Lee, William 157*
Leibniz, Gottfried Wilhelm
137–8, 142–3*
Protogaea 213, 216*
Leipzig Transactions 213
Le Kain 110
Le Lorrain, L.-J. 54, 54*
Lemercier, Jacques 23*
Le Moine, F. 59, 63*, 110, 124*
Leo X, pope 59, 63*
Le Sueur, Eustache 59, 117, 124*,
146, 154*
Le Vau 46*
liberal arts 9, 145
liberty
civil 254–5
intellectual 249–53
Linnaeus, Carl 160, 168, 169,
177–8, 189*, 217, 226*
literature
Greek 58, 130
history 127–9
influence on other artists 58–9
men of letters 237–9, 249,
251–3
patrons 237, 240–1
progress in 139–40
scientific 172–3
Locke, John 136, 138, 142*, 143*
*Essay Concerning Human
Understanding* 136
Lorrain, Claude 96, 101*, 102*
Louis VI, king of France 118
Louis XIV, king of France 8, 42,
45, 59, 140, 144
Louis XV, king of France 242
Loutherbourg, P.J. de 107
Louvre 12, 16, 17, 19, 22*, 43,
46*, 51
Academy of Architecture 55

gallery 57, 123*
Lucan 140
Lucian 115, 124*
Lucretius 118, 124–5*
Luxembourg, Château de 18, 23*
Lysippis 41, 41*

magnetism 151
Maison Carrée, Nîmes 15, 23*
Malebranche, Nicholas 137, 142*
Mansart, François 52*
Mansart, J.H. 23*
Maratta, Carlo 31, 37*, 87, 92,
101*
marble, choice of 21
Marie-Antoinette, queen of France
63*
Marigny, Marquis de 42, 53, 54*,
57
Marivaux, Pierre de 143*
Marlborough, first duke 47
mass production 153
Massuci, Agostino 92, 101*
materials, building 21, 32
mathematics 30, 133, 137, 140*,
149–50, 160, 185–9
Matlock Bath 86
mechanical arts 145–6
study of 147–53
mechanics 30, 135, 149–50, 188,
211
interdependence of parts 156
inventions 148, 151
Medicis 128, 140*
memory, as learning method
78–9, 129, 167
Mendelssohn, Moses 249
Mengs, Raffael 92, 101*
Mercure de France 144
Merlin's cave, Richmond Park 44
metal-working 49
metaphysics 134, 136–7, 142*,
145, 212
Michelangelo 12, 29, 34, 37*, 63*,
90
Milton, John 58
mirrors
Archimedes' 152, 154*
effect on painting 59–60
increase in use 59, 63*
Molière 46
monads 138
Montaigne, Michel de 152, 154*

Montesquieu, Charles Louis de
xiv, 126
Morine, M de 79
Moses 210, 213
movement, and beauty 69–70
Mozart, Wolfgang Amadeus, *Le
Nozze di Figaro* 242, 246
music 9, 87
Myron 41, 41*
mythological/historical inspiration
to architects 31–2
to painters 58–9, 96–7, 104,
124*

Nattier, J.-M. 63*
natural history 147, 160–89
animals, geographical
distribution 227–35
animals, interrelation 220–2
animals, relative sizes, Old/New
World 230–1
beginning to study 162–3
botany 166–9, 180, 189*
in classical times 179–83
classification systems 160,
165–70, 174–83, 217, 223
degeneration 220, 221, 223–5,
230
description in 171–2, 173–4,
183
false connections 162, 164, 171
human variation 223–4, 232
multiplicity in 161
'the savage' 230
species, concept of 217, 221,
222–3, 227, 228, 235
superiority of man 234–5
'natural state' of man 8, 13–14
nature
and art generally 64, 79, 109,
139–40, 173
and beauty 64
imitation, in architecture 14,
15, 19, 37
imitation, in gardens 82–3, 85
imitation, in painting 104, 121
Newton and 135
and straight lines 85
neo-classical
architecture 24, 42, 47*, 53–4
interiors 55–6
painting 101–2*
Newcastle, duke of 88*

Newton, Sir Isaac 134–6, 138,
141–2*, 187, 192
Nichols, John Bowyer 77

optics 30–1, 135, 188
optimism (Leibniz) 138
Orléans, Duc d' 63*
ornament, architectural 1, 11,
21–2, 34, 35, 36
classical 21–2
effect on painting 59
English 44
French 45
and mythology/history 31–2
taste and 43

painting 9, 11, 31
Dutch 96, 97
emotional response to 103–4,
109, 114, 119, 123
English 91
Flemish 57, 95, 97, 101*
French 57, 59–62, 113
'grand style' 90, 96
Greek 41, 41*
Italian 57, 91–2
and literature 58–9
and mirrors 59–60
moral intent 103, 108
at night 93
novelty in 98
painters' struggle for success
110–11
and poetry 59, 97
sale of bad 80
Palladio, Andrea 22*, 23*, 34,
35–6, 37*, 40, 41*, 46*
Palladianism 24
Pantheon, Rome 35, 38*
Paris Salons 103
Parrocel, Charles 110, 124*
Pascal, Blaise 137
patrons, literary 237, 240–1
Patte, Pierre 55
patterns, architectural 1, 24
pediments, essentialness of 14
Pelham, Henry 88*
Perrault, Charles 12, 22*, 46*, 156,
157*
perspective 30, 61, 83, 107
Peruzzi, Baldassare 34, 37*
Peterborough, earl of 84, 88*
Petrarch 112, 124*

Phidias 41, 41*
Philopoemon 238, 239*
philosopher's stone 166
philosophy 127, 184
    abuse 139
    and Christianity 130–1
    classical 128, 130
    history 129–39
    and mechanical arts 147
    systems 138–9, 143*, 192
physics 133–6, 137, 185–9, 192
    and theology 210, 214
Piazza Navona 86
Pierre, Jean-Baptiste 107, 124*
pilasters 16–17, 23*, 36–7
    orders of 37
Plato 205, 209*
Pliny the elder 180,–182–3, 190*
Pluche, Abbé 157*
Plutarch 239*
poetry 9, 11, 128
    and painting 59, 97
Polidoro 34, 37*
Pompadour,Marquise de 42, 48,
    54*
Pond, Arthur 66, 75–6*
Ponte, Lorenzo da 242, 246
Pope, Alexander xiii, 80, 81*, 84,
    88*
portrait painting 61–2, 63*, 90,
    94, 99, 101*
Potain 53
Poussin, Nicolas 59, 99, 100,
    101*, 102*
Praxiteles 41, 41*
prejudiced attitudes 13, 130, 134,
    184, 251
prestige, sources of 238–9
printing 128–9, 148, 151
Prior, Matthew 88*
proportion
    architectural 1, 2, 8, 11, 20, 31,
        34, 40, 43, 44
    generally 49, 67
Puget, Pierre 46, 47*
pursuit, innate love of 68

Quesnai, François xiv

Racine, Jean 105, 123*
Raphael 34, 37*, 59, 63*, 90, 100,
    101*, 105
Ray, John 214, 216*

reason
    and Christianity 130–1
    definition 2
    inductive reasoning 193, 209*
    men of letters and 249, 251–3
    need for guiding principles
        9–10
    reasoning cf imagination 130,
        140*, 192–3
    sufficient reason 138
    superstition and 128
    suppression, private 251
    travel and 33
    use of 15, 251
religion
    and enlightenment 252, 254
    as inspiration to art 59, 105,
        123*
    theology and earth's formation
        210–16
    theology and philosophy 130–1
Renaissance 12, 20
    aesthetic theories 64
    architecture 38*
    factors assisting 128, 140*
Revett, Nicholas xiv, 39
Reynolds, Joshua xiv, 24, 57, 90,
    100–1*, 104
Richardson, Jonathan 64, 75*
Rochefoucault, Duc de la 63*
Rococo
    architecture 22, 23*, 47*, 48,
        50–2,53, 55
    ornamentation 49–50
    spread of 52*
Romano, Giulio 59
Romans 31
    architecture 12, 19–20, 39– 41,
        43
    fall of empire 40
    literature 58
    natural history 180, 182–3
    Roman Order 35
Rosa, Salvator 97, 101*
Rousham, garden at 84, 88*
Rousseau, J.-B. 59, 63*
Rousseau, Jean-Jacques xii, xiv,
    8, 126
Royal Academy of Arts 90
Rubens, Sir Peter Paul 59, 95, 97,
    100, 101*, 107
Ruisdael, Jacob von 95, 101*
rulers, duties of 253–4

Sacchi, Andrea 92, 101*
St Bartholomew's Hospital 81*
St Geneviève, church of, Paris 8
St Gervais, church of, Paris 16
St Judule, church of, Brussels 100
St Paul's, London 43, 81*
St Paul and St Louis, church of,
    Paris 16, 19
St Peter's, Rome 18, 37*, 43, 86
    piazza 31
St Petersburg Academy of Fine
    Arts 54*
Sanmichele, Michele 34, 37*
Sansovino, Andrea 34, 37*
Savery, Capt Thomas 154*
Scamozzi, Vincenzo 35–6, 37*
Scheutzer, J.J. 213–14, 215
Schwab, Richard M. 143*
science 126–7
    astronomy 131, 133, 137, 142*,
        188, 192
    early scientists 128
    as facts 173, 180
    functions 139
    geology 191, 193–208
    mathematics 30, 133, 137,
        140*, 149–50, 160, 185–9
    method 133, 138–9, 141*,
        147–8, 160, 165–71,
        185–9
    natural history 147, 160–89,
        217–35
    origins 145
    physics 133–6, 137, 185–9, 192
sculpture 31
    in architecture 21–2, 31
    Greek 41, 41*, 68, 90
Sedaine, Michel-Jean 124*
Seneca, Lucius Annaeus 140
serpentine line, and beauty 69,
    71–4
Shaftesbury, third earl 64, 75*
Shakespeare, William xiii, 64
simplicity 8, 14, 35, 37, 44–5
Smith, Adam xii, xiv
Society of Dilettanti 39
Soubise, Hôtel de 18
Soufflot 8, 42, 48, 53, 54*
Southcote, Philip 86, 88*
steam engine 154*
Stensen, Niels (Steno) 214, 216*
Stourhead grotto 86
streets, design 8

Stuart, James xiv, 39, 41*
sufficient reason (Leibniz) 138
superstition 128
Sweden, queen of 103
Sydenham, Mr 137, 142*
Sylvester II, pope 140*
symmetry 45, 82
synthetic art 64
systems, philosophical 138–9,
    143*, 192

talent 10, 11
    importance 237–8
tapestry 61, 62, 63*
Tasso, Torquato 58, 63*
taste 11, 17, 18, 19, 33, 111
    architecture dependent on 43
    and criticism 58
    defined 46
    establishment of rules 64
    formation 34
    see also fashion
Teniers, David I 101*
Teniers, David II 120, 125*
Theocritus 105, 123*
Theophrastus 180, 190*
Thomas, St 223, 226*
Thornhill, Sir James 76*, 81*
Tintoretto 106, 124*
Titian 87, 93, 101*
Toland, John xiii
Tournefort, J.P. de 168, 189*, 210,
    216*
travel, broadening the mind 33–4
truth 184–9, 249
Tuileries palace 18, 51
Turgot, Jacques 126
Tuscan Order 20, 35–6
Tuscany, grand-duke of 103

understanding see reasons

Val de Grâce, church, Paris 18,
    23*
Vanbrugh, Sir John 47*, 88*
Van Dyck, Sir Anthony 101*
Van Loo, L.-M. 63*
Varignon, Pierre 149, 154*
Vernet, Claude-Joseph 110,
    113–15, 124*
Versailles, palace of 63*
    chapel 17, 19, 22, 59, 63*
Vesalius, Andreas 137, 142*

Vien, Joseph-Marie 116–17, 124*
Viète, François 133, 141*
Vignola, Barozzi da 12, 23*, 34,
    35, 37*
Virgil 58, 140, 241, 241*
visual perception 65, 69
Vitruvius Britannicus (Campbell)
    42, 44, 46*
Vitruvius Pollio, Marcus 9, 19,
    22*, 28, 35, 37*
Voltaire xiii, xiv, 8, 42, 61, 105,
    123*, 126, 237
    Temple du Goût 61, 63*

Walpole, Horace xiv, 48, 82,
    88–9*
Walpole, Sir Robert 88*
water
    Flood 191, 197–8, 210–16
    fountains 83, 86
    in gardens 83
    grottoes 86
    seas 194–5

waving line, and beauty 69, 70–1
Webb, Daniel 113, 124*
Wedgwood, Josiah 37*
Weymouth, first viscount 88*
Whately, Thomas 88*
Whiston, William 192, 208*,
    211–12, 213, 214
Whitefield, George xii, xiii
Whitehall, banqueting house at 44
Wilson, Richard 96, 101*
Winckelman, Johann Joachim
    101*
windows 51
Woburn Farm 88*
Woodward, John 192, 209*, 211,
    213–14, 215
World, The 240
Wouwerman, Philips 101*
Wynants, Johannes 101*

Zachary, pope 131
Zeuxis 41, 41*, 107, 124*
Zöllner, J.F. 249

Index by Ann Edwards

264